Pick Me Up

Created by
David Roberts
and Jeremy Leslie

Editor
David Roberts
Creative Director
Jeremy Leslie
Art Director
Ian Pierce

Managing Editor
Rosie Mellor
Deputy Editor
Martin Skegg
Assistant Editor
Becky Lucas
Staff Writer
Oliver Horton

Designers
Izabella Bielawska
John Critchley
Corinna Drossel
James Grubb
Katharina Rocksien
Emmi Salonen

Picture Research
Marianna Sonnenberg
Luisa Nitrato-Izzo

Account Management
Caroline Sims
Rachel Webb

Writers
Simon Adams, Stephen
Armstrong, Clare Birchall, Alex
Hanks, Roger Highfield, Will
Hodgkinson, Andrew Holmes,
Dr. Jo Littler, Andrew Losowsky,
Jennifer Lucas, Fiona McGowan,
Will Petty, Tom Sandham, Alex
Silcox, Robert Smith, Debbie
Sperry, Rebecca Spooner,
Andrew Staffell, Nick Taylor,
Richard Walker, Mo White,
Mathew Willis

Consultants
Roger Bridgman, David Burnie,
Clare Bell, Jacqueline Mitton,
Olly Phillipson, Philip Wilkinson,
Andrew Shields

Inspired by and dedicated to
Hannah and Nadia
Cameron and Ewan

Cover illustration:
Eboy

Devised and produced
for DK Publishing by
John Brown Citrus Publishing
www.jbcp.co.uk

John
Brown
Citrus
Publishing

Andrew Jarvis, Chief Operating Officer
Dean Fitzpatrick, Managing Director
Andrew Hirsch, Chief Executive Officer

For DK
Reference Category Publisher, UK
Laura Buller
Children's Publishing Director, US
Beth Sutinis

First American Edition, 2006
Published in the United States by
DK Publishing
375 Hudson Street
New York, New York 10014

DK books are available at special discounts
for bulk purchases for sales promotions,
premiums, fund-raising, or educational use.
For details, contact:
DK Publishing Special Markets
375 Hudson Street
New York, New York 10014
SpecialSales@dk.com

A catalog record for this book
is available from the Library of Congress.

ISBN-13: 978-0-7566-2159-9
ISBN-10: 0-7566-2159-3

Color reproduction
by JBCP, London, UK
Printed and bound in Hong Kong by
Toppan Printing Company Ltd.

Discover more at www.dk.com

Stuff you need to know...

LIBRARY DISTRICT NO. 1
206 SOUTH BROADWAY
P.O. BOX 398
LOUISBURG, KS 66053

PAGE 74
This is all about how "Every mountain tells a story," and is full of fascinating stuff about **Mount Kilimanjaro** and **Mount Everest**—as well as what to do if you're ever caught in an avalanche. You have to dribble! Why? A little thing called **gravity**...

PAGE 130
The first page you open asks a question: "Which animal is man's best friend?" Your favorite has always been **cats**—and there's lots to learn about them here. But your brother prefers **dogs**. They sound pretty cool, too, when you read how they help in **avalanches** and get sent to...

START HERE!

PAGE 6
If you know the kind of subject you want to read about first, you can turn to "**Where to find stuff**." Here, you'll see eight areas to choose from (each with its own color). So, if you want to read about **Planet Earth** (**dinosaurs**? recycling?), check out all the pages under the big red box. Or, you can open the book at random to find...

How to use me

So, how do you find the stuff you want to know? You can start anywhere in this book if you like. But if you want to find something you're really interested in, look it up in the index, or check out the contents pages. Then, you can take an incredible trip all around the book, and you'll see how everything around us is connected —often in surprising ways

1 You can always find stuff in the index at the back of the book. Or, you can turn to the next page and look in Where to Find Stuff to get started. There are eight main subject areas, shown by eight different colors. So, if you want to find all the Planet Earth stuff, you can look up all the pages under the big red box.

2 There's another way to get into Pick Me Up. All through the book, you will find words underlined in bold with a page number, like this: cats 130. This shows you that if you turn to page 130, you can read lots of cool stuff about cats. On that page, you will find more underlined words sending you to connected subjects on other pages...

3 In the top left corner of each page is a box. Its color matches the colors on the contents page, to tell you the main subject area of the page. The words tell you what you're going to read about. So, when you turn to page 74 to read about avalanches, the red box says "Mountains to Water to Mexico." This shows the main subject is Planet Earth, the topic is mountains, and other stuff includes water and Mexico...

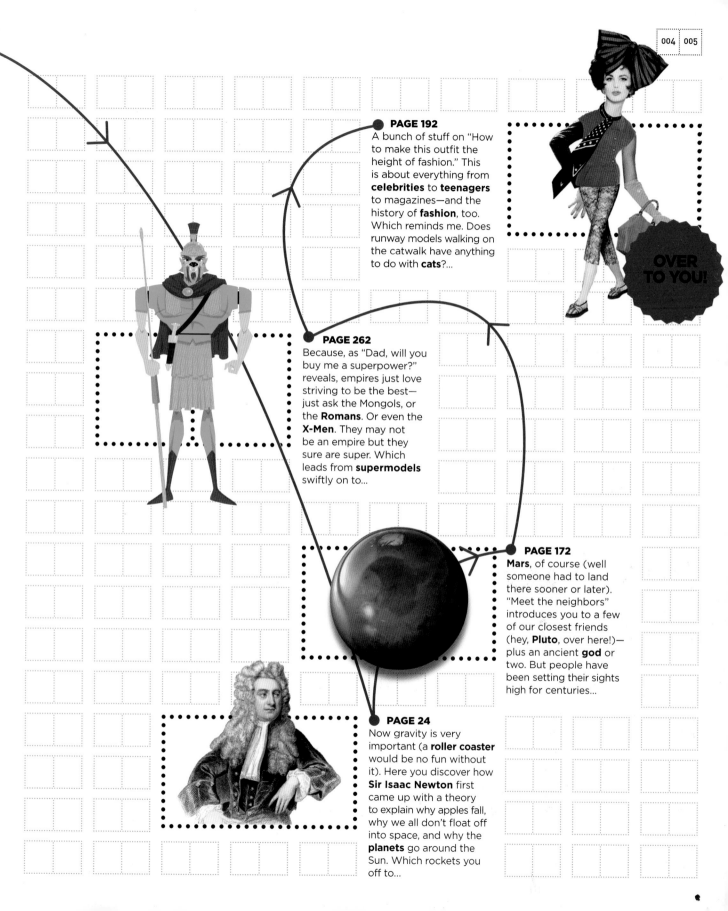

PAGE 192
A bunch of stuff on "How to make this outfit the height of fashion." This is about everything from **celebrities** to **teenagers** to magazines—and the history of **fashion**, too. Which reminds me. Does runway models walking on the catwalk have anything to do with **cats**?...

OVER TO YOU!

PAGE 262
Because, as "Dad, will you buy me a superpower?" reveals, empires just love striving to be the best— just ask the Mongols, or the **Romans**. Or even the **X-Men**. They may not be an empire but they sure are super. Which leads from **supermodels** swiftly on to...

PAGE 172
Mars, of course (well someone had to land there sooner or later). "Meet the neighbors" introduces you to a few of our closest friends (hey, **Pluto**, over here!)— plus an ancient **god** or two. But people have been setting their sights high for centuries...

PAGE 24
Now gravity is very important (a **roller coaster** would be no fun without it). Here you discover how **Sir Isaac Newton** first came up with a theory to explain why apples fall, why we all don't float off into space, and why the **planets** go around the Sun. Which rockets you off to...

The Natural World

People who made the world

Arts, entertainment, and media

You and your body

Planet Earth

Where to find stuff

HOW TREES TALK TO US

Trees are talking to us—you just have to know how to listen. One story they tell is about the changing **seasons 196** of the year. In spring and summer, most trees are green and the pigment that causes this color is chlorophyll. As sunlight falls on the leaves, chlorophyll absorbs the light as energy. **Plants 018** use this energy to turn carbon dioxide (from the air) and water (sucked up through their roots) into carbohydrates (the tree's lunch) and oxygen (released into the air for us to breathe). This process is called photosynthesis.

TROUBLE is, trees need a fairly decent amount of sunlight to keep this process going. During winter, there is not enough light for photosynthesis. The trees downsize, drop their leaves, and live off the food they stored up in the summer months. (Evergreens, with their cold-resistant leaves, continue to photosynthesize, only much more slowly.) So, in the fall, as sunlight fades, the green chlorophyll disappears from the leaves. Carotene pigment (which is "hidden" under the green) emerges, turning the leaves yellow and orange.

ANOTHER story is found beneath the bark. Trees grow bigger as new layers of wood grow around the old layers. This happens once a year (mainly in the spring and summer), leaving an annual ring, or tree ring (you can see this on the stump after a tree has been cut down). By counting the number of rings on its trunk, the tree will tell you its age. But that's not all. Historians can date past events by looking at tree rings—information about weather, fires, **insects 232**, and disease can be read from them.

CHRISTMAS TREES

A spangly, dead spruce tree in the living room is a Christmas symbol throughout Europe and the US. The custom started in Germany. One Christmas Eve, around about the year 1500, church reformer **Martin Luther 216**, noticed the beauty of a group of evergreens. So he brought one back to his pad and decorated it with candles. Prince Albert, the German husband of Queen Victoria, introduced the practice to England in the mid-1800s and from there it spread to other countries.

TOUCHING TREES

The idea of touching or knocking on wood probably derives from an ancient belief that a tree (often an oak) had the power to ward off evil. Before Christianity spread through Europe in the fourth century AD, people worshipped nature. Known as pagans, they thought that protective spirits lived in the trees.

MOON TREES

In 1971, seeds from redwood, sycamore, Douglas fir, and other trees went into **space 048** with Apollo 14 and orbited the Moon 34 times. They were planted all over the Earth and former President Gerald Ford described them as living symbols of "our spectacular human and scientific achievements." Sadly, no one kept a record of where all the trees went. And because the Moon Trees are exactly the same as normal trees—Houston, we have a problem (we can't find them).

MORE TALKING TREES

The Family Plot

Talk about old relatives, in *The Lord of the Rings*, Aragorn son of Arathorn can trace his family history back to Isildur, the prince who fought the evil Saruman but failed to destroy the One Ring. Not bad when you consider that Isildur lived 3,000 years before. (Somewhere, Aragorn must have a family tree the size of a football field.) The tree is a device for plotting your ancestors and their relationships. This study of family pedigrees is called genealogy. It's a way of **mapping 068** the story of our relatives—and another way to answer the question, where do I come from?

great grandma

grandma — grandpa

dad — mom

You

MEMBERSHIP: TREE CLUB

NAME: tree
DESCRIPTION: At least 16 ft (5 m) tall and 4 in (10 cm) thick
RESTRICTIONS: Woody plants of diminished height are called shrubs

EXCEPTIONS: Japanese Bonsai trees, despite being tiny. Their small size is the result of careful pruning: left alone they'd grow to full tree height

OLDER THAN NOAH'S GRANDDAD

*The oldest living tree is nicknamed Methuselah, after (the biblical character) Noah's grandfather. It's a 4,700-year-old bristlecone pine that lives way up in the White Mountains in California. Here's a tree that was a seedling when **the pyramids 314** went up, that hit maturity when Jesus was alive and entered old age just as you were being born. Still, it's a youngster compared to polar lichen (plantlike fungus) and North American creosote bushes, which can be over 10,000 years old.*

JUST WHAT IS A FRACTAL?

You may have seen fractals in a math textbook. But they also appear in nature in the design of a tree leaf. A fractal (part of chaos theory) is all about pattern and repetition. In a tree, the same basic "Y" shape of the trunk and branches is repeated within the branches and then repeated in the twigs and then in the leaves. This gives a strong, compact structure that needs less energy to grow. In leaves, the spread of Y-shaped stems lets trees absorb the greatest amount of water and carbon dioxide.

In our **lungs 134**, the tubes are broccoli-shaped to supply the greatest amount of oxygen. One famous fractal is the Sierpinski Triangle (left). If you zoom in on it, the pattern will repeat itself endlessly, without ever leaving the borders of the original triangle (it just gets really, really small).

THE SCARIEST DINOSAUR THAT NEVER LIVED

*"Terrible lizard"—that's what dinosaur means. British geologist Richard Owen combined two **Greek 240** words to invent it in 1842. Here, Pick Me Up presents the most terrible dinosaur of them all. We've called him Hideousaurus. He really is a **Frankenstein's monster 206**: the best parts of all the others stitched into one supersized beast.*

DEADLIEST BITE
Tyrannosaurus Rex
(65 million years ago)

If they were around today, *T.rex* could swallow you—yes, you—in one single gulp. Their sawlike teeth would tear your flesh to ribbons. These powerful meat-eaters were extremely scary, with strong jaws and huge teeth. *T.rex* stood over 41 ft (12.4 m) long and up to 20 ft (6 m) tall—that's bigger than a double-decker bus. But their little arms were just over 3 ft (1 m) long (making them terrible at tennis).

(fig. 1)

MOST INTELLIGENT
Troodon
(75 million years ago)

A man-sized meat-eater, *Troodon* was probably the smartest of the dinosaurs—it had a large brain for the size of its body. *Troodon* also had great eyesight. And a cool name that means "wounding tooth." Sadly, being the smartest dinosaur didn't mean he could read the **newspaper 292** or do algebra. He was still more stupid than modern birds and **mammals 124**. D'oh!

(fig. 2)

LONGEST NECK
Mamenchisaurus
(156 million years ago)

Mamenchisaurus ("ferry lizard") would make today's giraffe look positively squat. Their necks were 43 ft (13 m) long on a body that was 112 ft (34 m) in length. The modern giraffe can barely reach up 20 ft (6 m)! With tiny heads and tiny brains, they needed an extra nerve center near their hips to control the back legs and tail. Because of their sheer size, they would have had to eat nonstop.

(fig. 3)

fig. 5

fig. 8

fig. 6

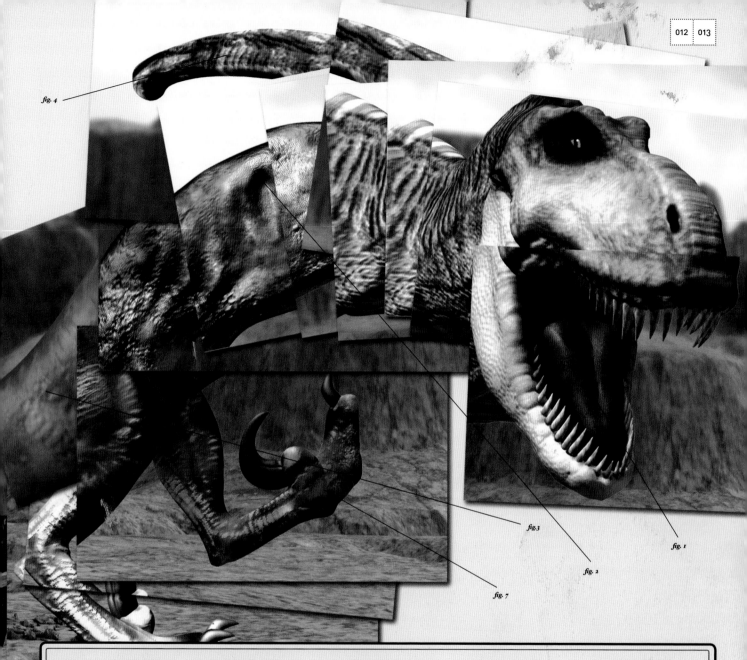

fig. 4

fig. 3

fig. 1

fig. 2

fig. 7

FREAKIEST SOUND
Parasaurolophus
(65 million years ago)

The "similar crested lizard" boasted a long, hollow crest that emerged from the back of its head. Through this, it could make a sound like a trumpet. Paaaarrrrrrrrrrrpppppp! No one's quite sure why. Maybe it was to cause fear, maybe to attract a mate. Maybe it wanted to start a band.

(fig. 4)

BEST PROTECTION
Ankylosaurus
(65 million years ago)

Built like a tank, *Ankylosaurus* was armor-plated with a strong club tail. Even its eyelids were armored, making it one tough lizard. You wouldn't want to stand behind it: if the clublike tail didn't get you, its terrible farts certainly would. The name means "stiff lizard," which would be a good name for a rock group. Hey, *Parasaurolophus*, over here!

(fig. 5)

MOST LETHAL TAIL
Stegosaurus
(152 million years ago)

Stegosaurus translates as "covered lizard." Its tail was blessed with four, three-foot-long (1 m) spikes. Sadly, old *Stego* was as thick as two short planks. Its brain was the size of a pingpong ball in a body the size of a truck. Lucky *Stegosaurus* had all that armor, or it would probably have spiked itself to **death 162**. Ouch!

(fig. 6)

MOST VICIOUS CLAWS
Utahraptor
(127 million years ago)

On each foot, *Utahraptor* had retractable, slashing claws that measured 8 in (20 cm). And he was also quick, making *Utahraptor* one of the most deadly dinosaurs around. The name means "robber from Utah"—Utah being the state where this dinosaur was discovered.

(fig. 7)

FASTEST LEGS
Dromiceiomimus
(65 million years ago)

Dubbed "emu mimic" because they looked a little like emus, these beak-faced dinosaurs were 11 ft (3.4 m) long and 6 ft (1.8 m) high (as tall as tall men), with great, athletic thighs. They could run at speeds of up to 37 mph (60 km/h)—faster than a tiger. Their **brains 038** were around the same size as an ostrich's, making them quite bright by dinosaur standards.

(fig. 8)

HOW TO TELL TALES

Stories twist and turn through our lives like snakes. As toddlers, they are read to us, at the movies we watch them, and on the playground we hear at least a dozen a day. But where do stories come from? The starting point is usually the plot (the sequence of events that happen). Some believe that every single story can be reduced to basic plots like the ones below, no matter where, when, or by whom they were written.

1 CHARACTER vs. NATURE

Your sailing trip is hit by a freak storm and you find yourself on a totally deserted island. Surviving on coconuts and a strange blue fruit like an apple, you build a raft from tree branches and sail to safety. Fortunately, you pack some fruits—naming them "blues"—and become a famous trader on your return.

Spot the plot: *Robinson Crusoe, Lord of the Flies, The Perfect Storm*

2 CHARACTER vs. CHARACTER

The new kid in class, you accidentally upset the **school 160** loudmouths by sitting at "their" cafeteria table. After eating packed lunches outside for two weeks, you face up to them. In a 12:30 p.m. showdown they fling spaghetti all over you, but you ignore them, becoming a pasta-covered idol for weaker pupils.

Spot the plot: *Othello,* **Rebel Without a Cause 274**, *David and Goliath*

3 CHARACTER vs. ENVIRONMENT

All you've ever wanted to do is draw cartoons, but everyone insists you take up teaching, banking, or some stable profession. You endure brief social isolation with only your drawings as comfort, but eventually become a millionaire computer game designer. Ha!

Spot the plot: *Oliver Twist, The Canterbury Tales, Cinderella*

4 CHARACTER vs. GOD

You've got a chess match against God, and you think you have a good shot. It's after school in front of a massive crowd. God checkmates your king before you make the first move. You feel foolish—you should have known it would be a tough match. Maybe you're going to have to respect Him.

Spot the plot: *The Odyssey,* **Moby Dick 114**, *Book of Job*

5 CHARACTER vs. SUPERNATURAL

It's the middle of the night. It's dark. And you're sure an old woman just leapt out of your bedroom mirror. Once your heart removes itself from your mouth, you start chatting with her. She tells wonderful stories. Before she disappears, she says she lived in your room 100 years ago. Next morning you think it was a dream, but then you notice her handbag by your bed. Creepy.

Spot the plot: *Ghostbusters, Metamorphosis, Harry Potter*

6 CHARACTER vs. SELF

It's the end of your birthday party. As you look around at the bobbing balloons and leftover cake a voice in your head dejectedly shouts: "I wanted more people! I wanted more presents!" You then feel guilty for being so ungrateful. "I have it all," you think, "and I'm still not happy." Downer.

Spot the plot: *The Bell Jar, The Catcher in the Rye, Finding Nemo*

7 CHARACTER vs. MACHINE

Thanks to your new robotic rollerboots, you can do all those tricky moves you've been practicing in the local park. A crowd flocks, and you do a fancy routine in time to music. But suddenly you're flung from the skates and they speed away, kicking and twirling into the distance, leaving you feeling pretty foolish.

Spot the plot: *The Iron Giant, Watership Down, I, Robot*

8 YOU DECIDE!

Can you write an eighth plot? It might be completely different from these—or a mixture of them all!

THE HEAVYWEIGHT CHAMPIONSHIP OF YOUR SPARE TIME

BOOKS vs. TELEVISION

A CLASH OF TWO HIGHLY ADDICTIVE PASTIMES

IN THE BLUE CORNER
BOOKS

No ads
Increases concentration span
More portable than TV 330
The story comes to life in your head—and is sometimes way better than the movie version
Much more information than a 30-minute TV show
Can borrow books for free from the library

TICKETS AVAILABLE
BOTH

Escapism
Can make you ignore people around you… or encourage chitchat if you've seen the same program or read the same book
Make you more aware of the world and other people = make you a more interesting person!

IN THE RED CORNER
TELEVISION

Full of celebs
You don't need to concentrate as hard
Easier and quicker to watch the movie than read the whole book
You learn lots if you watch documentaries or the news
Big choice of programs (especially if you have cable)
Annoys parents

LIVE FROM YOUR LIVING ROOM!

Libraries are full of hot air

Many well-known stories originated from spoken tales, changing as they were repeated from person to person, before eventually being scrawled onto paper

All's Well That Ends Well, Romeo and Juliet, King Lear
Although **Shakespeare 222** had a powerful imagination, his stories weren't always original. Some started as 12th-century folktales, which, in turn, were based on earlier stories.

Alice in Wonderland
British author Lewis Carroll (1832-1898) first told the story to Alice Liddell, the little girl who inspired his main character, in 1862. It was published, in 1865, after many retellings.

Sleeping Beauty, Cinderella, Rapunzel and Hansel & Gretel
Before they were published by the Brothers Grimm, these fairy tales were told to courtiers by Giambattista Basile (1575–1632), an Italian tale collector. His versions were more adult—Sleeping Beauty wakes up after having two children! In fact, even Basile heard them in Crete and Venice first. For all we know, *Sleeping Beauty* could originally have been called *Home Alone!*

Romeo loves someone—Rosalind—until he meets Juliet, that is.

Romeo and Juliet have a smooch, before Juliet realizes Romeo is part of the Montague clan—the enemies of her family, the Capulets.

They get married anyway. Then Romeo kills Juliet's cousin right after. Oops.

Juliet drinks a potion to look like she's dead and cleverly escape all the fighting for a happy life with her true love Romeo.

But he thinks she's really dead and kills himself. So Juliet kills herself when she wakes up. But their parents make up.

Hmmmm, interesting.

HOW TO TELL TALL TALES

Fritz Kreisler (1875-1962), a talented Austrian violinist, fooled everyone into thinking music he had written was by historically famous composers. Critics were amazed—and red-faced—when he later confessed. No one minded though—the music was too good.

In 1899 four journalists from Denver decided to spice up a slow news day by printing a fake story. They printed that the Chinese were tearing down the **Great Wall 264** and replacing it with a road, and that American firms were involved. The story made front-page news in California before the newsmen owned up. Years later, rumors spread that the Chinese had heard the story and attacked Westerners in rage. That wasn't true either.

The king of liars was millionaire Brian Hughes, a paper-box manufacturer who lived in New York City from 1849 to 1924 and founded the Dollar Savings Bank. A lifelong fibber, he once donated a public park in Brooklyn, which turned out to be a tiny plot of land Hughes had purchased for $35 (there was certainly no room for ball games). He also left imitation jewels outside Tiffany's (the famous jewelers) to watch passers-by steal them, and planted empty picture frames in front of an art museum, causing a panicked search for "stolen" paintings. What a card!

01. Co to jest?

02. YINI LENA?

03. ‎يعني ايش؟‎

04. QU'EST-CE QUE C'EST?

05. Mikä tämä on?

06. Bu nedir?

07. Что бы это значило?

08. यह क्या है?

09. Beth yw hyn?

10. O QUE É ISTO?

11. Τι είναι αυτό;

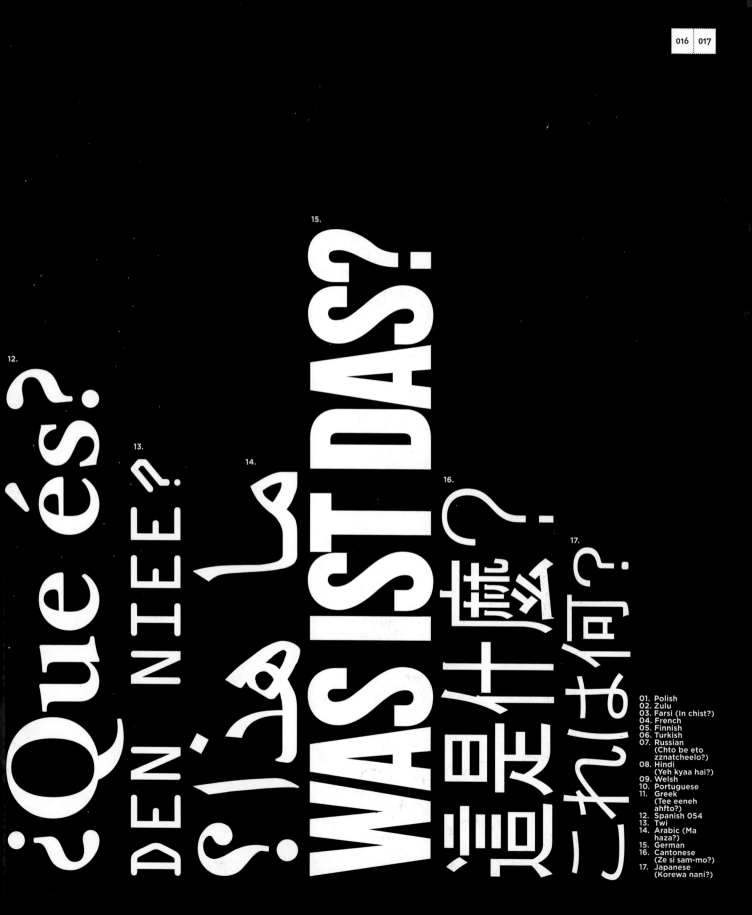

15.
12.
¿Que és?
13.
DEN NIEE?
14.
WAS IST DAS?
16.
17.

01. Polish
02. Zulu
03. Farsi (In chist?)
04. French
05. Finnish
06. Turkish
07. Russian
     (Chto be eto
     zznatcheelo?)
08. Hindi
     (Yeh kyaa hai?)
09. Welsh
10. Portuguese
11. Greek
     (Tee eeneh
     ahfto?)
12. Spanish 054
13. Twi
14. Arabic (Ma
     haza?)
15. German
16. Cantonese
     (Ze si sam-mo?)
17. Japanese
     (Korewa nani?)

THE SUPER POWERS OF PLANTS!

Plants serve living creatures in many diverse ways. They prevent **floods 136** and soil erosion, give off oxygen, provide food and shelter for animals and man, and are a source of **medicine 270** to fight diseases. But you knew all that. Now, it's time to discover their other, more surprising skills...

They can live for centuries!

The oldest living individual plants are the bristlecone pine trees (above and below) found in arid areas of North America. Some are over 4,000 years old. Scientists can study their annual **rings 010** to work out how the world's climate has developed. Other trees, such as the oak (leaves, left), don't produce seeds until they're over 20 (or sometimes even 50) years old—but can continue to produce them for 200 years.

They can invade!

Some species can establish themselves almost anywhere. The buddleia plant (above left) was originally found in China. In the late 19th century, it was brought over to England—now, the hardy species has spread across the globe and thrives in urban areas in Europe, New Zealand, Australia, and the US. The purple loosestrife (above right) is a herb native to Europe that was introduced to North America in the mid-1800s. A single plant can produce up to 300,000 seeds, and the loosestrife has now spread to more than 40 US states.

They can protect themselves!

Plants are under constant attack from all kinds of herbivorous (plant-eating) animals. So, many plants have **evolved 206** cunning defense tricks. Conifer trees (such as the caucasian fir, above) ooze gum to jam up greedy insects' mouths and feet. Nettles have sharp hairs that can break animals' skin to inject painful chemicals called histamines. To prevent animals stealing the water stored in cactus stems, the plant's leaves have developed into piercing spines. Perhaps the shrewdest plant of all is the passionflower vine (inset, above). Postman **butterflies 232** lay their eggs on the plant, so the caterpillars can eat the leaves when they hatch. But the butterfly won't bother if there are eggs there already. In response, the plant has adapted to grow fake "eggs" so the butterflies stay away.

They can sleep!

Well, kind of. Just like humans, plants take up more comfortable positions at night. Flowers, such as the wood anemone (above left) and cuckoo flower (above right), close their petals or droop at night to keep out the cold. Sweet.

They can fly!

Plant seeds need to be scattered widely to reach the best habitats—with plenty of nutrients and lots of light. Many seeds literally fly to their destination. Willow tree, milk thistle (above right), and dandelion (above left) seeds have tufts or plumes of hair. These act like parachutes to achieve gliding flight—so the seeds can fly many miles (or kilometers) without any power. The seeds of the ash (leaves, right), birch, maple, and elm (above center) trees have thin **wings 304** that work in a similar way. These wings keep seeds airborne by twirling in a "helicopter" motion.

How many of these things do NOT come from PLANTS?

Dye
Medicine
Beer
Cocoa butter moisturizer
Rubber
Tea
Coal
Rope
Chewing gum

They can come back to life!

Many plants die after one or two years. Downer. But wait—some plants, known as herbaceous perennials, only partly die at the end of their growing season, and can live for an indefinite time. Although they appear to have no life and the top portion dies, they retain reserves of food, such as starches and sugars, in their root systems. They then use this to sprout shoots the following year. For example, onion bulbs (above) are shortened stems that store food underground. If we didn't eat them first, they'd supply food for new plants to grow.

A short history of flower power

Ever wondered what—or who—a hippy really is? Well, they were people who got together to throw one long, nonstop party throughout the 1960s and 1970s, and were especially big in the US. They believed in peace, **rock'n'roll 152,** and loving everyone and everything, but thought the **Vietnam War 294,** consumerism (too much shopping), and the power of corporations "were a real downer, man." They decorated their long hair with flowers, and wore flared, tie-dyed clothes, plenty of beads, and big floppy hats (look, it was cool at the time, okay?).

And, of course, they use insects to their advantage!

The sundew (above) captures and eats insects. It has flat, bristled leaves that release a sticky liquid to trap an insect when it lands. The plant then pours digestive juices over its victim to absorb all its nutrients. But not every plant kills insects. Many, such as the ox-eye daisy (right), have worked out a happier deal. In exchange for nectar (a sweet, sugary liquid), bees help these plants to reproduce. Before plants produce seeds, their flowers must be fertilized. This occurs only when dustlike pollen, produced by stamens (the male parts of flowers) finds its way to a stigma (female part). While a bee drinks nectar from deep inside a flower, its body becomes dusted with pollen. It then carries this pollen to the next flower it visits, where stigmas brush it off. Job done.

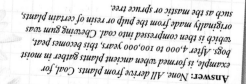

Answer: *None. All derive from plants. Coal, for example, is formed when ancient plants gather in moist bogs. After 4,000 to 100,000 years, this becomes peat, which is then compressed into coal. Chewing gum was originally made from the pulp or resin of certain plants, such as the mastic or spruce tree.*

Life in the real world

How the world looks if each country is sized by its share of world population

More than 1 billion people	
More than 150 million people	
More than 50 million people	
More than 25 million people	
More than 10 million people	
More than 5 million people	
Fewer than 5 million people	

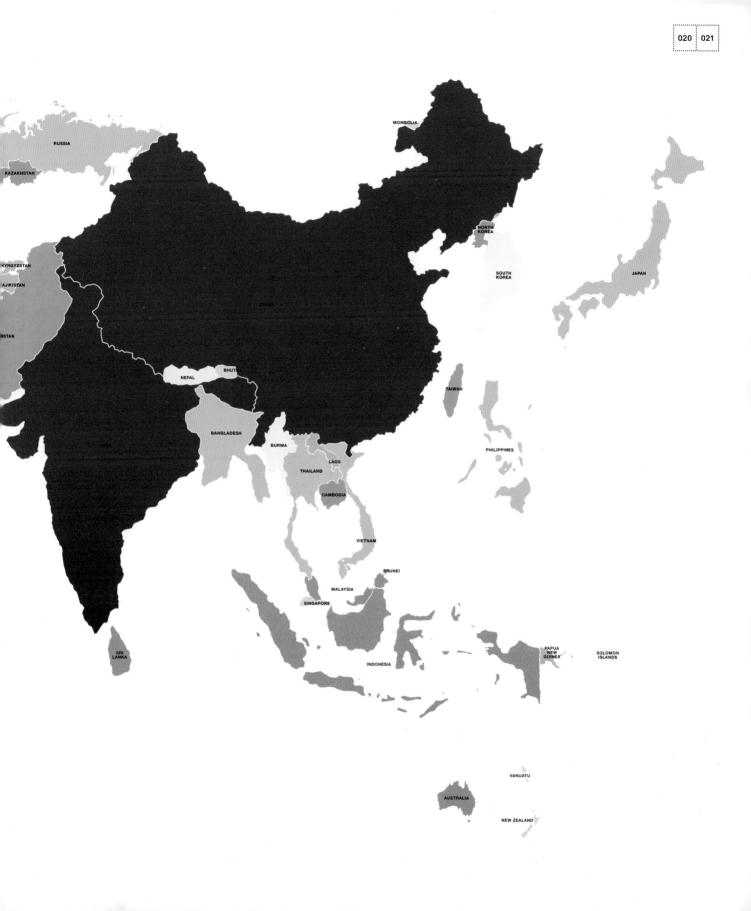

WAS BEETHOVEN A PUNK?

ONE OF THE MOST FAMOUS composers of all time, Ludwig van Beethoven was born in Bonn, **Germany 244**, in 1770. The road to success was not easy. His grandfather died, then his mother died and his dad became an alcoholic. The family spiraled into poverty. By the time he was 18, Beethoven was the main breadwinner. He was a determined and impatient character, as well as something of a loner. Famous for his hot-headed temper, he stuck out as an individual. His music reflected his extreme dislike for the rich and powerful and his dreams of rebellion. Some 200 years later, punk rock band the Sex Pistols took a similar line. They made punk famous with angry-sounding songs such as "Anarchy in the UK."

TURN THAT RACKET DOWN!

Beethoven began work on his controversial *Third Symphony* in the summer of 1803. This radical piece divided audiences with its brash directness. It was part of a musical trend called Romanticism, which began in the early 19th century. Composers broke away from pretty harmonies and served up drastic, dynamic key changes. They took new approaches to rhythm and melody, and tunes became much shorter. This was music about emotion. The new ideas were inspired by the turmoil of the **French Revolution 138**. Beethoven even dedicated his *Third Symphony* to the French leader **Napoleon Bonaparte 216**. But Beethoven's own radicalism ran deep. When Napoleon crowned himself Emperor of the French, flying in the face of all his previous revolutionary beliefs, the composer ditched the reference to him and named the work *Sinfonia Eroica* (meaning heroic symphony—a much better name anyway).

Bonaparte Crossing the Great St. Bernards Pass (1801) by Jacques-Louis David

PUNK is a set of social and political beliefs that rejects everyday thinking and conformity.

HOW TO PLAY THE OPENING TO BEETHOVEN'S *FIFTH* ON BOTTLES

1,2,3 4 1,2,3 4

BEETHOVEN'S RECORD SALES: 173 MILLION

SEX PISTOLS' RECORD SALES: 35 MILLION

DISCUSS

HOW MUSIC AFFECTS YOUR BRAIN

What is it about music that can trigger memories and change our moods, for better or worse? After all, it's just a collection of sounds and noises. When you hear a piece of music (or any sound), your ear converts the sound waves into vibrations. This movement is then converted into electrical signals that travel to your **brain 038**. These signals are then translated into their own **language 054** of electrical impulses, which generates various thoughts, feelings, and emotions. Major keys (A, B, etc.) and fast beats stimulate happiness, for instance, but minor keys (A minor, B minor, etc.) and slow tempos generate sadness. The pattern of impulses is recorded by your brain. And when you hear the music again, it triggers those same emotions. This is the same for all music, from classical to **pop 305**.

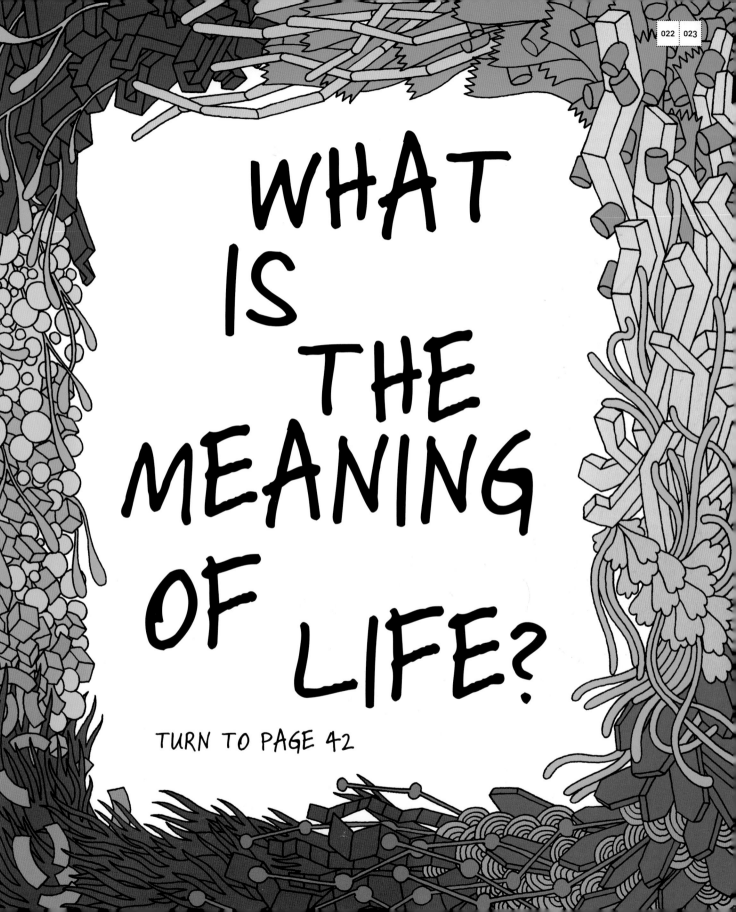

WHAT IS THE MEANING OF LIFE?

TURN TO PAGE 42

DROP THIS BOOK AND A PENCIL TO TEST GRAVITY

They hit the floor at the same time, right? Good, that means gravity is working. The heavier thing (the book) doesn't hit the ground first because gravity, though, slows things down, which is why feathers and leaves fall gently to the ground.

Air resistance, makes any object, heavy or light, accelerate (speed up) at the same rate.

Brain of Britain— 1687

The English scientist Sir Isaac Newton (1643-1727) had one of his best ideas after watching an apple fall from a tree—he came up with a theory of gravity. As a physicist, mathematician, astronomer, philosopher, and all around general egghead Newton wasn't short of ideas. In fact, he is regarded as a founder of modern science. He realized gravity was the same force that made apples fall and the Moon orbit the Earth. Gravity acts everywhere, between any two objects, no matter how small or large. It's the reason we don't float off into space, why the **planets 172** go around the Sun, and how the Moon creates tides. In 1687, Newton published his ideas in a book, *Mathematical Principles Of Natural Philosophy*, that, despite the boring title, is one of the most important books in scientific history. Newton was also an alchemist, a less than respectable occupation. Alchemists used a mix of chemistry and magic in an attempt to make gold. Newton has also been called the "last of the magicians."

SOME OTHER IMPORTANT APPLES

ADAM AND EVE: According to the Bible, Eve committed the first sin ever when she took a bite of the forbidden fruit.

WILLIAM TELL: The Swiss hero is famous for shooting an arrow through an apple balanced on his son's head. Don't try this at home.

BIG APPLE: The nickname for New York City was first used in the 1920s by a horse-racing columnist.

GRAVITY MACHINE

A roller coaster wouldn't be much fun without gravity. It is the Earth's gravitational pull toward its center that makes a roller coaster roll.

MEN'S WIGS

Newton's poodlelike wig was all the rage in the late 17th century. The French king Louis XIV made wigs ultrafashionable and it was quite the thing to wear them long with plenty of curls. Oh, yes.

SCIENCE
CAN GET YOU INTO TROUBLE

Newton was made a professor at Cambridge University in England for his work, but it isn't always straightforward being a **scientist 326**. The Catholic Church didn't like it when scientists came up with ideas that contradicted its views of the world. In 1633, the Italian scientist Galileo Galilei (1564-1642) was made to deny his beliefs about the universe, or face torture. The Church didn't like him saying that the Earth wasn't the center of the universe and he was arrested.

We're at the top, hold tight.

The higher we are, the more distance there is for gravity to pull us down and the faster we'll go.

During the day, gravity pulls on your spine so you are up to 1/2 inch (1.25 cm) shorter at bedtime. As you sleep, you return to normal.

Gravity is pulling the car, making us rush down the slope. This is the fun part.

As the rails head upward, we slow down, as gravity applies a backward force to the coaster.

We're being dragged up the hill...

Roller coasters can hit speeds of 120 mph (195 km/h)—as fast as an intercity train.

HERE WE GO...!

WHOOOOOAAAAA!!!

GRAVITY AIN'T ALWAYS HEAVY

How strong gravity is depends on an object's mass—that's how much stuff it contains. The Sun, because it is so large, has enough gravitational pull to keep all the nine planets of the solar system in orbit. The Moon, because it is smaller, has much weaker gravity (about one-sixth of the Earth's), which is why astronauts bounce around on it rather than walk. There is even a tiny gravitational pull between you and this book.

DO TRY
Golf. Tiger Woods hits a golf ball 360 yards (330 m). But on the **Moon 048**, his ball would travel over 2,160 yards (1,975 m).

DO'S & DON'TS ON THE MOON

DON'T TRY
Drinking a cup of coffee, since the liquid won't pour into your throat, but spill out onto your face. Ouch.

DO TRY
Jumping and throwing. The high jump record (on Earth) is 8 ft (2.45 m), but on the Moon, an athlete could jump nearly 49 ft (15 m). Other events such as the javelin or shot put would also be more fun.

DON'T TRY
Running, because you can't. You just end up taking long leaps. The stronger gravity on Earth helps you run faster by allowing you to take more steps.

As the Moon orbits the Earth, its gravitational force attracts the oceans, pulling them toward it. This creates tides. Fortunately, the Moon's gravity isn't strong enough to pull the water off our planet.

1. **The**
2. **Philosopher's**
3. **Stone**

4. Alchemy dates back to **ancient Egypt 100** and China. Alchemists hoped to change common metals into gold or silver. The mythical substance that would make this happen was called the philosopher's stone. It could also be used to create a potion that would make humans immortal. Alchemists' experiments helped lay the foundations of modern chemistry. In 1997, J. K. Rowling used the name for the first Harry Potter book.

5. **Au** Gold
6. **Ag** Silver
7. **Ma** Magic

But as we reach the top again, gravity drags us back down.

If you weigh 80 lbs (36 kg) on Earth, you'd be heavier on Jupiter—nearly 207 lbs (94 kg)—because gravity there is so strong.

To break away from the pull of Earth's gravity, a rocket must fly at 7 miles (11 km) a second. This is the "escape velocity."

Hey, is that a black hole...?

Gravity is weird. The closer you are to a gravitational field's source, the slower time passes. A clock high on a mountain runs slightly quicker than one at sea level.

I want to get off.

They have such a large gravitational pull that nothing can escape from them—not even light.

I feel sick.

Not in my face.

How'd that get here? Black holes are found in space.

Who turned the lights out?

Spot

the

odd

IT'S THE LESSER WEEVER (11), THE ONLY SPECIES HERE NOT EATEN BY MAN. WE GOBBLE ALL THE
REST, AND LOTS OF OUR FOOD COMES OUT OF THE OCEANS 202. THE LESSER WEEVER IS FOUND AROUND
WESTERN EUROPE. THEY MAY BE ONLY 4-6 INCHES IN LENGTH (10-15 CM), BUT THEY HAVE AN ENORMOUSLY
PAINFUL STING. THEY HIDE THEMSELVES UNDER SAND, SO WATCH WHERE YOU STEP!

1.	BLACK SEA BASS	4.	CRAB	8.	HADDOCK
2.	CATFISH	5.	HALIBUT	9.	ROCK FISH
3.	OPAH	6.	SQUID	10.	PUFFER FISH
		7.	SPEARFISH	11.	LESSER WEEVER

one

out

21.

22.

23.

24.

25.

26.

27.

28.

29.

30.

31.

32.

33.

34.

35.

36.

37.

38.

39.

40.

41.

42.

43.

12. POMFRET	16. TUNA	20. FLOUNDER	24. WAHOO	28. MARLIN	32. SEAL	36. SCAD	39. WHALE	42. POLLOCK
13. OCTOPUS	17. CONCH	21. TREVALLY	25. CRAYFISH	29. COD	33. CLAM	37. WHITE	40. ORANGE	43. MONKFISH
14. SOLE	18. SHRIMP	22. SALMON	26. SCALLOP	30. SHARK	34. TROUT	SEA BASS	ROUGHY	
15. WRECKFISH	19. SNAPPER	23. SAND DAB	27. MACKEREL	31. DORADO	35. ABALONE	38. HERRING	41. LOBSTER	

Japan...

10%

Almost one in 10 active volcanoes are in Japan

The country has more than 75 active volcanoes 136

One in five of all major earthquakes* occur in Japan
(*over 6.0 on the Richter scale)

→ There are 5.5 million **vending machines** in Japan, one for every 23 people. Around half sell drinks. The rest dispense items such as fresh flowers, single pages from newspapers, live lobsters, toys, rice, and underwear.

Drinks

Underwear   Newspapers   Lobsters

Toys   Flowers   Rice

↓ More patents—registers of **new inventions**—are granted in Japan than anywhere else in the world. In 2001, 118,535 patents were awarded to residents of Japan. Second was the **US 256**, with 85,528 patents.

Japan 118,535

USA 85,528

← Japan is made up of more than **3,000 islands**: 600 are occupied. Three-quarters of Japan is hills or **mountains**.

← One-third of all **tuna** caught in the world is eaten in Japan. Seafood is often served raw, either plain (sashimi) or rolled with rice (sushi). Fugu (a pufferfish) is poisonous if the bad bits aren't removed.

Famous Japanese inventions include the **digital watch** and the **portable music player**.

Biggest city
Tokyo is the heart of the biggest conurbation (urban area) in the world, home to 35 million people—around one in four Japanese

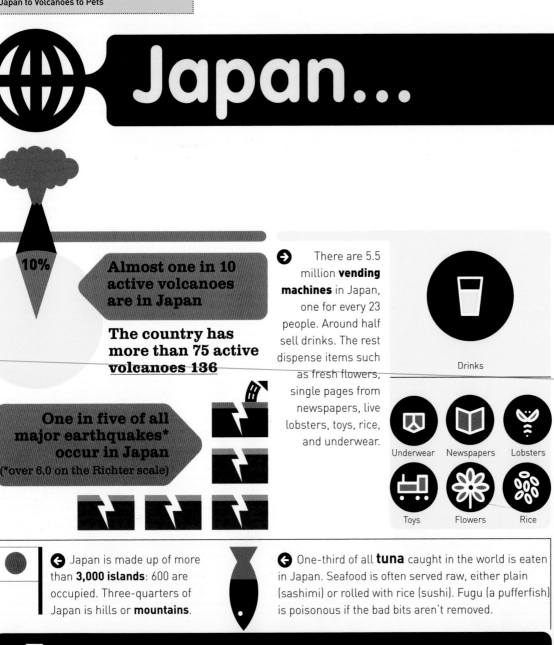

Tokyo	Mexico City	LA	Moscow	Paris	London
35 million	**18.7 million**	**12 million**	**10.5 million**	**9.8 million**	**7.6 million**

↑ **Where is Japan?**

↑ **Nation knowledge**

 Population **127 million— holding steady**

 Life expectancy for men: **78 years**

Life expectancy for women: **84 years**

❓ There are **135,000** karaoke booths in Japan

Vacations

Minimum days' vacation from work per year

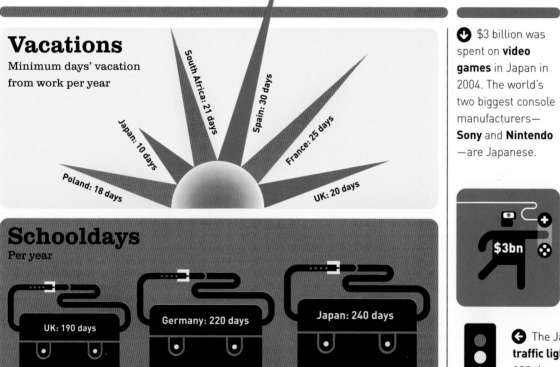

South Africa: 21 days

Spain: 30 days

Japan: 10 days

France: 25 days

Poland: 18 days

UK: 20 days

Schooldays

Per year

UK: 190 days

Germany: 220 days

Japan: 240 days

⬇ $3 billion was spent on **video games** in Japan in 2004. The world's two biggest console manufacturers— **Sony** and **Nintendo** —are Japanese.

⬇ Japan is home to an estimated 19 million **pets 130**. There are more pets in Japan than there are children under 15.

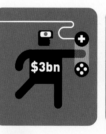

$3bn

19m

 ◀ The Japanese call green **traffic lights** "blue"—the **color 128** they were when first introduced.

Greeting cards

The Japanese send **four billion cards** to celebrate New Year's Day. That's more than 30 cards for every person in the country.

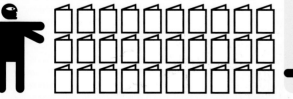

Travel

Japanese who traveled abroad in 2003—16.5 million
Foreigners who traveled to Japan in 2003—5.2 million

In 5.2m

Japan

Out 16.5m

PMU'S ALL-STAR FEARLESS FEMALE FIGHTERS

SELECT YOUR FIGHTER

CLEOPATRA VII PHILOPATOR
69 BC–30 BC, Egypt

QIU JIN
1875-1907, China

ELIZABETH I
1533-1603, England

HER STORY

She was the last Greek monarch of <u>ancient Egypt 100</u>, coruling with members of her family, including her brother-husband. In those days, kings and queens had to marry their siblings to ensure their right to the throne. Yuk!

She organized an uprising against the old-fashioned Qing dynasty that ruled <u>China 264</u>. This helped change forever the lives of Chinese people. She opposed foot binding and in 1906 founded a radical women's journal in Shanghai.

She was Queen of England and Ireland. During her reign, English power increased dramatically. She led her subjects through war with Spain, improved the national economy, and survived various treasonous plots.

HER KILLER POWER

She refused to take the back seat while sharing the crown. Her independence made her unpopular. But she had kids with two Roman rulers, <u>Julius Caesar 216</u> and Mark Antony. They helped secure her reign (now that's lucky in love).

She was brave enough to leave her family and start a revolution. When her plans were exposed, she became the first woman martyr of the rebellion. Her courage motivated others to join it.

Despite being surrounded by male advisers who disapproved of a female monarch and demanded she provide an heir, Elizabeth never married. Instead, she used her single status as a political weapon.

TRIPLE BONUS KNOWLEDGE POINTS

She killed herself by allowing a poisonous snake to bite her, after the Romans invaded Egypt. On a lighter note, she learned Egyptian—the rest of her family spoke Greek during their 300-year reign.

She began practicing martial arts during childhood, even though she had little use for such skills. Under the Qing dynasty, <u>girls 080</u> were confined to doing traditional tasks, such as housework.

She was a writer and poet (like her father Henry the Eighth), and could speak six <u>languages 016</u>. The US state of Virginia is also named after her, as she was nicknamed the Virgin Queen.

FIGHTING TALK

"Be it known that we, the greatest, are misthought."

Cleopatra suspected that the invading Romans would accuse her of using her lovers to gain power. Rather than suffer this slur, she killed herself.

"Though I was not born with a man's body, I was born with a mind stronger than man's."

This was her self-styled motto. She used it to inspire herself to succeed in a male-dominated society.

"I would rather be a beggar and single than a queen and married."

This was her famous response when Parliament pressured her to marry. Normally, she hid her inner thoughts and feelings from the public.

ROCKING RATING

THIS TEMPTRESS IN A HEADDRESS WAS ONE OF THE FIRST TO BRAVE THE BATTLE OF THE SEXES.

THIS LADY HIGH-KICKED HER WAY TO EQUALITY—NOT JUST FOR THE LADIES, BUT FOR THE MEN, TOO.

THE SASSY SPINSTER KEPT HER HEAD —WHEN OTHERS WANTED TO CHOP IT OFF. A WORLD-CLASS MONARCH.

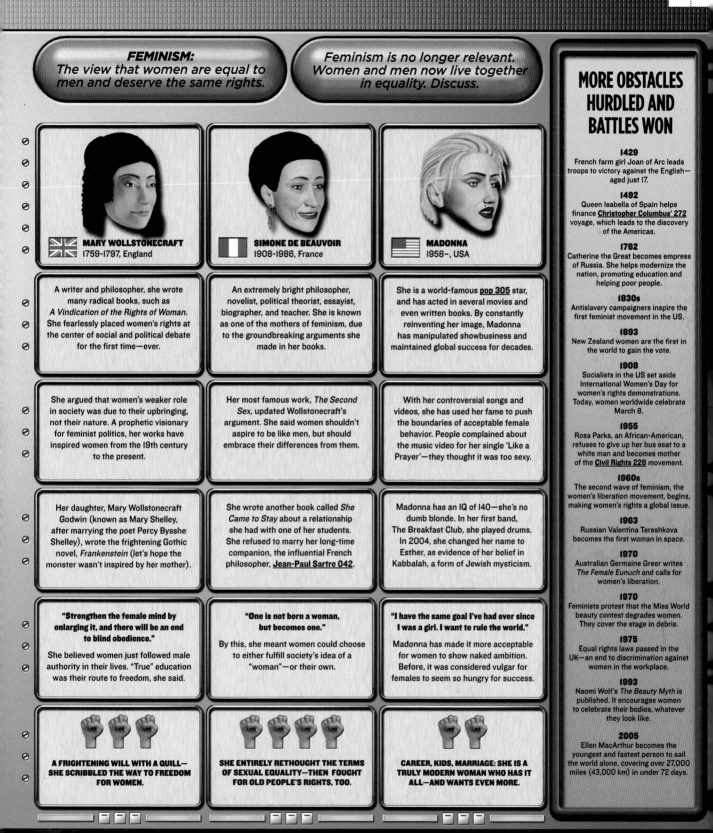

FEMINISM:
The view that women are equal to men and deserve the same rights.

Feminism is no longer relevant. Women and men now live together in equality. Discuss.

MORE OBSTACLES HURDLED AND BATTLES WON

1429
French farm girl Joan of Arc leads troops to victory against the English—aged just 17.

1492
Queen Isabella of Spain helps finance <u>Christopher Columbus' 272</u> voyage, which leads to the discovery of the Americas.

1762
Catherine the Great becomes empress of Russia. She helps modernize the nation, promoting education and helping poor people.

1830s
Antislavery campaigners inspire the first feminist movement in the US.

1893
New Zealand women are the first in the world to gain the vote.

1908
Socialists in the US set aside International Women's Day for women's rights demonstrations. Today, women worldwide celebrate March 8.

1955
Rosa Parks, an African-American, refuses to give up her bus seat to a white man and becomes mother of the <u>Civil Rights 226</u> movement.

1960s
The second wave of feminism, the women's liberation movement, begins, making women's rights a global issue.

1963
Russian Valentina Tereshkova becomes the first woman in space.

1970
Australian Germaine Greer writes *The Female Eunuch* and calls for women's liberation.

1970
Feminists protest that the Miss World beauty contest degrades women. They cover the stage in debris.

1975
Equal rights laws passed in the UK—an end to discrimination against women in the workplace.

1993
Naomi Wolf's *The Beauty Myth* is published. It encourages women to celebrate their bodies, whatever they look like.

2005
Ellen MacArthur becomes the youngest and fastest person to sail the world alone, covering over 27,000 miles (43,000 km) in under 72 days.

MARY WOLLSTONECRAFT
1759-1797, England

A writer and philosopher, she wrote many radical books, such as *A Vindication of the Rights of Woman*. She fearlessly placed women's rights at the center of social and political debate for the first time—ever.

She argued that women's weaker role in society was due to their upbringing, not their nature. A prophetic visionary for feminist politics, her works have inspired women from the 19th century to the present.

Her daughter, Mary Wollstonecraft Godwin (known as Mary Shelley, after marrying the poet Percy Bysshe Shelley), wrote the frightening Gothic novel, *Frankenstein* (let's hope the monster wasn't inspired by her mother).

"Strengthen the female mind by enlarging it, and there will be an end to blind obedience."

She believed women just followed male authority in their lives. "True" education was their route to freedom, she said.

A FRIGHTENING WILL WITH A QUILL—SHE SCRIBBLED THE WAY TO FREEDOM FOR WOMEN.

SIMONE DE BEAUVOIR
1908-1986, France

An extremely bright philosopher, novelist, political theorist, essayist, biographer, and teacher. She is known as one of the mothers of feminism, due to the groundbreaking arguments she made in her books.

Her most famous work, *The Second Sex*, updated Wollstonecraft's argument. She said women shouldn't aspire to be like men, but should embrace their differences from them.

She wrote another book called *She Came to Stay* about a relationship she had with one of her students. She refused to marry her long-time companion, the influential French philosopher, <u>Jean-Paul Sartre 042</u>.

"One is not born a woman, but becomes one."

By this, she meant women could choose to either fulfill society's idea of a "woman"—or their own.

SHE ENTIRELY RETHOUGHT THE TERMS OF SEXUAL EQUALITY—THEN FOUGHT FOR OLD PEOPLE'S RIGHTS, TOO.

MADONNA
1958–, USA

She is a world-famous <u>pop 305</u> star, and has acted in several movies and even written books. By constantly reinventing her image, Madonna has manipulated showbusiness and maintained global success for decades.

With her controversial songs and videos, she has used her fame to push the boundaries of acceptable female behavior. People complained about the music video for her single 'Like a Prayer'—they thought it was too sexy.

Madonna has an IQ of 140—she's no dumb blonde. In her first band, The Breakfast Club, she played drums. In 2004, she changed her name to Esther, as evidence of her belief in Kabbalah, a form of Jewish mysticism.

"I have the same goal I've had ever since I was a girl. I want to rule the world."

Madonna has made it more acceptable for women to show naked ambition. Before, it was considered vulgar for females to seem so hungry for success.

CAREER, KIDS, MARRIAGE: SHE IS A TRULY MODERN WOMAN WHO HAS IT ALL—AND WANTS EVEN MORE.

Remember the last time you wanted to buy something?

How to make *PMU*: the movie

Cast your mom. Hire your friends as extras. Here are six essential techniques to get you started in the world of movies. Action!

01 COMPUTER-GENERATED IMAGES

CGI is the use of computer graphics to create special effects. Highly flexible, it can be used to replace **actors 240** and create monsters, to add thousands to a battle scene, or to summon up an ancient city. The actors do their bit and the special effects are added during postproduction (when all the film footage is edited down to a watchable length, and sounds, like gunshots or music, are added).

02 FORCED PERSPECTIVE

The camera can be used to make very small things appear giant or very large things seem tiny. For instance, objects nearer the camera always appear bigger. If you place two characters at a distance from each other but frame the scene as if they're next to one another, you create an optical illusion: the one nearest the camera will appear substantially bigger.

03 CAMERA ANGLE

Usually, cameras are positioned at eye level. But if you want to make someone look troubled, put the camera in a high position and point it down at them. When shooting a dominant character, put the camera at a lower level and point it up at them (unless they're fighting a giant monster, when you need them to appear fragile, too).

04 LIGHTING

By hiding detail, you create fear of the unknown. This is known by the Italian word 'chiaroscuro.' A low backlight, pointed up at the character, obscures their features. A "fill light" removes shadows—without it, the image fills up with scary contrasts. Lighting with different **colors 128** also creates mood: red for passion, green for calm, and blue for detachment.

FILM: THE PLOT SO FAR

CINEMA BEGAN IN France, as a novelty. The Lumière Brothers (Auguste and Louis) developed a camera that could record and project moving pictures. They started exhibiting 50-second movies to a paying public in 1895. *Workers Leaving the Lumiere Factory* and *Arrival of a Train at a Station* were big hits.

FELLOW FRENCHMAN Georges Méliès brought stories 014 and fantasy to the movies—as well as special effects. *A Trip to the Moon* (1901) was the first movie to show space travel.

MOVIES WERE SILENT in these early days and a live orchestra supplied the sound. This changed in 1927 with the US film, *The Jazz Singer*. By this time, Hollywood, California was already the center of the global movie industry. Talking pictures were the start of its "golden age," a period that lasted until the late 1940s.

IN HOLLYWOOD, a handful of movie moguls owned all the movie sets and kept stars under contract—actors could only work for one studio. Different studios became known for different styles: glossy musicals at MGM and gangster pictures at Warner Bros.

THE STUDIOS' POWER was challenged in the 1960s and 1970s. Beginning with *Star Wars* (1977), movie-related toys made fortunes for filmmakers.

SINCE THEN, ACTORS have become more important. Superstars like Tom Cruise are the new Hollywood moguls: they make any movie they like, thanks to their audience appeal.

BUTTER AND SALT?

POPCORN DATES right back to the **Aztecs 298**. By the early 1900s, street vendors pushed popcorn machines around North American towns. These vendors targeted those wating in line at the movies—to the frustration of movie theater owners, who thought snacking was an unwelcome distraction. But soon enough they realized that snacks were good business. Popcorn soon spread all over the world: hotdogs, nachos, ice cream, and soda are now served everywhere. But some countries do it differently. In Hong Kong, they serve dried seafood, such as crispy squid (yikes). In India, they take a snack break halfway through the movie and munch on samosas. Mmm!

WHO'S BEST BOY?

(AND OTHER ODD JOBS IN FILM)

LINE PRODUCER Not someone who draws lines, but a manager responsible for the day-to-day running of the film. They keep it to budget and on time, and resolve arguments or setbacks.

CLAPPER LOADER The clapboard is marked with information about the scene. It is clapped every time the camera rolls, so that editors can easily identify what footage is on each reel. The clapper loader does the clapping. He also helps prepare the cameras.

TO BE CONTINUED...

05 STOP TRICK

If you want to make someone or something disappear, this is the oldest trick in the book. Stop filming, remove the person or thing from the shot—start filming again. So long as nothing else within the frame has shifted. Pop! It seems to have vanished.

06 FAST, FRENETIC CUTS

In action scenes, shots are short and quick. They chop and change rapidly between close-ups and shots taken from farther away. The camera position moves to different points around the action: the idea is to amplify the drama. One second you're close to the character's face, witnessing their desperation, the next, we're far back, worrying about the jump they're about to make. It's very exciting!

ODD JOBS IN FILM (PART TWO)

KEY GRIP
Grips move props and arrange equipment (but don't look after actor's car keys). The key grip is their leader.

SET DESIGNER
Most movies are shot partly in a studio. The set designer is the person responsible for building the backdrop required by the story.

BOOM OPERATOR
Responsible for microphones, not explosives.

DIRECTOR OF PHOTOGRAPHY
Also known as the cinematographer, the "DP" is responsible for the way the movie looks. He's in charge of the camerawork and the lighting.

GAFFER
The gaffer is the chief sparky. Sparkies are electricians.

BEST BOY
This is not decided by **vote 194** and no award is given—the best boy is the name given to the gaffer's assistant. Even if she's a girl.

WANT TO SMELL A FILM TONIGHT?

FIFTY YEARS AGO FILMMAKERS WENT TO AMAZING LENGTHS TO TRY AND FILL SEATS...

SMELLOVISION
In the 1950s, Smellovision used pipes to bring odors into the movie theater to coincide with key moments in the movie. But all the smells mingled together. Later, in 1981, the movie *Polyester* used a scratch-and-sniff card to add odors to the movie experience. One of the smells was a fart. Careful where you scratch!

PERCEPTO
The 1959 horror flick *The Tingler* employed Percepto: movie seats equipped with vibrating buzzers. The movie was about a creature that lives in your **spine 044** and grows when you're scared. The only way to stop it was to scream. Every so often, the seats "tingled." Needless to say, everyone screamed. A lot.

3-D
Three-dimensional movies (when the picture appears to leap out at you) hit boomtime in the 1950s. Unfortunately, getting a decent picture was expensive. The format is now enjoying a second life in special Imax 3-D movie theaters.

SENSORAMA
This was a 1950s virtual reality machine. A one-person booth combined the effects of motion, 3-D images, sounds, artificial breezes, and smells. Sadly, it looked like a carnival attraction and flopped.

★ THROW UP LIKE A FILM STAR ★
(and other movie tricks)

What you'll need is makeup, food coloring, dishwashing liquid, talcum powder, and cream of mushroom soup. And be sure not to wear your best clothes. This will get messy...

VOMIT
Mushroom soup is best for this. Sip it into your mouth cold (to up the disgusting factor), then, with the cameras rolling, let spew! Don't do this on your mom's new carpet. Outside is best.

FAKE BRUISES
Grab a makeup sponge and dab it into some red makeup. Pat it gently over the area—you don't want a solid color, so don't paint it on. (A real bruise is rarely solid in color. Your **skin 134** should remain visible.) Now repeat, this time using maroon and purple makeup. (Whenever applying makeup, it's best to start with the lighter colors and move on to the darker ones.) Every new layer should be less thick. Adding some powder should help dry it out.

FAKE BUCKETS OF BLOOD
Add a few drops of red food coloring, and one drop of blue coloring, to cheap dishwashing liquid. The result is runny, foamy "blood."

FAKE BLACK EYE
Use red and blue eye shadow on the shallow parts around the eye. This is a good way to get your annoying brother into trouble.

FAKE OLD AGE
Douse your face with baby powder. To make wrinkles, draw thin, dark lines on your skin with an eye pencil and smooth the edges to blend in the lines. Cover your face once again in baby powder, and splash some on your hair to make it gray. Tell your mother: "All this homework's putting years on me!"

"I'LL BE BACK"

* * *

and 10 other movie lines as memorable as The Terminator's

"I'll make him an offer he can't refuse"
The Godfather

"ET phone home"
ET the Extra-Terrestrial

"Frankly my dear, I don't give a damn"
Gone with the Wind

"Mama always said, life is like a box of chocolates"
Forrest Gump

"To infinity—and beyond!"
Toy Story

"May the Force be with you"
Star Wars

"Show me the money"
Jerry Maguire

"Go ahead, make my day"
Sudden Impact

"There's no place like home"
The Wizard of Oz

"Shaken, not stirred"
Dr. No

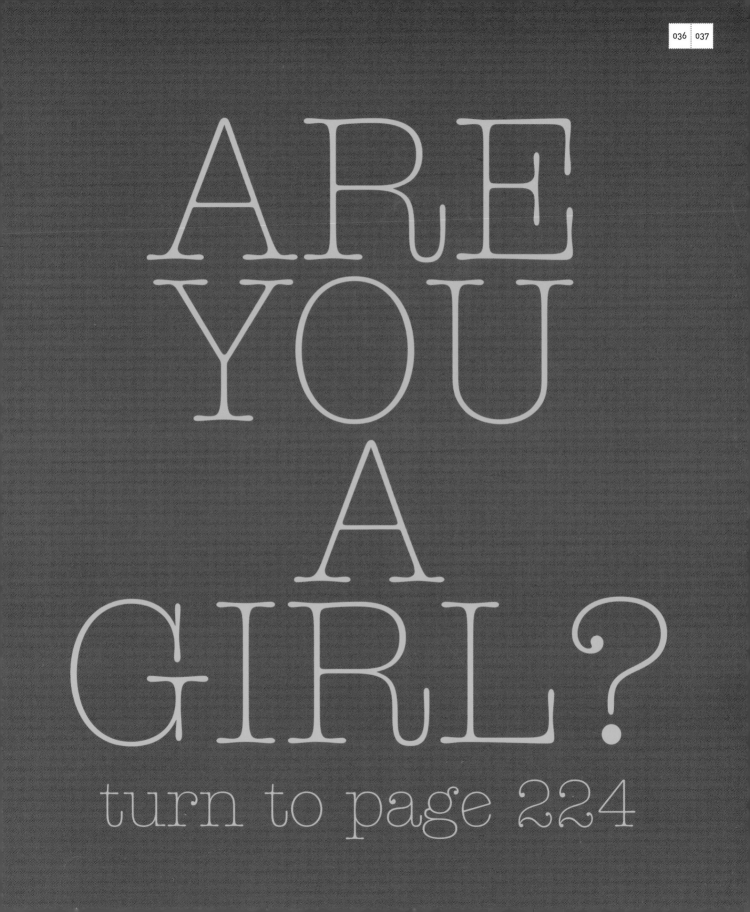

ARE
YOU
A
GIRL?

turn to page 224

HOW OUR BRAINS MAKE US DIFFERENT

The human brain differs from the brains of other animals for one very simple reason—it is by far the most complex thing in the world. It can perform many functions an animal brain is simply incapable of, including talking, figuring out difficult things (like how a brain works), and planning for the future. The ability to communicate thoughts, emotions, and abstract ideas through spoken and written words is one of the most important features that distinguishes humans from other animals. When the human brain is compared with the brain of our nearest relatives, the apes, there are several obvious differences. While the centers for the sense of **smell 066** and foot control are larger in apes, in humans the centers for hand control, airway control, vocalization, language, and thought are far more developed. Our brains know how important they are, too. While your brain accounts for only about two percent of your body weight, it takes 20 percent of your body's oxygen supply and uses up 20 to 30 percent of your body's energy. Now that's smart thinking.

RIGHT BRAIN:
Rhythm
Color
Listening to music
Daydreaming about
your boy/girlfriend

FRONTAL LOBE:
Creativity
Imagination
Guessing what's
on the next page

LEFT BRAIN:
Numbers
Logic
Making a list
Trying to speak French

TEMPORAL LOBE:
Speech
Language
Organization
Arguing with
your brother

CEREBELLUM:
Position
Balance
Standing up straight
Playing soccer

BIGGEST MAMMAL BRAIN: SPERM WHALE
17 LBS
(7,800 GRAMS)

SMALLEST MAMMAL BRAIN: SHREW
0.0001 LBS
(0.0584 GRAMS)

WHOSE BRAINS ARE THESE?

Different species of animal have completely different brain shapes

ALBERT EINSTEIN'S BRAIN WAS

15%

WIDER THAN THE AVERAGE HUMAN'S

PHYSICS GENIUS EINSTEIN 132 had a brain the same as any other except in one particular area—the region responsible for mathematical thought and the ability to think in terms of space and movement. Einstein's brain's extensive development in this region meant that it was actually 15 percent wider than average. His brain was unusual in another way, too—the groove that runs from the front of the brain to the back disappeared partway along. Perhaps this allowed more **neurons 044** to connect and work together. In other words, the two halves of Einstein's (very wide) brain could have talked to each other much more fluently. How do we know all this? After he died, curious scientists removed his brain to check it out.

VIKING

CORINTHIAN

SAMURAI

POLICE

THE IMPORTANCE OF HATS

```
_WHEN
 WILL
 COMPUTERS
 HAVE
 BRAINS?
 WHEN
 WILL
 COMPUTERS
 HAVE
 BRAINS?_
```

WORKER

AVIATOR

SINCE YOUR HEAD IS HOME TO THE MOST important organ of all—your brain—it makes sense to look after it well. The Assyrians and **Persians 120** were the first to come up with the idea of the helmet, thousands of years ago. Ever since then, head protection has been an important feature not just for soldiers, but also for construction workers, police officers, and anyone going for a ride on their bike. Hats also protect against other things—rain, wind, sun, and even flies. Why do Australians wear hats with corks hanging off them? To keep away the bugs (and to save on insect repellent). It's also worth remembering that you can lose 40 percent of your body heat through your head—so it makes good sense to get a good hat and stay on top of things.

> From science fiction books to movies like *The Terminator*, the thought of a robot with a brain is a frightening concept. But how long will it be before a Terminator-style figure is no longer just the stuff of Hollywood movies?

> Scientists estimate that the biggest computers today have one-hundredth the power of a human mind. In less than 20 years, though, they could match the human brain for processing power. But even then, computer technology will still have a long way to go before cyborgs decide to take over the planet (we hope).

What is a headache?®

All of us get a headache at one time or another. But although it may feel like it, a headache is not a **pain 084** in your brain at all. Your brain quickly tells you when other parts of your body hurt, but it can't actually feel pain itself (which is why people can have brain surgery while they are still awake). So most headaches come from outside your skull—from swellings or constrictions in the nerves, blood vessels, and muscles that cover your head and neck.

I play the timpani—these great big drums at the back. Despite all the noise, I have perfect **hearing 066**—sometimes I have to retune the drums halfway through a piece.

I play the clarinet. People say it's the most **beautiful 190** of all the woodwind instruments—it has a range of over three octaves. I really like taking a breather when the flutes come in.

concert hall

horns

harps

looking for mom

2nd violins

dying for the bathroom

I'm the leader of the orchestra. After the conductor, I have the most important job here. It's true: usually I lead the melody (the tune) of the music that the orchestra's playing.

1st violins

wobbly seat

podium

rustling candy wrappers

moved to tears

Is the world getting better?

We have the internet. We have jet airplanes. And even our laundry detergent is new and improved. Surely, life is getting better? Well, this certainly shows progress. But the question of whether the world is getting better is a very different matter. It may seem like a modern problem, but actually it's very old. Plato (427-347 BC), who lived in **ancient Greece 240**, said we should try to make the world as flawless as possible, even though it would never match the perfection of another world that he called the World of Forms. The World of Forms is not an actual place we can live in. It is more like a set of standards we can aspire to. Our world, the physical one we inhabit, is just a bad version of the World of Forms. But Plato described how we could use our power of reason to understand the World of Forms and to use our understanding to make our world a better place.

How do I know I'm not dreaming?

Try pinching yourself. Did that hurt? Even if it didn't, you certainly felt it, so you must be awake. Hmmm, maybe. Couldn't the pinch have been a dream? So how can you be sure that you aren't dreaming right now? René Descartes (1596-1650) must have pinched himself a lot because he wrote (with his non-pinching hand) whole books about this question. He thought that philosophy should be about doubting everything until you can prove it to be true. And he even doubted his own existence, as if it were all a dream. But he realized that he could only doubt his existence if he existed to doubt it (clever, huh?). If he could think about not existing, then—hey!—he must exist: "I think, therefore I am," or "Cogito, ergo sum" as he put it back then (one bit of Latin worth remembering).

How can anyone know me better than myself?

Okay, so you pretty much know who you are, and the idea of someone else knowing you better is pretty strange. After all, who lives in your head except for you? But have you ever done something you didn't mean to do, like leaving your homework on the bus? Why would you do that—a failure of **memory 302** or somehow on purpose? For **Sigmund Freud 239**, the fact that we make mistakes means that we don't know ourselves inside out. There's a part of us that knows ourselves and a part of us that doesn't. He called the first part conscious and the second part unconscious. The unconscious affects our behavior, even though we can't actually control it. "But over time it is possible for another person to see what mistakes I make and to suggest reasons why. I myself might be able to spot that pattern, too. Between us, we might be able to get to know me better!" That's what Freud called "psychoanalysis": two people talking abou~ one of their unconscious minds.

WHEN IS PHILOSOPHY NOT REALLY PHILOSOPHY?

Zen Buddhism isn't really a philosophy, but it has philosophical features. Koans, for instance, are like paradoxes, or contradictions. The most well-known koan is to think about the sound of one hand clapping (give it a try). The point is not to make logical sense of the koan, but to realize that logic ~ry far, anyway.

WHAT IS THE MEANING OF LIFE?

For a long time, many religions taught that the meaning of life was found in following God and being good. But since the **Enlightenment 150**, people have questioned religion's view of the world. One of the most famous philosophers to ask about the meaning of life was French intellectual Jean-Paul Sartre (1905-1980). He was pretty certain that God didn't exist and that life had no meaning at all. That may sound rather depressing, but Sartre had his own answer. He thought that if life is meaningless you can make meaning out of it for yourself. Sartre reckoned that the best way to give life meaning was to get involved in politics—and he himself was a committed member of the Communist Party. So for Sartre, the meaning of life is that it has no meaning—until you create it for yourself, that is.

If God exists, why do I get spots?

Well, spots may not be important enough to get God's attention, but what about really serious stuff like war? Christian philosophers spent a lot of time thinking about this. They concluded that **God 185** allows bad things to happen for the same reason that He lets good things happen (good and evil are **binary opposites 098**). And why would He want that? Well, the Christians thought it was to give us humans some freedom. Otherwise, we'd be just like robots, doing what God commands with His remote control in the sky. Only if we are free can we choose to have a belief in God—it's the choice that has meaning. Questions like this were really important to medieval thinkers like Thomas Aquinas (1224-1274), whose main concern was to understand the relationship between Christian truths and human knowledge.

Why can't people agree on what the truth is?

These days, we're very comfortable with people having different opinions—it shows we're all individuals. But the downside is, it becomes difficult to decide what the truth is. Which is better—this song or that? Immanuel Kant (1724-1804) thought that we can't rely on personal preference. If we just have opinions, there's a risk we will end up with nothing in common and we'd all just go our own way. So he set out to prove that we have a set of "right" judgments already wired into our minds. When we disagree about a song, one of us is wrong and one is right. The more we can all see the truth, said Kant, the better we can form a society and the more rational we'll all be.

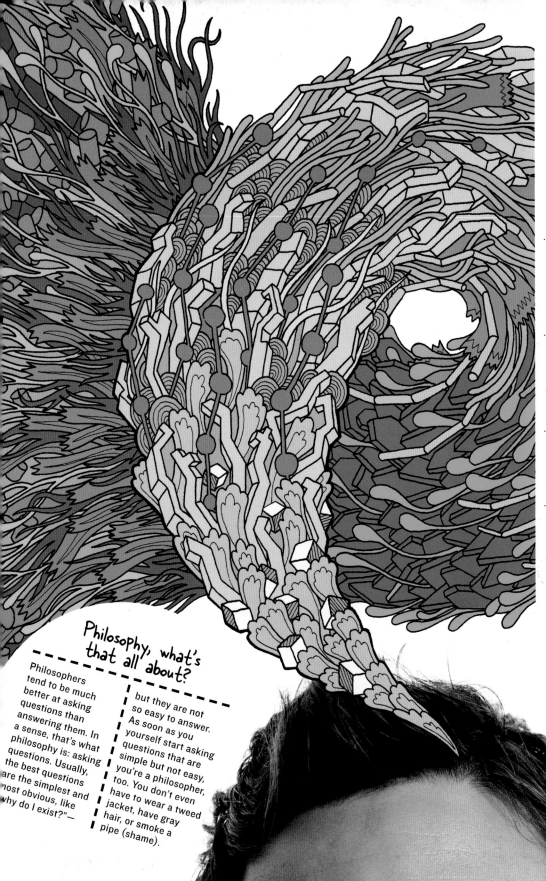

WHAT ARE THEY ON ABOUT?

EPISTEMOLOGY

Epistemology explores the theory of knowledge. What is it possible for us to know? And can we be certain of what we think we know? How do I know I know something? How do I know I know I know something? (You get the idea.)

ONTOLOGY

Ontology is the study of being. It's not about who we are or what our identity is, but about what lies beneath who we are. Ontology might look at what it means to say "I am": what is that "am-ness" about? How can you explain it? Answers on a postcard, please.

LOGIC

There are different kinds of logic. Math is a logical way of putting <u>numbers 212</u> together, and arguments are a logical way of putting thoughts together. Studying logic means looking at how well you have put things together and if you've made any false moves.

METAPHYSICS

Metaphysics relates to those big questions that can't be answered by science—like, "why is there something rather than nothing?" or "do we have a fate?" Stuff like the "nature of reality" is dealt with here.

ETHICS

Ethics looks at moral and social questions from an independent point of view. For example, a philosopher talking about whether the death penalty is right or wrong would try to get clear what we mean by "right" and "wrong" in the first place.

Philosophy, what's that all about?

Philosophers tend to be much better at asking questions than answering them. In a sense, that's what philosophy is: asking questions. Usually, the best questions are the simplest and most obvious, like "why do I exist?"— but they are not so easy to answer. As soon as you yourself start asking questions that are simple but not easy, you're a philosopher, too. You don't even have to wear a tweed jacket, have gray hair, or smoke a pipe (shame).

100 BILLION IN YOUR HEAD

THERE ARE 100 BILLION NEURONS IN YOUR HEAD. NEURONS ARE SPECIALIZED CELLS OF THE NERVOUS SYSTEM, DESIGNED TO CARRY MESSAGES THROUGHOUT YOUR BODY VIA AN ELECTROCHEMICAL PROCESS. EACH NEURON HAS BETWEEN 1,000 AND 10,000 CONNECTIONS TO OTHER BRAIN CELLS.

It's Behind You!

Without your spine, your brain wouldn't be able to carry out almost all complex everyday interactions. That means you wouldn't be able to sleep well, run fast, or turn the next page.

Along with your brain, your spine is part of what is called the central nervous system. This is connected to every part of the body by 43 pairs of nerves—12 pairs go to and from the brain and 31 go to and from the spinal cord (a bundle of nerve fibers and tissue enclosed within the spine). Messages pass along the nerves as electrical impulses. There are nearly 45 miles (72 km) of nerves in your body, but the messages can travel up to 250 mph (400 km/h)—faster than the speediest Formula One racing car.

The spinal cord runs through 33 bones down your neck and back, called vertebrae. The first seven of these bones are in the neck (even giraffes only have seven vertebrae in their necks). The rest come in different groups to make up the curve of the spine down your back. They are (from top to bottom): thoracic, lumbar, sacrum, and coccyx. The spinal cord controls many of our reactions and responses to what's going on—without the brain getting involved at all. If we put our hand too close to something hot, our instant reaction is to pull it away. This response is called a reflex response, and it is controlled by the spinal cord. Only after we have pulled our hand away from danger, does our brain feel the heat and understand what has happened.

WHAT HAPPENS WHEN YOUR BRAIN STOPS WORKING?

1
2
3

WHAT DID THIS ACTOR, FORMER PRESIDENT, AND WRITER HAVE IN COMMON?

EH?

THE FIRST REAL COMPUTER

AT THE HEIGHT OF **World War II 294**, Britain and the US needed to find ways to decrypt the coded messages of the German high command. These messages were encoded with the ENIGMA machine, a small typewriterlike device that used rotating disks. The Germans believed that the codes produced by the machines were unbreakable. But largely thanks to the work of an English mathematician named Alan Turing, the German codes were, in fact, broken. At first, the code breaking—basically a matter of comparing different lists—had to be done by hand or on a small machine called Heath Robinson. To be able to break the codes of numerous, complex messages as fast as possible, a new machine was needed. In December 1943, Colossus was switched on. It was the first computer to be digital, programmable, and electronic.

This huge machine was an immediate success. Colossus 2 followed in time for the crucial 1944 D-Day landings, when German-occupied **Europe 216** was invaded by Britain, the US, and their allies.

"WE ALL LIVE IN A YELLOW SUBMARINE, A YELLOW SUBMARINE, A YELLOW SUBMARINE"

Nasal Cavity

Oral Cavity

Vocal Tract
Larynx

Lungs

THE POWER OF SPEECH

Being able to speak is key to living our everyday lives with our families, friends, and neighbors. If we couldn't speak, we wouldn't have words to write down. And we wouldn't be able to speak if it weren't for the physical makeup of our lungs, vocal chords, mouths, and tongue. Some scientists believe that the exact way these have evolved explains why humans (*Homo sapiens*) have survived when Neanderthal Man became extinct. So much for the strong, silent type!

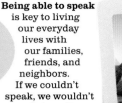

LOOK, MOM! HALF-MAN, HALF-LION…

THROUGHOUT HISTORY, PEOPLE HAVE WONDERED WHAT IT WOULD BE LIKE TO HAVE A HUMAN HEAD ON AN ANIMAL'S BODY

For thousands of years, men have conjured up mythical creatures made up of human heads and animal bodies: for example, the centaur (horse's body, man's torso and head) or the god Pan (head and body of a man, legs of a goat). Eeek! For the ancient Egyptians, the sphinx was a memorial to a dead king, made up of the head of a man and the body of a lion. (Egyptian gods, meanwhile, had human bodies and animal heads.) The most famous sphinx is the Great Sphinx at Giza (above), a colossal figure sculptured out of natural rock, near the pyramid of Khafre. It was considered by the ancients to be one of the **Seven Wonders 308** of the world.

Why free will is French

Philosopher Jean-Jacques Rousseau (1712-1778) was born in Geneva but lived much of his life in France. His writings on the relationship between people and the societies they live in explored issues such as government and freedom. His most famous **book 292**, *Du Contrat Social* (The Social Contract), was published in 1762. Rousseau argued that the will of the people was the most important thing in a society. He called this the *volonté général* (general will), and said that this should decide the laws of a country, not the whims of rulers. These ideas were embraced by French revolutionaries at the end of the 18th century, and Rousseau's phrase "Liberty, Equality, Fraternity" became their rallying cry (it is now part of the French constitution). Rousseau's work has remained influential in the two centuries since the **French Revolution 138**.

Because the brain is such a complicated thing, there are many ways in which it can go wrong. One way that is becoming more and more common is Alzheimer's disease. This irreversible brain disorder slowly steals the minds of sufferers, causing increasing levels of memory loss, confusion, personality change, and language difficulty. It usually strikes people over the age of 65. Our three famous sufferers:

1. Charles Bronson
2. Ronald Reagan
3. Iris Murdoch

ALZHEIMER'S DISEASE IS INCREASING FAST AROUND THE WORLD

Can you guess what I'm thinking?

Imagination is, in general, the power or process of producing mental images and ideas. Think for a moment about what you are going to do when you've finished reading this book. Are you going to go outside? Eat your dinner? Tell someone a joke and make them laugh? As soon as you start to think about these things, you begin to imagine what it will be like to do them. Understanding this process is very important to psychologists, who can learn a lot about the way people's minds work by studying how they imagine things. Imagination is also important when you want to tell someone a good story. Once upon a time…

WHO LIVES HERE?

This area is home to over 300 million people and one language. Its different countries tell one big story.

SAUDI ARABIA (1)
Language and religion

The term Arab originally applied to the nomadic (wandering) people of Saudi Arabia. Today, it's applied to anyone living in a country that has Arabic as its official language —that's more than 300 million people. (The actual number of Arab speakers is closer to 200 million, as other **languages 054** are still spoken in many regions.)

Around AD 570, an Arab called Mohammed was born in Mecca, a city in current-day Saudi Arabia. He became a merchant and then a great spiritual and political leader. By AD 630, he had united the Arab tribes and converted them to a religion called **Islam 186**. According to the followers of Islam (Muslims), Mohammed was a prophet who received instructions from God—and these are recorded in a book called The Koran (which is Arabic for "The Recitation").

Not all Arabs are Muslim, but Saudi Arabia is considered the spiritual home of Islam. Strict Muslims pray five times a day, always facing in the direction of Mecca. They make a pilgrimage (a spiritual visit) to the city at least once in their lives if they can.

MOROCCO (2) and ALGERIA (3)
Conquest and achievements

After Mohammed died in AD 632, his followers spread the Islamic faith through conquest (conquering other lands). By the beginning of the eighth century, Arabs had taken over North Africa, marching through what is now Algeria and founding the great city Fez in Morocco (now, interestingly, world-renowned for birdwatching). These places became the center of a thriving civilization.

Arabs were among the most advanced doctors, **scientists, 326** and mathematicians of their day, at a time when science in Europe was very primitive. They also preserved the ancient Roman and Greek books that they found on their travels. This knowledge was crucial for the later intellectual revival in Europe from the 1300s, known as the **Renaissance 148**.

The Arabs and the Berbers (the nomadic tribes that lived in North Africa at the time) expanded into Spain and got as far as Poitiers in France before turning back in AD 732. Most Arab rulers were tolerant, allowing Christians and Jews to practice their faiths and customs.

But the Christian countries of Europe didn't like having their holy places under Muslim control. The city of Jerusalem, in modern-day Israel, was especially dear to them: it's where Jesus was crucified. In the late 11th century, the Pope called for a Crusade (a military expedition of Christian troops) to reclaim the so-called Holy Lands. In 1099, the Crusaders captured Jerusalem. Despite further Crusades (there were seven major ones), the Arabs drove the Europeans out at the end of the 13th century.

EGYPT (4) and IRAQ (5)
The modern Arab world

From the 1500s to the mid-1900s, much of the Arab world was under foreign control or influence, either by the Ottoman Turks (who ran a huge empire from Turkey) or European powers such as Britain and **France 290**. Now, since winning their independence, some Arab countries have fared better than others. The discovery of oil (and lots of it) has brought huge wealth to some of the region, such as Saudi Arabia. But it has also created struggles over who runs things and caused meddling from other countries. Arab nations lacking oil are generally poor.

Egypt doesn't have much oil, but it has a lot of land and lots of people —over 77 million. In fact, about a quarter of all Arabs are Egyptian, and many see Egypt as the leader of the Arab world. It is often considered more modern than some of its neighbors (too forward-thinking for some—in 1981 Islamic radicals murdered Egyptian president Anwar Sadat because of his policies).

Iraq has about 10 percent of the world's oil. From 1979, Saddam Hussein ran the country as a ruthless

AL WORDS

In Arabic, "al" means "the." The word "Allah" comes from al-Ilah—which just means "the God." Many modern Spanish words derive from Arabic, such as "azuca." From this, we get the English word "sugar," as well as the French "sucre" and German "Zucker." The English word "coffee" comes from the Italian "caffé," which draws from the Turkish "kahveh," which comes from the Arabic "qahwah." One azuca or two?

SYRIA (6) and JORDAN (7)
Conflict with Israel

The state of Israel has been an issue for Arab countries, and none more so than for neighbors Syria and Jordan. The Jewish people consider Israel their historic homeland. The region was under British control from the end of World War I until 1948, during which time it was known as Palestine. When the British left in May 1948, the Jewish state of Israel was declared. It was immediately recognized by the **US 256** and Soviet Union. But Syria and Jordan supported Egypt in attacking Israel. The Arab states were beaten, and hundreds of thousands of Palestinian refugees fled to Jordan. In 1967, the Six Day War again brought Syria and Jordan into conflict with Israel and both Arab countries lost territory. There were further conflicts, but Israel survived. Arabs who live in the region still consider much of the land theirs. In the 1990s, a peace deal, involving Syria and Jordan, was only partially successful.

dictator for over two decades. In 1980, he started a war with neighbor Iran, which lasted eight years and cost a million lives. In 1990, he invaded Kuwait. This brought together an international coalition to liberate the country. Then, in March 2003, the US and its allies invaded Iraq and removed Saddam from power.

Stretching from Morocco to Egypt, the Sahara is the largest desert in the world. That's an awful lot of sand...

Estimated number of sand grains in the world
700,500,000,000,000,000,000

Estimated number of stars in the Universe
70,000,000,000,000,000,000,000 (that's 70 sextillion)

Estimated number of atoms in an adult human body
7,000,000,000,000,000,000,000,000,000 (incidentally, zero is another word derived from Arabic)

PUT A MAN ON THE WHAT?

Getting a man to the Moon was never going to be easy. It's a long way—238,000 miles (384,000 km)—in a hostile environment (there's a reason people don't live in space). Cue the scientists in lab coats...

A TO B, KIND OF

Working out a trip to the Moon is a bit of a headache. There aren't any road maps. Also, the Earth is spinning, the Moon is spinning, the Moon is orbiting the Earth and your spacecraft is moving—it's enough to make you dizzy. Tricky calculations had to be made (worse than the worst algebra exam you've ever taken). What a nightmare!

HEAT ISSUES

Heat was a big problem. The spacecraft would become superhot when reentering the Earth's atmosphere. A heat shield had to be invented to protect the astronauts so they didn't burn up.

AIR SUPPLY

There's no air in space. The astronauts needed oxygen on board the spacecraft, plus an air supply on the Moon (the round trip took six days). They also needed spacesuits to walk on the Moon (these were tested in swimming pools).

INVENTING THE TECHNOLOGY

The Americans already had a rocket program they could use to get men into space. The rest of the journey was more tricky. New machines and devices—from the lunar lander to pens that write in a weightless environment—had to be invented. There was also the problem of how NASA could talk to the astronauts while they were in space. Special receiving stations were set up in Spain and Australia.

LUNCH AND BODILY FUNCTIONS

The astronauts needed to eat, so special food had to be invented—in packets that stopped the food from escaping as it was being eaten (apple sauce floating around a spacecraft could cause problems). The scientists also weren't sure what effect weightlessness would have on the astronaut's bodies (would the bones and **muscles 156** act strangely?). And then there was the issue of the bathroom (a combination of urine tube and plastic bags was the solution). And what if one of them sneezed with his helmet on? Yuck.

OKAY, BUT THEY DIDN'T REALLY GO ALL THAT WAY, DID THEY?

Some people don't believe that Neil Armstrong and Buzz Aldrin ever walked on the Moon (footprint, above). They think the 1969 Moon landing was filmed in a studio. This is called a conspiracy theory: the idea that a group of people tell the same lie to the rest of the world. The idea is that the US was so desperate to beat the Soviet Union to the Moon that they cheated (this is the premise of the 1978 film *Capricorn One*). But there's plenty of evidence to indicate that the first Moon landing was genuine.

GUESS WHAT?

NEIL ARMSTRONG FLUFFED HIS LINES IN 1969. HE MEANT TO SAY: "THAT'S ONE SMALL STEP FOR A MAN, ONE GIANT LEAP FOR MANKIND." LEAVING OUT THE "A" MAKES IT PRETTY MEANINGLESS. D'OH!

HOW ON EARTH DID MAN GET TO THE MOON?

RACING TO THE MOON

» THE CHALLENGE

After World War II (during which they had been allies), the US and <u>Soviet Union 260</u> did not get along. They couldn't agree how the world should be run and were continually squabbling. This period was known as the Cold War, because they didn't actually fight each other. In 1961, the Soviet Union sent the first man, cosmonaut Yuri Gagarin, into space. He did a quick orbit of the Earth and came back to a hero's welcome. The Americans were seriously peeved and decided to go one better. John F Kennedy, the US president, declared America's intention to put a man on the Moon before the end of the 1960s. The space race was truly on.

» EARLY DAYS

The US government opened its checkbook and NASA (the National Aeronautics and Space Administration), which was running the program, began researching and testing. In 1962, John Glenn became the first American in space, unmanned craft were sent to the Moon to check out the conditions, and space toilets were tried and tested. Meanwhile, the Soviets kept up the pressure with a bunch of firsts: first spacewalk, first woman in space, and first animals to orbit the Moon (including turtles, who lost weight, but still had an appetite for lettuce when they returned).

» MAKING IT WORK

By the end of 1968, NASA was getting close (men had orbited the Moon in Apollo Eight), but President Kennedy's deadline was looming. The early months of 1969 were like a crazy sprint to the finish line. NASA had designed a spacecraft with two sections. The main section, called the command/service module, would propel the astronauts to and from the Earth. Attached to this, a smaller section—the lunar module—would take the astronauts down to the Moon once close enough. A huge Saturn rocket, 363 ft (111 m) tall, would blast the whole lot into space. It would burn 560,000 gallons (2,120,000 liters) of fuel in under three minutes. Apollo 11 was designated as the mission to make history.

» THE LANDING

Apollo 11 launched without a problem. The toilet worked and it was all systems go. The difficulty came when the lunar module was descending to the Moon to land. The computer on board became overloaded (back then, computers were relatively primitive—it would have had all the processing power of a modern calculator). Mission commander Neil Armstrong and his colleague Buzz Aldrin had to land the module manually. They found they were not quite in the position they had predicted and in danger of landing on rocky terrain and damaging the craft. A <u>speech 093</u> had been prepared for the US president to read in case a disaster happened. Fortunately, it wasn't required, though by the time the lunar module finally touched down, there was only 30 seconds of fuel left.

On July 20, 1969, more than 500 million people back on Earth watched the black-and-white images of Armstrong stepping onto the surface of another world. Aldrin (below, in a picture taken by Armstrong) joined him and they explored the Moon's surface. When they were done, they returned to the command/service module orbiting above (piloted by Michael Collins) and headed to Earth.

The mission was a complete success. The US had won the space race—the Soviets never attempted a manned Moon landing.

HOW TO GO TO THE MOON (OR OTHER ALIEN WORLD) – WITHOUT LEAVING EARTH. One day it might be possible to take a vacation to the Moon (you'd better start saving now, though). In the meantime, there are a few places on Earth that look pretty similar...

DESTINATION	DESCRIPTION
Craters of the Moon National Preserve in Idaho	Lava, which flowed here millions of years ago, has given this area its craggy, moonlike appearance
Tunisian desert	This doubled for the planet of Tatooine in Star Wars—some of the film sets are still there to visit
Atacama desert, Chile	It hardly ever rains in this rocky desert, giving it a very eerie, otherworldly look

VOYAGE EARTH

While Hollywood creates incredible sci-fi settings with intergalactic travel and exotic worlds, real-life space travel can seem a little dull. But remember that a man blasted off into space little more than 50 years after the first **airplane 304** flew, and that humans have visited an alien world. How man (sorry, no women have visited, yet) went to the **Moon 170** is a tale of global rivalry, tremendous bravery, and computers as powerful as a pocket calculator.

WHAT IS CAPITALISM?

Capitalism is the main economic system in the world (capital refers to wealth—money, property, or anything used in a business). Companies compete with one another to sell their products. They want to make profit (cold, hard cash) by selling products for more than they cost to make. Like to be a capitalist yourself?

YOU WILL NEED:

Pen and paper, a calculator (if you're not good at math), a token to mark your position, and a die.

HOW TO PLAY:

Begin at the bank. It loans you $20,000 to start a toy business.

Move forward, one square at a time. Make your business decisions, noting down changes to your fortune as you go.

Each player takes a turn before you all move to the next square.

Each time you pass the bank, you must pay back $5,000 (except on your first turn).

The winner is the one with the most money after you've been around the board three times. If you run out of money, sorry—you're out of the game.

1. THE BANK

Banks have existed for 4,000 years. Their function is to store and lend **money 058**. Businesses often get loans from them so they can expand or to get through a tough period.

2. FACTORIES

One of the most important features of capitalism is that the factories and offices are owned by individuals or companies. (Under other economic systems, such as communism, the state owns everything.)

Decide how much of your money you want to invest in a factory, then roll a die. If you roll a one, two, three, or four, then double this investment. A five or six: you lose your whole investment.

3. THE LAW

Capitalism can only exist where there is a reliable rule of law. Otherwise, how do individuals protect their property? And who's going to stop people from cheating?

You've been hit with a legal bill. Roll the die and if you get a one, two, or three, add three zeros to the number to make $1,000, $2,000 or $3,000 and subtract it from your fortune. If you roll a five or six, you're in the clear. If you roll a four, gain $5,000—you've won a lawsuit!

4. PRICES

In capitalism, the principle of supply and demand decides prices. Supply is the amount of goods available and demand is the number of people who want them. Prices are high when the supply of something is low but lots of people desire it (think **cool sneakers 192**). But if there's lots of a product and no one wants it (like food that's starting to smell a bit) then prices will be low.

Roll the die. If you get a one, three, or five, you've overestimated demand and produced too many toys. Lose half your fortune. If you get a two, four, or six, you sell everything at a good price. Double your fortune.

5. COMPETITION

A monopoly occurs when there is only one source for a particular product. Not fair! Competition between many companies generally ensures the best products are made for the best price.

You have a rival. Roll the die. If you get a one or two, your competitor takes a big bite out of your business. Lose half your money. If you roll a three, four, five, or six, the competition has made your company more efficient. Double your fortune.

6. THE FREE MARKET

In a completely free market, everyone has a fair crack at trading. In real life, there are regulations and things such as tariffs (taxes on imports and exports).

You want to sell your products overseas. Decide how much you want to invest. Then roll the die. If you rolled a one, two, or three, double your investment—your toys all sold without a hitch. If you rolled a four, five, or six, a foreign government puts a big tariff on your products. Lose half of your investment.

THE BANK

FACTORIES

THE BY-PRODUCTS OF CAPITALISM

THE STOCK EXCHANGE

MARXISM

THE GOVERNMENT

7. PROFITS

Capitalists want to make a profit. Selling goods for more than they cost to produce is what makes a profit. (This profit can then be used to invest in the business or splash out on a big house and a nice car.)

Roll the die. If you get a one or two, double your fortune—you've had a record year. If you roll a three or four, increase your fortune by half—you've done okay. If you roll a five or six, you "broke even" (your costs equaled your income)—you make no money.

8. PEOPLE

Most companies have employees working for them. They get paid wages in return for turning up and doing their jobs.

Roll the die. If you get a one, three, or five, wages don't affect profits: add a $20,000 bonus to your fortune. If you roll a two, four, or six, the workforce goes on strike because of your miserly wages. Lose $20,000.

9. THE GOVERNMENT

Free enterprise means that businesses are allowed to do what they want (within the law) and without regulation. In practice, governments act to prevent monopolies or, for example, to make sure moms get paid maternity leave (a break from work while they look after their newborn child).

Roll the die. If you get a one or six, a new law lets you pay your workers in cookies. Double your fortune. If you roll a two, three, four, or five, the government demands that your toys conform to expensive new safety standards, which will cost an arm and a leg. Lose half your fortune.

10. MARXISM

German-born thinker **Karl Marx 216** believed that capitalists exploit (take advantage of) working people to make themselves rich. He believed communism was a fairer system. The idea is that all wealth is shared equally among the people—bad news for capitalists.

A new government comes to power. Roll the die. If you roll a one, three, or five, your country turns to communism and all your factories are nationalized (taken over by the state). You're left with just $5,000. If you roll a two, four, or six, the free market is restored so nothing changes.

11. THE STOCK EXCHANGE

Ownership of companies can be broken into thousands of pieces and sold as shares. People buy and sell these at a market called the stock exchange, where the share prices are constantly changing. If shares are popular (for instance, the company is doing really well), the price rises. Then shareholders may want to sell them to make a profit.

Roll the die. If you get a one or two, your company's shares sell well at the stock market. Double your fortune. If you roll a three or four, it's all a bit flat—no change. If you roll a five or six, it's a gigantic nosedive. Lose half your fortune.

12. THE BY-PRODUCTS OF CAPITALISM

Adam Smith, a Scottish philosopher, more or less invented economics in the 18th century. He believed that by trying to get **rich 246**, people would benefit the whole community—for example, by providing goods that people need. However, capitalism can cause pollution and create large inequalities in wealth (lots of poor people, only a few rich).

Are you using environmentally friendly chemicals to make your toys? Roll the die. If you roll a one or two, lose $20,000 on a clean-up operation. If you get three, four, five, or six, double your fortune—you get new customers by going green.

Many people say that Muhammad Ali (born in 1942) was the best sportsman in history—including Ali himself. The American boxer often claimed in interviews that he was "the greatest"—and his record backs him up. He began a successful amateur career at just 12 years old and turned professional after winning a gold medal at the 1960 Olympic Games. Four years later, he knocked out Sonny Liston to secure the World Heavyweight Championship, and later became the first fighter ever to win the title on three separate occasions. He successfully defended it 19 times and lost only five fights during his entire career.

But he wasn't only skilled in the ring. By combining poetry, extreme boasting, and fancy foot-work with trash-talking (verbally abusing opponents), he took sports showmanship

WHO'S THE GREATEST?
(SPORTS STAR EVER)

to new heights. His fights, such as the epic 1974 clash with George Foreman in Zaire, Africa (nicknamed "The Rumble in the Jungle"), won him worldwide fame like no sportsman ever before. Ali also had a lot to do with the massive pay checks sportsmen get today: he received "purses" of up to $2.5 million per fight. He made news headlines everywhere when he converted to the Islamic faith, and again when he refused to serve in the **Vietnam War 294** because of his religion.

Today, boxing is surrounded by controversy. Competitors have often suffered serious injuries, and even death, since the sport first appeared as an Olympic event in the Games of the 23rd Olympiad back in 688 BC. In 1984, Ali was diagnosed with pugilistic Parkinson's syndrome, a brain disorder that slows responses and which has been linked to boxing.

TIGER WOODS
(born in 1975)

By the time he was 29 years old, American golfer Tiger Woods had already won 10 major championships, including the Masters (a yearly tournament held in Augusta, Georgia) and the British and US Opens. Golf requires extreme precision, a skill that normally grows with age (so the average age of US players in the 2004 Ryder Cup, a famous tournament between US and European teams, was 37). Woods is widely regarded as the best golfer ever. Because of his background—he's a quarter African American, a quarter Chinese, a quarter Thai, an eighth **Native American 096** and an eighth Dutch—he has also been credited with attracting more ethnic diversity to a typically white sport.

STEVEN REDGRAVE
(born in 1962)

The rower from Marlow, England, won an incredible five gold medals over five Olympic Games. He also broke the world record for coxless pairs (races with no coxswain—the person who commands and steers the boat) in 1994 with Matthew Pinsent. Rowing first emerged as a competitive sport with rules in England in the 1800s. It is so physically grueling that Olympic competitors must consume 6,000 calories a day to maintain strength (an average man needs 2,500 calories). After his fourth Olympics, in 1996, Redgrave said: "If anyone sees me go near a boat again, they have my permission to shoot me." No one did (phew!), and he rowed and won again at the 2000 Olympics in Sydney, Australia.

PELÉ
(born in 1940)

Edson Arantes do Nascimento, or Pelé (a school nickname), is arguably the best soccer player the world has ever seen. The Brazilian learned the sport using a sock wrapped around a grapefruit as a ball. He became an exceptional goal-scorer, dribbler, and passer, and even an expert tackler, despite being a striker (translated for non-soccer fans: he was really, really good). Pelé was involved in three of Brazil's five World Cup victories, and was just 17 when he helped his country first win the tournament in 1958, scoring six goals. During his 22-year career, he scored 1,281 goals. Even his near-misses were so skillful that they are still regularly televised today.

DENG YAPING
(born in 1973)

Deng Yaping is a giant in the world of table tennis. After holding the world's number one female title for eight years and claiming four Olympic gold medals, Deng was voted China's "Athlete of the Century" in 1999. Table tennis is played at high speed on a hard, small table of only 9 ft (2.7 m) by 5 ft (1.5 m). It was developed in the 1800s by upperclass English people who were tired of outdoor sports in gloomy **weather 196**. It has now been mastered particularly well in China—where Yaping achieved more than anyone by the time she retired, aged just 24.

KATARINA WITT
(born in 1965)

German Katarina Witt made her name on ice. She won more figure-skating titles than any other competitor, including two Olympic gold medals, four World Championships, and six European Championships. She also raised a few eyebrows with costumes that were sometimes considered "too revealing." Not content with just a sports career, she went on to become an actress, winning an Emmy Award for her role in the 1989 film *Carmen on Ice*.

Pelé

GOOD LOSERS

JACK NICKLAUS, from the US, offered British opponent Tony Jacklin the benefit of the doubt during the 1969 Ryder Cup. Jacklin's ball was two ft (60 cm) away from the hole. Nicklaus assumed Jacklin would make the shot and told him not to bother playing it. It meant the match was a draw. Now that's sporting.

DEREK REDMOND of Great Britain completed his 1992 Olympic 400 m race in last place, and was carried over the line by his father, Jim, because he had torn his hamstring **muscle 156**.

TREND–O–METER

DIEGO MARADONA of Argentina, then the best soccer player in the world, scored a goal using his hand to secure a 2–1 victory over England in the 1986 World Cup quarterfinal. That's, er, cheating.

MICHAEL SCHUMACHER crashed into Formula One opponent Jacques Villeneuve in a Grand Prix in 1997 in a deliberate—and unsuccessful—attempt to deny his rival the World Championship.

BAD WINNERS

Katarina

Tiger

Deng

Steven

WHO WANTS TO BE A RECORD BREAKER?

You too can break a world record. Just make sure you have plenty of witnesses when you try it

In 2005, the world's **largest crossword puzzle** was made by a family in southern Russia. The 64,000 word puzzle will keep your grandad quiet for hours.

The world record distance for **a human fired from a cannonball** is 185 ft 10 in (56.54 m). This was achieved by David "Cannonball" Smith on 29 May, 1998 in Pennsylvania. He traveled at an estimated 70 mph (112 km/h). Smith has eight children, five of whom are human cannonballs—the others are too young to blast.

In 2006, Kimberly Yeo, a student from Singapore, scooped the world record for composing the **fastest text message** on a mobile phone. She tapped the 160-character message (using both upper and lower cases) in a mere 43.24 seconds. Bt tht!

Nearly 7,000 different languages are spoken around the world. But a handful dominate. Most of the smaller ones are spoken by just a few thousand speakers. In fact, 96 percent of the world's languages are spoken by just four percent of the people.

Do you speak **ENGLISH?**

TAMIL
65 million speakers

PORTUGUESE
175 million native speakers

Because Portuguese is spoken in Brazil, and Brazil accounts for over half of South America's population, Portuguese is the biggest language in South America.

ENGLISH
400 million native speakers

English may not have the most speakers, but it is now the "global language." It is spoken in more countries than any other language: large numbers of English speakers exist in over 100 countries, while Mandarin spans only 16. English spread through British **colonization 096** and trade links, and is important today thanks to US business and culture.

HINDI
180 million native speakers

Hindi is mainly spoken in north and central India. It became the official language of India in 1965.

PANJABI
73 million speakers

CANTONESE
55 million speakers

WU CHINESE
91 million speakers

ARABIC
200 million native speakers

Arabic is spoken through-out the Arab world. It first appeared in literature in the 7th century. It is the sacred language of **Islam 046**.

RUSSIAN
170 million native speakers

Russia is the world's largest country. Its language has the most speakers in Europe. It is also an official language of the United Nations and has major political importance.

LATIN*

*With currently zero native speakers, Latin is considered a dead or extinct language—even though it is the basis of many modern languages, including French, Spanish, and Portuguese, and its alphabet remains the most widely used in the world. A version of the language, however, called Ecclesiastical Latin, remains the formal language of the **Roman Catholic 185** Church to this day, and is therefore the official national language of the Vatican, the home of the Pope in Rome. The Vatican uses it for religious texts, but uses Italian in daily life.

MANDARIN CHINESE
885 million native speakers

Yep, the language spoken by the most people on the planet is found in the most populated country. Mandarin is made up of a number of different dialects (variations of the language) spoken across north and southwest **China 118**.

JAPANESE
125 million speakers

The language has nouns and verbs to indicate a speaker's social status.

SPANISH
332 million native speakers

Spanish is spoken in 47 different countries, from Mexico to Melilla, Africa. In the US, the Hispanic population (people of Spanish origin) is growing. The number of Spanish-speakers is predicted to reach 40 million by 2025 (compared with 28 million in 2000). As a result, many non-Hispanic Americans are learning the language, and Spanish radio and television stations are booming. Olé!

BENGALI
168 million native speakers

Bengali (known as "Bangla") is India's number two language. Bengali enjoyed a cultural boom in the 19th and 20th centuries, when many works of poetry and literature were written.

FRENCH
72 million speakers

KOREAN
75 million speakers

GERMAN
100 million speakers

German is also spoken in Austria and Switzerland.

ITALIAN
57 million speakers

WHY IS THE SKY DARK AT NIGHT?

YOU MAY THINK it's dark at night because the <u>Sun 168</u> is on the other side of the Earth and it's time for bed. But think again. The light around us is given off by the Sun and other stars. Starlight takes a very long time to get here (the twinkle from our nearest star, Proxima Centauri, takes over four years to arrive). If the universe were of infinite age (if it stretched back in time with no beginning) and infinite size (if it had no edges), then wherever you looked in the sky there would be a star. And all these dazzling stars would light up the sky at night—because the light from them would have

had forever to travel here. So, the sky is dark at night because the universe is not infinitely old. It had a beginning—which scientists call the Big Bang—and is, in fact, expanding. In the 1920s, US astronomer (and junior pole vault champion) Edwin <u>Hubble 102</u> realized that there was more than one galaxy (or collection of stars) out there and, even more revolutionary, that they were moving away from from each other.

(Draw dots on a balloon and blow it up and you get an idea of how the universe is expanding.) In fact, Hubble realized, the more distant the galaxies were, the faster they were moving. Rewind time like a movie and the galaxies come back together to a single, tiny point—and this is the Big Bang. The thing is, if there was a beginning to the universe, will it also have an end?

AVERAGE DISTANCE FROM EARTH TO SUN
93,000,000 miles
(150,000,000 km)

LIGHT-YEAR 132
5,900,000,000,000 miles
(9,500,000,000,000 km)

DISTANCE TO NEAREST LARGE GALAXY, ANDROMEDA
14,000,000,000,000,000,000 miles
(23,000,000,000,000,000,000 km)

DISTANCE TO EDGE OF VISIBLE UNIVERSE
81,000,000,000,000,000,000,000 miles
(130,000,000,000,000,000,000,000 km)
OR 8.1×10^{22} miles (1.3×10^{23} km)
(WHEN NUMBERS GET THIS BIG, WE WRITE THEM IN SHORTHAND AS "POWERS" THAT SHOW THE NUMBER OF TIMES 10 IS MULTIPLIED BY ITSELF.)

Scientists have a pretty good idea of what they think happened when the universe formed in the Big Bang. What eventually happens to the universe depends on whether or not it continues to expand. Most astrophysicists (the people who study this stuff) believe it will do just that until it becomes a cold, dark, and deslolate place. Here's a timeline to cheer us all up, then...

The birth and (possible) death of the universe

Zilch

Before the Big Bang, there is nothing. It's impossible to imagine, but there is no time, no space. In fact, it's not worth thinking about, you'll hurt your brain.

14-13

Then, the Big Bang. And boy, is it big! In a split second, the universe—an incredibly hot bundle of energy and matter—expands from being smaller than an atom to the size of a galaxy.

12.0003

The universe is expanding, but it's still pretty basic. It's another 300,000 years before any <u>atoms 060</u> form.

12

Massive clouds of hydrogen gather together and collapse inward under the force of <u>gravity 024</u>. The centers heat up as atoms fuse in nuclear explosion. These are the first stars.

9-6

There's not much more than hydrogen and helium around. But as stars begin to die and explode in <u>supernovas 262</u>, they form more complex elements. Things are getting a bit more interesting.

5

Our Sun is born in a cloud of gas and dust when a supernova goes off nearby. The planets in our solar system form in a disk of stuff spinning around the new Sun.

0

There are at least 100 billion galaxies, each containing an average of 100 billion stars. New stars are still being formed (about 10 a day in our galaxy).

Billions of years ago

CONSTELLATIONS, OR WHY A RANDOM COLLECTION OF STARS IS A GREAT BEAR

ON A CLEAR NIGHT you can see around 1,000 stars in the sky, and some of them seem to form patterns. We call these constellations. Thousands of years ago, people began naming constellations, often after animals. **Farmers 086** might have been the first to notice that certain constellations appear at certain times of the year, and this could remind them to start planting or harvesting. Although the stars in a constellation may appear to be close together, they can be many light-years (the distance light can travel in a year) apart. From here, they just, well, *look* connected.

When sci-fi misses the science...

Noisy explosions
Every explosion, rocket sound, and collision noise that filmmakers give us in space is wrong. There is no sound in space as there is no air (sound needs to travel through a medium like air or water). Space is a vacuum (empty of all matter), so when the Death Star in *Star Wars* blows up it should be silent. (Nor should there be any flames—fire needs oxygen to burn, and there's none of that in space.)

Intergalactic travel
Einstein 132 proved that nothing could go faster than the speed of light, so even the fastest spacecraft would take more than four years to get to our nearest star, Proxima Centauri, and 30,000 years to get to the center of the Galaxy. Of course, *Star Trek* and the like would be a bit dull if it took centuries to get anywhere. Though, there are worm holes, of course (see right).

Communication
There's a similar problem with instant radio conversations between ships and planets thousands of light-years apart. Even a chat between Earth and **Mars 172** would be a long-winded affair (it would take about 20 minutes for a message to reach Earth).

What happened?

WOW WHAT A RIDE.

Turns out the black hole on p025 was connected to another one—it was a worm hole. You travel into one black hole, through a "tunnel" and pop out in a different location.

I thought that was only a theory.

It's one way of scooting around the universe.

It is. Einstein's General Theory says they can exist, but the technology required to use them would have to be amazingly advanced.

Okay. I'm not leaving this page.

3
As the Sun ages, it heats up—so the Earth gets as much sunlight as Venus does today. The oceans boil as **global warming 266** occurs on a gigantic scale. The Earth is dead and barren.

3.027
More bad news—the Sun uses up all its hydrogen and becomes unstable. It expands and engulfs the Earth. No school today, then.

4
The Sun becomes a white dwarf—small, but very hot and dense—and eventually cools down and dies, taking the solar system with it.

17
The rest of the universe continues to expand. But the material that stars are made from is running out.

24
Stars are no longer forming. When the old stars die, the universe darkens. The lights are going out. The universe can no longer make complex objects.

10^{14}
Now, most stars are dead. What's left is mainly cold—dead planets and black holes (collapsed stars so dense that nothing can escape from them).

10^{106}
By now, even black holes have evaporated. What a dump. There's not much going on and certainly nothing to look at.

$10^{10^{76}}$
It's impossible to be sure about things this far in the future. But from what we know, you wouldn't want to be here. The universe is cold and dark, containing only tiny particles. All the fun is over.

Billions of years in the future

WHY IS BILL GATES THE RICHEST MAN IN THE WORLD?

William Henry Gates the Third, better known as computing superstar Bill Gates, is the cofounder and chairman of the Microsoft Corporation, the world's largest computer software company. Software is essential to computers because it allows people to use them without learning a programming language. Because of this, it's a highly profitable industry. At just 18 years old, Gates (born in 1955) and a friend adapted the popular programming language BASIC for the Altair 8800, a highly successful early **personal computer 316**. In 1975, he formed Microsoft. The company's first big hit was the operating system (the most important part of software you need to use the computer)

MS-DOS, which made computers more accessible. Then, in 1985, Microsoft launched Windows. This operating system used graphics to navigate the programs. These days, Windows is installed on 90 percent of desktop and laptop computers. Gates's efforts have meant more people have computers in their own homes. In 2005, *Forbes* magazine ranked him as the world's wealthiest person, worth $51 billion. If his money (in dollar bills) were lined up, it would go to the Moon and back seven times.

IT'S THE GIVING THAT COUNTS

In 1994, Bill Gates and his wife founded the Bill and Melinda Gates Foundation. This charitable organization provides grants for causes ranging from funds for college scholarships to AIDS research. The foundation was set up with a gift from Gates of $28 billion.

A philanthropist is someone who gives time or money (or both) toward helping others. Meet two other big givers:

ALFRED BERNHARD NOBEL
(1833-1896)
A Swedish chemist, engineer, and inventor of dynamite. He left $4 million (worth about $173 million now) in his will to fund the Nobel Prizes—five annual awards given to exceptional achievers in different fields.

JOHN DAVISON ROCKEFELLER
(1839-1937)
This US businessman was one of the richest men that ever lived. After making his fortune in the oil industry, he retired to full-time philanthropy, giving away an estimated $500 million (well over $5 billion in today's dollars) to good causes before his death.

WHAT WE USED TO USE FOR MONEY

9000 BC
With the development of **farming 086**, cows, sheep, and camels are used. Carrying small change is not commonplace.

1200 BC
Roman soldiers are partly paid in salt. The word "salary" is born.

AD 1
Wampum is a string of beads made of clam shells. These are used by **Native North Americans 096**.

AD 1535
Tobacco is used in the North American colony of Virginia as a currency. Careless people are in danger of smoking their savings. Oops.

WHY WE LIVE IN THE INFORMATION AGE

THE TERM "INFORMATION AGE" REFERS TO THE POSTINDUSTRIAL WORLD WE LIVE IN—THAT'S THE TIME, SINCE ABOUT 1970, WHEN MAKING GOODS FROM RAW MATERIALS WAS NO LONGER THE BIGGEST INDUSTRY. INSTEAD, THE BIGGEST BUSINESS IN DEVELOPED COUNTRIES HAS BECOME INFORMATION, WHICH WE HAVE MORE ACCESS TO THANKS TO EMAIL, THE INTERNET, TV, AND **CELL PHONES 144**. INFORMATION CAN ALSO BE BOUGHT OR SOLD. FOR EXAMPLE, SOME COMPANIES MAKE MONEY BY TELLING OTHER BUSINESSES ABOUT THE KINDS OF THINGS YOU AND YOUR FAMILY LIKE DOING, SO THEY CAN SELL YOU THINGS.

AND THE SMALLEST THING IN THE WORLD IS...

THE ~~ATOM~~
-THE QUARK-

It's pretty obvious that things in the world can be broken up into smaller pieces—if you've ever dropped a plate by accident or smashed a ball through your neighbor's window, you'll know all about this. But keep breaking things down into smaller and smaller pieces and what are you left with?

THE ancient **Greek 240** philosopher Democritus was way ahead of his time. Known as the "laughing philosopher" (he liked being cheerful), Democritus had the idea that the universe was made up of really small stuff called atoms.

DEMOCRITUS had no microscope to see atoms—he was simply using his head. It was more than 2,000 years before scientists proved that atoms really exist. And they are amazingly small—you could get five trillion on the head of a pin. An atom consists of protons and neutrons in the nucleus (or center), and electrons that spin around outside. The number of protons dictates what type of substance the atom is. The gas hydrogen has just one proton, the gas helium has two protons—and so on, through the **periodic table 288**.

IN the 20th century, quantum physics (the study of incredibly small things, like atoms) opened up a new and exotic world when scientists discovered quarks. Even smaller than atoms, these particles are now thought to be the basic building blocks of all things. Quarks are what make up the protons and neutrons. And leptons (another quark-like tiny particle) form electrons. So Democritus was kind of right. He just wasn't thinking small enough.

A PEEK INSIDE THE ATOM

ELECTRON

NEUTRON

ATOM

PROTON QUARK

NUCLEUS

THE CRAZY WORLD OF QUANTUM PHYSICS

A LOT OF VERY, VERY WEIRD THINGS HAPPEN IN QUANTUM PHYSICS—MANY OF WHICH SCIENTISTS ARE STILL TRYING TO EXPLAIN. HERE ARE A FEW MIND-BENDING TRUTHS ABOUT THE WORLD OF QUARKS

Particles are a little difficult to pin down. A German physicist called Werner Heisenberg (1901-1976) discovered that if you measure the position of a particle (where the little critter is), you can't find out how fast it's going at the same time. But if you want to know its speed, you can't pinpoint exactly where it is. This rule is called the Heisenberg Uncertainty Principle, because you can't be certain of both momentum and position at the same time. How weird is that?

Quarks are particles, so you would expect them to behave like tiny marbles, bouncing around. But actually they seem to behave like waves, as if they moved like ripples across a pond. So scientists accept they are both waves and particles (sort of like you being two things at once: a person and a fish).

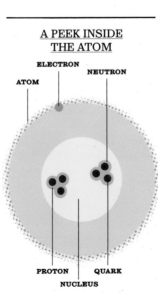

Some particles have an electric charge—either positive or negative, like one of the two ends of a battery. But every electric particle in the universe also has a twin with the opposite charge. For example, an electron has a negative charge, but its twin, called a positron, has a positive charge. Yet we hardly find any of this oppositely charged "antimatter" in our corner of the universe (no one is quite sure why). When matter and antimatter meet, they annihilate each other. That's game over, buddy.

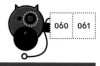
WHEN SCIENTISTS LET THEIR HAIR DOWN

YOU MIGHT THINK THAT SCIENTISTS ARE NERDS WHO NEVER TAKE OFF THEIR GOGGLES OR LEAVE THE LABORATORY. BUT MANY OF THEM KNOW HOW TO HAVE A GOOD TIME…

DMITRI MENDELEYEV
The chemist who invented the periodic table figured out and patented the official formula for Russian vodka!

CHARLES DARWIN 206
Evolution made his name, breeding pigeons was his game. Darwin's hobby helped with his work.

RICHARD FEYNMAN
One of the most important quantum physicists, the American was a drummer, too!

ALBERT EINSTEIN 132
Dear old Al was another musician: he played the violin. He also loved sailing!

LEONARDO DA VINCI 254
Mixed up his science with art—as well as thinking about physics, he loved to paint!

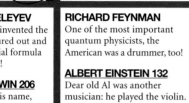

Particles are able to appear and disappear as if by magic. Often in experiments, scientists watch some particles just vanish and completely different ones appear in their place (no abracadabra or wand required).

GETTING TIED UP IN SUPERSTRINGS

SCIENTISTS are always refining their theories. The latest thinking is called superstring theory. It's pretty complex stuff. But try looking at it this way…

Imagine you are a little insect, sleeping peacefully on the surface of a pond. Although you don't know it, a person is holding a string from above the pond which goes right through the water and is attached to a rock lying at the bottom. The water is still until the person starts plucking the string. Suddenly the water starts to ripple. You, the innocent little insect, wake up, thinking there must be something on the surface of the pond. But it's not just something on the surface of the pond; it's a whole string going through the pond that's causing the ripples.

IN a similar way, scientists think that particles are like the disturbances on the surface of a pond. And maybe humans are like the insect. Perhaps we can't see the rest of the string because it crosses into other dimensions (maybe as many as 26).

WHAT'S ALL THIS ABOUT ATOMIC BOMBS?

In the early 20th century, scientists realized that some materials, like uranium and plutonium, were made of unstable atoms. Bombard them with neutrons and they release a huge amount of energy, starting a chain reaction or a process called fission. So much energy is released in such a short space of time that a massive explosion occurs. This is, in essence, an atomic bomb (nuclear power plants utilize a controlled fission reaction to generate power).

The only atomic bombs ever used in war were dropped on Japan in 1945 by US planes. The first was used on the city of Hiroshima, instantly killing 70,000 people, and the second on the city of Nagasaki 204, which killed 40,000. Many more died of radiation sickness afterward. Since then, atomic weapons have become even more powerful, but they (fortunately) have never been used again.

HOW THE QUARK GOT ITS NAME

The physicist Murray Gell-Mann named the fundamental particles "quark" after a line in Irish writer James Joyce's book *Finnegans Wake*. "Three quarks for Muster Mark" is sung by some seabirds (it's a pretty crazy book). *Finnegans Wake* is considered one of the most brilliant (if least read) novels in literature. It is written in a dreamlike language and is packed with wordplay and puns.

Tiny particles: detect me if you can!

DETECTING particles (like quarks or leptons) requires very large and expensive machines. Even the most powerful microscopes can't do it. Instead, the atoms need to be accelerated to incredible speeds and then smashed into each other. Scientists use detectors to find traces of the particles (that's as near to seeing them as we can get). The machines, called particle accelerators, are so big because the atoms travel through miles of special tubing to reach the high speeds. Many particles only exist at the high energy levels produced through smashing atoms together at these speeds. The largest particle accelerator in the world is being built in Switzerland (left). Called the Large Hadron Collider, it is over 26 miles (42 km) round. Scientists want to look at the structure of matter and to re-create conditions after the Big Bang 056.

Imagine a world

without

printed words

WEBLOG OF A VIKING GIRL— 1001 AD

NAME
Hilde
Torfadottir

AGE
13

DATE OF BIRTH
6 Corn cutting
time AD 988

ADDRESS
Fifth wooden
house past
the fields,
Turfbygate
village,
Greenland

34 FREYJA'S DAY ***SEED TIME***

Oh my Odin, I'm so excited I hardly ate my evening meal of juicy horseflesh. Father is negotiating plans for my engagement! Today, after a typical morning spent tending the pigs and baking bread, I was just weaving tunics for my brothers, Asmund, Bjorgolf, and Frothi, when father came in from the fields and told me to make more cloth for Bork Snorrason and his family because Bork wants to marry me! He's a **trader 324**, so I'm hoping for gifts like Asian silk or kohl eyeliner from Egypt. But he had better hurry up with the marriage plans, or my family will kill him—literally!

36 MANI'S DAY

Too tired to write—been practicing warrior moves with Aestrid. I so admire the Shieldmaidens, those brave warriors in the sagas. Every part of me aches!

37 TYR'S DAY

Fed the horses, made some pots, the usual… talked to mother about what it will be like after I'm married. She said if Bork doesn't provide for me properly, I can always divorce him. Sigrid and Bolla kept their houses, children, and inheritance after divorcing their husbands! Mother said I'll feel really powerful running my own household. Can't wait.

39 THOR'S DAY ***HAY TIME***

Everyone from the village was at the Sacred Grove today, partying at the summer blot. It's my favorite festival. We all stood round cauldrons while the chieftain (who's ancient—at least 45) sacrificed and boiled some horses and pigs. After we'd sprinkled their blood over religious statues and ourselves (great look!), we sat down for a HUGE feast. I love blots. The more sacred food and beer we consume, the more Odin, the god of war, will help our warriors in England and France at raiding. Everyone was at the ceremony—black, white, tanned, freckly. Us Vikings have happily adopted people from across the world's flat disk. Diarf (one of my warrior friends) says it's the same in the other Scandinavian Viking lands, too.

42 SUNNA'S DAY

Head buzzing from chieftain's meeting this morning, so went to local runemaster for a reading. I love the way you can learn about your future just from picking rune pebbles from a bag! I found out I'm going to have a long marriage and plenty of children. Cool. Skipping home, I spotted some men lifting a huge longship that they'd just paddled up a stream. Lief Erikson, the guy in charge, offered me a bunch of grapes. He said he'd found lots of them in the **New World 272**, or somewhere—it can't have been that nice if he didn't stay there! He's a bit of a nut anyway, always talking about some religion thing called Christianity. I mean, how can he say that only one god exists when we all know Odin, Thor, Frey, plus all the elves and dwarves, live over the rainbow in Asgard, battling away with those slobby giants?! Crazy people like Erikson will be the end of us Vikings, you know…

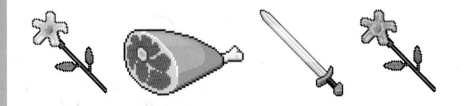

One small invention,
one giant leap for warfare

THE SIMPLEST IDEAS CAN REALLY MAKE A DIFFERENCE WHEN YOU'RE OUT TO WHACK YOUR FELLOW MAN. IN TIMES OF WAR, IT PAYS TO HAVE AN EDGE

WATER HAZARD

The Vikings' boats gave them a real advantage in conquering rival countries. Their narrow longboats were shallow enough to sail up rivers 140 and streams and light enough to lift up and carry. Such mobility gave them a great advantage when attacking—the enemy wouldn't know what hit them (probably a beautifully decorated silver spear).

GIDDY-UP

The stirrup changed the world forever. After its arrival in Europe during the eighth century, men who could afford horses began winning battles against those running round with a battle-ax. The same thing had already happened in China in AD 322. Xianbei, a scary military elite, started riding horses into battle and ruled northern China 264 right up until the sixth century.

HIP HOPLITE PHALANX

In 650 BC, an ancient Greek soldier had a lightbulb moment. He realized that if a group of soldiers marched into battle shoulder to shoulder, instead of in a disorganized gaggle, each hoplite (soldier) would be protected by the shield of the man next to him. This "human wall" technique, known as a phalanx, made the Greeks a powerful

military power for centuries and helped to create democracy 194 (by emphasizing the importance of every soldier). It was later adopted by the Romans to create their empire. Hey, centurion! Get your own ideas.

BULL'S EYE

The longbow made the English a terrifying fighting force in Europe in the 14th and 15th centuries. Even when they were outnumbered five men to one, such as in the Battle of Agincourt (1415), they could come out triumphant. The Welsh are probably a bit peeved though. The English stole the idea of the bow after seeing how well it worked for them in battle. All's fair in love and war, they say.

1. Viking longboat.
2. German knights in stirrups.
3. Viking sword.
4. Greek phalanx.
5. English fighters with longbows.
6. Viking helmet.

GUESS WHAT?

THE VIKINGS WERE EXPERT ICE-SKATERS. THEY USED REINDEER AND OXEN BONES AS BLADES, AND SPREAD THE SKILL ACROSS EUROPE DURING THEIR EXPEDITIONS

2

3

4

5

READ ABOUT TOMORROW, TODAY

Vikings used a different alphabet from us. It only had 16 symbols, called runes. They were used (and slightly altered) in some parts of northern Europe, Scandinavia, the British Isles, and Iceland between AD 150 and about AD 1200. Runes worked a bit harder than our ABCs, though. Each symbol refers to a Norse god and Vikings used them to find out about the future 104. Many people even turn to them for answers today. Similar to tarot cards, you simply choose runes at random and a runemaster translates them into predictions about your life.

BERKANO: birth and liberation. Mental, physical, and personal growth

Hilde picked the following at her reading:

JERA: expectations of peace and prosperity

FEHU: luck, success, fertility, and creation

1

6

How do you do? My name's Mister Holmes. Mister for short. You may not have heard of me, but you've probably heard of my father, Sherlock—the famous dog detective. Unfortunately, dad's not around at the moment, so it's up to me to solve today's mystery. And the crime is...

MURDER!

Looks like I'm going to need help on this one. Okay, owners—time to earn your keep.

You get a real sense of frustration when your owners can't be bothered to learn your language. You say, "Wake up, Hannah." She hears...

WOOF!

WOOF!

WOOF!

Hey, at least she hears it...

Mister! Why are you barking so loudly?

You ever hear a dog bark quietly?

Better wake Nadia, too. Her room today was blacker than a lucky cat in a coal shed. And when you can't see, you have to let your other senses do the talking. Let's see if a little tickle does the trick...

What's that I can feel on my feet? Something like a...

Hearing

My shouting (or "barking" as Hannah might call it) comes out as airborne sound waves that enter Hannah's ear. First, they go into the ear canal (which might be coated in earwax if Hannah hasn't washed—yuk). The ear canal funnels the sound waves to the eardrum, which vibrates like, well, a drum, passing the vibrations into the middle ear. Here, tiny little bones pass the vibrations into the inner ear where they are picked up by tiny hairs, which then send nerve signals to the **brain 038**. Hey presto—a sound. The inner ear is also responsible for helping you to balance, thanks to fluid-filled pouches and channels.

...MISTER!

What do you want?

You to learn how to speak dog would be good.

Touch

Unlike the other sense **organs 134**, the skin doesn't solely govern your sense of touch. It also keeps out water, dust, and germs, protects you from the sun, and helps to control your body temperature. The skin has an outer layer called the epidermis and an inner layer, which is the dermis. The epidermis itself is then split into four more layers, while the dermis contains hair follicles, sweat glands, blood vessels, and the sensory receptors that feed the brain information about touch, pressure, pain, and vibration. There are millions of these microscopic sensors, and different types of sensors pick up different feelings. Some parts of the body are more sensitive than others. The most sensitive area of the skin is on the fingertips—although Nadia has particularly sensitive toes. Ha, ha.

Next...

What's wrong with Mister?

Two things mainly: his owners!

Okay, okay, let's use some common sense. "Use your eyes," Dad always says. Seeing is believing, eh girls? Well, watch this...

Thirty seconds later...

MURDER?!?

At last we were getting somewhere. My dad would be proud. Then, Lady Luck threw me a stick and said fetch—I got another big break with my case.

EUREKA!

How fortunate. I thought I'd lost dinner tonight, but it turns out I'd left the sausages in the car. And at last I've found them. Looks like we're back in business, gang.

That night...

Mmm! These sausages taste good

Mister's enjoying them, too.

We never did find out what all that "murder" business was, did we, Mister?

Sight

Nadia and Hannah needed to see to believe, because of all of our senses, sight is the most important, with vision accounting for a massive two-thirds of all information stored in the brain. Light enters the eye through the pupil (the dark circle in the center of the eye). In bright light, the pupil gets smaller, while, in the dark, it grows larger to let in more light. The cornea (a clear layer that covers the front of the eye) focuses light toward the back of the eye (the retina), where receptor cells called rods and cones send messages to the brain. Each retina contains about six million cones and 120 million rods. The cones allow you to see in bright light, while the rods let you see in the dark—well, as best as they can. And did you know the eyes actually see upside down? The brain turns the image the right way up—and makes one image from two eyes. Smart brain.

Taste

The sausages were so good thanks to the sense of taste. This is detected by special cells called taste buds on the tongue. If you stick out your tongue, you won't be able to see your taste buds, but you can see the places where they're stored. See those tiny bumps? They're the papillae, and they're where the taste buds are. There are about 10,000 taste buds on the tongue. Taste buds to detect bitter things are at the back of the tongue, for sweet things on the tip of the tongue, for salty at the sides, and for sour at the back and on the sides. Different **foods 176** can taste differently depending on where they go on the tongue—sugar, for example, tastes much sweeter at the front of the tongue, where the sweet taste buds are located. But sausages just taste great all around.

Well girls, there never really was a murder—except there would be murder if I missed sausages. The real mystery is, how did I know dinner was missing? Well, Mrs. H smelled like the meat counter when she arrived home, but there was no meat when she emptied her bags. I put two and two together and came up with sausages. You don't understand a word I'm saying, do you?

Why's he barking like that?

Search me...

Smell

Because I'm a detective **dog 130**, I have an excellent sense of smell—that's how I was able to smell the sausages. Your sense of smell isn't quite as good as mine (of course), but it is still a source of great pleasure when you smell things you like, and can even save your life by smelling danger scents, such as smoke or gas. Smells travel up the nose to the olfactory (smell) center, which is about the size of a stamp. Here, there is soft tissue, which contains olfactory cells. These cells carry signals to the olfactory bulb (in the large, front part of the brain) where they are sorted and processed before traveling along the olfactory tract to other brain areas. So, the smell of those sausages set my brain on fire!

YOU ARE HERE

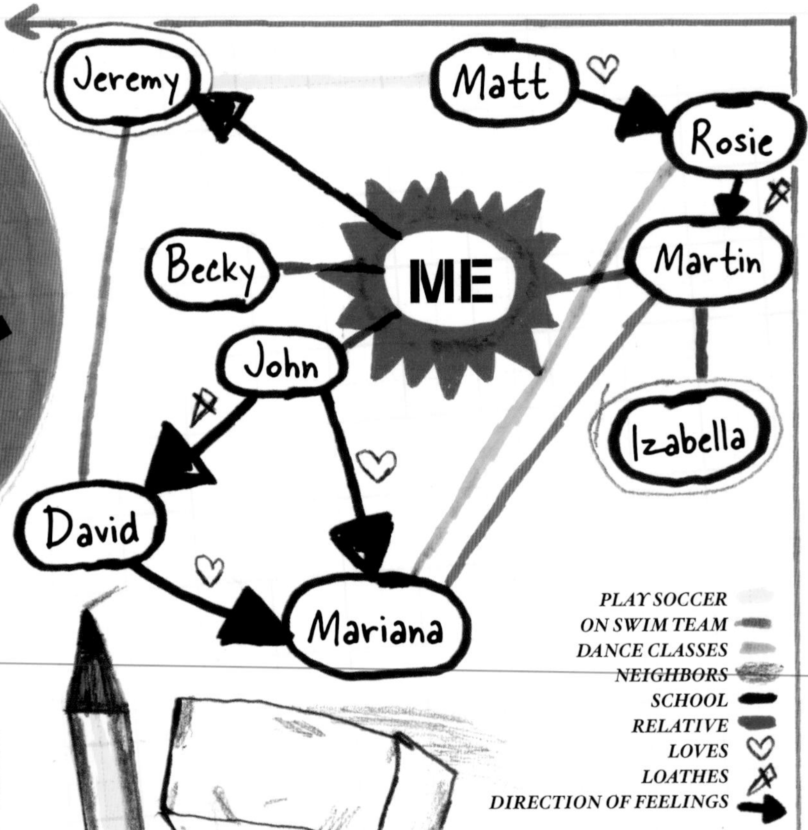

ME

Jeremy

Matt

Rosie

Becky

Martin

John

Izabella

David

Mariana

PLAY SOCCER
ON SWIM TEAM
DANCE CLASSES
NEIGHBORS
SCHOOL
RELATIVE
LOVES
LOATHES
DIRECTION OF FEELINGS

A map is a way of telling a story. What the story is about depends on who the map is for. It could be a political map that shows you where countries and territories begin and end. Or it could be a physical map that illustrates things such as **mountains 074**. Someone who makes a map is called a cartographer. Learn to be one. Right here. Right now.

HB

HOW TO MAKE A MAP OF ↑ EVERYONE AROUND YOU

If you want to make a map that's about relationships instead of geography, you can create a spider diagram. This is a little like a **family tree 010**. First, you need to decide who it's going to include. Perhaps it's a map of your friends, your family, or the people you know in your area. Write down the names of everyone you want to include, not in a list, but spread all over your piece of paper. Then draw lines between them to show which ones are related (they might be friends or neighbors). To make things interesting, use colored lines to show different types of relationship: black means school friend, yellow means soccer buddy, and red means relative, etc. Symbols like a dagger or the heart logo indicate love or loathing, and two-way lines let you show different feelings.

HOW TO MAKE A MAP OF... | YOUR LOCATION

Materials:
Compass, pencils, paper.

1. Who's this map for? Is it simply a way for someone to find your house? Or have you buried treasure for your buddy who thinks he's a pirate?

2. Use the compass to find north. Most place maps put north at the top of the page.

3. Your map should balance context and detail. You need to include reference points that the map's readers will understand. Perhaps there's a park five minutes away where everyone hangs out. Since they know where it is, the park is a landmark and gives context. The things between your house and the landmark are the detail.

4. Prepare your measurements. The length of your stride is probably about three feet (1 m). If you come up short, try and pace in 18 inches (half meters) since this will make it more exact. If your stride is longer than three feet—wow, do you have to duck when aircraft fly over?

5. Walk your map. Your first steps (literally) should be the route between your house and the landmark. What direction do you set out in? The road starts west and then veers south? Okay. Count out the number of paces you make until you change direction. Stop and make a note: 25 paces west. As you go along, you also need to note any interesting things to help direct the map-reader. Do you pass a big oak tree? Make a note. What about a post office or store? Get that down, too. And what's the road like? Is it a wide avenue or a narrow alleyway? Record this information as well. Temporary features, like ice cream vans and that fellow asleep on the bench, can be ignored.

6. And repeat. You're going to keep noting down turns and changes to the road, plus the features—and all the time counting out the number of paces—until you arrive at your landmark. This will give you the basic contents of your map and determine its dimensions. It will also give you an appetite, so bring a sandwich along.

7. At this point you need to figure out the scale. Perhaps 1 inch represents 1/2 mile (or 1 mm represents 1 m), so your map is much smaller than real life. And if your street stretches 2 miles, then it will be 4 inches on the map (or if it stretches 200 m, it will be 200 mm, or 20 cm). Mark this down. You also need to figure out symbols to represent the various features. The post office could be represented by an envelope symbol. And perhaps an acorn represents the big oak tree. These symbols are called keys and must be explained somewhere on the map.

8. Sketch it out. Draw out your basic route, using your notes from the walk. Make sure it's to scale. The lines should get thicker or change color for bigger roads.

9. Start filling in. Any road you walked or crossed should be plotted until you fill the map to its edges in the same manner as point five. Otherwise, you'll have one squiggly line, surrounded by trees and envelopes, which would look a little **silly 078**.

10. Extend your map. Use more sheets to stretch the map north, south, east, and west.

A map of a book, **magazine 330**, or newspaper is called a flat plan. Like a normal map, it's on a much smaller scale than the real thing. And also like a map, it's two dimensional (or flat). Each page looks like a rectangular block. And each page is numbered: the half-title page (the one that says 'Pick Me Up' in big black letters) is page one. Within each box is a quick, at-a-glance explanation of what's on that page. For instance, this page is described as "you are here (maps)."

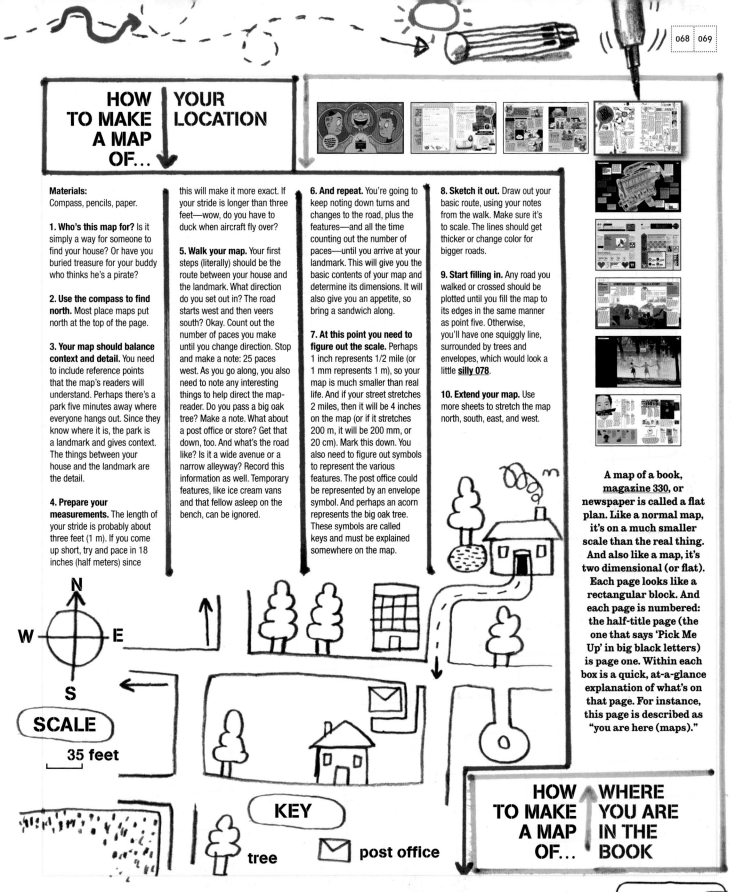

N
W   E
S

SCALE

⊢——⊣ **35 feet**

KEY

🌲 tree

✉ post office

HOW TO MAKE A MAP OF... | WHERE YOU ARE IN THE BOOK

THERE'S MORE TO AN ENGINE THAN FIRST MEETS THE EYE

The forerunner of today's car engine was designed by German engineer Nicklaus Otto in the 1870s. The combustion engine, as it's known, burns air and fuel to drive pistons. The energy they generate turns the wheels. Engines are dependent on the fuel that goes in them—a lot like people, in fact (the difference being that you don't eat fossil fuels, but tasty **food 176** instead)

The crankshaft is rotated by the pistons moving up and down, transmitting the power to the gearbox and then to the **wheels 282**.

Food is the fuel that contains energy to power your body. Carbohydrates (such as pasta and potatoes) and fats are burned up by the body to release energy. Any excess energy that the body doesn't use is stored as fat. It's a little bit like a battery storing energy for later use.

Food, such as meat, **fish 026**, and eggs, also contains protein and vitamins. Protein helps muscles and other tissues to grow, while vitamins benefit the eyes, skin, and lots more. The body also needs minerals, such as iron for healthy blood—though only in small measures.

The exhaust pipe removes gases produced during combustion.

The gases go straight into the atmosphere. One of these, carbon dioxide, is a contributor to the **greenhouse effect 266**. Many countries around the world have tried to regulate the pollution caused by carbon dioxide.

The gases created by vehicle engines can create smog in cities such as **Los Angeles 113**. When smog occurs, the atmosphere turns brown and the air feels thick and unhealthy.

The fuel injection system controls how much gasoline goes into the cylinder.

Fossil (or mineral) fuels such as oil, coal, and natural gas are formed from the remains of plant and animal life that died hundreds of millions of years ago. They provide nearly 90 percent of all the energy used by industrial nations.

All fossil fuels are hydrocarbons—a chemical (unsurprisingly, given the name) that is made up of hydrogen and carbon. Diamonds are a form of carbon and are the hardest known mineral. They are often used as cutting tools on saws and drills (don't try it with your mom's ring, though). Strangely enough, graphite is also a type of carbon. And it's one of the softest materials there is. Pencil lead is made of graphite, and not lead at all (which is poisonous).

Fuel mixed with air enters the cylinder and is ignited by a spark plug and burns rapidly. The gases created by the rapid burning expand, forcing the piston down, producing the engine's power.

Otto's engine had just one cylinder. The average sedan today has four. Ferraris and other high-performance cars have as many as 12 cylinders.

The sump contains oil, which is used to lubricate the engine.

The geological process that creates coal, oil, and natural gas also creates fossils. A fossilized animal or plant is usually one that has died in water and been covered with mud. When the fleshy part of the animal has decomposed, only the bones are left. And, as more layers of mud pile up, the remains turn to rock, and become fossils.

Fossils are an amazing document of the past. Without them, it would be a lot more difficult to know anything about the natural world in **prehistoric 234** times. The fossil record has been crucial for naturalists studying **evolution 206**. It makes it possible to trace the development of species.

WHAT'S THE MOST EFFICIENT WAY OF GETTING AROUND?

The chart shows the equivalent number of calories (a measure of energy) each form of transportation uses if taking one person one mile (0.6 km). The fewer calories, the better.

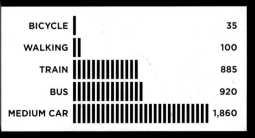

BICYCLE	35
WALKING	100
TRAIN	885
BUS	920
MEDIUM CAR	1,860

Street life

Population **186 million—** going up

In 2005, there were **10 million** children living and working on the streets in Brazil. They included orphans and children separated from their families.

Nation knowledge

Where is Brazil?

The Brazilian TV network, **TV Globo**, is the fourth largest **television 330** station in the world by audience. It comes in behind three US networks (ABC, CBS, NBC).

GLOBO

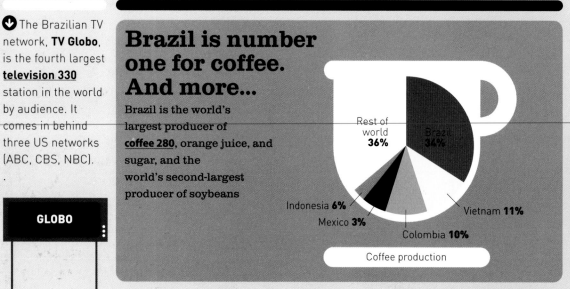

Brazil is number one for coffee. And more...

Brazil is the world's largest producer of **coffee 280**, orange juice, and sugar, and the world's second-largest producer of soybeans

Rest of world **36%**

Brazil **34%**

Indonesia **6%**

Mexico **3%**

Colombia **10%**

Vietnam **11%**

Coffee production

Brazil has the best **soccer team** in the world—it is the only country to have qualified for every **World Cup.**

The world's first Beach Soccer World Championship was held in 1995 on a Rio de Janeiro beach.

The shirt worn by Brazilian soccer player **Pelé** during the 1970 World Cup sold for **$228,738** in 2002 —the most ever paid for a soccer shirt.

Brazil is beefing up

Brazil has the world's largest commercial cattle herd, with 195 million cows. In 2004, the nation became the largest exporter of beef and veal in the world, too.

Brazil
2 million

Australia
1.65 million

Argentina
750,000

India
685,000

Canada
675,000

2005 beef and veal exports in tons

Brazil loves music

2004 Sales in South America of Latin American music

Brazil **$374**	●●●●●●●●●	
Mexico **$360**	●●●●●●●○	
Argentina **$84**	●●	
Colombia **$49**	●	(in millions of US $)
Chile **$38**	●	

70% of CDs sold in Brazil are by Brazilians

10

!

There are nearly **one million** Japanese in Brazil. Only **Japan 028** has more.

Brazil...

Brazilians know how to party

The Salvador Carnival is the world's biggest street carnival —it attracts two million people each year.

And Brazil is home to the most famous carnival, too. The Rio Carnival takes place every year, seven weeks before Easter Sunday.

The trees are coming down

Between 2001 and 2002, a total 9,840 square miles (25,486 sq km) of trees in the Amazon were cut down—an area 74 times .the size of nearby Grenada.

= 1,000 km² (386 miles²)

Wildlife wonderland

The Brazilian Amazon contains the largest single reserve of biological organisms in the world. Over one-third of the entire world's biodiversity is found there.

1.5m
Trees and other plants

3,000
Types of freshwater fish

950
Species of birds

300
Species of mammals

⌄ One-third of the world's **rain forests** are in Brazil, including the world's largest, located in the Amazon River basin.

⌄ The **Amazon River** has 20 percent of the Earth's freshwater. It is 4,000 miles (6,400 km) long— the **second longest river** in the world.

THE MIGHTY AMA2%N

⌄ Brazil is South America's **biggest country** and takes up almost half the continent: it is 3.3 million sq miles (8.5 million sq km)—this makes it the **fifth largest nation** in the world after Russia, Canada, China, and the United States.

MOUNT KILIMANJARO

Mount Kilimanjaro is a dormant (sleeping) volcano in east Africa. Its highest peak is 19,340 ft (5,895 m). <u>Volcanoes 136</u> are formed when molten rock from beneath the Earth's surface bursts out like a giant, exploding zit. The outflows of lava (rock so hot it's like liquid) pile up and cool (along with ash) into a mountain.

What are you doing here?

At the bottom of Kilimanjaro are slopes and forests where small animals like bush babies (wide-eyed primates) set up camp, as well as monkeys, leopards, and <u>elephants 130</u>. Reach 9,190 ft (2,800 m) and it's just the small or the vicious: moles, rats, and birds of prey such as buzzards and eagles. Hike up to the summit, and you'll find only the odd spider—they're all that survive the freezing temperatures (which makes the eight-legged freaks all the more scary).

What's at the other end of the faucet?

Mountains such as Kilimanjaro are the world's "water towers." They feed every major river on Earth—from the Nile to the Rio Grande. More than half the world's population, some three billion people, depend on mountains for their water. And that's not just to drink. It's also to grow food, to produce <u>electricity 300,</u> and to nourish industries, too. Melted snow and rainwater collect into mountain streams. These feed into other streams, which combine to form a river. This finally flows into a large body of water, like a bay, lake, or ocean. But somewhere between the mountain and the sea, there's always a system of pipes. Unless a city is right by a lake or natural source, its local water resources can only provide a fraction of the total needed. So the water is pumped in through massive channels called aqueducts. Along the way, it is treated to kill germs. Then it's sent into smaller and smaller pipes until it emerges from the faucet.

EVERY MOUNTAIN

RECORD HIGHS AT THE MEXICO OLYMPICS

Back in 1968, the summer Olympic Games took place in Mexico City. It's one of the world's highest cities: 7,546 ft (2,300 m) above sea level. Being way up, the air contains much less oxygen than at sea level. This had a devastating effect on many athletes in longer events, like the 10,000 m run, because they need lots of oxygen to sustain them during the race.

But there were world records galore in the men's races that were 400 m, or less. This is down to lower air resistance at higher altitudes. Most noteworthy was US athlete Bob Beamon's triumph at the long jump. Beamon trashed the world record by 22 in (55 cm) and his 29 ft (8.9 m) leap wasn't beaten for 22 years. What a result!

TELLS A STORY

HOW TO

SURVIVE AN AVALANCHE

An avalanche is a huge mass of snow sliding down a mountain. What happens is that **gravity 024** acts on the snow, forcing it down the slope. When they start moving, they cannot be stopped. Avalanches kill about 150 people every year. Just in case one gets you, here are some tips.

1. Keep snow out of your mouth. Wave one hand back and forth in front of your mouth, to create an air-pocket.

2. Drool. The direction of your dribble will tell you which way is down. So, dig upward!

3. Punch to the surface. Snow hardens like concrete, but if any part of you is sticking out, you'll be found quicker.

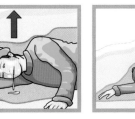

MOUNT EVEREST

The ground beneath our feet is made up of giant rock plates—between 50 and 250 miles (80 and 400 km) thick. Several are bigger than entire continents. These **tectonic plates 318** are floating on a layer of molten rock and move very slowly all the time (about as fast as your fingernails grow). If two plates push together for long enough (like, millions of years), the ground buckles under the pressure and produces hills and mountains. In fact, Mount Everest grows by 1½ in (4 cm) every year as the Indian tectonic plate slides north under the Eurasian plate (a growth spurt, but not as you know it).

Life on top of the world

Sheep can still be found in the upper alpine zone of Everest—14,750 ft (4,500 m) above sea level. There are also hares, wolves, wasps (imagine being up that high and getting stung), mountain finches, a hawk called a kite, Himalayan Griffons (left), and mice. At about 18,690 ft (5,750 m), you hit the permanent snow line in the Himalaya. Except for moss or edelweiss, the only other company in the rock and snow might be a friendly chough (little bird) or ominous vulture (big, scary bird).

Man versus mountain

At 8,850 m (29,035 ft), Everest is the highest mountain peak in the world. This makes it an irresistible challenge for people who don't mind cold, a lack of oxygen, and the chance of slipping off a rock face. Even airplanes could not get above the thing until 1933. The first people to climb Everest were New Zealander Edmund Hillary (a former beekeeper) and Tenzing Norgay, members of a British team. Tenzing was a Sherpa, one of the native people that live on the mountainous border of Nepal and Tibet. Their 1953 expedition was the ninth British attempt. Hillary and Tenzing reached the top of the world at 11:30 a.m. local time on May 29. Tenzing buried sweets (a gift to the gods) and Hillary took his picture. But their job was only half-done: they still had to get back down again. By the time they reached Kathmandu city, the newly crowned Queen Elizabeth II had knighted Hillary and awarded Tenzing the George Medal.

A picture paints a thousand words

And sometimes even more. Take a look at this picture. Can you tell what's happening at first glance? Or does it seem that the longer you look, the more possibilities there are? Are the three people in the middle holding hands because they are having fun? Are the people in the background watching them perform? Or are they watching something else we can't see? What's that blowing between the trees? Is it dust? Is it smoke? And who are these three people? Are they a family? Or friends? Where is this happening? And when?

The caption

Now read the description that goes with this picture: "May 4, 1963, Birmingham, Alabama. An African-American man and two African-American women hold hands and try to brace themselves against the harsh spray of a fire hose during an antisegregation protest. [Segregation forced African-Americans to live, work, and play separately from the majority white population.] Against 3,000 protesters, police released dogs, attacked with electric cattle prods, and used water sprayed with enough strength to rip bark off trees."

The full story?

So, have the 58 words of the caption told us everything? We now know why the three people are holding hands, and why the other people are here, too—demonstrating for their **civil rights 226**. But is that the full story? Or are there now more questions to ask? Why was a water hose turned on young men and women? Why did police release dogs against a crowd as peaceful as this one appears to be? And is the view that this picture gives us of these events the only view to take, or could someone else see things differently? A picture like this asks a thousand questions. Just as it did in May 1963, when it was televised across the US...

WHY DO WE SMILE?

'ONE MAY SMILE, AND SMILE,
AND BE A VILLAIN.'
WILLIAM SHAKESPEARE,
HAMLET

Every human being, no matter where they're from, is born with the ability to smile. We know this because even children who can't see still grin. A smile is a natural reaction to a positive moment, like a friendly face or a clever joke. But this isn't the first reason we smile. Most babies first smile between six and eight weeks old. It's usually an accident: an expression made when exercising their facial muscles or passing wind. But once they realize a smile gets them a lot of attention—huge smiles in return, happy noises, extra treats—they learn to try it again. And why wouldn't they? It takes 43 muscles to frown but only 17 to smile.

Not every creature can smile. Although it may look like your pooch is smiling back at you—it's not. Animals feel some of the same emotions as us, but they don't smile. A dog's chirpy face is more likely to be a sign of confusion, while dolphins lack the muscles for facial expressions—their mouths are permanently turned upward (like a **celebrity 218** after too many facelifts). Animals show their joy through other movements, like a wagging tail or backward flip. Some even laugh, such as chimps and rats (when the pesky rodents are being tickled).

WHAT WOULD HAPPEN IF WE DIDN'T BRUSH OUR TEETH EVERY DAY?

1.
You'd have to wear false teeth like your granddad. Dirty teeth get covered in a film called plaque. This attracts bacteria, which breaks down sugar (candy, ice cream...) on your teeth into acids. Acids eat away tooth enamel and holes called cavities grow.

2.
You'd only be able to eat soup. Teeth are essential for chewing (mastication) before you swallow food. As you chew, salivary glands automatically secrete saliva, which moistens the food and begins the digestion process.

3.
Your face would change shape. Not only are healthy, sparkly teeth vital for that all-important smile, but they also provide essential structural support for the face muscles. Without strong teeth, the lower half of your face would be loose and rubbery.

4.
You'd make funny noises when you tried to talk. With the lips and tongue, teeth create words by controlling air as it flows from the mouth. So, when making the "th" sound (theory, theater, etc.), you put your tongue against your upper row of teeth.

LET YOUR BODY DO THE TALKING

NODDING YOUR HEAD
In most places, shaking your head from side to side means "no." However, this gesture is not universal.

In many places, such as southern Italy, Bulgaria, and Sri Lanka, shaking your head from side to side means "yes," while nodding your head up and down means "no." Next time someone offers you extrahot chilli in Sri Lanka—be very careful.

THUMBS-UP SIGN
This means "everything is okay" almost everywhere. Pilots, race-car drivers, and **astronauts 102** use it. In Germany, it means "number one." Don't try it in Iran, though, or they'll think you're very impolite. And think twice about using it underwater, where it means, "I'm going up."

THE A-OKAY SIGN
In the US, the A-okay sign means "good job" or "I agree." In Japan, the gesture symbolizes money. In France, it means "zero," and that something is worthless. However, in Latin America the sign is extremely insulting: the American and English equivalent is the raised fist with the middle finger extended.

NO!

NO!

YES!

YES!

GRIN POLICE: WE KNOW YOU'RE FAKING

We smile when we're happy. We smile when we see people we know. But what happens when you're not happy to see someone you know? You smile anyway—you fake a smile. Unfortunately, however, a fake smile never looks quite the same as a real one.

GENUINE:
The Duchenne smile. This is named after Guillaume Duchenne, a 19th-century French doctor who analyzed facial expressions. You show your lower teeth and fully use the risorius muscle running all the way around the mouth. Only when this muscle is flexed does the skin around the eyes becomes tighter—and your smile is real.

FAKE:
The Pan-Am smile. When someone smiles politely, rather than because they really want to, they only use the zygomaticus major muscle. This raises the sides of the mouth, but doesn't move the muscles at the corners of the eyes. This smile is named after the former airline whose flight attendants welcomed every passenger with the same, forced smile.

A   B   C   D

CAN YOU SPOT THE FAKE SMILES FROM THE REAL?
Answers on page 199

HAVE YOU SEEN THIS FACE?

In 1963, graphic artist Harvey Ball from Massachusetts designed the smiley face symbol so that a not-so-happy company could put it on work stationery. By the 1970s it had taken on a life of its own, and people everywhere wore smiley badges, T-shirts, and bags. In the late 1980s it became the symbol for the Acid House music movement, and today it has morphed into happy face "emoticons," where people use punctuation marks to make different expressions in their texts or emails ;-)

HOW THE MONA LISA CHANGED PORTRAITS FOREVER

People have been guessing about the *Mona Lisa*'s mysterious smile for centuries, but that's not the only reason this painting is so famous. **Leonardo da Vinci's 254** 1506 painting, along with others by Italian Renaissance artists, completely changed the way people were painted. The background is hazy, with fewer distinct outlines than the foreground. This technique is known as aerial perspective. Leonardo was one of the first to use it to give paintings more depth and a lifelike quality.

BEFORE THE MONA LISA

Some of the earliest portraits were by **ancient Egyptians 100** from 3100 BC. Most paintings of people were "flat" and two-dimensional. Later, from the fifth century AD, Christian painting (above) was about ideas rather than painting what you could actually see. Icons (pictures of saints and Biblical figures) illustrated beliefs about God.

AFTER THE MONA LISA

Portraits became increasingly lifelike. Artists such as Dutch painter Rembrandt (1606-1669) loved to capture facial expressions. But by the late 19th century, **Modernism 322** was rewriting the rules. Art was now more about how the artist saw the world. Pablo Picasso painted abstract faces, made up of crazy lines and angles (below).

Try being a girl for a day. Don't know where you're going? Ask people for directions. It will be difficult, but resist the urge to work it out for yourself.

When you talk to people today, don't only focus on the words they use. Take note of their body language, voice tones, and expressions. This will make you more sensitive to other information they may be communicating, so you can empathize better with them.

When you're doing your homework, don't do one subject at a time. Switch between tasks. Break it up with other things too, like sorting out your photo collection or decorating your bedroom wall. It's okay to juggle— you may even find it more stimulating.

Think about how you are feeling today. Write down all the emotions you have experienced. What caused you to feel that way? What could you change to feel more positive?

It's a common joke that boys hate asking for directions if they're lost, while girls turn to people who know the area for advice because it's the quickest solution. **Evolutionary 206** psychologists (people who study how the way we think has changed) believe this is linked to the hunter-gatherer distinction: boys feel compelled to explore independently, while girls prefer to work as a team. Others, like American academic Joseph Pleck, think that the the society you live in teaches males and females to display distinct sex-typed behaviors and attitudes—boys must appear **aggressive 154** and strong, girls must be passive and weak. Whichever is true, boys should overcome their resistance to seeking help. According to some research, boys visit the doctor less frequently over their lifetimes than girls, have higher suicide rates, and a shorter life expectancy. Playing the tough guy isn't always so smart, eh?

Girls are more sensitive and caring than **boys 224**. Okay, this is a huge generalization (before you boys start blubbing), but there is a biological reason. Girls are born physically and mentally equipped to have children and then raise them into adults. They are biologically programmed to be more adept than boys at identifying with others. This is reinforced by society: girls are often given baby dolls to look after, for instance. This encourages them to be carers. However, some people think the differences between boys and girls are completely set by nature (fixed from birth), while some believe they are totally learned. This is called the "nature versus nurture" debate, which pops up a lot when people talk about gender differences (the contrasts between the sexes).

Generally speaking, girls are better at multitasking, while boys tend to focus on one job at a time. Evolutionary theories can also explain this difference. During mankind's earliest times, it was advantageous for females to be good at doing lots of things at once, such as rearing children, keeping them safe, feeding them, managing relationships, and so on. It may have been more useful for males to concentrate on one thing at a time, such as hunting down dinner. Today, each skill is advantageous in different situations: it's handy to be single-minded during an exam, but better to be multifocused when trying fit in cramming for all your different subjects. Of course, sometimes boys excel at multitasking (such as talking with their mouths full) and girls can still be very focused.

Boys can find it difficult to relate to their feelings, while girls tend to feel more in touch with a wider range of emotions. This common distinction may stem from boys' and girls' different brains. Recent research has suggested that emotions may be processed more on the left side of the brain in girls, but more on the right side in boys. The left part of the **brain 038** is most often linked to language and communication skills—explaining why boys find it harder to verbalize (say) their right-brained feelings. However, some researchers claim boys and girls do, in fact, experience exactly the same emotions. Girls just show them, while boys hide them. So, boys may be less likely to cry at sad **films 034** because it's not as socially acceptable (their friends might laugh at them).

TRY BEING A GIRL FOR A DAY

Write a list of the best relationships in your life. Who could you not live without? (If you have a very short list, work on making it longer.) Healthy relationships make you a stronger person—they are not a sign of weakness.

According to a famous psychologist called **Sigmund Freud 239**, boys and girls have opposite ideas about the value of human relationships—linked to the different relationships they have with their mothers. Boys only feel masculine once they have emotionally separated themselves from their mother (meaning that, if they feel upset, they can cope without her), while girls become feminine by attaching themselves to her and adopting her characteristics. Intimacy (feeling close to someone) therefore becomes scary to males, but a source of security to females. No wonder attempts to forge relations between the two often go so horribly, horribly wrong. (Wouldn't you know it?)

Phone a friend for a chat. No reason, just to see how they are. If you're afraid male friends will find this odd (or even frightening), call a female one. She won't think anything of it (unless you have a huge crush on her...).

You've probably already noticed that boys and girls communicate differently. At a party, boys are more likely to dominate the entire group with long stories or jokes, while girls separate and confide in each other about their (or other people's) personal lives. Boys and girls listen differently, too. Girls are more likely to nod and **smile 078** encouragingly, looking at the speaker's face, while boys appear less receptive. Evolutionary psychologists argue that this is linked to prehistoric sexual roles: males had to hunt, an activity that required focus on one thing and little conversation, while females gathered supplies, conversing with each other (to find the best berries). American professor John Gray wrote a famous book *Men are from Mars, Women are from Venus* about gender differences (how you behave if you're a boy or a girl). He argues that girls and boys talk to fulfill different personal needs. Girls chat about problems because they want emotional support. If you offer quick solutions, they feel they're not being heard. Boys, on the other hand, communicate issues in search of answers—they don't want your pesky empathy (when you identify with someone else's feelings)! No wonder we find each other so confusing...

Try being very aware of your appearance. Imagine that everyone is constantly sizing you up based on how you dress and comb your hair. See if this makes a difference as you go about your day.

Many sociologists (people who study cultures) argue that boys and girls act differently because they are treated differently by society. People are not born with built-in gender roles (there's that nurture argument again). So, many boys are taught from a young age that to be considered successful they need a high-powered job, lots of money, and complete independence. Society encourages girls to judge themselves (and each other) by their relationships and their appearance. In many societies, a beautiful, attractive female is deemed more successful than a less attractive one, no matter who has achieved more things. Therefore, girls learn how to wear makeup and jewelry to achieve the idea of **beauty 190** as defined by the society they live in. Of course, these days many boys spend more time in front of the mirror than anybody, while females have become more influential in the workplace since the **feminist 030** movement of the 1960s.

ARE YOU A GIRL? TURN TO PAGE 224

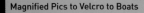

A

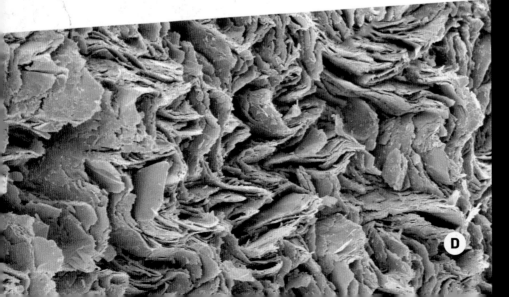

WHAT ARE YOU LOOKING AT?

These images were produced by a scanning electron

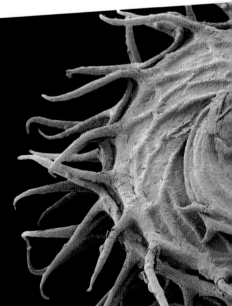

D

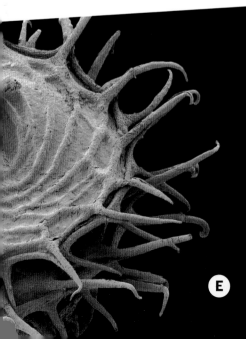

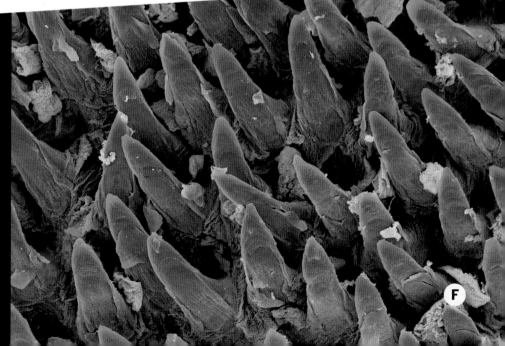

1. MAGNIFIED FLUORESCENT LIGHTBULB POWDER

Grains of a phosphor (light-emitting) powder coat the inside of a fluorescent lightbulb. A series of events, triggered by an **electric 300** *current passing through mercury vapor inside the bulb, cause the powder to emit light.*

2. MAGNIFIED TONGUE PAPILLAE

*These cone-shaped papillae (small projections of tissue) on the tongue contain nerve endings that transmit tactile (**touch 066**) information to the brain. There are more papillae on the tongue than taste buds (not shown).*

3. MAGNIFIED BURR MEDIC SEED CASE

This contains the plant's seeds. The long, hooked spikes get caught on the wool or hair of passing animals, helping the seeds to disperse far from the parent plant. This mechanism was the inspiration for Velcro fastening.

4. MAGNIFIED SHARK SCALES

These sharply pointed scales are also known as dermal (skin) teeth. They give the shark the feel of sandpaper. The scales seriously reduce resistance on the shark as it swims. This design is being investigated by engineers for use on the surfaces of aircraft and boats.

5. MAGNIFIED FLY'S FOOT

These are pulvilli (tubular hairs) on the base of the foot of a fly. Each pulvillus releases a solution that forms a bond with the surface on which the fly is standing— allowing the pesky insect to walk on ceilings and walls.

6. MAGNIFIED GRAPHITE PENCIL CORE

These graphite layers make up the core of a pencil (lead's not used because it's poisonous). Graphite is a soft form of carbon, so the tip of the pencil crumbles under pressure, leaving marks on paper.

Answers: A=4, B=1, C=5, D=6, E=3, F=2

OW! THAT REALLY HURTS…

It may hurt, but pain is vital for humans and other animals. Pain tells us that a part of the body is damaged. Without it, we couldn't defend ourselves and we couldn't help our bodies heal. Dogs might bite us, things could hit us on the head and we wouldn't realize. Pain is our body screaming at us: "You're in trouble!"

Pain is like an exaggerated sense of **touch 066**. Your skin contains millions of sensory receptors: points around the body that can sense pain, pressure, or heat. They tell the brain (via electrical impulses) what's happening on the body's surface. Your sense of taste, smell, and hearing are all determined by specific sensory receptors. Pain receptors are activated only if there is a threat of damage. For instance, if you touch something hot enough to burn, heat receptors stop firing and specialized pain receptors take over. And they are not just confined to your skin—pain receptors are also found in your bones and body organs too.

HOW **YOUR BODY** LOOKS AFTER ITSELF

THE BODY'S INFANTRY

The body's defense system is known as the immune system. It protects the body against bacteria, parasites (tiny organisms that feed off other creatures, like you), and **viruses 214**. The first line of defense is the body's natural barrier—the skin. While the skin provides a permanent defense, the rest of the body's immune system is more reactive and deals with the nasty things that have gotten inside you. White blood cells are like soldiers on patrol, constantly on the hunt for harmful substances (as seen in the supermagnified picture, right). They are looking for antigens, which are usually found on the surface of bacteria or viruses and cause disease. When antigens are detected, white blood cells defend the body by producing antibodies: special proteins that cling on to the enemy antigens and neutralize them.

You know how you need a stake to kill a vampire? But werewolves are stopped only by silver bullets? Well, white blood cells have to produce a different antibody for every different antigen. And, like an elephant, your body's white blood soldiers never forget. If an antigen comes along that the immune system has dealt with before, the white blood cells recognize it and destroy it before you get sick. However, when the immune system is weak, white blood cells don't produce the antibodies to keep you from being ill. Bad **diet 176** is the most common cause of this. Cancers (diseases that cause the growth and spread of abnormal cells) or the abuse of alcohol or drugs can severely damage the immune system. HIV, the virus that leads to AIDS, produces antigens that attack the immune system itself, stripping the body of its defenses altogether.

YOU CAN REBUILD YOU

Geckos can lose their tails and regrow them. Crabs, lobsters, and spiders drop legs and grow them back. But the only parts of the human body that fully regenerate are hair, nails, and skin.

Scar tissue replaces skin after a deep wound. It is not as good as regular skin. For instance, it doesn't **tan 122** in the sun. And no sweat glands and hair follicles can grow in scar tissue. Scientists are hoping to beat scarring by studying frogs. The slimy creatures are able to grow back skin, even on deep wounds.

When a bone breaks, the body reacts by swelling around the site of the fracture. This helps to stabilize the broken bone fragments. Cells in your body called osteoblasts then spring into life, producing calcium to make a new bone.

LIMB BROKEN, humor intact: what to write on a cast

Dude, where's my arm?

Fashion accessory

That's the last time I arm-wrestle your sister!

Doctors are trying to mummify me!

Break a leg!

Push the human body to its limits and it can be incredibly sturdy. In 1985, British mountaineer Joe Simpson was coming down a dangerous peak in the Peruvian Andes with partner Simon Yates when he fell and shattered his knee. Things got worse when he dropped 100 ft (30 m) from an overhanging cliff into a crevasse (a deep crack). His partner thought he was dead, but Simpson survived and then started hopping and crawling across miles of glaciers without food, water—or painkillers. He spent three days sipping water from melting ice to survive, and arrived back at camp just as his friends were about to leave. In 2003, the whole amazing tale was made into a film, *Touching The Void*.

Help! I'm down here

HOW TO
MAKE A SLING

1. You need a piece of cloth about 40 in (1 m) square. Fold the square diagonally to make a triangle.

2. Slide one pointy end of the bandage under the arm and over the shoulder. Take the other end of the bandage around the other shoulder, cradling the arm. Tie the end of the bandage behind the neck.

3. Now, adopt a forlorn look, attract plenty of sympathy—and discover just how useful your right arm really was.

ANCIENT SUMERIAN

"You'd struggle to get your toast if it weren't for us. We were the first to really organize farming (about 3300 BC), in the Fertile Crescent (a bow-shaped area stretching north from Lebanon to Turkey and then south to the Iran-Iraq border). Before us, farming was rather primitive. We grew crops such as wheat and barley, and used them to make bread and beer. We also created the earliest irrigation methods (smart ways of keeping the soil watered), and trained a farming workforce. Those who weren't farming could concentrate on other things, like building the first civilization. Later, agriculture (the technical term for farming) was the foundation of early societies in **Egypt 100**, China, India, and Europe. So, the next time you munch on a grilled-cheese sandwich, just remember us Sumerians."

WHEAT FARMER

"Farming has come a long way since the Sumerians! The global trade in food really picked up in the 1500s, when explorers started moving plants and animals around the world. In the 18th and 19th centuries, there was an agricultural revolution in Britain. New techniques were introduced and new tools developed, such as the seed drill (a device for sowing seeds in even rows at the right depth) and the iron plow (a tool used for breaking up soil ready for seeds to be planted). Fewer people were needed to work the fields, yet more food was produced. There was a shift from subsistence farming (growing enough to survive) to profit-making farming (enough to sell and make money). Today, we have fully mechanized farms with tractors and combine harvesters that have computers on board. But in many poorer parts of the world traditional tools and animals are still used. Yikes, I wouldn't want to give up my combine harvester!"

GOVERNMENT OFFICIAL

"I may not wear galoshes, but I am very important when it comes to farming. We set the overall rules for agriculture in each country. These make sure food is of a certain quality and free of contamination (so it doesn't spread disease). Governments sometimes give farmers an agricultural subsidy, which is a type of payment. These help keep staples (basic foods, like bread) cheap to buy, while at the same time guaranteeing an income for farmers."

AGRICULTURAL ENGINEER

"At the beginning of the 20th century, it took four farmers to grow enough food for 10 people. By the end of the century, one farmer could feed 100 people. Much of this is thanks to us agricultural engineers. Farming is now possible in arid (dry) parts of the world, because of the irrigation systems we have designed. It can also exist in waterlogged areas because of the drainage systems we have invented. Today, we use **Global Positioning System (GPS) 316** receivers to decide which areas of farms need water, fertilizer (nutrients to help crops grow), and pesticide (a substance that kills pests, such as weeds and insects). One day, the farmer may control everything by home computer."

IT'S NOT JUST BAKERS
WHO MAKE BREAD

PILOT

"I release fertilizers and insecticides (chemicals to kill insects) over fields from my plane. This process is called crop dusting or aerial top dressing. Planes and helicopters are also used for hydroseeding. This involves spreading a slurry (a sloppy paste) of seed on the ground to make crops grow more quickly. We first did this using converted warplanes in the 1920s. Today, aircraft are an important element of intensive farming. This is when the most modern techniques and machines are used to make the farm produce as much as possible. But intensive farming is rare in developing countries because it is expensive. It can have negative effects too, such as soil damage."

SUPERMARKET MANAGER

"I'm the one who puts bread within your reach—on supermarket shelves. You can get almost any **food 176**, however exotic, at any time of year—all in a nice, neat package. More than 40,000 products can be stored in one store thanks to complex distribution methods. Even before the food reaches the store, it has been preserved (kept fresh) with special techniques to prevent it from spoiling. Freeze-drying, for example, is a process whereby frozen food (such as shrimp or strawberries) has the water removed to help keep it fresh. Then, when we scan your purchase at the check-out, the distribution center is automatically alerted and it can send deliveries for the next day, if necessary."

SCIENTIST

"So you thought agriculture was traditional and, if you're honest, a bit boring, huh? Well, us **scientists 326** do cutting-edge research to improve farm production. We investigate everything, from new, more effective fertilizers to the nutritional needs of farm animals. We look at how crops and livestock (cows, sheep, pigs, etc.) can grow faster or be made healthier. These days, we can change the **DNA 258** of plants to make them more resistant to disease. Foods created from plants and animals modified in this way are known as genetically modified foods. But not everyone thinks that what we do is great. Some believe crops and livestock are 'healthier' without the use of fertilizers and pesticides. They prefer things grown on organic farms, instead."

EARL OF SANDWICH

"Hello. I'm John Montagu, the fourth Earl of Sandwich (1718-1792), from England. While gambling (or even working), I would ask for meat between two slices of bread. Soon, everyone wanted a 'sandwich'. The word is an eponym—its origin is a (usually famous) person."

OTHER FAMOUS EPONYMS

Trendy among the British aristocracy, Wellington boots, or "wellies" were worn by Arthur Wellesley (1769-1852), first Duke of Wellington.

Pavlova cake was named after Anna Pavlova (1881–1931), a Russian ballerina who was as dainty as the dessert.

Garibaldi biscuits were named after Giuseppe Garibaldi, the 19th-century Italian general who fought to unify Italy.

GUESS WHAT?

THE AVERAGE AMERICAN EATS 230 SANDWICHES A YEAR. THAT'S A LOT OF CRUMBS

WHY BEIJING NEEDS ITS *BICYCLES*

Aside from walking, bicycles are the most popular way of getting around on this planet. There are more than one billion bikes in the world today. More than half of those are in <u>China 118</u>. Beijing is home to 10 million bikes—more than in any other city in the world. So many bikes fill Beijing's streets that they are now banned in some parts of the city.

Early bicycles, in the 1860s, had pedals connected directly to the front wheels. The High Wheeler (or Penny Farthing) was invented in 1871 and had a very large front wheel and small back wheel, which made it more efficient, but still not much fun to ride up a hill. In 1893, the modern diamond-shaped frame with a roller chain was introduced, which allowed faster speeds with less pedaling. (The 1890s also saw the first tandem bike built for two people.)

Bikes became popular in China after the Communist revolution in 1949. Only a very few people could afford cars, so the government encouraged everyone to buy bikes. Families often considered their bicycle a prized possession. Women sometimes refused to marry men who did not own one.

Beijing is flat, which makes it perfect for pedal transportation. The Old City district is divided by narrow alleys called hutongs. They are too tight for cars but perfect for bikes. Bicycle-rickshaws (pedicabs) became a fixture in Beijing in the 1950s and have been an icon of the city ever since.

But things are changing. More people can afford <u>cars 113</u> and are ditching their bicycles. Five years ago, 60 percent of all journeys in Beijing were by bicycle. Now, that's down to 40 percent. Meanwhile, the number of cars in Beijing has tripled to 1.6 million since 1993.

PEDALING INTO THE FUTURE

More than 110 million bikes were built last year. Increasingly, they are being made with new types of aluminum alloys (aluminum mixed with another metal), which make them stronger and lighter. Since 1984, carbon fiber has been used to make superlight but strong racing bikes. The lightest racing bikes of all are made of titanium alloys, which may weigh half as much as other alloy steels.

The greatest innovations are expected with electric bikes, which back up pedal power with a motor. The best electrics use efficient lithium-ion batteries and zip along at 20 mph (32 km/h). More than 7.5 million electrics have already been sold in China. As the technology develops—in other words, as they get faster and cheaper—they could become a realistic alternative for commuters going to work.

THE GREATEST INVENTION EVER (FOR YOUR BACKSIDE, THAT IS)

The <u>wheel 282</u> was man's first great mechanical invention, but for thousands of years it offered a bumpy ride. Early bikes had solid wooden wheels that were uncomfortable and liable to crack. Enter John Boyd Dunlop, a Scottish veterinarian, who came up with the idea of wrapping an air-filled sack around the wheels of his son's tricycle in 1887. The modern pneumatic (inflatable) tire was born. They quickly caught on with other cyclists who, after years of bruised butts, were suddenly riding on air (left).

A human on a bicycle is more energy efficient than any animal on Earth (when measured in terms of weight transported over distance).

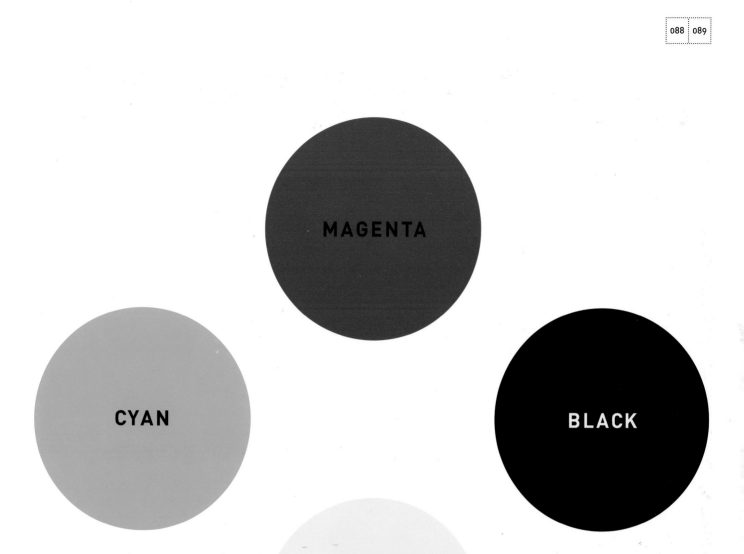

This entire book is made up of only four colors...
Don't believe it? Turn the pages

These four colors, when layered over each other in different combinations, create all the **colors 128** you've ever seen printed. Every page in this book, and all color magazines, newspapers, posters, and brochures, are made up of tiny, tiny dots of cyan, magenta, yellow, and black, too small for the eye to see. This is known as the CMYK (K is for black or "key" color) **printing 292** process. And what's the painting we've printed? It's *The Scream* by Edvard Munch (1863-1944)—clearly, it's all too much for him.

"**Freedom of choice is a universal principle to which there should be no exceptions**"

Mikhail Gorbachev (born 1931) became president of the Soviet Union in 1985. His 1988 speech to the United Nations marked the official declaration of the end of the **Cold War 294**.

FIVE SPEECHES THAT CHANGED THE WORLD

How does a strong vision and a few carefully chosen words transform the lives of millions?

"**I am here as a soldier who has temporarily left the field of battle**"

So said Emmeline Pankhurst (1858-1928), an English **suffragette 194**, while on a visit to the US. Pankhurst spent her life campaigning for British women to be allowed to vote in elections.

"**We should have today a free India**"

Mohandas (commonly known as Mahatma) Gandhi (1869-1948) was an inspirational campaigner for change. In this 1916 speech, he asked Indians to take back their culture and independence from their British **colonizers 096**.

"**Now we are engaged in a great civil war, testing whether any nation so conceived and so dedicated can long endure**"

Abraham Lincoln (1809-1865) was the US's 16th president. His 1863 Gettysburg Address inspired his countrymen to continue to fight to protect the idea of unity on which the US was first founded.

Martin Luther King, Jr (1929-1968) was a Baptist minister. His famous 1963 speech was made to 250,000 people in front of the Lincoln memorial in Washington, D. C., rallying supporters of the **civil rights movement 226**.

"**I have a dream**"

"The ballot [voting box] is stronger than the bullet" — Abraham Lincoln. DISCUSS

THE MAN WHO REUNITED THE UNITED STATES

Abraham Lincoln faced an almighty challenge when he became president in 1861. The country was splitting apart. The north's industrialized economy relied on paid labor. The south's agriculture-based wealth, though, depended on slaves—and they were determined to keep it that way, despite Lincoln's promise to stop the spread of slavery. Eventually, 11 southern states broke away from the Union to form the Confederate States of America.

The Civil War between the two sides began in April 1861 at Fort Sumter, South Carolina. With more manpower and weapons, the Union eventually had the edge in a war that cost some 600,000 lives. On April 9, 1865, the Confederacy surrendered. Days later, Lincoln was assassinated by John Wilkes Booth, an actor sympathetic to the Southern cause. Even so, in December 1865, the 13th Amendment ended slavery in the US. Although the nation's reunification period was still difficult, Lincoln had prevented a permanent division of the United States.

2 PEOPLE ARE IN SPACE

22 MILLION PEOPLE ARE BRUSHING THEIR HAIR

320 MILLION PEOPLE ARE WATCHING TV

2 BILLION PEOPLE ARE SLEEPING

11 MILLION CHILDREN ARE MISBEHAVING

1 MILLION PEOPLE ARE SENDING A TEXT MESSAGE

110 MILLION PEOPLE ARE USING THE BATHROOM

Joe's

WHAT HAPPENED NEXT?

Three snapshots of the story of colonization

When a country or city takes control of a territory in another country, this is called colonization. The practice is ancient —3,000 years ago the Phoenicians colonized areas around the Mediterranean—but it really began to take off in the 16th century. Then, European powers such as Portugal, **Spain 164** and Britain seized regions in the Americas, Australasia and Africa. The people already there (the indigenous people) often had to live, work and worship according to the wishes of the colonizers. In the decades after the **Second World War 178**, most colonies gained independence. But the story doesn't end there...

PAPUA NEW GUINEA'S TRIBES

When did they get there?
The first settlers arrived more than 40,000 years ago, crossing the sea from southeast Asia.

Who came along after?
In the late 19th century, Britain and Germany ran parts of the country. In 1905, Australia took over the British areas, and occupied the German territory in World War I. In 1946, the United Nations placed Papua New Guinea under Australian authority. But the indigenous tribes might not have noticed. Many lived in mountainous highlands, and some, until recently, were unaware of neighbors just a few miles or kilometers away.

How the indigenous people survived
Australia granted Papua New Guinea partial independence in 1973. Full independence followed in 1975. Today, foreign residents make up one percent of the population, while 97 percent of land is owned by indigenous people. Thousands of clans live there, with different customs and **languages 054** (over 800 tongues are spoken—a third of the world's total). Generally, they have traditional lifestyles with subsistence economies (wealth is measured by natural resources, not money).

Famous export
Locals claim their ancestors invented body board surfing.

WHEN GETTING THERE FIRST IS ALL THAT COUNTS...

'Queue' is a word to describe how people wait for things on a first-come, first-served basis. But not every culture queues in the same way. In some countries, such as Germany, people crowd around en masse. In other cultures, people form a single file 'snake line', as in the USA. Older people or those of high status in Japan do not have to queue. But British people queue so often that journalist Oliver Burkeman set up a series of fake queues in 2005, each leading to nothing. Bizarrely, confused passers-by joined them!

A SHORT HISTORY OF THE WESTERN

The Western is perhaps the most "American" of American genres, often revolving around the endless battle between "cowboys and Indians" in the Wild West. The Western-style story first featured in pulp magazines at the end of the 19th century. It then became one of Hollywood's earliest __film 034__ genres, first with silent flicks (no gunfire, no hoofbeats!). Movies tended to glorify frontier values ("goodie" cowboys defeated "baddie" Indians in the name of "civilization"). Since the 1970s, films such as *Dances With Wolves* (1990) have been more balanced and sympathetic to Native Americans. But there are still plenty of blazing shootouts and galloping horses.

NATIVE AMERICANS

When did they get there?
North America's first inhabitants walked across the Bering Land Bridge (now the Bering Strait) from Siberia around 20,000 years ago. Eventually, millions settled in semipermanent villages.

Who came along after?
__Christopher Columbus 272__ and the Europeans turned up in the late 15th century. They brought foreign diseases, such as measles, which Native Americans had no immunity to. These diseases killed at least 80 percent of the __population 020__. European colonizers seized their territory during the American Revolutionary war (1775-1783) and grabbed more as they expanded west. Millions were killed during centuries of war and conflict.

How the indigenous people survived
Today, 563 tribes are recognized, with their own governments, in the US. The current Native American population remains less than one percent (just over two million) of the US's total (296 million). However, in the late 1980s, tribes won the right to operate casinos. In 2004, these generated more than $18 billion dollars in revenue.

Famous export
The game of lacrosse was invented by the Iroquois tribe.

THE MAORIS OF NEW ZEALAND

When did they get there?
The group (whose name means "originals") migrated to the islands from eastern Polynesia about 1,000 years ago. They lived there independently for centuries.

Who came along after?
British Captain James Cook (1728-1779) and the Europeans arrived in the late 18th century. At first, Maoris liked these "Pakeha" (or "new arrivals") for their skills and trade. But not for long. After Britain annexed the country in 1840, the New Zealand wars caused many Maori deaths, as well as the loss of tribal land. As much as 10 percent of the original Maori population was wiped out by European diseases, and their customs and language were stifled. By the 1960s, it looked as though the Maoris might even cease to exist as a separate race.

How the indigenous people survived
During the 1970s, the Maoris had a renaissance (rebirth). European governments paid compensation for land and Maori language was introduced to many schools. Today, they make up nearly 15 percent of the population in New Zealand.

Famous export
The "haka," a warlike dance, is performed by New Zealand's rugby team before every game.

BEGINNING
MALE
ORDER
YOUNG
EXCITEMENT
CAUSE
RATIONAL
ABSENCE
DARK
GOOD
ALIVE
WAR
STRENGTH
NIGHT
HAPPY
SAFE
LOVE
RAW
IGNORANCE

Nothing on this page has
meaning 042 without the
words on the facing PAGE

END
FEMALE
CHAOS
OLD
CALM
EFFECT
EMOTIONAL
PRESENCE
LIGHT
EVIL
DEAD
PEACE
WEAKNESS
DAY
SAD
ENDANGERED
HATE
COOKED
KNOWLEDGE

Each pair of words is a binary opposite. You can't understand one without the other

Can YOU think of another binary opposite?

HOW THE ANCIENT EGYPTIANS TRIED TO LIVE FOREVER

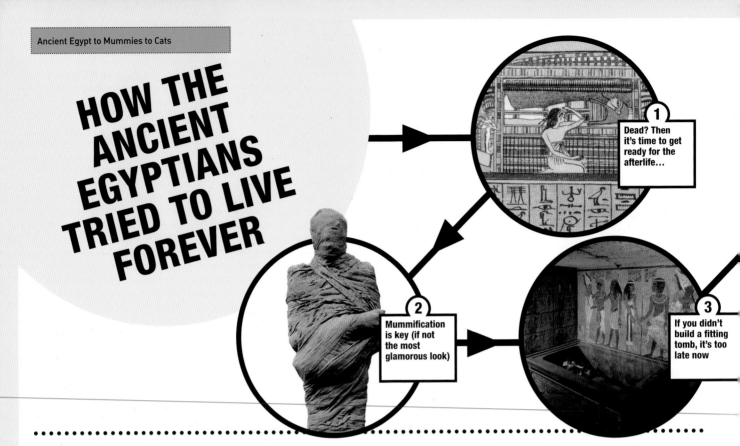

1 Dead? Then it's time to get ready for the afterlife…

2 Mummification is key (if not the most glamorous look)

3 If you didn't build a fitting tomb, it's too late now

The ancient Egyptians were blessed with a good climate, water from the Nile, and a talent for building almost anything they put their minds to. They created a civilization that lasted for more than 3,000 years. So why did they spend all their time worrying about the next life?

In ancient Egypt, nothing was more important in life than what happened in death. The pharaohs (Egyptian kings and, occasionally, queens) built elaborate tombs, such as the **Great Pyramid at Giza 314** to house their bodies and possessions for the journey to the afterlife.

According to ancient Egyptian religion, everyone was born with a ka (life-force) and a ba (personality) that would survive death. But for this to happen, your ka and ba had to be protected. The physical body was mummified (preserved) so the ka had something to live in during the next life. Mummification was a 70-day process. First, the body was washed in palm wine. Internal organs, such as the lungs, stomach, and brain, were then removed. These were dried and placed in jars (they also went into the tomb). The body was dried out using natron, a natural salt, for the next 40 days. It was then embalmed with oils and stuffed with leaves and sawdust so it kept its shape. Finally, the corpse was wrapped in lots and lots of linen and a priest read spells to aid the dead person's journey into the afterlife. It was then placed into a casket and moved to the tomb.

Meanwhile, the ba supposedly journeyed into Duat (the underworld) armed with the Book of the Dead, a handy guidebook for avoiding the perils waiting there. In the Hall of Two Truths, the **heart 134** was placed on weighing scales and assessor gods interrogated the ba to ensure it was being honest. If this test was passed, Thoth, the god of wisdom, allowed the ba to pass through to the kingdom of Osiris. This was like Egypt, but everlasting, and a bit nicer. Dishonest types instead met the "Devourer of the Dead" goddess, who gobbled up the heart and ended the person's existence for good.

HOW TO PASS A LIE-DETECTOR TEST

The scales used by the gods of the underworld were probably a lot better at spotting liars than today's equivalent—the polygraph machine. However, just in case your teacher whips one out when you next try "excusing" yourself from gym—here are three tips to trick it…

4 The moment of truth. Just how worthy are you?

?

?

5? Cool. You get to hang out in the Kingdom of Osiris

5? Uh-oh. It's the Devourer of the Dead, and she looks hungry…

How ancient Egypt nearly lasted forever

Ancient Egypt was around for a very, very long time. It existed even before the time of the first pharaoh, Narmer, around 2950 BC, and lasted until the death of the last, **Cleopatra 030** (top right), in 30 BC. Why? Because the Egyptians were very good at carrying on as before, no matter what was going on.

For example, around 2125 BC, the strain of building all those pyramids and a progressive drying-out of the region caused the economy to collapse and the country to split in two. Internal warfare kept Egypt divided until Mentuhotep II (reigned 2010–1960 BC) reunited both halves. Egypt was (pretty much) back to its old self.

Skip forward 300 years, and the Hyksos people (from what is now Lebanon) invaded Egypt and seized the throne. They got to rule, but everyday Egypt carried on much as it always had.

And there were plenty more foreign invaders who failed to upset the Egyptian way of life. From 1069 to 664 BC, the **Libyans 046** and Nubians from Sudan ran the country. The Persian kings twice conquered and ruled, first in 525 BC and then in 343 BC. And 332 BC saw the arrival of Alexander the Great, King of Macedonia (a region near ancient Greece). He identified so much with the place that he became more like an Egyptian than most Egyptians. Only the Romans, who occupied the country after the death of Cleopatra, managed to properly conquer it. But even they fell in love with Egypt, mummifying dead bodies and stealing Egyptian gods to worship. Oh well, when in Egypt…

1) Throughout the test, think about something embarrassing that has happened to you. The machine compares responses to different types of questions, from the straightforward (Is the light on in this room?), to personal ones (Have you ever been in love?), and those you might lie about (Were your sneakers really eaten by your dog this morning?). Concentrating on feeling embarrassed helps keep your reactions similar—the test is then in trouble.

2) Don't hesitate with your answers—you'll seem as though you're deciding how to respond. A lot of the test relies on the questioner's view of how you answer.

3) Control your breathing. The detector measures changes in your breathing and heart rate. Inhale deeply through the nose for two seconds, then release through the mouth for two seconds. You might appear strange, but (probably) not a liar.

WERE THE EGYPTIANS CAT PEOPLE OR DOG PEOPLE?

The ancient Egyptians liked their pet **cats 130** so much they mummified them after they died (left). They also made small bronze statues of them as offerings to Bastet, a feline god and symbol of motherhood. And their word for cat—"miu"—sounded just like a cat.

They also really liked dogs, and gave them individual names. Pet dogs were also buried with their owners—one royal mutt got his own tomb by the pyramids at Giza—and mummified. But dogs were used as insults, as when King Amenemhat I (reigned c1938–1908 BC) said, "I made the Asiatics do the dog walk." The Asiatics were probably the inhabitants of Palestine, and probably didn't enjoy being forced to heel. So sorry, dog-lovers, but the cats win.

EXPLORE_ The US stopped sending people to the **Moon 048** years ago (it was too expensive), and no one has set foot on its dusty surface since 1972. But budding astronauts may yet get a chance to travel to other worlds. In 2004, President Bush announced the US's intention to send people not just to the Moon again, but to **Mars 172** (right), as well. China and Europe are also interested in sending a manned mission to the red planet. Scientists want to find out if there is (or has ever been) life on Mars— that is, tiny microscopic creatures rather than little green men.

OBSERVE_ Space is a great place to check out the **universe 056**. The atmosphere on Earth interferes with telescope images, but from above Earth there are no such problems. Launched in 1990, NASA's Hubble Space Telescope (right), named after the astronomer Edwin Hubble, has provided sharper and more detailed images of the heavens than any land-based telescope. In 2013, the James Webb Space Telescope is expected to launch. This will study galaxies and stars at the very edge of the universe.

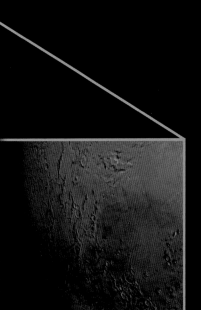

WHAT IS THERE TO DO IN SPACE?

EXPERIMENT_ Many things are different in space, so it gives scientists the opportunity to do **experiments 326** that they wouldn't be able to do on Earth. The effects of weightlessness on people and materials have been researched, and experiments have been done in biology, medicine, physics, and firefighting. Space is also ideal for climate study, as it's easier to examine **weather 196** patterns and the ozone layer when you're looking down from above. The International Space Station (right) is used as an orbiting laboratory and is permanently manned by a variety of international astronauts. It is scheduled for completion in 2010.

HOW TO
FIND ALIENS

The best bet is to listen for signals from alien technology. The Search for Extraterrestrial Intelligence (SETI) is doing just that, searching the galaxy for planets like our own and listening for radio signals from alien life. The spacecraft Pioneer 10 was the first to leave our solar system. It carries a plaque engraved with a map showing the location of Earth and what humans look like—just in case the craft

JUNK_ There is lots of **garbage 310** in space—big things like disused satellites and rockets, but also debris from previous missions, including nuts, bolts (below), and garbage bags. Scientists worry because even a speck of paint traveling at high speed could damage a spacesuit.

THE SPACE SHUTTLE_ First launched by the US in 1981, this was the first reusable spacecraft. It uses two rockets to launch, which parachute down to be reused once the fuel is burned up. The orbiter craft then carries out the mission in space, before returning to Earth. It has been used for deploying satellites, as a laboratory, and to help build the International Space Station. Two accidents, in 1986 and 2003, resulting in the loss of craft and crew, served as a reminder of the dangers of space travel. There are plans to retire the shuttle in 2010 and develop a successor.

WHAT MIGHT YOU MEET THERE?

TOURISTS_ Going into space is really expensive. When the first space **tourist 122** took a trip to the International Space Station in 2001, his ticket cost $20 million. Private companies plan to start short trips into space by 2008, and the business is expected to grow (and prices drop) in the coming decades. I can see my house from here!

ASTEROIDS_ An asteroid (right) is a rocky-metallic object in orbit round the Sun that is too small to be a planet. They are different from meteors, which are small enough to burn up in our atmosphere, and meteorites, which land but don't generally do too much damage. It's thought that an asteroid impact wiped out the **dinosaurs 162** some 65 million years ago. Today, an asteroid named Apophis is headed this way, and there is a very (very) small chance it could strike in 2036 (scientists are looking at a way of diverting it).

UFOS_ Alien intelligent life would have to come from habitable planets outside our solar system. Some people claim aliens are already visiting us—in Unidentified Flying Objects (UFOs). This picture (right) was taken in Ohio in 1966. The photographer described the object as a flying saucer.

WHAT WILL THE WORLD BE LIKE WHEN YOU GROW UP?

Take the future quiz and find out if you'll be living in a utopia (a near perfect society) or a dystopia (where things have turned out for the worse). Unless, of course, it's something in between.

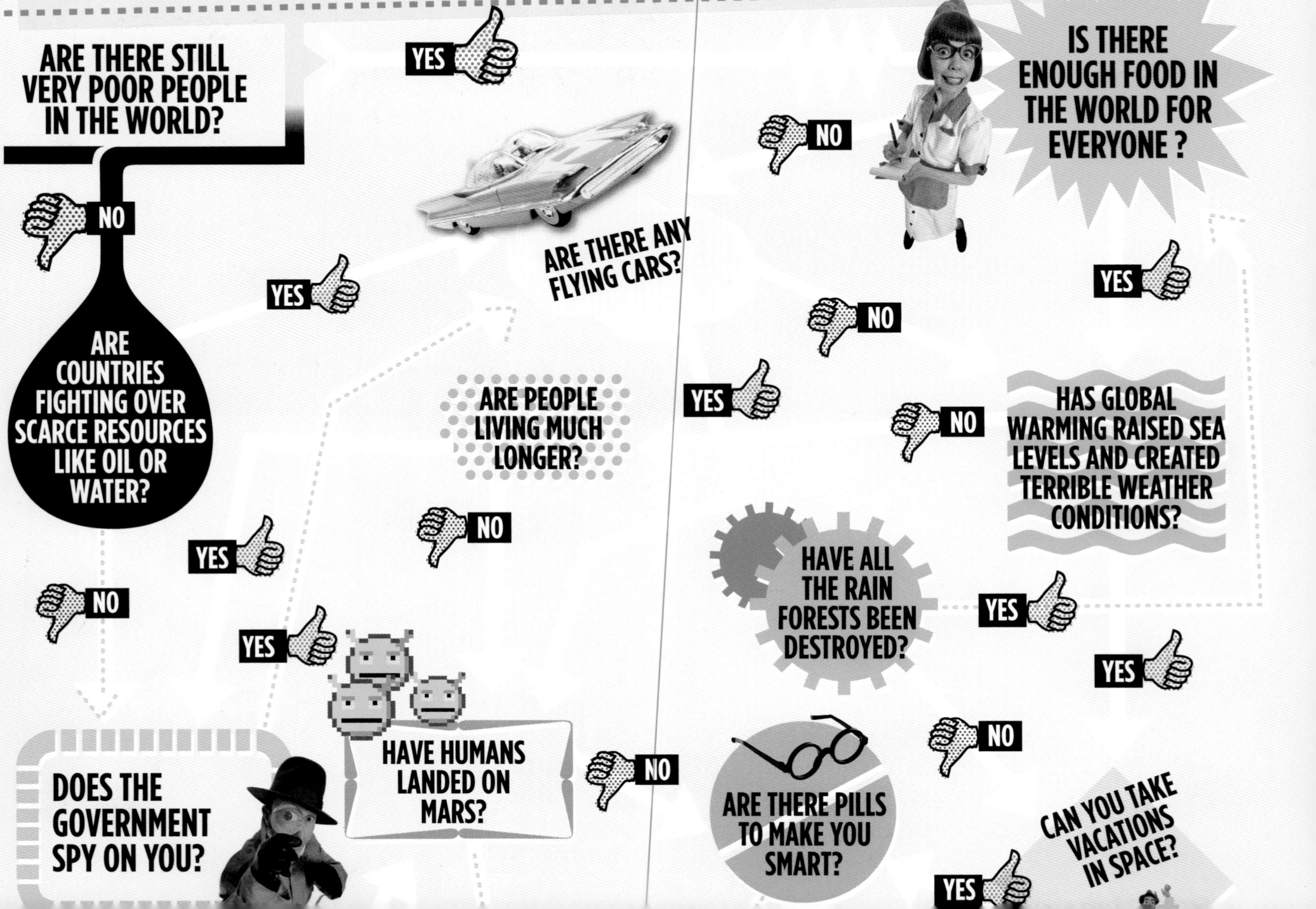

Will it be ruined by pollution, global warming 266 and overpopulation? Or, will there be an end to disease, lots more space exploration, and tons of groovy technology?

IS THERE ENOUGH FOOD IN THE WORLD FOR EVERYONE?

YES

NO

HAS GLOBAL WARMING RAISED SEA LEVELS AND CREATED TERRIBLE WEATHER CONDITIONS?

YES

NO

YES

NO

HAVE ALL THE RAIN FORESTS BEEN DESTROYED?

YES

CAN YOU TAKE VACATIONS IN SPACE?

NO

YES

ARE THERE PILLS TO MAKE YOU SMART?

NO

ARE THERE ANY FLYING CARS?

YES

ARE PEOPLE LIVING MUCH LONGER?

NO

YES

HAVE HUMANS LANDED ON MARS?

YES

YES

NO

ARE THERE STILL VERY POOR PEOPLE IN THE WORLD?

NO

YES

ARE COUNTRIES FIGHTING OVER SCARCE RESOURCES LIKE OIL OR WATER?

NO

DOES THE GOVERNMENT SPY ON YOU?

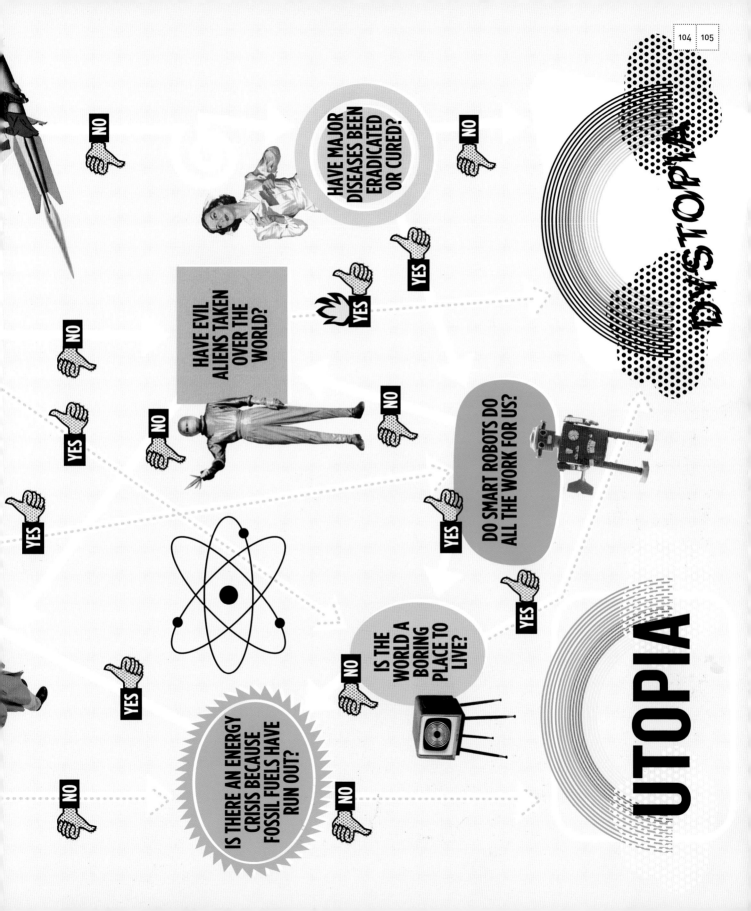

It can be a bit embarrassing to *SEX* is not just for the birds and deal for the human race.

REPRODUCTION:
IT'S THE ONLY
WAY FORWARD

The thing is, as a race, if we don't reproduce, humans are going to die out (no pressure or anything). So sex is important. Maybe not quite as important as breathing. Or eating. But close. Anyway, a man and a woman make a baby by having sex. During sex, one of the man's sperm fuses together with a woman's egg, and, over the course of nine months, a baby starts to grow.

GENDER:
JUST ONE LETTER
AWAY FROM BEING
A BOY (OR GIRL)

Confusingly enough, sex is also one of the words that refer to the difference between males and females. You probably think you know all about the difference between **girls 080** and **boys 224**. But the truth is, the reason we are different is down to just one little letter—an X or a Y. Both sexes will end up with two sex **chromosomes 258**—girls have two X chromosomes, and boys have an X and a Y. Whether an egg becomes a baby girl or a baby boy is decided by the fertilizing sperm. All eggs already have an X chromosome from the mother, and the sperm gives an X or Y one from the father (like a deciding vote). Your genes and chromosomes are a little like an instruction manual telling your body how to grow and develop (probably not worth trying to read it, though). They dictate not only whether you're a girl or a boy, but also your hair color, eye color, and almost all your physical features (not the scar you got at soccer camp). And of course, they'll cast a vote in the formation of your own baby when you're ready to be a parent.

talk about, but the truth is, the bees. It's a pretty big

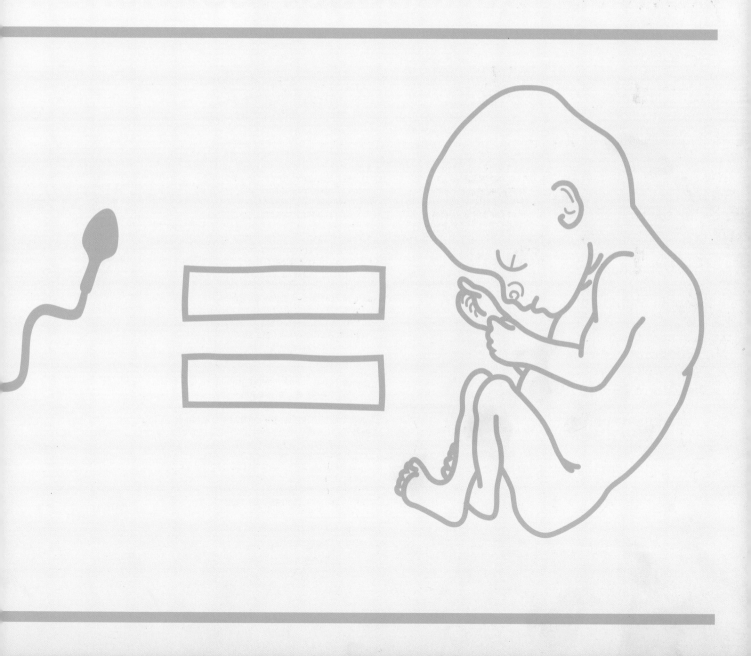

WHY PEOPLE ARE LIVING LONGER

If your great-grandparents were born in a rich country in the early 1900s, their life expectancy would have been about 50. Today, people in developed countries such as **Japan 028** or Sweden have a life expectancy of 80 or more. This is because of public health improvements (things like running water and flushing toilets), an understanding of how disease is transmitted, and improvements in medical care. Advances in agricultural technology also mean more food can be produced and diets are better (yum yum). But these improvements have mostly benefited richer, industrialized nations. There are still places in the world that don't have clean water or enough doctors, and so suffer from famine and disease. Today, a newborn baby in Angola, west Africa, has a life expectancy of just 37 years.

DEAD SPOOKY

Ghosts are meant to be the souls of dead people trapped on Earth, unable to move on to an afterlife. Without physical bodies (hence the ability to walk through walls), they wander around the places they lived, "haunting" them. The Tower of London is one place meant to have a fine collection of ghosts, including a headless Queen Anne Boleyn and explorer Sir Walter Raleigh. There is, of course, no scientific evidence for ghosts' existence. But they make great stories, especially late at night, with the lights off—and what was that noise you just heard?

The oldest recorded person living, in March 2006, was Maria Esther Heredia Lecaro, an Ecuadoran woman who was 116 years old. She was born in 1889, when Queen Victoria was on the throne in Britain.

What has happened in Maria's time to prolong life?

1954
The first successful human organ transplant is the kidney. Most organs can now be transplanted (except the brain—although sometimes you may wish it could).

1956
Ford installs seat belts in cars as standard. They are thought to have saved tens of thousands of lives since.

2000
US doctors monitor the location and well-being of at-risk patients with a new transmitter, inserted under the skin.

1912
In the US, the eight-hour working day becomes the norm, giving workers real time off.

1895
German scientist Wilhelm Röntgen figures out X-rays: the inside of the body becomes viewable (and the search for X-ray specs is on).

AND BEFORE SHE WAS BORN…

1862
Frenchman Louis Pasteur tests a process (pasteurization) to kill the harmful bacteria in milk.

WHY YOU CAN'T LIVE FOREVER— EVER

Without disease or the aging process, the only things to kill humans would be accidents, suicide, and murder. If that were the case, the average lifespan would probably be 1,200 years and the maximum 25,000 years (the longer you live, the greater the chance of accidental death). Not quite immortality, but still, that's a lot of birthday presents.

THE WHAT-WHY-HOW OF DEATH

BIOLOGICALLY, death occurs when the body (in particular, the brain and the **heart 134**) stops working. This happens because it is worn out (from old age) or broken (from disease, for example).

EVOLUTION suggests that people, animals, and plants die because their main purpose is to reproduce. Once they have had offspring or babies (and, if necessary, reared them), their job is done

and there's no (evolutionary) reason to hang around on the Earth any longer. Some people argue that having children is a version of immortality, as what makes up "you" (your **genes 258**) is passed on.

THE BIONIC (OLD) MAN

If medical science continues to progress, within 50 years it may be possible to replace half the human body. Already, key organs such as hearts can be switched. Knees and hips are regularly exchanged for plastic parts, which could become better than the originals. Imagine bones strengthened with carbon-fiber titanium to withstand impact better. Our brains might become equipped with electronic cards for better memory. And with plastic surgery advances, there'll be no need for people to look old. You'll run faster, think quicker, and look younger than ever. Bring it on!

Turtles

can live for up to 150 years. They're one of the few animals with a longer lifespan than humans. Most of a turtle's growth occurs during its first 10 years. After this age, it continues to grow, but at a much slower rate. Turtles are famous for their migratory behavior. The largest species—the leatherback—may swim hundreds of thousands of miles (or kilometers) during its long life. But even the oldest turtles have nothing on the baobab <u>tree 010</u>. It can live for 3,000 years.

GETTING OLD:
IT'S ALL THE RAGE

There's no such thing as acne

No one nags you if you spend all day online

You don't care what people think about you

Your kids might look after you for a change

You know it all. Really

Retirement = no need to find excuses not to work

Your best outfit is back in fashion

1854
<u>Florence Nightingale 270</u> lays the foundations of modern nursing.

1850s
Chloroform debuts as a general anaesthetic. Patients no longer feel the pain of surgery and more survive.

1880s
Thomas Crapper popularizes flush toilets in England, after installing them for the Prince of Wales (yep, even royals go to the bathroom).

1796
British doctor Edward Jenner tests whether vaccination can make the body immune to diseases (he's to blame for the painful shots).

Who lived the longest ever?
It was French-born Jeanne-Louise Calment, who died in 1997, aged 122

The oldest man alive today
is Emiliano Mercado. Born in 1891, he is a veteran of <u>World War I 294</u>. He lives in Puerto Rico

RELIGIONS tend to believe there is a specific purpose to life and death. Some <u>faiths 185</u>, such as Hinduism and Sikhism, believe in reincarnation, where your spirit is born into another body. What kind of body it is depends on how you behave during this life. Be good and worship regularly and you return as a human again. But break the rules and you could end up a rat or a fly.
In other religions, like Islam and Christianity, life on Earth is preparation for the afterlife: your soul either goes to heaven (a place for good people) or hell, where sinners (those who have seriously misbehaved) end up.

Look at the pictures on these pages—they are both from the same photograph. Can you see how different they are? The picture on this page is the girl exactly as the camera saw her. She looks pretty, doesn't she?

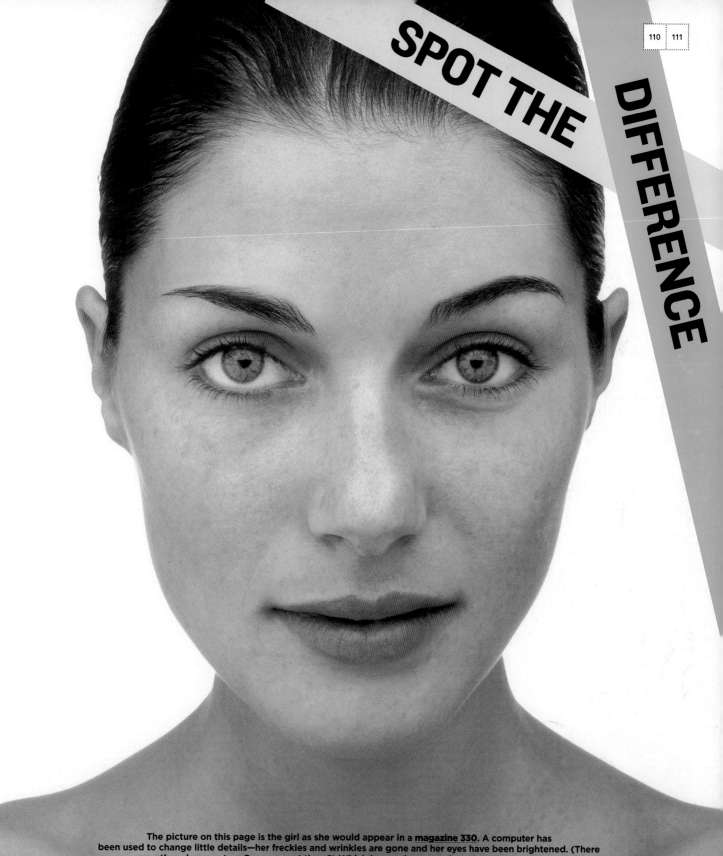

The picture on this page is the girl as she would appear in a magazine 330. A computer has been used to change little details—her freckles and wrinkles are gone and her eyes have been brightened. (There are other changes, too. Can you spot them?) Which image do you prefer? The one that tells the truth, or the one where the camera has been made to lie? Now turn the page for more lies...

THE CAMERA NEVER LIED

HOW THE CAMERA CAN BE MADE TO LIE

Leon Trotsky was an important figure in the **Soviet Union 260** after the revolution of 1917. That was until Joseph Stalin became leader in 1924. Then, Trotsky's days were numbered. Stalin had different ideas to Trotsky about how things should be run, and had him thrown out of the country. Photographs of the two revolutionaries that featured Trotsky were then altered so that he no longer appeared—he was cut out of history as though he hadn't existed. (Worse for Trotsky was Stalin's agents finding him in Mexico and killing him with an ice pick to the head.) And it wasn't only Trotsky. Hundreds of people, some of them Stalin's former friends, were snipped and painted out of pictures. Ironically, after Stalin's death in 1953, the new regime decided that Stalin was no good. So *he* was removed from important photographs. Poor old Trotsky had the last laugh—just a little too late.

Magic moments: *wedding photography now and then*

- Small, hand-held camera
- Digital memory chip holds dozens of photos
- Optical viewfinder or LCD screen
- Beep-beep—very quick exposures
- Glorious colour
- Easy electronic flash
- The happy couple are snapped on the move
- Big smiles all round

- Camera the size of a TV on a tripod
- Primitive glass plate only captures a single image
- Screen only viewable under black cloth
- Ssssnappp—hold that pose a little bit longer
- Choice of sombre black and white or brown sepia
- Don't jump when the scary flash pops
- The couple stand against a backdrop in the photographer's studio
- "Adopt a pleasant expression"—serious faces for a serious business

HOW TO
MAKE THE CAMERA LIE

SIX TIPS ON HOW TO LOOK YOUR BEST IN A PHOTO

1. Pose in front of a simple, but not boring, background. You'll stand out more.

2. Stand up straight. Put one foot slightly in front of the other and rest your weight on the back foot. You'll look more dynamic—or at least awake.

3. Don't put your hands in your pockets, but don't leave them hanging straight down like a goof, either. Don't hold your breath.

4. Turn your head slightly to your best side.

5. **Smile 078** with your mouth open revealing upper, but not lower, teeth. It will look more natural, even if you feel a bit stupid.

6. Enjoy yourself. If you're not projecting happiness with your whole face, it will show in the picture.

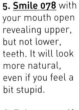

HOW THE PAINTERS LIED

JOHANNES Vermeer was a Dutch painter in the 1600s. His work is incredibly lifelike, photographic even (see left). Is it possible that he traced his paintings from a photograph? Well... the first photo was taken in 1826 so that would be impossible. But he might have used a camera obscura (a **Latin 054** word meaning dark chamber). This works like a camera but without the film. Early examples were large—the size of a room—but they soon became more portable. They work by allowing light in through a pinhole which projects an image onto the back of the box. With a properly placed canvas, **artists 322** could paint directly from the image, to achieve lifelike results. In the 1700s many of them did just that, including famous artists such as Canaletto and Joshua Reynolds (who disguised his camera obscura as a book). If Vermeer used one 100 years earlier, as some experts claim, he'd be a pioneer—and maybe a bit of a cheat, too.

HOW *CARS* SHAPED LOS ANGELES

Nowhere in the world has embraced the automobile as passionately as Los Angeles (**LA**). The city in California has three cars for every four people, is crossed by 27 highways, and has more than 10 million cars on its streets every day. Founded in 1781, LA started out like most other **US** West Coast towns—small and dusty. But by the 1920s, as mass production made cars more affordable, LA's streets filled up. Town planners expanded road building dramatically—a sprawling network of suburbs developed, joined by wide, straight roads, and the city's first highway opened on January 1, 1940. Soon, wider highways were built and the world's first four-level stack interchange (where two major roads cross using bridges and raised entrance ramps) was opened in 1952. Eventually, a backlash built as residents grasped the problems of **air pollution 070**, and "carpool" lanes were introduced in 1985. These can be used only by cars carrying more than one person, and are designed to reduce traffic.

Today, the 17 million people living in **LA** and its surrounding suburbs travel 100 million miles (160 million km) in their cars every day—a distance equivalent to driving to the **Moon 170** and back more than 200 times. The city struggles with a serious traffic problem and rush-hour jams (right, a downtown freeway) are as much a part of **LA** life as the Hollywood sign. Despite modern cars being less polluting than in the past, smog can still block out the California sunshine.

DRIVE SAFELY

It wasn't until the 1950s that car manufacturers around the world began to take safety seriously. The seat belt was introduced in the US by Kenneth Ligon, whose quick-release AutoCrat Safety Belt was offered by Ford in its 1956 models. (The company also came up with padded seats, dashboards, and rearview mirrors.) The three-point belt we all know today was designed by an engineer at Swedish manufacturer Volvo in 1958.

THE THREE BEST DRIVING SONGS EVER

"(GET YOUR KICKS ON) ROUTE 66"
Song about the famous highway that links Chicago and LA. Recorded by Nat King Cole in 1946. Covered by the Rolling Stones and countless karaoke singers.

"NO PARTICULAR PLACE TO GO"
A 1964 song by Chuck Berry, much loved by courting teenagers in the US in the 1960s. Often mistakenly called "Driving Along in My Automobile."

"LITTLE RED CORVETTE"
A worldwide hit for Prince in 1983, this pop song is all about a classic American sports car. Probably.

WHEN THE PRICE OF GAS GETS TOO HIGH

There are more than 600 million cars on the world's roads. That number could double by 2030, and oil reserves are in decline. The search for alternatives to gasoline made from oil is on. Ethanol—a distilled alcohol obtained from sugar or starch—is already sold as a cheap, clean alternative in Sweden and **Brazil 072**. In the US, California is leading the way with tough legislation to reduce greenhouse gas emissions. Hybrid cars use electricity as well as gas for power, but the best hope overall may lie in hydrogen fuel cells, a type of battery with no grubby exhaust discharge. In 2004, a BMW H2R (above) broke the speed record for a hydrogen car, hitting 186 mph (300 km/h).

THE LONGEST CAR CHASE IN MOVIE HISTORY IS IN THE 1974 VERSION OF *GONE IN 60 SECONDS*. THE CHASE LASTS FOR 40 MINUTES. DURING THE CHASE A TOTAL OF 93 CARS ARE WRECKED.

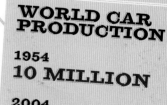

WORLD CAR PRODUCTION

1954
10 MILLION

2004
45 MILLION

US
HERMAN MELVILLE
(1819-1891)

Moby-Dick is a swashbuckling yarn about the search for a white whale. But it's much more than this. Melville's ambitious 1851 novel was revolutionary for its time. It mixed adventure, based on his own experiences on whaling ships, with big themes including religion, history, and **philosophy 042**. It was so radical it was shunned until it got noticed as a classic in 1920.

✳✳✳

CLEVER QUOTE:
"Ignorance is the parent of fear . . ."
Moby-Dick

CHILE
ISABEL ALLENDE
(1942-)

Allende's uncle was the president of Chile. When his regime was overthrown she was forced to emigrate. Perhaps this is why she only began to write on a large scale in the 1980s, when she was in her forties. Her famous novel, *House of Spirits*, started as a letter to her dying grandfather. Clara, a main character, can read peoples' minds and make objects move without touching them.

✳✳✳

CLEVER QUOTE:
"You will always be alone! Your body and soul will shrivel up and you'll die like a dog!"
House of Spirits

ARGENTINA
JORGE LUIS BORGES
(1899-1986)

This one-man writing machine penned essays, poems, and screen plays, but was best known for short stories with fantastical themes. *The Aleph* is a tale about an object that enables one to see the entire universe. Despite losing his sight as he grew older, Borges was appointed head of Argentina's national library.

✳✳✳

CLEVER QUOTE:
"No one is anyone, one single immortal man is all men."
The Immortal

SPAIN
MIGUEL DE CERVANTES
(1547-1616)

Cervantes was always strapped for cash and once held hostage by pirates, but managed to pour his difficult experiences into *Don Quixote*. The novel tells of a deluded "knight" and his put-upon squire and their (ridiculous) attempts to perform great deeds. It has since become one of the most famous novels in the world, and marks the shift from medieval to modern literature.

✳✳✳

CLEVER QUOTE:
"Straighten out the barber's basin you've got on your head."
Don Quixote

ENGLAND
VIRGINIA WOOLF
(1882-1941)

When she wasn't too ill to work, Woolf wrote books like *To the Lighthouse* using a "stream of consciousness style." You can read every thought her characters have—like who they secretly like. She also went to lots of parties in **London 159** with other writers and artists, known as the Bloomsbury Group.

✳✳✳

CLEVER QUOTE:
"Imaginative work... is like a spider's web, attached ever so lightly perhaps, but still attached to life at all four corners."
A Room of One's Own

YOU ARE WHAT

Impress your friends with vast knowledge about the novelist big-shots from around the world

CZECH REPUBLIC
FRANZ KAFKA
(1883-1924)

Imagine one day, out of the blue, you wake up as a huge, human-size insect. That's what Kafka did in *The Metamorphosis*. His bizarre style has lots of people baffled. And many think his short stories have messages about society. Unfortunately, we couldn't ask him as most were published after he died.

✳✳✳

CLEVER QUOTE:
"It is not necessary to accept everything as true, one must only accept it as necessary."
The Trial

NIGERIA
CHINUA ACHEBE
(1930-)

The "father of African literature," Achebe not only writes highly influential novels himself, but works hard to introduce fresh African talent to the rest of the world through his magazine and book series. *Things Fall Apart*, like most of his novels, focuses on the effects of Western customs on traditional African society, through the story of village leader Okonkwo.

✳✳✳

CLEVER QUOTE:
"A man who makes trouble for others is also making trouble for himself."
Things Fall Apart

INDIA
MUNSHI PREMCHAND
(1880-1936)

Hindi stories used to be all about religion or fantasy. Then, Premchand showed they could be about people like Hori—a peasant whose one ambition is to own a cow—and introduced India to "realism". He wanted them to get the message: he wrote 300 stories, 12 novels, and two plays—not including ones he wrote under the name Nawabrai!

✳✳✳

CLEVER QUOTE:
"It's only when something goes against our expectations that we're grieved by it."
Nirmala

RUSSIA
LEO TOLSTOY
(1828-1910)

Despite being a genius writer in later life, Tolstoy struggled as a **teenager 276** and dropped out of college. His anxieties were compounded by the death of his father and grandmother during his teens. His view of happiness, loss, and willful women formed the heart of his most famous works, such as *War and Peace* (that really long book).

✳✳✳

CLEVER QUOTE:
"Happy families are all alike; every unhappy family is unhappy in its own way."
Anna Karenina

JAPAN
MURASAKI SHIKIBU
(c. 973-1025)

So little is known about this ancient author, we're not quite sure what her real name was—many believe it was actually Takako. We do know, however, that she wrote *The Tale of Genji*, a story about a gorgeous emperor's son and his scandalous, secret affairs. It's often hailed as the first ever novel in human history.

✳✳✳

CLEVER QUOTE:
"In a life as short as a flash of lightning I was attracted to pleasures."
The Tale of Genji

WHAT MAKES THESE SOME OF THE FREAKIEST MAMMALS ON EARTH?

PLATYPUS

The platypus and the short-beaked echidna (which looks like a hedgehog) are the only mammals that lay eggs. All the 4,600 or so other mammals give birth to live babies. The two odd-mammals-out are known as monotremes. This means "one hole," because they have only one opening (called the cloaca), used for both excretion and reproduction. All young mammals rely on their mothers for **food 176** and stay with them until they can fend for themselves. Platypuses are ready to face the world alone after just four months (elephants don't leave their mothers for eight years).

STALLIONS

Boy horses are the only mammals you are likely to meet that don't have nipples. (Wild zebras and monotremes like the platypus don't have any either.) Mammals were even named after teets, since nipples are also known as mammary glands. Charles Darwin suggested male mammals used their nipples long ago, to yield milk and feed their young, like females do. These days, males don't use their mammary glands, but they're there all the same. But there's no room on a stallion where the nipples should go at the tail end. This is where he keeps his, ahem, penis.

NAKED MOLE RAT

Unlike all other mammals, this African rodent can't control its own body temperature. As mammals, our bodies maintain a constant level of warmth. It's why we're warm-blooded (**reptiles 146** are cold-blooded). Not only do we generate heat when it's cold, but we also find ways to cool down when it's hot, too (only mammals sweat). The naked mole rat doesn't control its own body heat because it lives underground in burrows that have a stable temperature—as though someone left the central heating on, permanently.

HEDGEHOGS

All mammals have hair or fur. Baby dolphins are born with a moustache to help them feel their mother. The stiff hairs on a cat's face are called whiskers. As with other hairs, these tell the cat about its surroundings because they are connected to nerves in the skin. But the hair of hedgehogs is among the strangest. Their spines (spikes) are hollow hairs made stiff by a protein called keratin. Adult hedgehogs have up to 5,000 spikes. These lie flat unless the hedgehog feels threatened. Then the spikes stick out and the hedgehog pulls itself into a prickly ball. Defending yourself with your hair? Freaky.

HOW CHEWING HELPED MAMMALS DOMINATE THE WORLD

Mammals are also unique because we can chew (masticate). Chewing gets digestion started while food is still in our mouths. Birds and reptiles gulp their food straight down—their mouths open and shut like a hinge. Our lower jaws contain one bone, the mandible, and our jawbones are firmly attached to our skulls, making them very strong. Reptiles and birds have several bones in their lower jaws, which are flexible, but cannot move sideways, like ours. Whereas they have more uniform teeth, we have different gnashers, from piercing canines to crushing molars. Our super teeth and jaw team means mammals have top munching skills. We can process many foods extremely well, survive in almost any habitat—and chew our way around the globe.

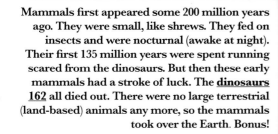

LIVING WITH DINOSAURS

Mammals first appeared some 200 million years ago. They were small, like shrews. They fed on insects and were nocturnal (awake at night). Their first 135 million years were spent running scared from the dinosaurs. But then these early mammals had a stroke of luck. The **dinosaurs 162** all died out. There were no large terrestrial (land-based) animals any more, so the mammals took over the Earth. Bonus!

TOP 5 MOST SUCCESSFUL MAMMALS

1. THE FLYING ONE

Bats are the only flying mammals. Flying squirrels can glide limited distances, but only bats can truly fly. They also boast the greatest number of species. There are almost 1,000 varieties—more than one-fifth of all mammal species.

2. THE FAST ONE

The **cheetah 206** is the fastest of all the mammals—and animals, for that matter—on land. It can reach speeds of 70 miles per hour (100 km/h) in short bursts, breaking most highway speed limits.

3. THE BRAINY ONE

The award goes to us humans. We may not quite have the biggest **brains 038** in comparison with our body size (the big-brained tree shrew beat us on that one) but we do have the most complex brains. We get extra points for having the longest **life expectancy 108** as well.

4. THE BIG ONE

Blue whales are the largest creatures in the world. Their tongues weigh as much as elephants, their hearts are the size of cars and some of their blood vessels are so gigantic you could swim down them, like water shoots at a water park. Woo-hoo!

5. THE STRONG ONE

The lion may be nicknamed king of the jungle, but tigers are the ones to watch out for. They can overpower prey from any angle, using their strength and body size to knock victims off balance. Tigers are the largest of all cats. They're one of the rare felines that can swim, too.

HOW TO
MAKE MAMMALS WITH SHADOWS

ELEPHANT	DOG

NO STILETTOS. ELEPHANTS WELCOME

What would do more damage to a kitchen floor: a lady in stilettos (high-heeled shoes) or a three-ton (6,000 lbs) elephant? Well, it's not the one with the trunk. An elephant may be heavier than a woman, but it spreads its weight over huge, soft feet. All the woman's weight is concentrated on a heel maybe 1/8 inch (0.3 cm) wide. Stand back... stilettos coming through.

China...

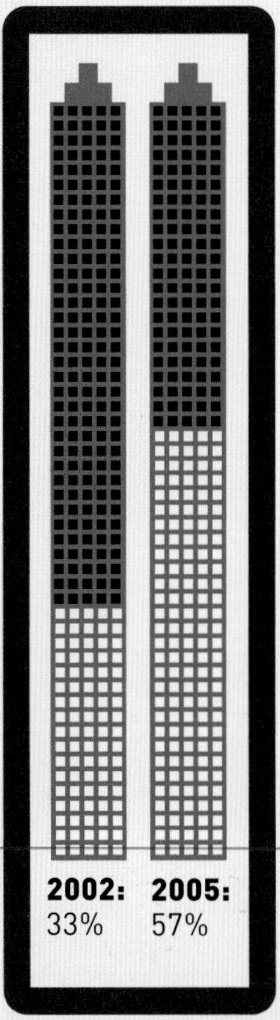

Half the world's pigs are Chinese

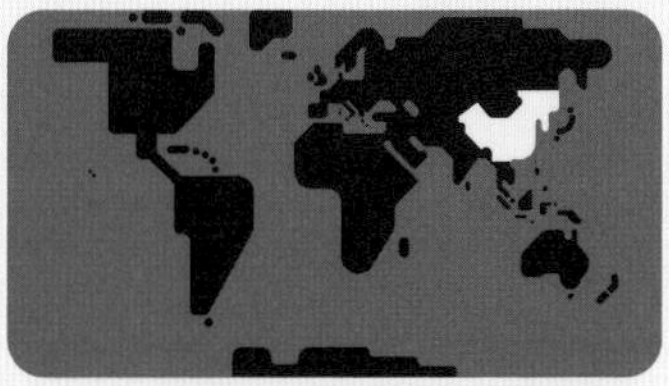

More than just people ↑ **Where is China?**

2002: 33% **2005:** 57%

← **Capitalism 050** is **accelerating** fast. How much private businesses add to China's GDP (Gross Domestic Product: the total output of goods and services)

There are 33 bikes to every car in China

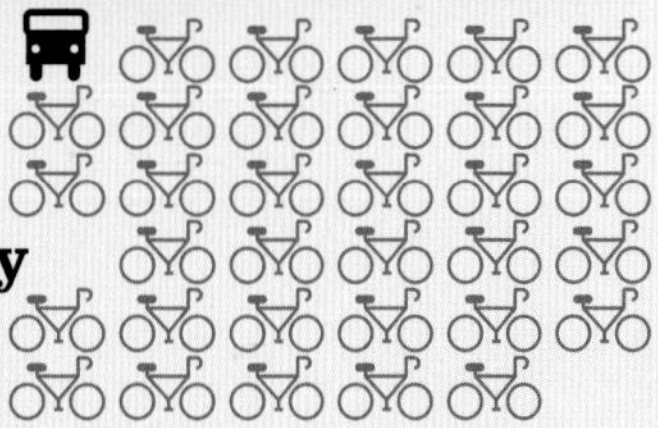

Bike sales are decreasing

1995

40 million bikes sold

33% of all trips

1999

23 million **bikes 088** sold

20% of all trips

Made in China

China produces a **large percentage of world goods**

29 Color TV sets

24 Clothes

70 Toys

37 PCs

49 DVD players

75 Clocks/watches

Pullovers exported from China to the European Union

2004: 40 million

2005: 300 million

The World Trade Organization removed the limit on the number of pullovers China could export on January 1, 2005. Chinese pullover exports shot up, though new limits on lots of clothing items were agreed in June 2005.

Car production is speeding up

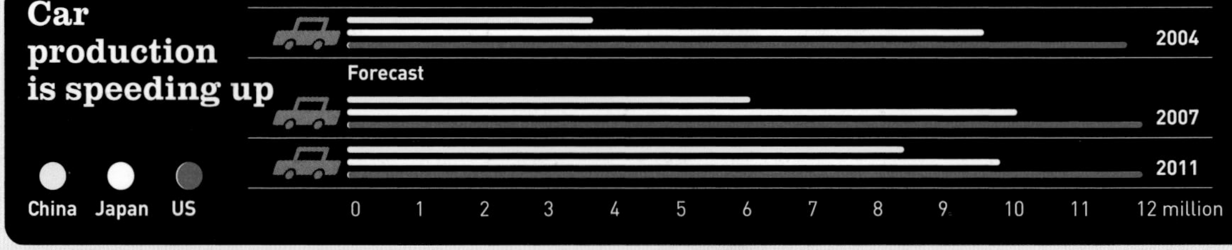

Forecast

2004

2007

2011

China Japan US

0 1 2 3 4 5 6 7 8 9 10 11 12 million

**Population
1.3 billion—
going up**

China is home to **one-fifth**
of the human race

| Li | Wang | Zhang |

One in every 24 people on the planet is named
either **Li**, **Wang,** or **Zhang**, China's three most
common family names

↑ **Nation knowledge**

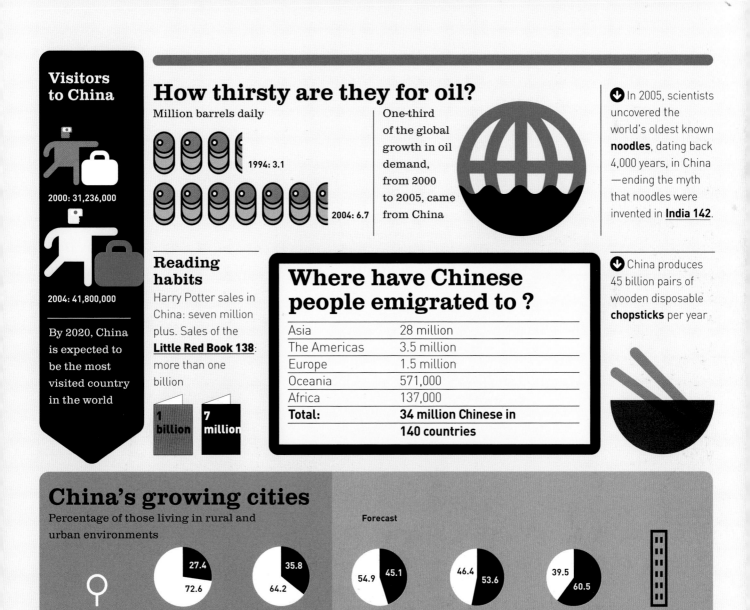

Visitors to China

2000: 31,236,000

2004: 41,800,000

By 2020, China
is expected to
be the most
visited country
in the world

How thirsty are they for oil?

Million barrels daily

1994: 3.1

2004: 6.7

One-third
of the global
growth in oil
demand,
from 2000
to 2005, came
from China

↓ In 2005, scientists
uncovered the
world's oldest known
noodles, dating back
4,000 years, in China
—ending the myth
that noodles were
invented in **India 142**.

Reading habits

Harry Potter sales in
China: seven million
plus. Sales of the
Little Red Book 138:
more than one
billion

1 billion

7 million

Where have Chinese people emigrated to ?

Asia	28 million
The Americas	3.5 million
Europe	1.5 million
Oceania	571,000
Africa	137,000
Total:	**34 million Chinese in 140 countries**

↓ China produces
45 billion pairs of
wooden disposable
chopsticks per year

China's growing cities

Percentage of those living in rural and
urban environments

Rural living

1990 — 27.4 / 72.6

2000 — 35.8 / 64.2

Forecast

2010 — 54.9 / 45.1

2020 — 46.4 / 53.6

2030 — 39.5 / 60.5

Urban living

The Persian regular army was called The Immortals. They didn't actually live forever, but as soon as a soldier was killed or wounded, another was there to take his place. The elite corps (the best fighters in an army) never dropped below 10,000 men—giving the illusion they were invincible. Although noblemen were trained to fight on horseback, the Persian military relied mainly on the horse-drawn chariot (below). When faced with better equipped enemies, such as Alexander the Great's troops, the Persian soldiers had little more than their bravery to protect them.

HOW HISTORY DID THE PERSIANS WRONG

The Persians didn't write much down—or whatever they did write has not survived. Greeks, such as Alexander the Great (356–323 BC, ruler of Macedon, a state in the Balkans), felt threatened by the Persians' vast territory and power. So, they encouraged myths about them. This _propaganda 292_ was believed for centuries. Since the early 1900s, however, artifacts have been discovered that reveal the real, forgotten Persian Empire

THE GREEK NEWS

450 BC

PERSIAN SHOCKER

WHEN IT COMES TO BATTLE, THEY SCATTER LIKE GUTLESS CHICKENS!

LAZY AND G

Instead of having a **democracy 194**, they are ruled by **MAD, TYRANNICAL DESPOTS** (rulers with all the power)!

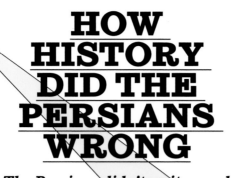

The Persians created the first "information superhighway." They built networks of roads so that information and troops could be transported at incredible speed—about 200 miles per day. New men and fresh horses waited at posting stations, ready to carry messages on. Many different languages were spoken in the Persian Empire. However, all official **messages 144** were written in Aramaic, a language used in the Near East from the sixth century BC. It still has about 200,000 speakers in scattered countries today.

After conquering the city of Babylon, Persian ruler Cyrus the Great (559-529 BC) allowed the **Jews 185** held captive there to return to Jerusalem. He also issued the Cyrus Cylinder (above), a document that promised not to destroy Babylonian institutions. This is sometimes referred to as the earliest declaration of **human rights 226**. The Persians were first to show that people from different cultures and faiths could live peacefully together (which isn't very tyrannical).

The Persians held burial ceremonies for their beloved dogs. They also wore fine robes and liked architecture. Ruler Darius I (521-486 BC) built palaces at Persepolis (above) and Susa.

IMAGINE A RACE SO BARBARIC THEY **KILL** SNAKES WITH THEIR BARE FISTS— **AND** TAKE PLEASURE IN DOING SO !

"History is written by the victors." WINSTON CHURCHILL 216 Discuss.

A SHORT HISTORY OF SPIN

Ancient Greeks 240 adapted facts about Persians to encourage people to fight them. This is spin—information that has "spun away" from the original truth. Some people say the 1980s term is an acronym (made up of the first letters of words) of the phrase Significant Progress In the News—but this could be spin too! In politics, spin doctors (people who create spin) may give selective information or phrase things so that the point of view they favor gets headlines. Public relations people (who manage the image of brands, people and products) will use spin, too. Feeling dizzy yet?

REEDY!

They eat lots of sickly dessert and are always drunk on wine! They spoil themselves in luxury.

DON'T BE MISTAKEN. THESE PEASANTS ARE **DANGEROUS** The Persians are ruthless, and they want to rule the world. They dream of turning everyone into SAVAGES—JUST LIKE THEM!

GUESS WHAT? THE PERSIANS WERE SO CONCERNED WITH LOOKING GOOD THAT NOBLEMEN KEPT PERSONAL MAKEUP ARTISTS

Advanced communication, road, and taxation systems created a profitable __trade 324__ income for the Persians. Whether or not they were greedy, they enjoyed luxury. The Persian kings paid for silver and golden tableware, and craftsmen made dazzling jewelry. Persian luxury goods were of such a high standard that Europeans were still trying to match them in the 1900s. The Persians also produced early luxury carpets in Turkey and Iran, where winters are extremely cold. Mmm, comfy.

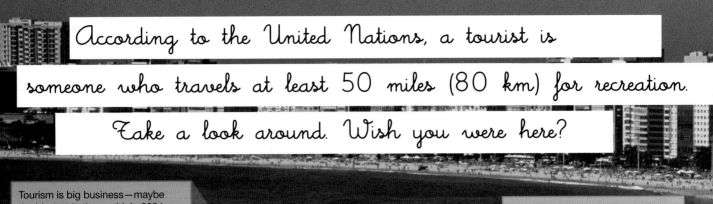

According to the United Nations, a tourist is someone who travels at least 50 miles (80 km) for recreation. Take a look around. Wish you were here?

Tourism is big business—maybe the biggest in the world. In 2004, $2,833 billion was spent on 400 million vacation trips abroad, compared to 360 million trips in 2003.

This is a picture of Rio de Janeiro in Brazil. The area has 45 miles (73 km) of almost continuous beaches. It is the country's top tourist destination.

Englishman Thomas Cook is credited with organizing the first vacation package—in 1841, he took 500 travelers to a nearby town. The price included a train ticket and a meal along the way. In 1845, he sold the first vacation package to Europe and, by 1866, his company was offering trips to the US.

Tourism is crucial to many countries' economies. It is estimated that eight percent of jobs in the world—that's more than 200 million people—depend on tourism. Though France welcomes the most tourists (75 million in 2004), it is the US that makes the most money from them (taking in more than $74 billion). The British Virgin Islands in the Caribbean are almost totally dependent on visitors. Some 95 percent of the islands' income comes from tourism.

Since 1949, when the first passenger jet plane took off, air travel has grown 70 times bigger. There have been environmental consequences—aircraft are the main source of carbon dioxide emission, a **greenhouse gas 266**.

She said she'd be under a yellow parasol. She didn't mention which one. Gulp...

Though tanning on the beach is popular, too much **Sun 168** can be bad for you. Skin cancer is caused by exposure to the Sun's ultraviolet radiation. It is important to use a suitable sunscreen and always wear a brimmed hat and sunglasses.

"Weather tourists" like to watch severe weather, such as tornadoes and storms. It's kind of a whirlwind tour.

A "labor tourist" is someone who lives in one country but travels to another for work (which isn't much of a vacation).

Hey! I told you it's important to stay in the shade during the middle of the day, when the Sun is strongest.

The Grand Tour, established in the late 17th century, was a way for rich kids in England, Germany, Scandinavia, and, later, the US to finish off their educations. They would travel around Europe, soaking up the culture. The key stop-off was Rome, where students gained an insight into art history and shopped for ancient artifacts.

Between 1990 and 2000, tourism in **Brazil 072** increased by a whopping 300 percent.

People in the US love taking trips. They spend more on vacations (some $883 billion in 2005, predicted to reach $1.6 trillion by 2015) than anyone else.

Wealthy **Romans 286** were eager to get away from it all (what with all that exhaustive empire building). One of the earliest seaside vacation resorts, 2,000 years ago, was the town of Baiae, on the modern Italian Bay of Naples.

Tourism is growing and growing. By 2015, it is estimated that $4,602 billion will be spent worldwide on vacations abroad. Regions in Asia, the Pacific, the Middle East, and Africa will see the greatest growth.

You know, jets today gobble up three to four percent of the fossil fuels produced.

Spot the odd

1. JAGUAR	5. MONKEY	9. TERRIER	13. BROWN RAT	17. POCKET
2. STRIPED HYENA	6. SHEEP	10. BABIRUSA	14. RABBIT	GOPHER
3. RHINOCEROS	7. TIGER	11. HARE	15. DRILL	18. ADDAX
4. TREE SHREW	8. ELEPHANT	12. GNU	16. WILD GOAT	19. CAMEL

one

out

20. SEALS	24. OKAPI	28. WOLF	32. HORSE	36. BLACKBUCK
21. KUDU	25. RIGHT WHALE	29. POINTER	33. SPIDER MONKEY	37. ARMADILLO
22. KANGAROO	26. ANTEATER	30. BEAR	34. ELEPHANT SHREW	38. CAT
23. ROCKING HORSE	27. WALRUS	31. TEDDY BEAR	35. BAT	39. GIRAFFE

Imagine writing all this stuff.

It all begins before anyone has written a single word (unless that word is "ideas," written in pencil at the top of a blank page in a notebook). First, the editorial team sits down together to talk. Around a table are the editor, the deputy editor, the art director, the assistant editor, and the staff writer. All these people have different jobs to do when they leave the room (hence the odd job titles), but right now everyone is getting together to do the first thing—to decide how to approach a new topic in the book. One of the big ideas of the exciting new book they are working on (do you know the one we mean?) is that every subject should be approached from "an angle." This means that a page about, say, cats and dogs doesn't just talk about cats and dogs in a normal, straightforward way but perhaps asks a surprising question, like "Which animal is man's best friend?" When an angle has been agreed upon, the idea has to be researched (a bit like doing homework) and, of course, the words have to be written. Sometimes the staff writer or one of the editors is given this job, and sometimes a writer who knows a lot about this sort of subject is asked to do the work instead. When the words are finished, they are edited by one of the editors (a bit like grading homework) and passed to the art director. It's his job to have a chat with the editor and then work out how the page will look. Will it use photographs? Will they be big or small? How about getting someone to draw an illustration instead? What sort of style should that be in? Even things like how the words themselves will look—the different styles or "fonts" that they're written in—make a big difference to the impression that the page will make and how interesting it will look. And when all this has been done, and the page is finished—with all the right words, fonts, photographs and illustrations—there is still more to be done. The page has to be sent to an expert on the subject, called a "consultant" (someone who knows almost everything there is to know about cats and dogs) for them to check that there aren't any mistakes to be corrected or better information to use. After this, another type of editor, called a subeditor, reads the page very carefully to make sure that all the commas, periods, and hyphens (among other things) are in the right places. Surely the page is finished by now? Well, aside from being worked on by three or four more people on its way to being printed (to make sure things like the colors look right and all the photographs look good), it is, at last, finished. Which means that everyone can get on with something else. So, the editorial team sits down together to talk. Around a table are the editor, the deputy editor, the art director, the assistant editor and the staff writer. All these people have different jobs to do when they leave the room (hence the odd job titles), but right now everyone is getting together to do the first thing—to decide how to approach a new topic in the book. One of the big ideas of the exciting new book they are working on (do you know the one we mean?) is that every subject should be approached from "an angle." This means that a page about, say, Beethoven doesn't just talk about him in a normal, straightforward way but perhaps asks a surprising question, like "Was Beethoven a punk?" When an angle has been agreed upon, the idea has to be researched (a bit like doing homework) and, of course, the words have to be written. Sometimes the staff writer or one of the editors is given this job, and sometimes a writer who knows a lot about this sort of subject is asked to do the work instead. When the words are finished, they are edited by one of the editors (a bit like grading homework) and passed to the art director. It's his job to have a chat with the editor and then work out how the page will look. Will it use photographs? Will they be big or small? How about getting someone to draw an illustration instead? What sort of style should that be in? Even things like how the words themselves will look—the different styles or "fonts" that they're written in—make a big difference to the impression that the page will make and how interesting it will look. And when all this has been done, and the page is finished—with all the right words, fonts, photographs and illustrations—there is still more to be done. The page has to be sent to an expert on the subject, called a "consultant" (someone who knows almost everything there is to know about classical music) for them to check that there aren't any mistakes to be corrected or better information to use. After this, another type of editor, called a subeditor, reads the page very carefully to make sure that all the commas, full stops and hyphens (among other things) are in the right places. Surely the page is finished by now? Well, aside from being worked on by three or four more people on its way to being printed (to make sure things like the colors look right and all the photographs look good), it is, at last, finished. Which means that everyone can get on with something else. So, the editorial team sits down together to talk. Around a table are the editor, the deputy editor, the art director, the assistant editor and the staff writer. All these people have different jobs to do when they leave the room (hence the odd job titles), but right now everyone is getting together to do the first thing—to decide how to approach a new topic in the book. One of the big ideas of the exciting new book they are working on (do you know the one we mean?) is that every subject should be approached from "an angle." This means that a page about, say, the stars doesn't just talk about the stars in a normal, straightforward way but perhaps asks a surprising question, like "Why is the sky dark at night?" When an angle has been agreed upon, the idea has to be researched (a bit like doing homework) and, of course, the words have to be written. Sometimes the staff writer or one of the editors is given this job, and sometimes a writer who knows a lot about this sort of subject is asked to do the work instead. When the words are finished, they are edited by one of the editors (a bit like grading homework) and passed to the art director. It's his job to have a chat with the editor and then work out how the page will look. Will it use photographs? Will they be big or small? How about getting someone to draw an illustration instead? What sort of style should that be in? Even things like how the words themselves will look—the different styles or "fonts" that they're written in—make a big difference to the impression that the page will make and how interesting it will look. And when all this has been done, and the page is finished—with all the right words, fonts, photographs and illustrations—there is still more to be done. The page has to be sent to an expert on the subject, called a "consultant" (someone who knows almost everything there is to know about stars and stuff) for them to check that there aren't any mistakes to be corrected or better information to use. After this, another type of editor, called a subeditor, reads the page very carefully to make sure that all the commas, full stops and hyphens (among other things) are in the right places. Surely the page is finished by now? Well, aside from being worked on by three or four more people on its way to being printed (to make sure things like the colors look right and all the photographs look good), it is, at last, finished. Which means that everyone can get on with something else. So, the editorial team sits down together to talk. Around a table are the editor, the deputy editor, the art director, the assistant editor and the staff writer. All these people have different jobs to do when they leave the room (hence the odd job titles), but right now everyone is getting together to do the first thing—to decide how to approach a new topic in the book. One of the big ideas of the exciting new book they are working on (do you know the one we mean?) is that every subject should be approached from "an angle." This means that a page about, say, the pyramids doesn't just talk about pyramids in a normal, straightforward way but perhaps asks a surprising question, like "Why build big?" When an angle has been agreed upon, the idea has to be researched (a bit like doing homework) and, of course, the words have to be written. Sometimes the staff writer or one of the editors is given this job, and sometimes a writer who knows a lot about this sort of subject is asked to do the work instead. When the words are finished, they are edited by one of the editors (a bit like grading homework) and passed to the art director. It's his job to have a chat with the editor and then work out how the page will look. Will it use photographs? Will they be big or small? How about getting someone to draw an illustration instead? What sort of style should that be in? Even things like how the words themselves will look—the different styles or "fonts" that they're written in—make a big difference to the impression that the page will make and how interesting it will look. And when all this has been done, and the page is finished—with all the right words, fonts, photographs and illustrations—there is still more to be done. The page has to be sent to an expert on the subject, called a "consultant" (someone who knows almost everything there is to know about ancient Egypt) for them to check that there aren't any mistakes to be corrected or better information to use. After this, another type of editor, called a subeditor, reads the page very carefully to make sure that all the commas, full stops and hyphens (among other things) are in the right places. Surely the page is finished by now? Well, aside from being worked on by three or four more people on its way to being printed (to make sure things like the colors look right and all the photographs look good), it is, at last, finished. Which means that everyone can get on with something else. So, the editorial team sits down together to talk. Around a table are the editor, the deputy editor, the art director, the assistant editor and the staff writer. All these people have different jobs to do when they leave the room (hence the odd job titles), but right now everyone is getting together to do the first thing—to decide how to approach a new topic in the book. One of the big ideas of the exciting new book they are working on (do you know the one we mean?) is that every subject should be approached from "an angle." This means that a page about, say, terrorism doesn't just talk about terrorism in a normal, straightforward way but perhaps asks a surprising question, like "Was Nelson Mandela a terrorist?" When an angle has been agreed upon, the idea has to be researched (a bit like doing homework) and, of course, the words have to be written. Sometimes the staff writer or one of the editors is given this job, and sometimes a writer who knows a lot about this sort of subject is asked to do the work instead. When the words are finished, they are edited by one of the editors (a bit like grading homework) and passed to the art director. It's his job to have a chat with the editor and then work out how the page will look. Will it use photographs? Will they be big or small? How about getting someone to draw an illustration instead? What sort of style should that be in? Even things like how the words themselves will look—the different styles or "fonts" that they're written in—make a big difference to the impression that the page will make and how interesting it will look. And when all this has been done, and the page is finished—with all the right words, fonts, photographs and illustrations—there is still more to be done. The page has to be sent to an expert on the subject, called a "consultant" (someone who knows almost everything there is to know about modern history) for them to check that there aren't any mistakes to be corrected or better information to use. After this, another type of editor, called a subeditor, reads the page very carefully to make sure that all the commas, full stops and hyphens (among other things) are in the right places. Surely the page is finished by now? Well, aside from being worked on by three or four more people on its way to being printed (to make sure things like the colors look right and all the photographs look good), it is, at last, finished. Which means that everyone can get on with something else. So, the editorial team sits down together to talk. Around a table are the editor, the deputy editor, the art director, the assistant editor and the staff writer. All these people have different jobs to do when they leave the room (hence the odd job titles), but right now everyone is getting together to do the first thing—to decide how to approach a new topic in the book. One of the big ideas of the exciting new book they are working on (do you know the one we mean?) is that every subject should be approached from "an angle." This means that a page about, say, empires doesn't just talk about empires in a normal, straightforward way but perhaps asks a surprising question, like "Dad, will you buy me a superpower?" When an angle has been agreed upon, the idea has to be researched (a bit like doing homework) and, of course, the words have to be written. Sometimes the staff writer or one of the editors is given this job, and sometimes a writer who knows a lot about this sort of subject is asked to do the work instead. When the words are finished, they are edited by one of the editors (a bit like grading homework) and passed to the art director. It's his job to have a chat with the editor and then work out how the page will look. Will it use photographs? Will they be big or small? How about getting someone to draw an illustration instead? What sort of style should that be in? Even things like how the words themselves will look—the different styles or "fonts" that they're written in—make a big difference to the impression that the page will make and how interesting it will look. And when all this has been done, and the page is finished—with all the right words, fonts, photographs and illustrations—there is still more to be done. The page has to be sent to an expert on the subject, called a "consultant" (someone who knows almost everything there is to know about world history) for them to check that there aren't any mistakes to be corrected or better information to use. After this, another type of editor, called a subeditor, reads the page very carefully to make sure that all the commas, full stops and hyphens (among other things) are in the right places. Surely the page is finished by now? Well, aside from being worked on by three or four more people on its way to being printed (to make sure that things like the colors look right and all the photographs look good), it is, at last, finished. Which means that everyone can get on with something else. It all begins before anyone has written a single word (unless that word is "ideas" written in pencil at the top of a blank page in a notebook). First, the editorial team sits down together to talk. Around a table are the editor, the deputy editor, the art director, the assistant editor and the staff writer. All these people have different jobs to do when they leave the room (hence the odd job titles), but right now everyone is getting together to do the first thing—to decide how to approach a new topic in the book. One of the big ideas of the exciting new book they are working on (do you know the one we mean?) is that every subject should be approached from "an angle." This means that a page about, say, trees doesn't just talk about trees in a normal, straightforward way but perhaps asks a surprising question, like "How trees talk to us?" When an angle has been agreed upon, the idea has to be researched (a bit like doing homework) and, of course, the words have to be written. Sometimes the staff writer or one of the editors is given this job, and sometimes a writer who knows a lot about this sort of subject is asked to do the work instead. When the words are finished, they are edited by one of the editors (a bit like grading homework) and passed to the art director. It's his job to have a chat with the editor and then work out how the page will look. Will it use photographs? Will they be big or small? How about getting someone to draw an illustration instead? What sort of style should that be in? Even things like how the words themselves will look—the different styles or "fonts" that they're written in—make a big difference to the impression that the page will make and how interesting it will look. And when all this has been done, and the page is finished—with all the right words, fonts, photographs and illustrations—there is still more to be done. The page has to be sent to an expert on the subject, called a "consultant" (someone who knows almost everything there is to know about trees) for them to check that there aren't any mistakes to be corrected or better information to use. After this, another type of editor, called a subeditor, reads the page very carefully to make sure that all the commas, full stops and hyphens (among other things) are in the right places. Surely the page is finished by now? Well, aside from being worked on by three or four more people on its way to being printed (to make sure things like the colors look right and all the photographs look good), it is, at last, finished. Which means that everyone can get on with something else. So, the editorial team sits down together to talk. Around a table are the editor, the deputy editor, the art director, the assistant editor and the staff writer. All these people have different jobs to do when they leave the room (hence the odd job titles), but right now everyone is getting together to do the first thing—to decide how to approach a new topic in the book. One of the big ideas of the exciting new book they are working on (do you know the one we mean?) is that every subject should be approached from "an angle." This means that a page about, say, mammals doesn't just talk about mammals in a normal, straightforward way but perhaps asks a surprising question, like "What makes these the freakiest mammals on Earth?" When an angle has been agreed upon, the idea has to be researched (a bit like doing homework) and, of course, the words have to be written. Sometimes the staff writer or one of the editors is given this job, and sometimes a writer who knows a lot about this sort of subject is asked to do the work instead. When the words are finished, they are edited by one of the editors (a bit like grading homework) and passed to the art director. It's his job to have a chat with the editor and then work out how the page will look. Will it use photographs? Will they be big or small? How about getting someone to draw an illustration instead? What sort of style should that be in? Even things like how the words themselves will look—the different styles or "fonts" that they're written in—make a big difference to the impression that the page will make and how interesting it will look. And when all this has been done, and the page is finished—with all the right words, fonts, photographs and illustrations—there is still more to be done. The page has to be sent to an expert on the subject, called a "consultant" (someone who knows almost everything there is to know about mammals) for them to check that there aren't any mistakes to be corrected or better information to use. After this, another type of editor, called a subeditor, reads the page very carefully to make sure that all the commas, full stops and hyphens (among other things) are in the right places. Surely the page is finished by now? Well, aside from being worked on by three or four more people on its way to being printed (to make sure things like the colors look right and all the photographs look good), it is, at last, finished. Which means that everyone can get on with something else. So, the editorial team sits down together to talk. Around a table are the editor, the deputy editor, the art director, the assistant editor and the staff writer. All these people have different jobs to do when they leave the room (hence the odd job titles), but right now everyone is getting together to do the first thing—to decide how to approach a new topic in the book. One of the big ideas of the exciting new book they are working on (do you know the one we mean?) is that every subject should be approached from "an angle." This means that a page about, say, space doesn't just talk about space in a normal, straightforward way but perhaps asks a surprising question, like "What is there to do in space?" When an angle has been agreed upon, the idea has to be researched (a bit like doing homework) and, of course, the words have to be written. Sometimes the staff writer or one of the editors is given this job, and sometimes a writer who knows a lot about this sort of subject is asked to do the work instead. When the words are finished, they are edited by one of the editors (a bit like grading homework) and passed to the art director. It's his job to have a chat with the editor and then work out how the page will look. Will it use photographs? Will they be big or small? How about getting someone to draw an illustration instead? What sort of style should that be in? Even things like how the words themselves will look—the different styles or "fonts" that they're written in—make a big difference to the impression that the page will make and how interesting it will look. And when all this has been done, and the page is finished—with all the right words, fonts, photographs and illustrations—there is still more to be done. The page has to be sent to an expert on the subject, called a "consultant" (someone who knows almost everything there is to know about satellites and spaceships) for them to check that there aren't any mistakes to be corrected or better information to use. After this, another type of editor, called a subeditor, reads the page very carefully to make sure that all the commas, full stops and hyphens (among other things) are in the right places. Surely the page is finished by now? Well, aside from being worked on by three or four more people on its way to being printed (to make sure things like the colors look right and all the photographs look good), it is, at last, finished. Which means that everyone can get on with something else. So, the editorial team sits down together to talk. Around a table are the editor, the deputy editor, the art director, the assistant editor and the staff writer. All these people have different jobs to do when they leave the room (hence the odd job titles), but right now everyone is getting together to do the first thing—to decide how to approach a new topic in the book. One of the big ideas of the exciting new book they are working on (do you know the one we mean?) is that every subject should be approached from "an angle." This means that a page about, say, geology doesn't just talk about geology in a normal, straightforward way but perhaps asks a surprising question, like "What makes Iceland the world's fastest growing country" When an angle has been agreed upon, the idea has to be researched (a bit like doing homework) and, of course, the words have to be written. Sometimes the staff writer or one of the editors is given this job, and sometimes a writer who knows a lot about this sort of subject is asked to do the work instead. When the words are finished, they are edited by one of the editors (a bit like grading homework) and passed to the art director. It's his job to have a chat with the editor and then work out how the page will look. Will it use photographs? Will they be big or small? How about getting someone to draw an illustration instead? What sort of style should that be in? Even things like how the words themselves will look—the different styles or "fonts" that they're written in—make a big difference to the impression that the page will make and how interesting it will look. And when all this has been done, and the page is finished—with all the right words, fonts, photographs and illustrations—there is still more to be done. The page has to be sent to an expert on the subject, called a "consultant" (someone who knows almost everything there is to know about tectonic plates and stuff) for them to check that there aren't any mistakes to be corrected or better information to use. After this, another type of editor, called a subeditor, reads the page very carefully to make sure that all the commas, full stops and hyphens (among other things) are in the right places. Surely the page is finished by now? Well, aside from being worked on by three or four more people on its way to being printed (to make sure things like the colors look right and all the photographs look good), it is, at last, finished. Which means that everyone can get on with something else. So, the editorial team sits down together to talk. Around a table are the editor, the deputy editor, the art director, the assistant editor and the staff writer. All these people have different jobs to do when they leave the room (hence the odd job titles), but right now everyone is getting together to do the first thing—to decide how to approach a new topic in the book. One of the big ideas of the exciting new book they are working on (do you know the one we mean?) is that every subject should be approached from "an angle." This means that a page about, say, revolution doesn't just talk about revolution in a normal, straightforward way but perhaps asks a surprising question, like "Which revolution was most revolting?" When an angle has been agreed upon, the idea has to be researched (a bit like doing homework) and, of course, the words have to be written. Sometimes the staff writer or one of the editors is given this job, and sometimes a writer who knows a lot about this sort of subject is asked to do the work instead. When the words are finished, they are edited by one of the editors (a bit like grading homework) and passed to the art director. It's his job to have a chat with the editor and then work out how the page will look. Will it use photographs? Will they be big or small? How about getting someone to draw an illustration instead? What sort of style should that be in? Even things like how the words themselves will look—the different styles or "fonts" that they're written in—make a big difference to the impression that the page will make and how interesting it will look. And when all this has been done, and the page is finished—with all the right words, fonts, photographs and illustrations—there is still more to be done. The page has to be sent to an expert on the subject, called a "consultant" (someone who knows almost everything there is to know about modern history) for them to check that there aren't any mistakes to be corrected or better information to use. After this, another type of editor, called a subeditor, reads the page very carefully to make sure that all the commas, full stops and hyphens (among other things) are in the right places. Surely the page is finished by now? Well, aside from being worked on by three or four more people on its way to being printed (to make sure things like the colors look right and all the photographs look good), it is, at last, finished. Which means that everyone can get on with something else. So, the editorial team sits down together to talk. Around a table are the editor, the deputy editor, the art director, the assistant editor and the staff writer. All these people have different jobs to do when they leave the room (hence the odd job titles), but right now everyone is getting together to do the first thing—to decide how to approach a new topic in the book. One of the big ideas of the exciting new book they are working on (do you know the one we mean?) is that every subject should be approached from "an angle." This means that a page about, say, the Enlightenment doesn't just talk about the Enlightenment in a normal, straightforward way but perhaps asks a surprising question, like "Who switched the lights on?" When an angle has been agreed upon, the idea has to be researched (a bit like doing homework) and, of course, the words have to be written. Sometimes the staff writer or one of the editors is given this job, and sometimes a writer who knows a lot about this sort of subject is asked to do the work instead. When the words are finished, they are edited by one of the editors (a bit like grading homework) and passed to the art director. It's his job to have a chat with the editor and then work out how the page will look. Will it use photographs? Will they be big or small? How about getting someone to draw an illustration instead? What sort of style should that be in? Even things like how the words themselves will look—the different styles or "fonts" that they're written in—make a big difference to the impression that the page will make and how interesting it will look. And when all this has been done, and the page is finished—with all the right words, fonts, photographs and illustrations—there is still more to be done. The page has to be sent to an expert on the subject, called a "consultant" (someone who knows almost everything there is to know about intellectual history) for them to check that there aren't any mistakes to be corrected or better information to use. After this, another type of editor, called a subeditor, reads the page very carefully to make sure that all the commas, full stops and hyphens (among other things) are in the right places. Surely the page is finished by now? Well, aside from being worked on by three or four more people on its way to being printed (to make sure that things like the colors look right and all the photographs look good), it is, at last, finished. Which means that everyone can get on with something else. It all begins before anyone has written a single word (unless that word is "ideas," written in pencil at the top of a blank page in a notebook). First, the editorial team sits down together to talk. Around a table are the editor, the deputy editor, the art director, the assistant editor and the staff writer. All these people have different jobs to do when they leave the room (hence the odd job titles), but right now everyone is getting together to do the first thing—to decide how to approach a new topic in the book. One of the big ideas of the exciting new book they are working on (do you know the one we mean?) is that every subject should be approached from "an angle." This means that a page about, say, dinosaurs doesn't just talk about dinosaurs in a normal, straightforward way but perhaps asks a surprising question, like "Where did all the dinosaurs go?" When an angle has been agreed upon, the idea has to be researched (a bit like doing homework) and, of course, the words have to be written. Sometimes the staff writer or one of the editors is given this job, and sometimes a writer who knows a lot about this sort of subject is asked to do the work instead. When the words are finished, they are edited by one of the editors (a bit like grading homework) and passed to the art director. It's his job to have a chat with the editor and then work out how the page will look. Will it use photographs? Will they be big or small? How about getting someone to draw an illustration instead? What sort of style should that be in? Even things like how the words themselves will look—the different styles or "fonts" that they're written in—make a big difference to the impression that the page will make and how interesting it will look. And when all this has been done, and the page is finished—with all the right words, fonts, photographs and illustrations—there is still more to be done. The page has to be sent to an expert on the subject, called a "consultant" (someone who knows almost everything there is to know about dinosaurs) for them to check that there aren't any mistakes to be corrected or better information to use. After this, another type of editor, called a subeditor, reads the page very carefully to make sure that all the commas, full stops and hyphens (among other things) are in the right places. Surely the page is finished by now? Well, aside from being worked on by three or four more people on its way to being printed (to make sure things like the colors look right and all the photographs look good), it is, at last, finished. Which means that everyone can get on with something else. So, the editorial team sits down together to talk. Around a table are the editor, the deputy editor, the art director, the assistant editor and the staff writer. All these people have different jobs to do when they leave the room (hence the odd job titles), but right now everyone is getting together to do the first thing—to decide how to approach a new topic in the book. One of the big ideas of the exciting new book they are working on (do you know the one we mean?) is that every subject should be approached from "an angle." This means that a page about, say, religion doesn't just talk about religion in a normal, straightforward way but perhaps asks a surprising question, like "Where does God live?" When an angle has been agreed upon, the idea has to be researched (a bit like doing homework) and, of course, the words have to be written. Sometimes the staff writer or one of the editors is given this job, and sometimes a writer who knows a lot about this sort of subject is asked to do the work instead. When the words are finished, they are edited by one of the editors (a bit like grading homework) and passed to the art director. It's his job to have a chat with the editor and then work out how the page will look. Will it use photographs? Will they be big or small? How about getting someone to draw an illustration instead? What sort of style should that be in? Even things like how the words themselves will look—the different styles or "fonts" that they're written in—make a big difference to the impression that the page will make and how interesting it will look. And when all this has been done, and the page is finished—with all the right words, fonts, photographs and illustrations—there is still more to be done. The page has to be sent to an expert on the subject, called a "consultant" (someone who knows almost everything there is to know about gods) for them to check that there aren't any mistakes to be corrected or better information to use. After this, another type of editor, called a subeditor, reads the page very carefully to make sure that all the commas, full stops and hyphens (among other things) are in the right places. Surely the page is finished by now? Well, aside from being worked on by three or four more people on its way to being printed (to make sure things like the colors look right and all the photographs look good), it is, at last, finished. Which means that everyone can get on with something else. So, the editorial team sits down together to talk. Around a table are the editor, the deputy editor, the art director, the assistant editor and the staff writer. All these people have different jobs to do when they leave the room (hence the odd job titles), but right now everyone is getting together to do the first thing—to decide how to approach a new topic in the book. One of the big ideas of the exciting new book they are working on (do you know the one we mean?) is that every subject should be approached from "an angle." This means that a page about, say, sleep doesn't just talk about sleep in a normal, straightforward way but perhaps asks a surprising question, like "Where did you go last night?" When an angle has been agreed upon, the idea has to be researched (a bit like doing homework) and, of course, the words have to be written. Sometimes the staff writer or one of the editors is given this job, and sometimes a writer who knows a lot about this sort of subject is asked to do the work instead. When the words are finished, they are edited by one of the editors (a bit like grading homework) and passed to the art director. It's his job to have a chat with the editor and then work out how the page will look. Will it use photographs? Will they be big or small? How about getting someone to draw an illustration instead? What sort of style should that be in? Even things like how the words themselves will look—the different styles or "fonts" that they're written in—make a big difference to the impression that the page will make and how interesting it will look. And when all this has been done, and the page is finished—with all the right words, fonts, photographs and illustrations—there is still more to be done. The page has to be sent to an expert on the subject, called a "consultant" (someone who knows almost everything there is to know about snoozing and dreaming) for them to check that there aren't any mistakes to be corrected or better information to use. After this, another type of editor, called a subeditor, reads the page very carefully to make sure that all the commas, full stops and hyphens (among other things) are in the right places. Surely the page is finished by now? Well, aside from being worked on by three or four more people on its way to being printed (to make sure things like the colors look right and all the photographs look good), it is, at last, finished. Which means that everyone can get on with something else. So, the editorial team sits down together to talk. Around a table are the editor, the deputy editor, the art director, the assistant editor and the staff writer. All these people have different jobs to do when they leave the room (hence the odd job titles), but right now everyone is getting together to do the first thing—to decide how to approach a new topic in the book. One of the big ideas of the exciting new book they are working on (do you know the one we mean?) is that every subject should be approached from "an angle." This means that a page about, say, Sigmund Freud doesn't just talk about Freud in a normal, straightforward way but perhaps asks a surprising question, like "Was Freud a nutcase?" When an angle has been agreed upon, the idea has to be researched (a bit like doing homework) and, of course, the words have to be written. Sometimes the staff writer or one of the editors is given this job, and sometimes a writer who knows a lot about this sort of subject is asked to do the work instead. When the words are finished, they are edited by one of the editors (a bit like grading homework) and passed to the art director. It's his job to have a chat with the editor and then work out how the page will look. Will it use photographs? Will they be big or small? How about getting someone to draw an illustration instead? What sort of style should that be in? Even things like how the words themselves will look—the

Which part of this picture has the most color?

Think about it—then read the balloon

My bright tail feathers win the attention of female peacocks (beats pick-up lines). That tree frog over there is lurid green to indicate it's poisonous (so don't eat it). And the wasps are bright yellow to warn us they've got a sting and they're not afraid to use it. As animals our colors reflect our environment and characteristics.

Color plays an essential role in human life. It quickly communicates life-saving information, for example, to drivers and pedestrians (when green means "go" and red, "stop"). Colors can irritate or soothe your eyes, raise your blood pressure, suppress your appetite, or even change your **mood 308**. Fabulous!

Whatever the sport, a team wearing red has a higher chance of winning. Visibility isn't usually the key to its success—it's the **psychology 239** of wearing red that's important. Of course, luck and ability are important, too.

I'm an artist, darling. I just need three colors: magenta (red), cyan (blue), and yellow. I can mix them together to create any colur in the rainbow and hundreds of other shades. Maaarvellous.

Hey, square eyes! Unlike in book and magazine **printing 089**, colors on television are created with a system called RGB (Red, Green, and Blue). These three colors are added to my blank, black screen to make up all the different tones of your favorite shows.

Believe it or not, the white part of these pages contains the most color. No, really. Color is the way our eyes see different kinds of light. All light is made up of waves of varying lengths. These different wavelengths produce colors. White is a combination of all the waves. So, white really does have more color. Who'd have thought it?

Why are snowflakes white? Each snowflake is made up of tiny ice crystals stuck together. When light hits a crystal, it is knocked onto the next crystal, and ends up bouncing around until it comes out of the snowflake—no color is absorbed. The flake is the color of sunlight—white.

Look—a rainbow! When sunlight (white light) shines through raindrops, it splits into many colors! Seen from above, a rainbow is circular, too.

Can you spot the chameleon on these pages? It changes color to camouflage itself and hide from predators. Tigers **evolved 206** stripes so that they could hide in undergrowth while waiting to pounce on antelope. In the same way, soldiers paint stripes on their faces to avoid being seen by enemies.

Excuse me for talking with my cheeks full. I'm a squirrel and I can't distinguish between colors, just like guinea pigs and bulls (that angry bunch will chase any flag, it doesn't have to be red). Color-blindness is not always a problem for animals—color-blind hunters are better at spotting prey against confusing backgrounds and I'm better at finding nuts. Humans normally inherit color-blindness, but it can be caused by eye, nerve, or **brain 044** damage.

WHICH ANIMAL IS MAN'S* BEST FRIEND?

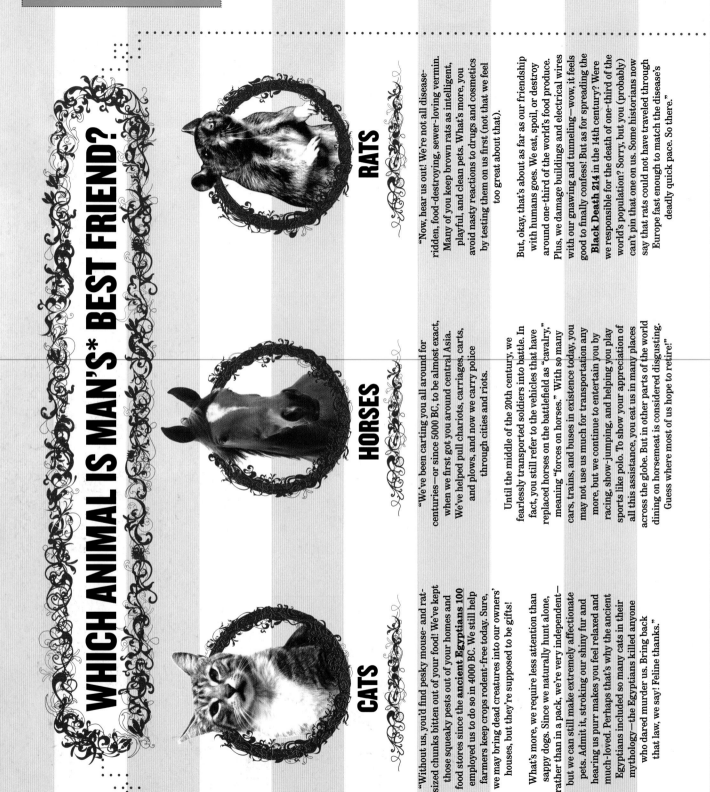

RATS

"Now, hear us out! We're not all disease-ridden, food-destroying, sewer-loving vermin. Many of you keep brown rats as intelligent, playful, and clean pets. What's more, you avoid nasty reactions to drugs and cosmetics by testing them on us first (not that we feel too great about that).

But, okay, that's about as far as our friendship with humans goes. We eat, spoil, or destroy around one-third of the world's food produce. Plus, we damage buildings and electrical wires with our gnawing and tunneling—wow, it feels good to finally confess! But as for spreading the **Black Death 214** in the 14th century? Were we responsible for the death of one-third of the world's population? Sorry, but you (probably) can't pin that one on us. Some historians now say that rats could not have traveled through Europe fast enough to match the disease's deadly quick pace. So there."

HORSES

"We've been carting you all around for centuries—or since 5000 BC, to be almost exact, when we first got you around central Asia. We've helped pull chariots, carriages, carts, and plows, and now we carry police through cities and riots.

Until the middle of the 20th century, we fearlessly transported soldiers into battle. In fact, you still refer to the vehicles that have replaced horses on the battlefield as "cavalry," meaning "forces on horses." With so many cars, trains, and buses in existence today, you may not use us much for transportation any more, but we continue to entertain you by racing, show-jumping, and helping you play sports like polo. To show your appreciation of all this assistance, you eat us in many places across the globe. But in other parts of the world dining on horsemeat is considered disgusting. Guess where most of us hope to retire!"

CATS

"Without us, you'd find pesky mouse- and rat-sized chunks bitten out of your food! We've kept those squeaky pests out of your homes and food stores since the ancient **Egyptians 100** employed us to do so in 4000 BC. We still help farmers keep crops rodent-free today. Sure, we may bring dead creatures into our owners' houses, but they're supposed to be gifts!

What's more, we require less attention than sappy dogs. Since we naturally hunt alone, rather than in a pack, we're very independent—but we can still make extremely affectionate pets. Admit it, stroking our shiny fur and hearing us purr makes you feel relaxed and much-loved. Perhaps that's why the ancient Egyptians included so many cats in their mythology—the Egyptians killed anyone who dared murder us. Bring back that law, we say! Feline thanks."

DOLPHINS

"Who wouldn't want one of us as a best pal: we're so brainy! We're at least as bright as dogs and monkeys—you train us to do tricks and one day, you may even be able to speak to us. At the moment, whether we have our own natural language is still open to question. But a few of us have learned to communicate with humans via hand gestures and computer-generated whistles. Thanks for taking an interest!

Plus, we just like you so much! We approach you when we spot you at sea, jump alongside your boats, and rescue you from **shark 082** attacks by swimming defensively around you. We also help the US military find people trapped underwater and discover mines. And some of us help autistic children simply by playing with them. Just think, 50 million years ago we might even have been land-dwelling mammals, like you! Our skeletons have two rod-shaped pelvic bones that scientists think could mean we once had hind legs. Imagine seeing us down at the mall or playing soccer (now that would be fun)."

ELEPHANTS

"We may be big and scary-looking, but we're great pals with humans. The Indian and **Persian empires 120** were the first to use our intimidating size as a war weapon during the 4th century BC. Excellent at carrying heavy humans (plus their gear), we charged through the enemy, trampling all and swinging our tusks as we went. In the battle of Heraclea in 280 BC, the **Romans 286** fled without even having a pop at us! That was until they discovered that we panic at the sound of pigs squealing and so started using the filthy little creatures against us.

Lately, however, you humans haven't been great friends. You've killed so many of us for our ivory tusks that we're in danger of **extinction 198**. And you've accused us of wrecking the environment just because we knock down the odd tree. You've even imprisoned us in circus cages and made us do tricks. I mean, how would that make you feel? Renowned for our long memories, we won't forget these grievances—we've been known to stampede through villages due to stress caused by your poor treatment of us, so watch out."

DOGS

"Ever since we evolved from wolves 10,000 years ago, we've always been there for humans, helping you hunt and herd animals. In the US, 68 million of us are kept as pets—that's one dog for every four people. And we can be professional, too. We help you seek out bombs and illegal drugs with our supersharp sense of smell. We guard your fancy houses and guide you if you're visually impaired. We rescue you if you get trapped under an **avalanche 074** or flounder at sea. (It's true! In Italy we let people cling to us and paddle them to safety.) And we tackle criminals when police can't do it themselves.

Laika, a Russian relative, even became the first living creature launched into space on November 4, 1957. She died of stress and exhaustion after surviving the takeoff and weightless atmosphere. Still, she paved the way for men to follow her. Most importantly of all, we're always happy to see you. We offer loyalty, unconditional love, companionship, and laughs.

Perhaps that's why you named the brightest star in the night sky Sirius, the "Dog Star.""

MAY THE BEST BUDDY WIN

*AND WOMAN'S

How ALBERT EINSTEIN did the math that proved time really does fly

Born in 1879, Einstein knew he was bright, but he didn't shine in school.

Teachers ignored him and he failed lots of tests. But he would sit in class and daydream about the future, and wonder about...

What if, one day, he could figure out what would happen if...

TWO TWIN BROTHERS LIVED IN A TIME WHEN HUMANS COULD TRAVEL BY ROCKET SHIP TO OTHER STARS, AND ONE OF THEM STAYED BEHIND ON EARTH WHILE THE OTHER ONE...

AND TRAVELED AT ALMOST THE SPEED OF LIGHT TO OUR NEAREST STAR, ALPHA CENTAURI (4.3 LIGHT YEARS AWAY), AND BACK...

BLASTED OFF TO SPACE (WITH A PACKED LUNCH AND AN APPLE 024, OF COURSE)...

WOULD THEY STILL BE THE SAME AGE WHEN THE SPACE BROTHER RETURNED 10 YEARS LATER (FOR MORE SANDWICHES AND A BANANA THIS TIME)? OR WOULD HE NOW BE FIVE YEARS YOUNGER THAN HIS EARTHBOUND BROTHER?

Well, after lots of thinking and calculations and walks in the park...

Einstein, in 1915, realized that that strange thing is exactly what would happen, because...

Time and space are relative, not fixed!
(Freaky, huh?)

I also came up with the famous equation $E=mc^2$ (energy equals mass multiplied by the speed of light squared). It's not all daydreaming!

What's so funny?

turn the page to find out

Why there's nothing funny about your pee and poop

Since this time last week, you've produced around 10 pints, or half a bucketful (4.5 liters), of pee, sufficient poop to fill a 3-pint (1.5-liter) ice cream container and enough farts to inflate several balloons. But why? Well, pee and poop (aka, urine and feces) are waste from various body organs. And they are the end products of some important goings-on...

Lungs
Without energy, your body cannot work—even when you're **sleeping 210**. This energy is released inside all body cells by combining oxygen and glucose, releasing carbon dioxide as waste. And here's where the lungs come in. These two pink, spongy, cone-shaped organs fill your chest, get oxygen into your bloodstream, and remove carbon dioxide before it poisons you. Breathing gets fresh air into, and flushes carbon dioxide-laden air out from, your lungs via your throat and windpipe.

Skin
Your body's biggest, heaviest organ, skin is vitally important for survival. It keeps water in and germs out. It repairs itself and filters out harmful UV rays in sunlight. It lets you touch and feel **pain 084**. And it helps keep body temperature at a steady 98.6 °F (37 °C). One of the ways it does that is by releasing sweat that evaporates from the skin's surface and cools it down. Sweating also disposes of tiny amounts of urea, the waste found in urine. And when it mixes with bacteria on the surface of the skin, it takes on that particular smell we are all familiar with. Nice.

Kidneys
Your two kidneys make urine 24/7. As blood flows through them, millions of microscopic filters remove excess water and unwanted waste to make urine. This trickles down to your bladder which, as it starts to bulge, sends a message to your brain so you know it is time to go to the bathroom. Without all this, your body's water content would be out of control, making you dehydrated one minute and bloated the next. And the toxic waste released by chemical reactions—known collectively as metabolism—inside your trillions of busy body **cells 258** would poison you.

Heart

Just below the surface of your chest, your fist-sized heart is a **muscle 156** that tirelessly pumps blood around your body. Your heart has two sides—the left pumps blood to your lungs to pick up oxygen and the right pumps blood rich in oxygen (and food and other goodies) to the cells. As blood courses along a 93,000 mile (150,000 km) network of blood vessels, it delivers essential oxygen and nutrients to cells and removes their metabolic wastes. These are then removed in pee, sweat, and breathed-out air. Blood also contains germ-eating white blood cells and wound-healing platelets.

Liver

Wedge-shaped and dark red-brown in color, your liver keeps the composition of your blood constant. It processes and stores newly digested food. This includes turning excess amino acids (which perform important activities in the cells) into urea, a waste found in urine. It removes drugs and poisons from the blood and recycles worn-out red blood cells. These are then released into the small intestine, before bacteria in the colon converts them into the brown pigments that color feces. And your liver also churns out heat to help keep you toasty warm. Busy body, eh?

Intestines

Your intestines are made up of around 25 feet (7.5 meters) of pink, slimy tubing. Of this, 20 ft (6 m) is the small and 5 feet (1.5 m) is the large intestine. They are both coiled into your abdomen. As a key player in your digestive system, the small (narrower) intestine digests—breaks down—churned food squirted into it from your stomach. It then absorbs this into your bloodstream. Your large intestine, or colon, then accepts the leftover, runny waste and dries it out to make feces (poop). Bacteria inside your colon help digest the waste, make the smelly gases in farts, and color your poop brown.

GOOD POOP

RICHEST: The semisolid droppings of birds and bats from the coastline of Peru in South America. Highly prized by the ancient **Inca 298** people as a super soil-enricher.

MOST ECOLOGICAL: In the United Arab Emirates, camel dung is used to clean up after oil spillages. Bacteria in the dung break down the oil and leave soil clean again.

MOST NUTRITIOUS: At six or seven months, a baby koala stops drinking mother's milk and begins to feed on a soft, runny poop called "pap." This is a rich source of protein.

POOP-O-METER

MOST REPELLENT: Not a single deer was run over on a Japanese railroad when lion dung was spread along the tracks. But the safety measure was abandoned because passengers hated the stench.

MOST DEADLY: Owls on the American prairies arrange lumps of animal dung around the entrance of their ground burrows to lure dung beetles. If the owl is patient, his dinner comes to him.

MOST AGGRESSIVE: To make a territorial claim, male hippopotami blow powerful showers of manure and urine from their back ends, while twirling their short tails like little propellers to get good coverage. Take cover!

BAD POOP

GUESS WHAT?

UROKINASE, AN ENZYME PRESENT IN HUMAN URINE, IS USED IN TABLETS TO TREAT VICTIMS OF HEART ATTACKS. PEE FOR THE PURPOSE USED TO BE COLLECTED FROM PORTAPOTTIES AT OUTSIDE EVENTS. ONE SPLASH OR TWO?

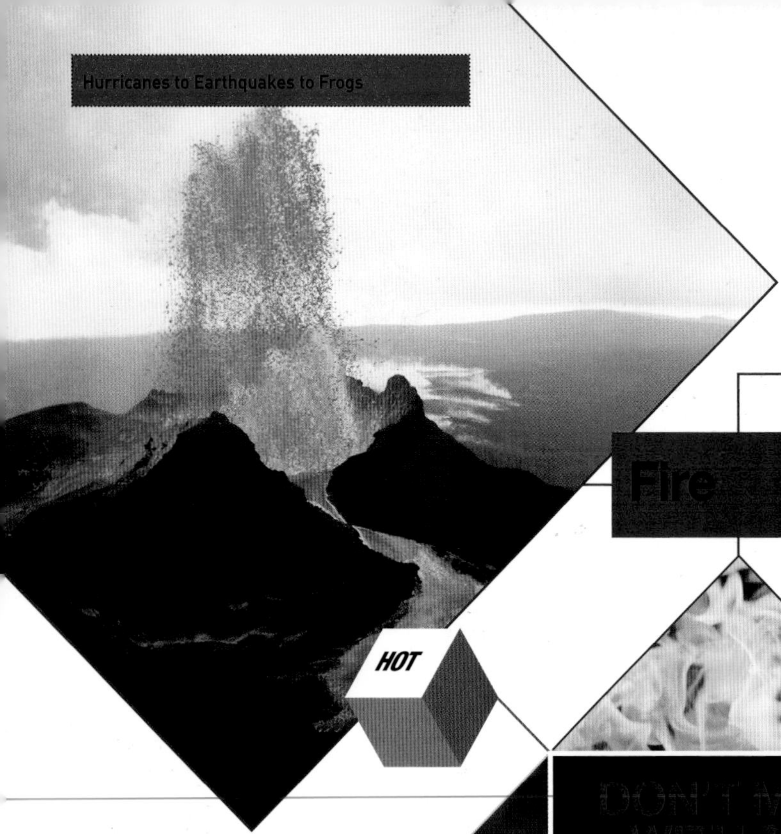

VOLCANIC ERUPTIONS

CAUSE Sometimes, the molten hot rock under the Earth's surface (called magma) forces its way to the surface. With enough pressure, this spurts out of the ground, just like when you shake up a can of soda and then open it. Only worse.

DAMAGE Fires, mudslides, poisonous gases, tsunamis (see below). When the Nevada del Ruiz volcano erupted in Columbia in 1985, rivers of volcanic rubble swept through towns dozens of miles (or kilometers) away from the volcano's base.

WHERE They're found all over the world, but only 500 are active. The volcano in Yellowstone Park caused the largest eruption ever 640,000 years ago. If it blows again, the western United States would be buried in dense ash deposits and volcanic gases would drastically affect the world's climate. In AD 79, Mount Vesuvius erupted in southern Italy, covering the

Fire

HOT

DRY

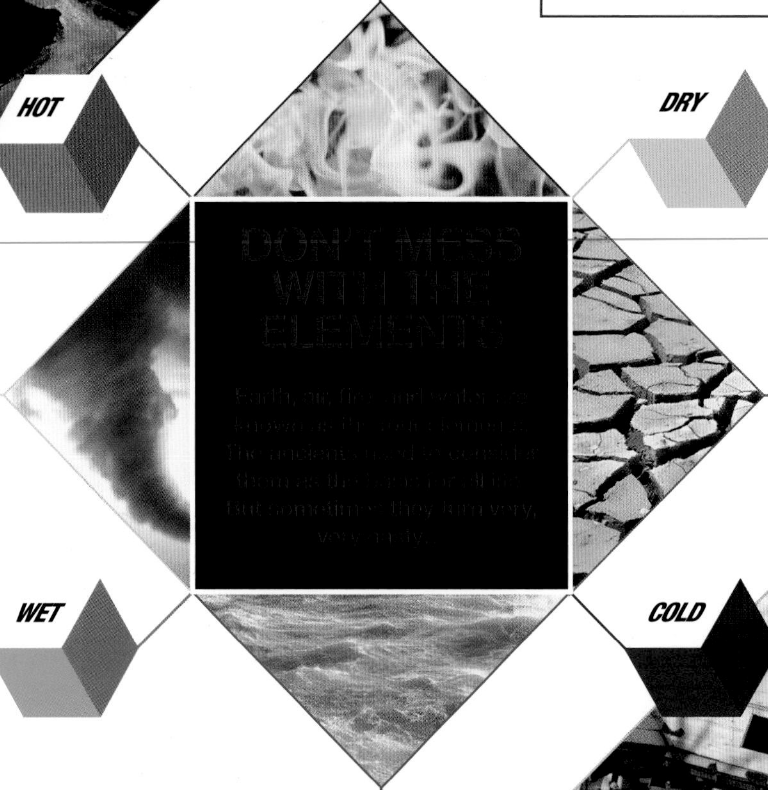

DON'T MESS WITH THE ELEMENTS

Earth, air, fire, and water are known as the four elements. The ancients used to consider them as the basis for all life. But sometimes they turn very, very nasty...

Air

Earth

WET

COLD

Water

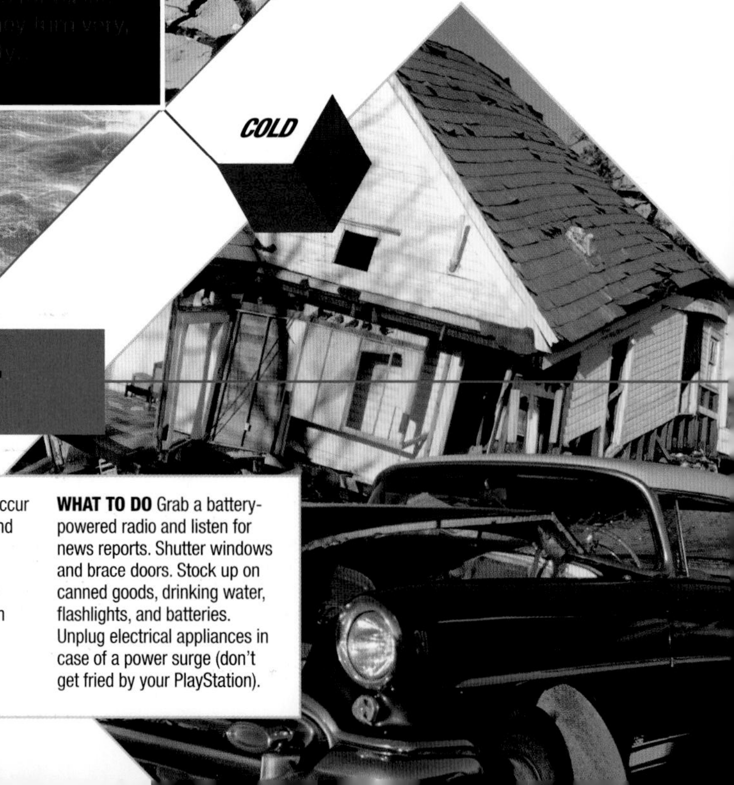

HURRICANE

CAUSE Warm water, moist air, and winds near the equator pull together into a swirling vortex that spins at speeds higher than 75 mph (120 km/h). Can be quite compact or spread over thousands of miles (or kilometers).

DAMAGE Massive flooding, turned-over cars, wrecked houses. In 2005, Hurricane Katrina left the US city of New Orleans underwater.

WHERE Hurricanes often occur in the US, the Caribbean, and Central America. But they also turn up in **India 142**, Australia, and southeast Asia (where they are known as cyclones).

WHAT TO DO Grab a battery-powered radio and listen for news reports. Shutter windows and brace doors. Stock up on canned goods, drinking water, flashlights, and batteries. Unplug electrical appliances in case of a power surge (don't get fried by your PlayStation).

town of Pompeii in thick layers of ash and killing thousands. The town was rediscovered, perfectly preserved, in 1748. Other volcanoes can be found in countries including Japan and Iceland, as well as on other planets, such as Venus and Mars.

WHAT TO DO Leave. The only safe thing to do is to put some serious distance between you and the fire-spurting **mountain 074**.

OTHER TERRIBLE WINDS

The average person lets 14 farts a day. Sometimes, they're caused by swallowed air that you didn't burp. Sometimes, it's leftover gas from the breakdown of **food 176** in the intestines. Most of this gas is absorbed into the intestines but, occasionally, a combination of oxygen, nitrogen, hydrogen, carbon dioxide, and methane squeaks out. Those deadly, rotten egg stinkers contain a twist of hydrogen sulfide, as well. Munching on foods with fiber, sugar, or carbohydrates is likely to make your backside whistle, as will eating too fast.

EARTHQUAKES

CAUSE The Earth's crust is made up of huge tectonic plates that fit together like a rocky jigsaw puzzle. As these plates move, pressure builds up until one plate suddenly rides over the other. The "sound" of this event includes powerful, low-frequency waves that make the ground shake—an earthquake.

DAMAGE Buildings are destroyed, the ground is cracked open, and there is also the danger of landslides and tidal waves. Ships are tossed out of the sea and onto land. When an earthquake hit Kashmir (in India and Pakistan) in 2005, around 75,000 people were killed and up to three million left homeless. Most of the main city, Muzaffarabad, was destroyed.

WHERE Earthquakes are most troublesome on the edges of tectonic plates, such as the San Andreas Fault in California, which threatens San Francisco and Los Angeles.

WHAT TO DO You'll need a flashlight when the lights go out. Hide under a stable piece of furniture like a table and HANG ON. Go outside once the tremors have stopped and move to open ground. But beware of falling debris and broken glass. There probably won't be any **school 166** today.

Not 4 but 5 elements

Chinese philosophers believed there were five elements. They were wood, fire, earth, metal, and water. The philosophy of these five elements was applied to music, **medicine 270**, and military strategy. Each element was assigned its own season (for example, wood = spring), planet (fire = Mars) and even finger (the little pinky meant water). The five elements also have a role in Chinese astrology. Just like in Western horoscopes, the Chinese have 12 signs of the zodiac. These are: rat, ox, tiger, rabbit, dragon, snake, horse, sheep, monkey, rooster, dog, and boar. People are assigned a star sign by year of birth, not month of birth. Each year is also a water year, or a fire year, and so on. Curiously, the five elements existed in Japanese and Hindu philosophies, as well. They even inspired the five-tier design of Japanese pagodas (religious towers).

NOT WHAT THE FORECAST PREDICTED

ICE BALLS
Megacryometeors are giant chunks of ice the size of basketballs. They fall out of the sky in oversized hailstorms. North and South America, Australia, and Spain have all suffered downpours.

LIVE SHOWERS
Tornadoes can suck all kinds of creatures into the sky. Well, what goes up must come down—in 1873, during a storm, Kansas City, Missouri, was doused with frogs. Ick.

BLUE MOON
After the explosion of the Indonesian volcano Krakatau in 1883, volcanic dust stayed in the Earth's atmosphere for years. This created the illusion of beautiful rings of blue, brown, and white around the **Sun 168** and Moon.

GREAT BALLS OF FIRE
In 1996, a tennis ball-sized sphere of blue and white light flew into a UK factory. To the amazement of workers, it bounced around, sending sparks flying. Such lightning balls occur frequently but are not dangerous.

TSUNAMIS

CAUSE Underwater earthquakes kick up giant waves called Tsunamis. These start out small in the open ocean but grow to be hundreds of miles (or kilometers) long and over 100 ft (30 m) high when they hit land. A tsunami travels at around 435 mph (700 km/h). Wave after massive wave may follow for 90 minutes after the initial strike.

DAMAGE People, cars, boats, and houses are all washed away. In December 2004, an earthquake off the coast of Sumatra triggered a major tsunami in the Indian Ocean. More than 200,000 people died in countries as far apart as Indonesia, the Maldives, Sri Lanka, and Somalia.

WHERE Most tsunamis occur in the Pacific Ocean. Beneath the deep water is a **tectonic plate 318** that is slowly moving. This movement has left deep underwater trenches at the plate's edges. It has also created the "Ring of Fire," a highly active volcano and earthquake zone.

In the Atlantic, a megatsunami could destroy New York City if the Cumbre Vieja volcano in the Canary Islands blows and forces a chunk of the island into the ocean. This could happen in 10 or 10,000 years' time.

WHAT TO DO Get away from the coast. The worst affected areas will be within 1 mile (1.5 km) of the shore. Get to high ground: anything under 50 ft (15 m) above sea level and the waves can get you.

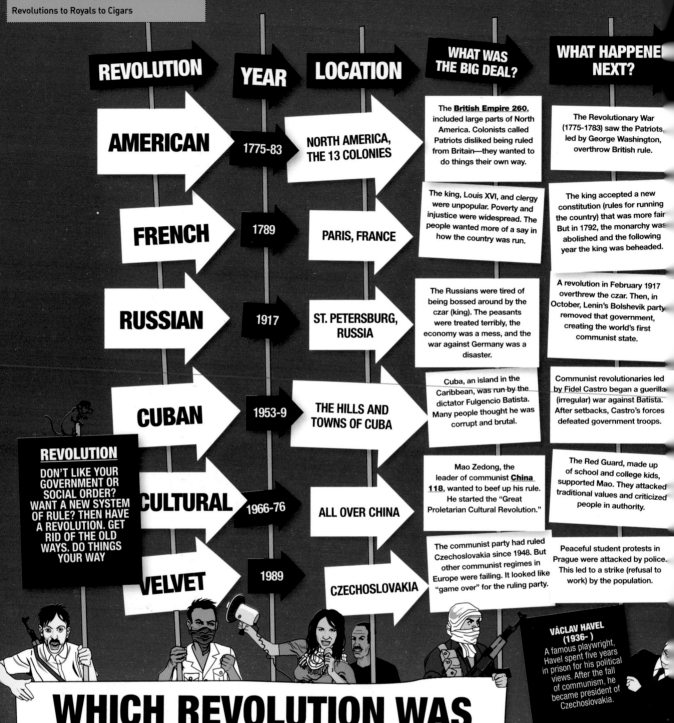

REVOLUTION	YEAR	LOCATION	WHAT WAS THE BIG DEAL?	WHAT HAPPENED NEXT?
AMERICAN	1775-83	NORTH AMERICA, THE 13 COLONIES	The British Empire 260, included large parts of North America. Colonists called Patriots disliked being ruled from Britain—they wanted to do things their own way.	The Revolutionary War (1775-1783) saw the Patriots, led by George Washington, overthrow British rule.
FRENCH	1789	PARIS, FRANCE	The king, Louis XVI, and clergy were unpopular. Poverty and injustice were widespread. The people wanted more of a say in how the country was run.	The king accepted a new constitution (rules for running the country) that was more fair. But in 1792, the monarchy was abolished and the following year the king was beheaded.
RUSSIAN	1917	ST. PETERSBURG, RUSSIA	The Russians were tired of being bossed around by the czar (king). The peasants were treated terribly, the economy was a mess, and the war against Germany was a disaster.	A revolution in February 1917 overthrew the czar. Then, in October, Lenin's Bolshevik party removed that government, creating the world's first communist state.
CUBAN	1953-9	THE HILLS AND TOWNS OF CUBA	Cuba, an island in the Caribbean, was run by the dictator Fulgencio Batista. Many people thought he was corrupt and brutal.	Communist revolutionaries led by Fidel Castro began a guerilla (irregular) war against Batista. After setbacks, Castro's forces defeated government troops.
CULTURAL	1966-76	ALL OVER CHINA	Mao Zedong, the leader of communist China 118, wanted to beef up his rule. He started the "Great Proletarian Cultural Revolution."	The Red Guard, made up of school and college kids, supported Mao. They attacked traditional values and criticized people in authority.
VELVET	1989	CZECHOSLOVAKIA	The communist party had ruled Czechoslovakia since 1948. But other communist regimes in Europe were failing. It looked like "game over" for the ruling party.	Peaceful student protests in Prague were attacked by police. This led to a strike (refusal to work) by the population.

REVOLUTION

DON'T LIKE YOUR GOVERNMENT OR SOCIAL ORDER? WANT A NEW SYSTEM OF RULE? THEN HAVE A REVOLUTION. GET RID OF THE OLD WAYS. DO THINGS YOUR WAY

VÁCLAV HAVEL (1936-)

A famous playwright, Havel spent five years in prison for his political views. After the fall of communism, he became president of Czechoslovakia.

WHICH REVOLUTION WAS THE MOST REVOLTING?

FAMOUS BITS

WINNERS AND LOSERS

HOW IT CHANGED THE WORLD

REVOLTING RATING

HERE COMES MORE TROUBLE

THE BOSTON TEA PARTY
The final straw came when the Americans couldn't even enjoy a decent cup of tea without the British taxing it. In 1773, protesters in Boston threw all the tea in the harbor.

The Brits were kicked out for good and, in 1783, they recognized the United States of America (then with just 13 states on the East Coast).

Ideas of liberty and equality were influential on the French Revolution. The phrase, "No taxation without representation!" took off. The US would eventually grow to 50 states.

Revving up the world for lots more risings

1688 GLORIOUS REVOLUTION (England)

1798 IRISH REBELLION

1830 JULY REVOLUTION (France)

STORMING OF THE BASTILLE
A prison in Paris, the Bastille was a symbol of oppression. In 1789, demonstrators seized it, but there were only seven prisoners to free.

The ruling royals were overthrown. Radicals took over and began chopping the heads off nobles and other unlucky folks. A European war 174 started as France tried to spread the revolution abroad.

Massive impact throughout Europe. The revolution ended when Napoleon Bonaparte 216 seized control in 1799, but the idea of democracy 194 had taken root.

Heads roll, and roll...

1848 REVOLUTIONS (all across Europe)

1851 TAIPING REBELLION (China)

1857 INDIAN REBELLION

THE WINTER PALACE
The uprising was mostly blood-free. Later accounts portrayed it as a heroic struggle, especially the taking of the czar's Winter Palace in St. Petersburg.

The Soviet Union (USSR) was formed and land redistributed to the peasants. Most Western countries were unhappy about the revolution.

A key event of the 20th century. It inspired other revolutions around the world, and made communism the opponent of capitalism 050, leading to the Cold War 294.

Shaking up the world for years to come

1871 PARIS COMMUNE (France)

1910 MEXICAN REVOLUTION

1918 GERMAN REVOLUTION

CASTRO AND HIS CIGAR
Castro had an iconic image: beard, combat gear, and big Cuban cigar. Right-hand man Che Guevera shared his style.

Batista and his generals fled and Castro took the island, setting up a communist regime. Anti-Castro Cubans fled to the US and vowed revenge—their 1961 invasion attempt (the Bay of Pigs) ended in disaster.

Though only a small island, Cuba was important during the Cold War, especially with the Cuban missile crisis 295 in 1962. In February 2006, Castro remained in power.

Small, but sizzling

1936 SPANISH REVOLUTION

1956 HUNGARIAN REVOLUTION

1969 LIBYA

THE LITTLE RED BOOK
This book contained the sayings of Mao. The Red Guards waved it around and shouted slogans.

There was huge unrest, the radical students got out of control. Millions of people were forced to do manual labor. Teachers and intellectuals were tortured or even killed for being educated.

After Mao's death in 1976, the leaders of the revolution were arrested. Tens of thousands had been executed. A whole generation had missed out on education.

Lashings of suffering all around

1968 STUDENTS' & WORKERS' REVOLT (France)

1974 CARNATION REVOLUTION (Portugal)

1975 ANGOLA

"VELVET"
Named "Velvet" by a journalist because it was peaceful, this is one of the better-named revolts. Mind you, Estonia's Singing Revolution of 1988 is charming, too.

The people got what they wanted. Elections were free (you could vote for who you wanted), censorship ended, and the borders opened.

The collapse of this and other communist regimes ended the Cold War and brought democracy to Eastern Europe.

A riotous revolt— minus the riot

1979 IRANIAN REVOLUTION

1989 ROMANIAN REVOLUTION

2003 ROSE REVOLUTION (Georgia) TULIP REVOLUTION (Kyrgyzstan)

GEORGE WASHINGTON (1732-1799)
A modest soldier with terribly bad teeth who led the Patriots' Continental Army against the British. He is lauded as "father" of his country. The capital city is named after him.

ROBESPIERRE (1758-1794)
A disciple of the philosopher Jean-Jacques Rousseau 044, Robespierre oversaw the "Reign of Terror" in France. Thousands were executed. And, in the end, he was, too.

VLADIMIR LENIN (1870-1924)
Bolshevik leader and, later, premier of the Soviet Union, Lenin inspired revolutionaries around the world. Soviet citizens lined up to view his embalmed corpse in Red Square, Moscow.

FIDEL CASTRO (1926-)
The only communist revolutionary leader still alive and still in power. Some praise him for his social policies, others claim he is a nasty dictator. The US once even tried to poison his cigars.

MAO TSE-TUNG (1893-1976)
Mao may have rid China of foreign interference but his policies were a disaster, killing tens of millions through starvation. Critics say he cared more about superpower status than his own people.

WATER River water is extremely precious. Global water consumption rose sixfold between 1900 and 1995. The average human can survive only three to four days without the stuff. Unfortunately, 97.5 percent of the world's water is undrinkable—it is found in oceans and is saline (full of salt). The remaining 2.5 percent is salt-free freshwater of the kind humans and animals can drink. But rivers and lakes contain a measly 0.3 percent of the world's freshwater supply—the rest is tied up in ice-caps and glaciers, or buried deep underground.

HABITAT Rivers provide an essential habitat for **fish 026** and other wildlife. An estimated 12 percent of all animal species live in freshwater. They rely on river ecosystems (communities of interacting plants, animals, and microorganisms), which include not only the river itself, but the surrounding area (its watershed). Man-made threats, such as dams and pollution, have rendered freshwater species among the most endangered in the world.

TRANSPORTATION Rivers have always been an essential means of conducting trade. Today, the Rhine River is the busiest river in the world for cargo ships. Millions of tons of goods are carried annually along it to cities in Germany, France, and Switzerland. Where there are no rivers, people have built their own waterways, called canals, ever since the Chinese started building the Grand Canal of China in the sixth century BC. Canals are either short extensions to natural rivers, or created where a river is required but doesn't exist. The great age of canal building in Britain (aaah, the memories...) was between 1760 and 1820. This new, cheap transportation spurred the **Industrial Revolution 184**.

WHY WE ALL WANT TO LIVE BY A RIVER

A river is fresh water that flows across the land's surface, usually to the sea. It may not sound as exciting as a buzzing city center, but humans and animals have flocked to be by rivers for centuries, for good reasons...

FARMING Agriculture accounts for 70 percent of all human water use. Ever since the ancient Egyptians farmed land around the Nile, humans have used fertile soils created by river valleys and plains for crops. Farmers 086 in dry regions irrigate (supply water to) land using irrigation ditches from nearby rivers.

ENERGY A river's flow contains huge kinetic energy (that is, the energy of a moving object). At the beginning of the 19th century, factories were built near fast-flowing rivers, where water could be used to power machines. Today, hydropower converts kinetic energy from falling water into electricity through water turbines (rotary engines). The Three Gorges Dam is currently being built on the Yangtze River in China 118. It will be the world's largest hydroelectric dam, more than 1 mile (1.5 km) wide and 600 fts (183 meter) high. The dam is expected to provide about one-ninth of China's total electrical production.

WHERE ARE ALL THE RIVERS RUNNING?

Rivers always flow downhill. They form in high areas from melted glacial water, mountain springs or waterlogged areas. This early stage is called the upper course, when the river's path is steep and straight. Gravity 024 pulls the water downward. The river then reaches its middle course, and starts to twist and turn. As it does so, it picks things up, such as rocks. This load erodes (wears down) parts of the riverbed and bank, while building up areas where it's dropped off.

By carving up the landscape, rivers create waterfalls (when passing from hard rock to softer rock), canyons (when erosion cuts a gorge into the earth), and oxbow lakes (when water is cut off from the main channel). The lower course is the river's last stage and has the slowest flow—like a tired runner at the end of a race.

MAD AS A FISH

Salmon are famous for swimming upstream, sometimes hundreds of miles (or kilometers), back to where they were born in order to spawn (reproduce). But this isn't the only creature that goes to crazy lengths for the young generation…

A single male wrasse fish dominates a group of females. If he dies, the principal female will begin to change sex within hours (apparently, she tells bad jokes within minutes).

The female green spoon worm inhales the male after mating. He rests inside her in a chamber called the androecium—literally, the "small man room." He spends the rest of his life fertilizing eggs. Talk about a man-eater.

A queen ant (the egg-layer in an ant colony) and a prince male ant mate 100 feet (30 meters) in the air. The male dies shortly afterward. The queen lands, removes her wings, then lays eggs fertilized from the encounter for 14 years.

1,900,000,000

By 2075, there will be more people in India than were on the entire planet in 1900. **The population will be 1,900,000,000—** and it'll be the most populated country in the world

On average, **2.7 people** live in each room of each house, the most in the world

One child is born in India every **1.26 seconds**

⬆ Some facts about India's population. . .

⬇ India has 22,000 **newspapers**—of which 1,800 are dailies. The average Indian spends 11 hours per week reading.

There is only one **television set** per 17.2 people in India.

⬇ The official **languages** of India are Hindi and English—with 21 other languages also recognized by the national constitution. There are more than 800 different languages or dialects in the country.

Hindi
English
+ 21 others

Computer software

India's computer software industry grew at more than 50 percent per year during the 1990s. Over half of the US's 500 largest companies set up offices in India for computer support services because it was cheaper.

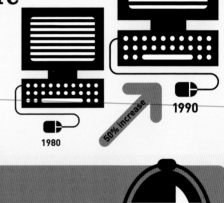

50% increase
1990
1980

Call centers

India has many call centers set up by foreign companies to take advantage of cheaper, well-educated labor. The business grew by more than 100 percent, to be worth $810 million, in 2003.

100% increase
January 2003
December 2003

The Taj Mahal

This world famous building was built in the 17th century as a tomb by the Mogul Emperor Shah Jahan for his beloved wife, Mumtaz Mahal. It took 22 years and 20,000 workers to complete.

➡ Every 12 years, northern India is the location of the largest human gathering on the planet. India's biggest **religious festival**, the Maha Kumbh Mela, lasts more than a month and takes place where the Ganges and Yamuna rivers meet. In 2001, approximately 70 million Hindus traveled there to bathe in the waters—more people than live in the **United Kingdom 200**.

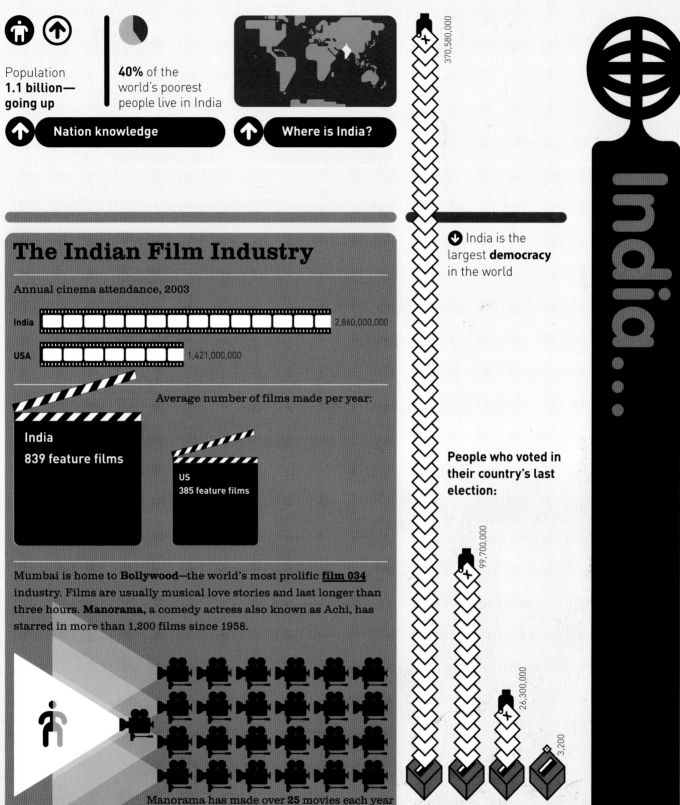

Population **1.1 billion—going up**

40% of the world's poorest people live in India

Nation knowledge

Where is India?

370,580,000

India is the largest **democracy** in the world

The Indian Film Industry

Annual cinema attendance, 2003

India	2,860,000,000
USA	1,421,000,000

Average number of films made per year:

India
839 feature films

US
385 feature films

Mumbai is home to **Bollywood**—the world's most prolific <u>film 034</u> industry. Films are usually musical love stories and last longer than three hours. **Manorama,** a comedy actress also known as Achi, has starred in more than 1,200 films since 1958.

Manorama has made over **25 movies each year**

People who voted in their country's last election:

99,700,000

26,300,000

3,200

India   US   UK   Monaco

India

MIND YOUR HEAD! THE WORLD IS GETTING SMALLER...

01 "Hello. I'm afraid our talk begins slowly, since it's **776 BC** and I'm using a homing pigeon to send my message. <u>Ancient Greeks 240</u> used the winged wonders to let people know who'd won the Olympics. It's air mail, but not as you know it!"

02 "Forget pigeons. It's **200 BC** and I'm using a human messenger in Egypt. They travel on foot or horseback and sometimes use fire and smoke signals. They're certainly more efficient than the ancient Greek soldier Pheidippides, who in 490 BC ran from the town of Marathon to Athens with his message, and promptly dropped dead. This was the first marathon."

03 "So why not get one messenger to deliver lots of messages at once? Oops—the Romans have already thought of that. I'm sending this to you via their postal service in **14 BC**."

04 "Forget snail mail! The postal service was fine until I, Claude Chappe, and my brothers, invented the semaphore line in **1792** in <u>Revolutionary France 138</u>. A series of people stand on top of high buildings. They each use manual machines to communicate different flag signals, one to the other down the line. Between them, it takes two to six minutes to get a message 120 miles (193 km) from Lille to Paris. Actually, the Romans also used a system of flags to communicate messages, but the idea was forgotten for more than 1,000 years."

05 "I'm American scientist Joseph Henry. It's **1830** and I've just found out that electricity can travel through wire and strike a bell at the other end: the principle of the electric telegraph. It's fast, but we can only talk with bell rings."

06 "Very good, Joseph, considering you can only use bell sounds. In fact, you're doing well to make sense of me now since I'm using the Morse code. I, Samuel Morse, invented it in **1835**. By sending pulses of current down a wire, I can move a marker to produce dots and dashes on a strip of paper."

07 "Dots and dashes aren't personal, though. I'm a rider with the Pony Express, a fleet of hardy horses fit enough to cross the deserts and mountains of new territories in the American West. Before we galloped to the rescue, the colonists only got mail once a month. It took us just seven days and 17 hours to hotfoot it from Washington, D. C., to California with President Abraham Lincoln's speech in **1861**. That was our fastest delivery. We travel 75-100 miles (120-160 km) a day to make our deliveries. Giddy up!"

08 "Woah now, Bessy. I'm Alexander Graham Bell. It's **1876** and I've just invented the first electric telephone after I realized sounds can be transmitted on a wire. What a shame there's almost no one to call, since hardly anyone has a phone yet."

09 "I'm afraid I can't take your call at the moment, Mr. Bell. I'm Valdemar Poulsen from Holland. I invented the telephone answering machine in **1898**. Please leave a message for me after the beeeeeep."

10 "Er, hi, Valdemar. Such a pity you're not there as it's **1914** and I'm making the first cross-continental telephone call. Drats."

11 "Never mind. In **1965** electronic mail is invented so academics can send messages to each other (probably tips on tweed jackets). As the message system becomes more popular, emails spread to all corners of the world. But that takes about 30 years to happen."

12 "Of course, if you still want to hear people's voices, wait until **1979**, when the earliest cell phone networks emerge in the US and Japan. In less than 20 years, cell phones will go from being heavy and pricey, to cheap and funky. Soon, though, you'll be so sick of being constantly available, you'll start using your caller ID to screen calls. Then you'll start texting to keep from having to speak to people at all—or even write full sentences. C U L8R."

700 MILLION
PEOPLE ARE TALKING ON A CELL PHONE RIGHT NOW...*

*FIGURE ACCURATE AT TIME OF PUBLICATION. IT'S PROBABLY RISEN A FEW HUNDRED THOUSAND BY THE TIME YOU READ THIS...

HOW TO

MAKE THE WORLD SHRINK

Next time you're watching your favorite soap opera on TV—the one that's set halfway across the country—take a closer look at your favorite star. Because according to American sociologist Stanley Milgram, you know him. Actually, a friend of yours knows him. Or one of their school friends does. Or maybe it's the friend's cousin that has met him.

Confused? Milgram's theory, called Six Degrees of Separation, explains that every person on the planet is connected to every other person through a chain of no more than five acquaintances. Milgram would randomly choose a person who lived thousands of miles away. Then, he would send a package to someone he thought might be connected to

the stranger. That person would do the same in turn, until the package reached the target person. The average number of links in the chain was six. In 2001, the theory was tested with emails. The average email chain to a random person was, again, six.

Not convinced? Try the experiment yourself.

1. Get yourself a white coat. All scientists need one.

2. Ask your parents to think of someone they know who lives as far away as possible (but who none of your friends already know).

3. Send a message to a friend who you think could have a link with the stranger. Explain that if they do know them, they must ask them to send a text to your parents. If they don't know them, they must send a text to one of their friends who might know the target person.

4. Eventually, your parents will receive a text from the far-off friend. The chain is complete. Try it several times with different target people and the average number of texts in the chain will be six.

ME

MY FRIEND

HER COUSIN

HER FRIEND IN AUSTRALIA

HIS UNCLE IN JAPAN

DAD'S FRIEND

RUOK? AFAIK WRE MEETIN B4 SHOW 2NITE @ STN. HRD IS XLNT. CUL8R, CNT W8! BFN

BEFORE CELLS, THAT TEXT MESSAGE SOUNDED SOMETHING LIKE THIS:

How are you? As far as I know, we're all meeting up before the performance tonight at the train station. I've heard the show is excellent. See you later—can't wait! Bye for now.

13 "Ha! Now you can see me through your computer because emails have popularized the internet. In **1994**, the worldwide web is released for use by the public. Described as 'a never-ending worldwide conversation' (like this one), it's spawned chat rooms, message boards, personal websites, and instant messaging. Now, ordinary people can see and hear each other anywhere in the world using a webcam, personal computer, and broadband internet connection. Like my new haircut?"

14 "Actually no, it looks like some kind of **wig 024**. Luckily, webcam man didn't hear that cutting remark—it's around **2015** and I'm communicating my message via light-emitting diodes (LEDs). These are lights so small that humans can't see them. Instead, they are picked up by receiving devices worn on other people. I guess you could call me a flash guy."

OTHER SMALL WORLDS

An object named Ceres was found orbiting between Mars and Jupiter in 1801. With its 590 mile (950 km) diameter and roughly spherical shape, it was thought to be a **planet 172**. But, after smaller objects were found with a similar orbit, it was classified as a mere asteroid.

In 2005, an object larger than Pluto, called 2003 UB313 (mmm, catchy), was discovered near Neptune. Like Pluto, it is part of the Kuiper Belt of icy asteroids (small objects orbiting the Sun). Astronomers are trying to decide which of these is really a planet. Is it both? Or neither?

15 "That sounds far too much like hard work. Now, soon after **2025**, I don't even have to connect to the internet to send a message—I just think about it. My brainwaves make the request and the internet—now called the OmniNet—responds with the information I want. A step on from homing pigeons, eh?"

✉ THUMBS DOWN TO TEXTING

The number of teenagers suffering Repetitive Strain Injury (RSI: when you repeat the same action until it hurts) in their thumbs has risen due to excessive texting. Thumbs **evolved 206** to help us grasp things—they're not meant for repetitive movement. The smaller phones become, the more difficult it is to navigate the keypad and the more the number of teens suffering RSI will continue to... swell.

WHAT MAKES THIS REPTILE SO SCARY?

BECAUSE IT'S COLD-BLOODED?

Actually, no. The blood of the Australian frilled lizard (*Chlamydosaurus kingii*, main picture) can be warmer than ours. This is true for all reptiles, including lizards, snakes, crocodiles, and turtles. They're not cold-blooded, but ectothermic. This means "heated from outside," because a reptile's body temperature depends on that of its surroundings. The warmer a reptile is, the more likely it is to be active, which is why reptiles are generally found in warmer parts of the world—so, no pythons in Greenland. How do reptiles control their temperature? By basking in the Sun to warm up, and sheltering to cool down. <u>Birds 182</u> and mammals are endothermic (heated from inside). Our body temperature stays high and constant, so we can be active in summer or winter. The downside is that we have to eat regularly to maintain that warmth. Reptiles, on the other hand, don't have to eat to keep warm, so can consume less food, less often. Sneaky.

BECAUSE IT CAN RUN FAST?

Well, yes. A frilled lizard can run fast—and on two legs for a real burst of speed—although usually they run away from you. Most lizards run fast to escape enemies, or to grab prey. But their legs are splayed outward, rather like a person's arms during push-ups. This stance makes movement hard work, so lizards generally move their low-slung bodies at high speed only over short distances. Crocodiles and alligators have the same sort of leg arrangement. They usually walk slowly on land, dragging their bellies along the ground, though in water they can swim rapidly, propelled by a lashing tail. Out of water, turtles (right) are slow and clumsy, but in the <u>ocean 202</u> they use their flipperlike legs to swim with real grace. And how do legless snakes move? The most common technique is the slithering movement. Broad belly scales anchor the snake against the ground, while its muscles push the body forward in S-shaped curves.

BECAUSE IT'S GOT PIERCING, HYPNOTIC EYES?

Most reptiles, including our frilled lizard, have good eyesight, with some seeing in color. But their eyes won't send you into a trance. Snakes such as boas and pit vipers have an extra way of "seeing," whether it's day or night. They have infrared sensors that detect heat given off by warm-blooded prey, such as mice.

Snakes, such as the red rattlesnake (right), and many lizards can also "taste the air." That familiar flicking in and out of the tongue captures scent particles floating in the air. Hearing, while adequate in most reptiles, is poor in snakes. Their simple ears only pick up the vibrations (from the ground or air) that pass through their skull bones.

BECAUSE IT'S GOT SLIMY, SLIPPERY, SCALY SKIN?

It's definitely scaly, but this skin is neither slimy nor slippery—it's smooth and dry. The overlapping scales are made of keratin, the same stuff that forms our nails. Scaly skin provides armor plating that protects against wear and tear, as well as hungry predators. What's more, it's waterproof and prevents the reptile from drying out. That's why so many reptiles—including the frilled lizard—can survive in hot, dry, inhospitable places. The only problem with external armor is that it makes growing difficult. So, reptiles shed their skin every so often, to allow for expansion. Lizards usually shed theirs in bits, but a snake's skin comes off in one piece. Skin scales vary, too. In crocodiles, the back scales are reinforced with bony plates, some lizards have spines and crests, while snake belly scales are like wide plates, ideal for slithering.

BECAUSE IT'S AGGRESSIVE?

This frilled lizard certainly looks aggressive. But the gaping mouth, outspread frill, upright stance, and lashing tail are simply a threat display— look how big I am! The lizard will often avoid a <u>fight 154</u> by scooting up the nearest tree. In fact, most reptiles prefer to maintain a low profile—they either run away from enemies or lie low when they sense danger. Many lizards lose the tips of their tails if they are grabbed—leaving behind a distracting, wiggling stump as they make their escape. Some reptiles, such as forest snakes and chameleons, have incredible camouflage that makes them difficult to spot. Of course, there are some aggressive reptiles. Crocodiles (right) and king cobras don't usually hold back when they're looking for lunch. Nor would a western diamondback rattlesnake, but it will rattle a warning first.

BECAUSE IT'S DANGEROUS TO HUMANS?

Only if you provoke it and put your finger in its mouth. People tend to be fearful of reptiles but, of the 8,000 species, few are a threat to us. Still, don't fall asleep outdoors on certain Indonesian islands, in case a 10-foot (three-meter) long Komodo dragon (right)—a giant lizard—sinks its bacteria-laden teeth into you. Of the lizards, only two are venomous (poisonous). These are the Mexican beaded lizard and the Gila monster, that holds its prey—or your finger—in a harsh grip while it chews in venom. Snakes, like most reptiles, are carnivores and some use venom to subdue prey. But not many are harmful to humans. The most dangerous, the cobras and vipers, cause around 30,000 deaths a year. Big constrictors—the snakes that crush and suffocate prey—such as reticulated pythons, are long and strong enough to eat a person. As are big crocodiles, that usually grab their prey with razor-sharp teeth, then drag it down and drown it.

RADICAL!

WHAT HAPPENS WHEN YOU CROSS TURTLES WITH RENAISSANCE ARTISTS? In 1984, four teenage, mutant (they'd been exposed to radiation), ninja (they were experts in martial arts) turtles took over the world (from their base in the sewers of New York). Named after four of the top artists from the **Renaissance 148**, Donatello, Leonardo, Michelangelo, and Raphael—The Teenage Mutant Ninja Turtles—became a global phenomenon. Kids across the world played with mini, muscle-bound turtle figures, brushed their teeth with turtle toothpaste, spoke in turtle phrases ("Radical!," "No Problemo!" "Mondo!") and followed turtle comics, TV shows, video games. and feature films. The turtles even went on a world tour, following the release of their 1989 album, *Coming Out of Their Shells*. Cowabunga!—as a turtle would say.

WHO SWITCHED THE LIGHTS ON?

THE MIDDLE AGES

This is the period from the end of the Classical Age (around AD 500 and the end of the Roman Empire) to the Renaissance. In terms of intellectual achievement (brainy feats in philosophy, science, and so on), it's a little dull—hardly anyone can read or write and religious thinking dominates.

Scholasticism takes off. Thinkers attempt to merge the parts of classical philosophy they know with Christianity. This is a little tricky, since the ancients worshipped many different gods. Later, philosopher and religious teacher Thomas Aquinas (c.1225-1274) emphasizes the importance of human reasoning and **logic 042**.

1000

1080s

1088

Bologna university is founded in Italy, possibly the oldest in Europe. Paris, Oxford, and Salamanca become other key centers of learning.

Anonymous Benedictine monk

"I'm a member of a Cluniac monastery in France. We're an order of monks that was established in 910. Monasteries (places where monks live) are important centers of learning. We monks spend a lot of time copying manuscripts by hand (it takes longer to write a book out than it does to read one). Mainly we copy religious texts, but I do copy some of the smart stuff the **ancient Greeks 240** and **Romans 262** wrote about science and medicine, if I can get hold of it."

Peter Abelard (1079-1142)

"I've been described as the first important philosopher of the Middle Ages. Some people also think I'm a bit too clever for my own good, but they're just jealous. I mean, just look at the numbers of pupils from all over Europe I attract to Paris. In my work, *Sic et Non* ("For and Against"), I look at contradictions in the Bible and use logic to resolve them. I also investigate what it is to be good or bad (goodness is all down to having the right intentions, you know). Apparently, **Aristotle 322** had similar ideas. I wish I had his books to read. Sigh."

Or the story of how Europeans got their brains working, from the Middle Ages to the Enlightenment, and discovered new things in philosophy, art and science

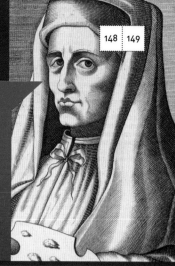

Giotto di Bondone (c. 1267-1337)

"The paintings I'm doing (here, in Italy) are much more realistic than traditional Christian art. The people are more lifelike and have real expressions. I'm interested in how things are in the real world. Like Petrarch, I can be considered a "humanist"—that means I am interested in man for his own sake, in what he is and what he can do."

THE RENAISSANCE

Lasting from the early 1300s to the 1650s, the Renaissance is a period of "rebirth" in western European art, culture, and thought. It starts in Italy and spreads north, affecting art, architecture, and philosophy.

1200

1300

1360

Giovanni di Bicci de' Medici

(1360-1429) makes the Medici family the richest in Italy. Over the next 200 years, the Medicis finance many of the painters, architects, and thinkers of the Renaissance, and make Florence (right) the cultural center of **Europe 216**.

Francesco Petrarca (1304-1374)

"Known as Petrarch, I'm an Italian poet and scholar who's a big fan of the classical world of ancient Greece and Rome. That was the period of greatest human achievement—myself (and other bright lights like me) search for old manuscripts in castles and monasteries, to read what the ancients thought and adapt their ideas. Though some of us are **Christians 185**, our thinking is a million miles away from gloomy priests who are always going on about sin."

Voyages of discovery

Portuguese navigators, in search of new markets and trade routes, spearhead European expansion around the globe. Later, the discovery of new lands by explorers such as **Christopher Columbus 272**, makes Europeans sit up and think. There were peoples and species that the ancients hadn't known anything about. The natural world was a lot more diverse than previously thought.

THE SCIENTIFIC REVOLUTION

Though historians argue over exact dates, the next 150 years are a period of great scientific discovery and investigation.

Polish astronomer **Nicolaus Copernicus** (1473-1543) argues that the Earth is just another planet that orbits the Sun, and is not the center of the universe. Man's place in the scheme of things drops a notch.

1400

1450s

1500

1543

1580 **1600**

Johannes Gutenberg's 292

advances in printing begin in Germany. Monks are put out of the scribe (manuscript copying) business and it is easier for the general public to get hold of books and pamphlets. The smarty-pants of Europe are increasingly found outside of universities and monasteries.

Michel de Montaigne

(1533-1592) publishes *Essays*, and invents the, ah, essay. His goal is to describe man, but he's also something of a sceptic, questioning everything. "What do I know?" is his motto.

Niccolò Machiavelli (1469-1527)

"I'm an Italian who writes about politics, but in a way that doesn't rely on using religion to justify the state of things. My books, for example *The Prince*, are rough guides to politics in the real world. If you want to get ahead, my friend, sometimes you have to ignore your conscience and be a little callous."

Francis Bacon (1561-1626)

"English statesman, philosopher, and sometime spy, that's me. I'm not much of a scientist myself—in fact, I've got a bad cold from stuffing a chicken full of snow to see how cold affects meat (I'm sure it will be the death of me). But I'm helping lay the foundations of modern science by popularizing the idea of **experimentation 326** and observation. Aah-choo!".

THE ENLIGHTENMENT

The early 1700s sees the start of the Enlightenment. Superstition and tradition are out. Reason, inquiry, and learning are in. There's a lot of talk about freedom and progress. These idea have a huge influence on the centuries to come.

German-born astronomer **Johannes Kepler** publishes his laws of planetary motion. He realizes their orbits are elliptical (oval), not circular, as Aristotle had thought.

In England, the **Royal Society** is founded. Scientists get together to discuss their work and show off experiments.

The Social Contract is published. Brainbox **Jean-Jacques Rousseau 044** explains how everyone has political rights, not just the wealthy.

Scot, **Adam Smith** publishes *An Inquiry into the Nature and Causes of the Wealth of Nations*. It's about **capitalism 050**, and pretty much invents modern economics.

1609

1610

1641

1660

1687

1700

1751

1762

1776

1784

1800

Galileo Galilei uses his home-built telescope to discover four of Jupiter's moons— evidence that not everything is orbiting the Earth.

French philosopher **René Descartes 042** publishes *Meditations on First Philosophy*, explaining how thinking is the only thing that can't be doubted.

Isaac Newton 024 publishes his work on motion and gravity. His insights are hugely important for science and for an understanding of the natural world— including apples.

Between 1751 and 1776, the 28 volumes of **Denis Diderot**'s *Encyclopédie* are published. It's an ordered collection of human knowledge, banned in France because of its anti-Catholic tone.

German philosopher **Immanuel Kant** publishes *What is Enlightenment?* He answers his own question by stating: "Have courage to use your own understanding." In other words, think for yourself. How enlightened are you?

Wolfgang Amadeus Mozart (1756-1791)

"I was known as a child genius—at age five I was already composing music. I'm famous for my operas, such as the *The Marriage of Figaro*. All my characters— even the servants—are treated as real human beings. I'm more independent than many composers. I don't write just for one noble patron or the church, but give public performances. It allows me more artistic freedom."

SNEAKY FAN: "The concert is live during the evening in Tokyo, but in <u>London 159</u>, it's the middle of the morning. I've got internet access on my cell phone, so I can watch the band playing. As long as my teachers don't catch me!"

SOUND MAN: "I have a mixing desk out here in the audience. This controls the house sound (what the audience hears)."

ONLINE FAN: "I'm a member of the band's official fan site, so I can watch all the action on my computer. The way they put the video footage live on to the internet is called streaming."

ADDICTED FAN: "I can watch the concert live from across the world. I've got the latest digital TV, so I can see it 100 times if I like!"

LIGHTING TECHNICIAN: "All the lights have to work in time with the music, so it looks amazing (even when it doesn't sound so great)."

SCREAMING FANS: Standing in front of speakers at a rock concert can expose a person to 130 decibels, almost as much as a jet plane. This damages your hearing in as little as eight minutes.

SECRET MEMBER: During some concerts, other musicians play backstage out of sight. It's a clever way of making the band <u>sound 066</u> more impressive.

THE GEAR: On really big tours, each stage takes seven trucks to transport, 24 hours to set up, and 24 hours to derig (take down). Another 22 trucks carry the sound, lights, rigging (ropes), video, pyrotechnics, and band gear. That's 43 trucks carrying 1,200 tons (1,100 metric tons) of equipment!

HAIRY ROADIES: On a big tour there are about 150 roadies—they make up the largest section of staff. They haul equipment around, fix lighting, put up sound systems, and generally look a bit weathered.

TWEAKING TECHNICIANS: Each instrument has its own technician to ensure it works and is in tune just before the show. They run on stage and fix broken strings—or guitars.

PRIME TIME ENTERTAINMENT 2006

50,000 crazed music fans in Ajinomoto stadium, Tokyo

PYROTECHNICS: Over 500 shots are released a night.

TV CREW: The band travels with its own TV studio. Four cameras capture the show, transmitting it on to two large screens flanking each side of the stage.

BURLY SECURITY: Security is provided by the venue, and the band has personal security to protect their equipment—and themselves (from autograph-hunters or **obsessed fans 220**).

DANCERS: "We have to wear earplugs—not because the music's bad, but because it's so loud and we don't want to go deaf."

SPEAKERS: The sound system totals 400,000 watts of power (that's over 40,000 times more powerful than your bedroom hi-fi) and weighs 30 tons (27 metric tons)—that's 45 average-sized cars.

SINGER: "I have a personal microphone attached to my head, so I can run around and do a zillion fancy dance moves without tripping over cables."

STAGE MANAGER: "Look out for that carelessly placed amp...ouch!' I am responsible for everything that happens in front of the audience. I'm kind of like a **film director 034**."

TOUR MANAGER: "I'm already planning the next stop on the tour—everything from food and hotels to glitzier stage costumes. In any given week, three different stages are either up, going up, or coming down. Show me the money!"

WHO WANTS A FIGHT?

Whether it's an ARGUMENT with your sister, a SCRAP on the playground, or a WAR between nations, humans are good at FIGHTING. But what happens when we are aggressive? And why do we do it?

You shouldn't have messed with my head. My brain's going to kick off the rest of my body now...

MODERN-DAY DANGERS

The body's reaction to danger is left over from when our hairier ancestors had more immediate threats to contend with on a daily basis. The body prepared for "fight or flight"—having a scrap or running away. Problem is, such a response is often unsuitable for the pressures of modern life (jostling for space in the lunch line is not the same as facing a wild animal with sharp claws). The result is that the body goes into threat mode when it doesn't face any physical hazard. This is what happens when you feel stressed. Too many false alarms can lead to stress-related disorders such as heart disease, immune system problems, migraine **headaches 038**, and an inability to sleep.

FALSE ALARM

RED ALERT

See? My heart's pumping faster than you can say, "I take it back!"

BODY RESPONSE

The moment your body senses a threat, a whole host of automatic responses kick in. Urgent messages from the brain override normal body operations, so that **nutrient 176** rich blood is pumped to the muscles at up to five times the normal rate. The lungs, throat, and nostrils expand while breathing speeds up. This allows the increased blood flow to pick up oxygen more quickly (one of the functions of blood is to transport oxygen around the body). Endorphins (nature's painkillers) are released from the brain and pituitary gland, while fat from fatty cells and glucose from the **liver 134** is used to create instant energy. Sweat glands open to allow the supercharged system to keep cool. And tiny blood vessels under the surface of the skin close to limit potential blood loss. Even the eyes dilate to aid sight. Activities not required for the emergency are shut down—the digestive system halts, sexual function stops, and even the **immune system 084** is temporarily turned off. The body even tries to get rid of excess waste (which is why very scared people poop their pants). The result is a body more aware and ready to react—to run faster, hit harder, see better, hear more acutely, and think more quickly than only seconds before.

And my digestion's stopped, too. Just when I've eaten dinner. Boy, are you in trouble now!

GUESS WHAT?

IN 1969, POP STAR JOHN LENNON AND HIS WIFE YOKO ONO STAGED A PEACE DEMONSTRATION BY SPENDING FIVE DAYS IN BED TO PROTEST AGAINST THE WAR IN VIETNAM

WHEN IS A FIGHT NOT A FIGHT?

WHEN IT'S A RAP BATTLE

Rappers like to show their mental agility and lyrical skill by making up rhymes on the spur of the moment. In a battle, when **rappers 306** go head-to-head to improvise the best lines over a hip-hop beat, this usually involves insulting their opponent with witty put-downs. In his early career, rap star Eminem used battles as a way of gaining respect from the hip-hop community.

WHEN IT'S A CAPOEIRA DANCE-OFF

A martial art created by African slaves in **Brazil 072** around 400 years ago, Capoeira is a type of fighting—but with little contact. Instead, your weapons are dance, acrobatics, and self-defense moves, all made to stirring, hypnotic music. Different rhythms and lyrics (traditionally in Brazilian Portuguese) call for various types of battle between the two fighters.

BACKYARD STADIUMS PRESENT

RUMBLE IN THE KITCHEN

MIFFI v SABER

You're dog food

FIGHTING LIKE AN ANIMAL

Take a look at the animal world to see what fighting is about. Animals use violence to get what they need. Resources—whether it be food, water, or a female to mate with—are generally scarce, and fighting is an effective (if not pleasant) way of deciding who gets access to them. Sometimes, the fighting can be very bloody, with rivals being killed (male lions will not only attack other males from another pride, but kill their young as well). But often it's enough for an animal to demonstrate its dominance without killing and maiming (watch puppies playing together: they are figuring out the pecking order between themselves but without really hurting each other). Humans usually like to see themselves as above this kind of animal behavior. Some scientists, though, point out that our animal instincts are never that far from the surface. The difference is, unlike animals, we have **evolved 206** to know the consequences of violence.

MEET YOUR MUSCLES

They make up roughly 50 percent of your body weight. Stand on the scale and halve the weight reading—say hello to your muscles. Without them, you couldn't even move your eyes. And as for running, jumping, lifting, and getting out of bed— forget about it

BICEPS

TRICEPS

SKELETAL MUSCLE

There are three different types of muscle to keep you alive and mobile— skeletal, smooth, and cardiac. Of the 650 or so muscles in your body, most are skeletal muscles (check out the next page for more on the other two). Skeletal muscles cover your skeleton (obvious, huh?) and give your body its shape. They also hold your bones in their correct position, preventing your joints from dislocating (becoming separated). Attached to the skeleton by springy tendons, or stuck straight onto rough patches of bone, skeletal muscles obey messages from the brain to contract and relax—so allowing you to walk, swim, bounce

on a trampoline, and **text 144** your friends. These muscles also work almost constantly to maintain your posture, making one tiny adjustment after another to keep your body upright. At the same time, they generate body heat, which is vital for maintaining a normal body temperature.

WHY ARE WE ALL PUPPETS?

Skeletal muscles come in pairs. The reason for this is that muscle can only pull a bone one way—a muscle can't push. So, something as simple as raising and lowering your lower arm works like this: the muscles at the front of the top of your arm (biceps) pull on the bone to bend it at the elbow. Then the muscles at the back of the top of your arm behind that bone (triceps) pull the lower arm back down. All over your skeleton, pairs of muscles operate to bend and straighten your body parts. Like a marionette (puppet on strings), your muscles pull your bones around. With your brain as the **conductor 040** of all this activity, you are the ultimate puppet master.

INSIDE A MUSCLE

Muscles are all made of the same material: a type of elastic tissue, like a rubber band. Each muscle is made up of thousands and thousands of these small fibers. When skeletal muscle is relaxed, layers of fibers lie in long slim lines, overlapping just a tiny bit. At a "move" command from the **brain 038**, they slide past each other, overlapping completely and making the muscle thicker and shorter. This is known as contraction. Even when a muscle is relaxed, your brain keeps it moving a little bit. This way, they are firm and ready for action—stopping the muscle from ending up like an old rubber band.

TWITCHIN'

There are two different fibers in skeletal muscle. Slow-twitch muscle fibers, which contract slowly but keep going for a long time, are good for endurance activities like long-distance running or **cycling 088**. Fast-twitch muscle fibers, which contract quickly but get tired in a short time, are good for rapid movements, such as jumping to catch a ball or sprinting. Beneath the skin, the endurance-type muscles are very red because they contain a lot of blood vessels. These bring plenty of oxygen-rich blood to supply the muscles with energy. This is quite different from fast-twitch muscles, which are much lighter in color. They don't need oxygen for energy, so they don't need such a rich blood supply. To see the difference between the two types, check out a cooked chicken. The legs have dark meat—they're full of blood vessels. But chicken wings have white meat. They're full of fast-twitch fibers, since chickens need lots of energy to flap off.

Turn the page for more muscles..

✱ MUSCLE MEMORY ✱

To kick or catch a ball with the ease of a professional football or soccer player requires muscle memory. This means that your muscles have a finely tuned sense of the position of the joints. Through repetition, you improve the link between the eyes (and brain) and the muscles used in the activity. Then, the eyes can concentrate solely on the position of the ball—and there's no need to think about how to do the kicking or catching.

HANDS UP—WHO LIKES PUPPETS?

A puppet is an object that can't move by itself, but is moved by a human puppeteer for a theatrical show. Puppet shows have been performed in almost all time periods and civilizations. They were mentioned as early as the fourth century BC by a Greek historian called Xenophon. And it's thought they might have been around even before people could write. A puppet with strings is called a marionette. The word is French in origin and was originally used to describe puppet replicas of the Virgin Mary when, during the **Middle Ages 148**, the church used puppets to illustrate stories from the Bible. Some of the most famous puppets are Punch and Judy, which are glove puppets. This kind of puppet can be made of any hollow tube of material that a hand can be put into, and is controlled from below (it's not rocket science). Admittedly, Punch and Judy's morals are more than a bit lacking (Punch hits his wife and throws his baby around, for starters), but the same storylines have kept audiences giggling for centuries.

Middle Ages 148; China 264

GUESS WHAT?

HUMANS USE MORE THAN 70 MUSCLES TO SAY JUST A SINGLE WORD TRY NOT TO WEAR THEM OUT

BURY ME WITH MY CHICKEN

It's strange to think of chickens as wild, but they were: running amok in Thailand until about 9,000 years ago. That's when they were first tamed and domesticated (probably not as pets). By about 5000 BC, people in China 264 were also keeping chickens, to eat the birds and their eggs. From here, their tasty reputation spread to India and Africa, and bones from chickens have even been found in ancient Egyptian tombs. (They must have been very special chickens.) The (very) long-term popularity of chickens as livestock is easy to understand—they don't need much space and they don't eat much. So they're cheap to keep. And there's another important factor: a chicken can be eaten in a single meal, which, before the days of fridges, was very important.

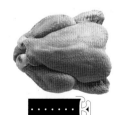

Why women are more muscly than men

There are other types of muscle working away inside your body that you have no control over. Smooth muscle is found in the walls of hollow organs, including your intestines, stomach, throat, and **eye 066**, and is responsible for the many "housekeeping" functions of the body. It works automatically, with you being scarcely aware of it. So, the muscular walls of your intestines contract to push food through your system, muscles in your bladder wall contract to expel urine from your body, and the muscles in your throat contract to push food into your stomach. To allow them to be mothers, women have extra muscle in their bodies. Made of smooth muscle tissue, the uterus carries a foetus (the unborn baby) during **pregnancy 106**. It eventually pushes each of us out into the world. The uterus is one of the strongest muscles in the human body.

WHY THE TONGUE IS LIKE THE LEG OF AN OCTOPUS

The tongue is the only muscle attached to you at only one end. Strictly speaking, the tongue is a bundle of 16 muscles —extrinsic muscles that attach the tongue to you, and intrinsic muscles that change its shape. These facilitate the chewing and swallowing of food, which is vital for life, and speech. So, while you're gabbing to your friends or snacking, you are actually exercising quite a few muscles. Since it contains no skeletal structure to support it, the tongue is called a muscular hydrostat. Other examples of muscular hydrostat include elephant trunks, some worms, and the legs of an octopus. Shake it, baby.

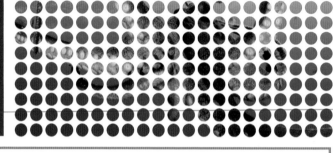

BIGGEST MUSCLE
YOUR BUTT
1.8 KG (4 LBS)

SMALLEST MUSCLE
MIDDLE EAR
1.27 MM (0.05 INCHES)

The heart and lungs

Your heart is made up of cardiac muscle—a type of muscle that exists nowhere else in the body. This muscle never gets tired. And, unlike skeletal muscle, cardiac muscles can contract all by themselves. Your heart acts as a double pump. One pump carries oxygen-poor blood to your lungs, where it unloads carbon dioxide, picks up oxygen and delivers oxygen-rich blood back to your heart. The second pump sends this oxygen-rich blood to every part of your body—especially your skeletal muscles, which require oxygen for fuel.

HOW COME GROWING UP IS SO PAINFUL?

During childhood, and especially puberty, muscles and bones grow at different rates —the bones can grow very quickly, with the muscles struggling to keep up. Since the two are connected by tendons strong enough to last a lifetime of pulling and yanking, this can make the bones ache as they are pulled at by those sluggish muscles. During a growth spurt, some athletic people find themselves unable to perform as well as they could before this war between their muscle and bones started. So, growing pains are real—as if being a **teenager 274** wasn't hard enough…

Your **lungs 134** are not made of muscle which means they can't inflate and deflate on their own. The muscle that actually allows you to breathe is your diaphragm—a dome-shaped muscle extending across the bottom of the ribcage. The diaphragm works hand-in-hand with your muscle-bound ribcage, contracting and relaxing as you breathe. The diaphragm is also vital for more essential bodily functions —pooing, hiccupping, and vomiting. Nice work.

The first railroad to carry passengers as well as goods opened in 1803, in south London. Devised by British engineer William Jessop, <u>**horses 130**</u> pulled wagons running on rails.

The arrival of efficient steam locomotives in the 1820s created rail mania. As the capital city, London was the center of this hubbub. Euston Station, London's first great rail terminus, opened in 1837, the same year that Victoria became Queen. Euston linked London with Birmingham, the second largest city. Soon the railroads connected the capital to other cities across the country.

London was growing fast: from one million people in 1800 to more than six million in 1900. To cope with the growth, it needed its own railroad, to move goods and people within its boundaries. This was the beginning of the London Underground (left). The first section of the world's first underground passenger railroad opened in 1863. It ran from Farringdon in the east to Paddington Station in the west. The first really deep-level subway line opened in 1890. Now part of the Northern line, it was also the first to be powered by <u>**electricity 300**</u>.

Trains became part of the landscape over the next 100 years. In 1994, the Channel Tunnel opened, connecting London with Paris, France, via 23 miles (37 km) of underwater tunnel. But London's growth had slowed: by 2001 the population had only increased by a million since 1900. The train-powered growth of the 1800s has never been repeated.

DID GEORGE STEPHENSON INVENT SPEED?

Imagine a land of green countryside with no <u>**cars 113**</u>, no trains—without even bicycles. This was England in the early 1800s. If you didn't want to walk, the only way to get around was by horse. George Stephenson's locomotive, the Rocket (right), changed all that in 1829. The Rocket could hit speeds of 24 mph (38 km/h). Alright, so a horse can gallop at about 40 mph (65 km/h), but it's hard to hang on and you

have to leave your luggage at home. After the Rocket, trains (and man) got faster and faster. The fastest ever steam train was The Mallard. In 1938, it managed 126 mph (202 km/h)—not too bad for a duck.

FASTER THAN A SPEEDING BULLET

In the <u>**future 254**</u>, trains will fly. Sort of. Maglev trains (right) don't have <u>**wheels 282**</u>, they use magnets to float just above the tracks. (Maglev is short for "magnetic levitation.") Because nothing touches the rail, there's no friction so they go faster. Maglevs are already running in Germany and <u>**Japan 028**</u>. They have reached speeds of 361 mph (581 km/h)—better not miss your stop! By 2020, it's estimated that Maglev trains will go as fast as 500 mph (800 km/h). Pretty good, when you consider that a jumbo jet travels at 565 mph (909 km/h).

FIVE HOBBIES AS GEEKY AS BEING A "TRAIN-SPOTTER"

PLANE-SPOTTER
They hang around airports, recording details of the planes they see.

GONGOOZLER
Someone who is crazy about canals and barges.

ANIME OTAKU
Japanese geek obsessed with cartoon books or films.

TREKKIE
Someone obsessed with the sci-fi world of TV's *Star Trek*.

TWITCHER
He sits in a converted shed, spying on birds through binoculars.

THE FIRST UNDERGROUND STATION TO BE BUILT WAS BAKER STREET, NEAR THE HOUSE WHERE THE FAMOUS FICTIONAL DETECTIVE SHERLOCK HOLMES WAS SUPPOSED TO LIVE.

NUMBER OF PASSENGERS ANNUALLY ON THE LONDON UNDERGROUND

1863/64: 10 MILLION

2000/01: 970 MILLION

Remember your best birthday present?

Where did all the dinosaurs go?

What happened to them?

These ancient creatures dominated life on Earth for 160 million years. Then, 65 million years ago (mya), they suddenly became extinct. Many experts believe that a six-mile (10-km) wide **asteroid 102** struck Earth (where Mexico is now) at 60,000 mph (100,000 km/h). It left a crater 40 miles (65 km) wide. The impact sent a cloud of vaporized asteroid (including the really rare element iridium) and dust into the atmosphere, blotting out the Sun for 12 months. Without light, **plants 018** withered. Herbivorous (plant-eating) dinosaurs were wiped out through lack of food. Their predators, the carnivorous (meat-eating) dinosaurs, starved to death. Where's the evidence? Scientists have discovered really high levels of iridium—known as an iridium spike—in 65 million-year-old rocks.

---

228 mya
Herrerasaurus

Bipedal (two-legged) carnivore —one of the earliest known dinosaurs (Argentina)

155-145 mya
Compsognathus
(not pictured)

Turkey-sized bipedal carnivore (Germany)

155-144 mya
Stegosaurus

Plated quadrupedal (four-legged) herbivore (US)

154-145 mya
Apatosaurus

Giant quadrupedal herbivore (US)

132-100 mya
Iguanodon
(not pictured)

Bipedal herbivore (western Europe, US)

115-100 mya
Ouranosaurus

Sail-backed, bipedal/ quadrupedal herbivore

How do we know?

The fossil record tells us lots about ancient life. Fossils formed when animals, including dinosaurs, died and were rapidly covered by mud or silt. The soft parts of their bodies decayed, leaving just the bones and other hard parts. Over time, these parts broke down into minerals, leaving behind a rocky replica of the original. Fossils show paleontologists (scientists who study fossils) that life forms living millions of years ago were different to those around today. This is key evidence for **evolution 206**. And there's more. Fossils are laid down in layers of rock that can be dated, with each layer older than the layer above. By dating fossils we can create a timetable for evolution.

What were they?

Dinosaurs were first discovered in Britain in 1818. Or, more accurately, the fossilized jaw of a giant reptile was discovered in Oxfordshire, England. Geologist William Buckland described the jaw as belonging to an extinct meat-eating reptile he named Megalosaurus ("giant lizard"). However, this was a time when biblical notions of creation were taken literally—the idea of "extinct" animals just did not fit. In 1842, anatomist Richard Owen devised the name dinosaur ("**terrible lizard 012**") to describe all extinct giant reptiles. No one took much notice. But, in 1854, the public flocked in their thousands to see (hopelessly wrong) life-size representations of dinosaurs in a London park (right). By the end of the 19th century, more discoveries showed that dinosaurs were very diverse and millions of years old. Dinosaurs had finally been accepted.

What survived?

The mass extinction at the end of the Cretaceous period 65 mya exterminated more than just dinosaurs. Also wiped out were most big reptiles (including flying pterosaurs and marine plesiosaurs) and many land plants. Microscopic, plantlike phytoplankton—the primary food source for ocean creatures—perished, too. But there were survivors:

BIRDS—warm-blooded, feathered descendants of bipedal dinosaurs called theropods

MAMMALS—small, warm-blooded and insulated by fur

SMALLER REPTILES—crocodiles, turtles, snakes, and lizards

MANY FISH—especially bony fish and sharks

AMPHIBIANS – frogs and salamanders

INSECTS 232—and many other invertebrates

SOME PLANTS—especially types of fern and conifer

I'm still here!

110-100 mya
Deinonychus

Pack-hunting, bipedal carnivore (US)

76-65 mya
Pachycephalosaurus

Bone-headed, bipedal herbivore (Canada, US)

76-74 mya
Parasaurolophus

Duck-billed, crested bipedal/quadrupedal herbivore (Canada, US)

76-70 mya
Euoplocephalus (not pictured)

Club-tailed, quadrupedal herbivore (Canada, US)

68-65 mya
Tyrannosaurus

Large, bipedal carnivore (Canada, US)

67-65 mya
Triceratops

Horned, quadrupedal herbivore (US)

65 mya

Extinction of dinosaurs (everywhere)

HOW TO

PREPARE FOR ARMAGEDDON

During the **Cold War 294**, the superpowers—the US and the Soviet Union—built up vast arsenals of nuclear weapons. By the early 1980s, many governments in Europe felt there was a real threat of nuclear armageddon (destruction) and published survival instructions for their populations. These were unlikely to help in the face of a nuclear blast, but were useful as **propaganda 292** to stop people from getting too worried.

Great advice included:

• **Stay at home**

• **If at school, get under your desk and cover head and neck**

• **Construct an inner refuge by removing a door and leaning it against a wall—you will shelter under this for 14 days**

• **Listen to the radio: "You should receive instructions on what to do next."** Well, if there's anyone left, that is

GUESS WHAT?

A MAJOR ASTEROID IMPACT—LIKE THE ONE THAT PROBABLY WIPED OUT THE DINOSAURS—ONLY HAPPENS EVERY 100 MILLION YEARS OR SO, AND THERE'S A 99.95 PERCENT CHANCE THAT NO ASTEROIDS (NOT EVEN LITTLE ONES) WILL HIT EARTH IN THE NEXT 50 YEARS. SO YOU CAN COME OUT FROM UNDER YOUR DESK NOW

Spain...

↑ **Where is Spain?**

↓ The south of Spain is incredibly **sunny**. Every July in Seville, the heat tops 104 °F (40 °C)

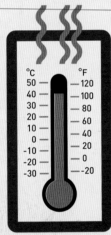

↑ Madrid's symbol is a bear and fruit **tree 010**. There used to be **bears** all over Spain —the area around Madrid was known as Ursaria, or "bear country". Now, there are less than 200

Tourism

In 2004, 53.6 million **tourists 122** visited Spain. The six most popular destinations lured 91 percent of them (in order):

1) Barcelona 2) the Canary Islands 3) the Balearic islands (Ibiza, Mallorca, Menorca) 4) Andalucia 5) Valencia 6) Madrid

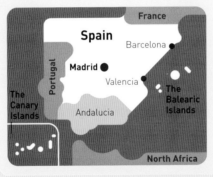

Spain
France
Barcelona
Madrid ●
Valencia
Portugal
The Canary Islands
Andalucia
The Balearic Islands
North Africa

UK **16.7 million**

Germany **10 million**

France **7.5 million**

The three countries providing the most tourist visitors

83%

Percentage of all tourists who had visited Spain before

Madrid is the highest capital city in Europe

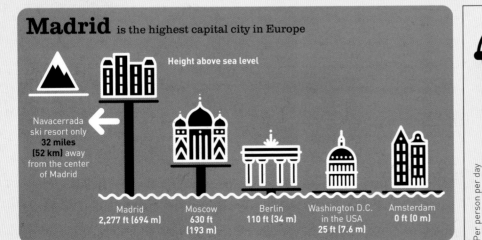

Height above sea level

Navacerrada ski resort only **32 miles (52 km)** away from the center of Madrid

Madrid **2,277 ft (694 m)**

Moscow **630 ft (193 m)**

Berlin **110 ft (34 m)**

Washington D.C. in the USA **25 ft (7.6 m)**

Amsterdam **0 ft (0 m)**

Spain **70 gallons (265 liters)**

Portugal **42.5 gallons (161 liters)**

Per person per day

→ Spain is very dry but uses a lot of **water**. Some 31 per cent of the land is under threat of **desertification**. Spanish households **consume the most water** per person per day in Europe—58 gallons (265 litres). Neighbor Portugal consumes only 35 gallons (161 litres) per person per day

Population **44 million—going up**

Nine per cent of **people living in Spain** are from another country—about 3.75 million people. **Morocco** (511,000 people) and **Ecuador** (498,000 people) provide the largest groups

There are also 227,000 **Britons** living in Spain

Nation knowledge

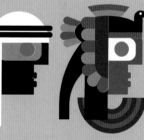

Spain was **united** as one country in 1492. Before, there were **separate kingdoms**, some with their own languages. Other languages sharing official status with Spanish: Basque (600,000 speakers), Catalan (6.4 m), and Galician (3 m)

Spain has the largest **commercial fishing fleet** in the EU. It is the top seafood consumer in the European Union, following only Japan worldwide. Spanish cooks prepare 1.7 million tons of seafood a year

Languages spoken in Spain

Galician **7%** Basque **2%**

Castilian Spanish **74%** Catalan **17%**

Castilian is the official language nationwide; the other languages are official regionally

The sunniest desert

The southern Tabernas desert gets 3,000 hours of sun per year. It's so sunny here that there is a solar energy plant producing enough energy for 10,000 homes and the area is often used as a setting for desert **movies 034**

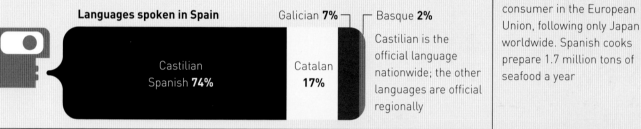

Films that have been shot here include:

The Good, the Bad and the Ugly **Indiana Jones and the Last Crusade** **Lawrence of Arabia** **Cleopatra**

 Olive Oil: Forty-four percent of the world's olive oil comes from Spain

Jamon, anyone?

A common sight in Spanish bars is a "jamon"—an entire leg of ham. The best come from pigs fed nothing but acorns. After the pig is killed, the hams are covered in salt and hung up for up to three years before they're eaten. Top "jamons" can cost hundreds of dollars

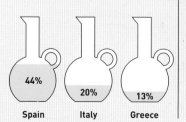

44% Spain **20%** Italy **13%** Greece

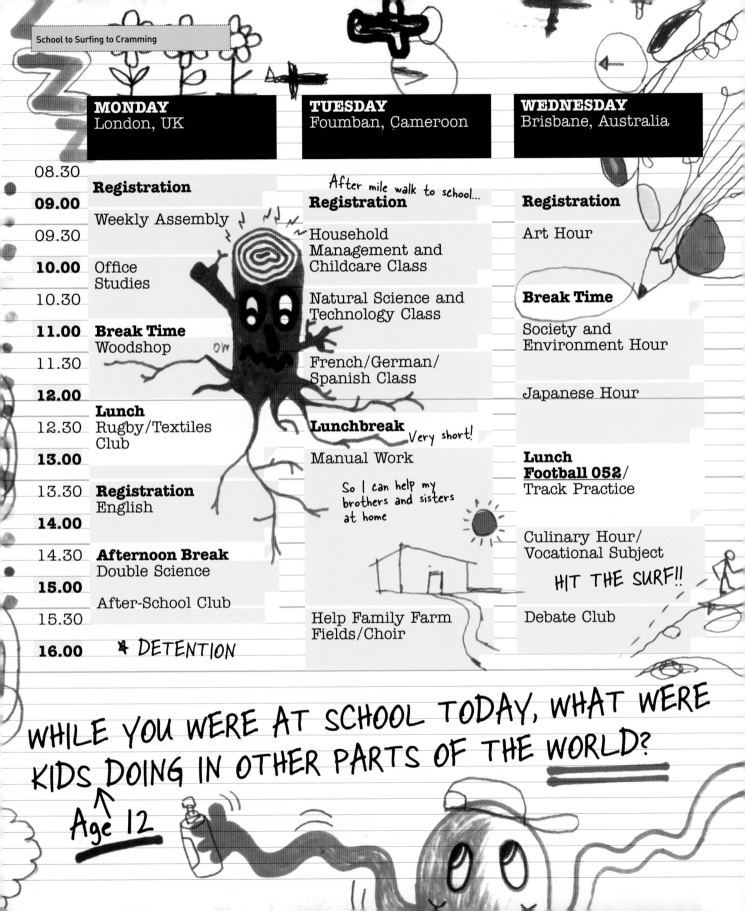

MONDAY London, UK	**TUESDAY** Foumban, Cameroon	**WEDNESDAY** Brisbane, Australia

08.30

09.00 — **Registration**

09.30 — Weekly Assembly

After mile walk to school...

Registration (Tuesday)

Registration (Wednesday)

Art Hour

10.00 — Office Studies

Household Management and Childcare Class

10.30

Natural Science and Technology Class

Break Time

Society and Environment Hour

11.00 — **Break Time**
Woodshop   *OW*

11.30

French/German/Spanish Class

Japanese Hour

12.00

Lunch
12.30 — Rugby/Textiles Club

Lunchbreak   *Very short!*

13.00

Manual Work

Lunch
Football 052/
Track Practice

So I can help my brothers and sisters at home

13.30 — **Registration**
English

14.00

14.30 — **Afternoon Break**
Double Science

Culinary Hour/
Vocational Subject

HIT THE SURF!!

15.00

After-School Club

15.30

Help Family Farm Fields/Choir

Debate Club

16.00 — ♣ DETENTION

WHILE YOU WERE AT SCHOOL TODAY, WHAT WERE KIDS DOING IN OTHER PARTS OF THE WORLD?

↑ Age 12

THURSDAY
Baghdad, Iraq

All single-sex classes

Registration

Religion Class

If you're not Muslim you don't have to go!

English Class

Lunchtime

Gym

Breaktime

Math Class

Algebra—my favorite! No, really!

History Class

Shop Work/Extra Study After School

For the talented—or those who like to work harder!

FRIDAY
San Diego, CA

Student Roll-call

English

Selected American Classics

Breaktime

Social Studies

Don't forget American history homework!

Lunch Period
Cheerleading

Honors Class

For really smart kids

Break Time
Computer Class

Health Class
Learn why drugs are bad for you

Soccer Practice

Watch or cheer

SATURDAY
Tokyo, Japan

Registration
Moral Studies

Learn to be a good person

Preparation for Annual School Festival

Japanese Studies

Teachers move around classrooms, not us!

Cleaning Session/ Calligraphy Club/ Cram School

We sweep floors, clean chalkboards, and empty garbage.

MEET THE NEIGHBORS

THE SOLAR SYSTEM, MADE UP OF THE SUN AND EVERYTHING IN ORBIT AROUND IT, WAS FORMED ABOUT 5 BILLION (THAT'S 5,000,000,000) YEARS AGO. IT WAS BORN IN A MASSIVE CLOUD OF GAS AND DUST, INCLUDING THE REMAINS OF OLDER STARS THAT HAD EXPLODED. **GRAVITY 024** PULLED THIS MATERIAL TOGETHER AND, OVER THE COURSE OF 100,000 YEARS, THE SUN AND SOLAR SYSTEM TOOK SHAPE. SO, MUCH OF WHAT IS HERE ON EARTH WAS ONCE THE STUFF OF STARS—INCLUDING YOU

THE SUN

DIAMETER: 865,000 miles (1,392,000 km)

←←←
It's so huge that it contains over 99 percent of all the matter in the solar system. The Sun is one big ball of hot gas with a fusion reactor in the middle (turning hydrogen into helium). The result is light and blazing heat—its core temperature is 27 million °F (15 million °C). The Sun will continue to burn like it does now for another five billion years.

←←
Ancient Egyptians worshipped the Sun god Ra, who rowed the Sun across the sky every day in a boat. He had to fight off the snake-god Apep, who wished to cover the world in darkness—a solar eclipse would mean Ra had temporarily failed.

←
You would need to swim the 50 meter race 3,000,000,000 times to get there.

SPACE

It's not quite as empty and lonely as you might think out here. There's energy, dust, gases, and even a solar wind. This is made of electrically charged particles from the Sun (called plasma) which could be used to propel starships in the same way the **wind 196** moves a sail boat.

VENUS

AVERAGE DISTANCE FROM SUN: 67,000,000 miles (108,000,000 km)
ORBIT: 225 Earth days
DIAMETER: 12,100 km (7,500 miles)
←←←
Named after the Roman goddess of love and beauty, the planet itself isn't so pretty. Clouds are made of sulfuric acid, the temperature is a baking 900 °F (480 °C) and there are no oceans. Venus rotates in the opposite direction to Earth, so the Sun rises in the west.
←←
Venus the goddess was popular as a subject for **Renaissance 148** painters, who usually depicted her unclothed (va va voom!). It became common to refer to any nude painting as a "Venus," whether of the goddess or not.
←
Running around Earth 1,100 times would be the same as running to Venus—exhausting.

MERCURY

AVERAGE DISTANCE FROM SUN: 36,000,000 miles (58,000,000 km)
ORBIT: 88 Earth days
DIAMETER: 3,000 miles (4,880 km)
←←←
The closest planet to the Sun, it's much smaller than Earth (40 percent the size). Mercury is awash with sunlight (over six times as intense as it is on Earth). But it's no place for sunbathing—the radiation would kill any visiting **astronauts 048** foolish enough not to pack the proper protection.
←←
Mercury was the fleet-footed messenger of the Roman gods. The Romans named the planet after him because it seemed to move so quickly across the night sky.
←
If there were a highway to Mercury, it would take 95 years to drive there.

EARTH

AVERAGE DISTANCE FROM SUN:
93,000,000 miles (150,000,000 km)
ORBIT: 365 Earth days
DIAMETER: 7,926 miles (12,800 km)
←←←
Earth moves at 67,000 mph
(108,000 km/h)—you don't notice
because you're on the planet moving
at the same speed. It's the only
planet in the solar system known to
support life—the atmosphere and
magnetic field shields us from most
of the harmful radiation coming
from the Sun.
←←
Earth has been seen as a goddess
in various cultures. In Norse
mythology, Jord is the Earth
goddess. The modern Gaia theory
views Earth as a single living
organism that regulates itself to
keep conditions suitable for life.

IT'S TOO HOT AROUND HERE

The highest recorded temperature
was in Libya in 1922, when the
desert town of El Azizia was sizzling
in sunshine at almost 136 °F (58 °C).

LANDLUBBERS BEWARE

Around 70 percent of Earth is
covered with water. Most of this is
seas and **oceans 202**.

WHEN IT'S COLD, IT'S REALLY COLD

Especially in Antarctica, where it gets down into the -170s °F (-80s °C).

MOON

AVERAGE DISTANCE FROM EARTH:
239,000 miles (384,000 km)
ORBIT: 27.3 Earth days
DIAMETER: 2,160 miles (3,476 km)
←←←
It looks the same size as the Sun from down here, but that's because it is 400 times closer than the Sun (and also 400 times smaller). We only ever see one side of the Moon, as it rotates in the same time that it takes to orbit Earth. It circles Earth about once a month.
←←
Aningan was Moon god for the Inuits of Greenland. He was always chasing Malina, the Sun goddess, across the sky. He replenished himself by eating for three full days (during the new Moon).
←
Flying 70 times from London to New York is equal to a trip to the Moon.

DEEP IMPACT

The largest crater on Earth is over 311 miles (500 km) wide, partly located beneath Mexico. It was created by an asteroid impact 65 million years ago that may have led to the extinction of the **dinosaurs 162**.

WHAT A WEIGHT

If you could ever find scales big enough, it's reckoned that Earth would weigh in at nearly 6,000,000,000,000,000,000,000 metric tons. Heavy, man.

SCARED OF HEIGHTS?

If you want to be at the top of the world, go to **Mount Everest 074** and climb the 29,035 ft (8,850 m) to the summit.

COMETS

Comets are bodies of rock and ice in orbit around the Sun. They are celebrated for their glowing tails; the comet begins to evaporate as it approaches the Sun, producing a trail of dust and gas. Some tails are 93 million miles (150 million km) long.

MARS

AVERAGE DISTANCE FROM SUN:
141,600,000 miles (228,000,000 km)
ORBIT: 687 Earth days
DIAMETER: 4,200 miles (6,800 km)
←←←
Mars was long considered a likely candidate for supporting life, and Martians made regular appearances in science fiction. Though scientists no longer believe aliens reside on Mars, there is a possibility that the planet could have once supported primitive life forms.
←←
Appearing red in the sky, the planet takes the name of the **Romans' 263** god of war. According to legend, the sons of Mars, Romulus and Remus, founded the city of Rome itself.
←←
Marching as fast as a Roman legionnaire, you could get to Mars in 1,344 years (how many pairs of sandals would that take?).

JUPITER

AVERAGE DISTANCE FROM SUN:
484,000,000 miles (778,000,000 km)
ORBIT: 4,332 Earth days
DIAMETER: 88,800 miles (143,000 km)
←←←
As planets go, it's big—318 times the mass of Earth and 11 times the diameter. It has no hard surface (no land), but layers of gaseous material that get denser towards the middle. **Galileo 024** discovered Jupiter's four largest moons, but it has many others.
←←
Jupiter had the top job as supreme ruler of the Roman gods. To the Greeks, he was Zeus and the **Olympic Games 180** were held in his honour.
←
As an Olympic marathon runner, you'd have to complete 14,952,400 races to make it as far as Jupiter.

SATURN

AVERAGE DISTANCE FROM SUN:
887,000,000 miles (1,427,000,000 km)
ORBIT: 10,750 Earth days
DIAMETER: 74,900 miles (120,500 km)
←←←
The second largest planet, Saturn is not very dense and would actually float in water. Saturn's wondrous rings are believed to be the wreckage of shattered moons.
←←
The feast of Saturnalia was held by Romans at the Winter Solstice. No war could be declared, slaves and masters switched roles (the slaves gave the orders) and gifts were exchanged. Christians later adopted it and called it Christmas.
←
If you had the fastest space ship around today, it would still take about two years to reach Saturn.

MAIN ASTEROID BELT

Between Mars and Jupiter, tens of thousands of pieces of rock orbit the Sun. The largest asteroid is Ceres, about 600 miles (1,000 km) in diameter.

URANUS

AVERAGE DISTANCE FROM SUN:
1,780,000,000 miles
(2,870,000,000 km)
ORBIT: 30,707 Earth days
DIAMETER: 31,800 miles (51,100 km)
←←←
Uranus was discovered by German-born astronomer William Herschel in 1781 (who wanted to name it after King George III of Britain). Like Saturn, it has rings that are made of dust and ice. It is tipped on its side, possibly because of a collision with another planet. Bad driver!
←←
Uranus was the deity of the heavens, who locked his children away deep in the Earth. Gaia, their mother, was upset, and organized a rebellion to depose him (worse than kids, these squabbling gods).
←
You'd need 1,813,000,000 friends to make a chain of people linked by hands from Earth to Uranus.

NEPTUNE

AVERAGE DISTANCE FROM SUN:
2,800,000,000 miles
(4,500,000,000 km)
ORBIT: 60,200 Earth days
DIAMETER: 30,700 miles (49,500 km)
←←←
A pretty big planet—you could fit 60 Earths inside it. It's probably a mixture of ice, rock, and gases. It has rings but they are rather faint.
←←
Neptune was the god of the seas —he had a trident to start storms, hurricanes and tides. Weirdly, he was also held in higher regard as the god and patron of **horses 130** (which he supposedly created).
←
Fancy cycling to Neptune? It'll take you around 30,900 years—and a heck of a lot of stamina.

PLUTO

AVERAGE DISTANCE FROM SUN:
3,674,000,000 miles
(5,913,000,000 km)
ORBIT: 90,600 Earth days
DIAMETER: 1,400 miles (2,300 km)
←←←
Pluto is part of a belt of icy asteroids out beyond Neptune that are orbiting the Sun. There are thousands of other small, cold worlds like Pluto. But astronomers haven't yet decided if these are real planets, or not.
←←
Pluto was the god of the underworld. He kidnapped Persephone, daughter of the grain goddess Demeter. Obviously, Demeter was upset, and all the crops failed. As a compromise, Pluto got Persephone for half the year, a time when no crops grew—the cold months, in other words.
←
If you had a space craft that went at the speed of light 132, you could reach Pluto in just over five hours.

B-2 BOMBER

RADAR

LAND MINES

V2 ROCKET

WAR:
WHAT IS IT GOOD FOR?

WAR IS BAD. BUT IT DOES
PRODUCE ONE GOOD THING:
TECHNOLOGICAL INNOVATION

**WHICH MILITARY TECHNOLOGY
LED TO WHICH INNOVATION?**

USA

MINUTEMAN
BALLISTIC MISSILE

_ARPANET

RATIONS

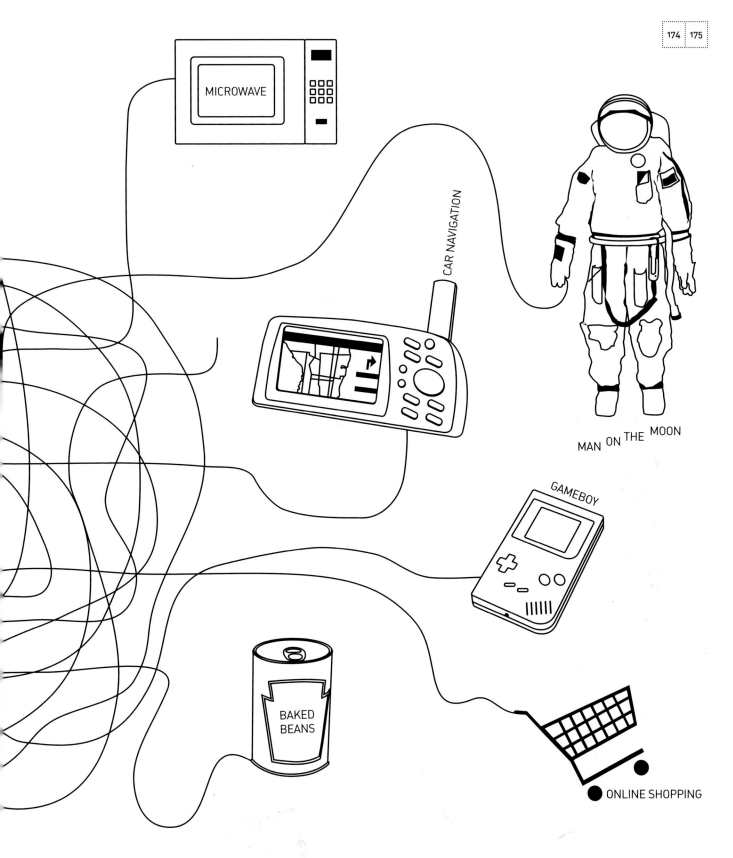

MICROWAVE

CAR NAVIGATION

MAN ON THE MOON

GAMEBOY

BAKED BEANS

● ONLINE SHOPPING

TURN TO PAGE 248 TO FIND OUT WHY...

AN APPLE A DAY

An apple a day
Keeps the doctor away

Apple in the morning—
Doctor's warning

Roast apple at night—
Starves the doctor outright

Eat an apple going to bed—
Knock the doctor on the head

Three each day,
seven days a week—
Ruddy apple, ruddy cheek

There's a nursery rhyme, popular in England since the 16th century, that talks about the benefits of eating an apple every day. While not wholly scientific ("Eat an apple going to bed, knock the doctor on the head") the basic message of the rhyme—that eating the right food keeps us healthy—is just as true today as it was 500 years ago.

So, how come lots of apples are good for you, but lots of apple pie isn't?

It's all about what's inside each apple. Like most fruit and vegetables, apples are a great source of fiber. This is the stuff that keeps food moving through your body (sort of like traffic police), and makes your poop 134 soft. Fruit and vegetables also contain lots of vitamins. These are key nutrients that the body takes from food to power growth and keep you healthy. Different vitamins are needed for different things—apples contain vitamin C, which is essential for the body to function normally and fight infection. Apples also provide some carbohydrate, which is the main source of energy for the body. It's no surprise, then, that a diet high in fruit and veg can keep you feeling good and prevent diseases later in life.

Apple pie, on the other hand, isn't quite so great (even if it is delicious). Cooking the apples removes many of the vitamins (a bad start). The pastry is high in a type of fat—saturated fat. This can increase the amount of cholesterol (a natural, waxy substance) in your blood. Too much cholesterol can eventually cause heart disease in later life. (The other type of fat—unsaturated fat—is much better for you.

It is found in oily fish 026 such as mackerel, and nuts and seeds.) Apple pie also contains quite a lot of sugar, which is high in taste but low in goodness. So, it's best not try for an apple pie a day to keep the doctor away.

What *should* you be eating every day?

The answer is that you need a variety of foods.
To work properly, our bodies need to take different
nutrients and vitamins from the foods we eat.
On an average day, a good mix would include:

Three things from the milk and dairy group (milk, cheese, and yogurt). Foods in this group contain calcium as well as vitamin B12, vitamin A, and vitamin D. These help keep your bones and teeth healthy. They are also an important source of protein, which is essential for building bone, **muscle 156**, skin, organs, and blood. Many hormones are also made of proteins.

No more than two or three things from the fat and sugar group (candy, cake, potato chips, and soft drinks). These foods provide very few nutrients, but lots of energy (which is why your little brother gets hyper after eating chocolate).

Five portions of fruit and veg. Fruit (including apples) and vegetables are an essential source of fiber, vitamins, and minerals.

Two to three servings from the meat, fish, and vegetarian alternatives group (made up of lentils, legumes, nuts, seeds, and beans). Foods in this group are a rich source of protein and some also contain iron, magnesium, zinc, essential fatty acids, and B vitamins. All these are needed for good growth and body repair.

Five things from the bread 086, cereal, and potato group (which also includes pasta, rice, and crackers). These foods provide the body's main supply of carbohydrate. Although potatoes are a vegetable, they are included here because they have a high starch content, a type of carbohydrate.

Why the potato is an apple

It's true! The Latin term "pomum" means any fruit in general. Because apples were the first fruit grown by man, they got the name (in French, la pomme). After that, some other fruits derived their names from the word for apple, such as pomegranate in English, or la pomme de terre in French. This means potato, or literally "the apple of the earth." So, spuds are really apples—until you taste them, that is!

WHAT NURSERY RHYMES ARE REALLY ABOUT

Nursery rhymes are more than nonsense verse—some may be about historical events. The lyrics were often used to make jokes about the political events of the day. The English nursery rhyme, "Ring Around the Rosies" is thought to be about the Bubonic **plague 214** that swept across Europe in the 14th century ("we all fall down" refers to people dying). And "Jack and Jill" might sound like a fun story of two children trudging up a hill, but is said to be about the French King Louis the Sixteenth (Jack), who was beheaded ("lost his crown"). The German nursery rhyme, "May-bug, fly!" ("May-bug, fly! Your father's in the war. Your mother's in Pommerland, Pommerland has burned down. May-bug, fly"), isn't really about insects. It became popular when Swedish troops occupied Pommerland (now eastern Germany) during the Thirty Years' War (1618-48). It's about children going to stay with relatives in other parts of the country.

You're not going to eat that!

Northern Thailand
Giant water bugs served with chilli and sticky rice are a tasty treat. And dung beetles are used to add flavor to curry.

Ghana
Edible frogs are made into a soup or roasted.

Southeast Asia
The much-loved durian fruit is said to smell like sweaty socks. Yum.

Scotland
Chocolate bars coated in batter and deep fried in oil are a cult delicacy. Just don't tell your doctor.

HOW MIGHT THE HISTORY OF WORLD

WHAT

...Franz Ferdinand's driver had not missed his turn?

...The Allies hadn't been vengeful after World War I?

...Chamberlain hadn't appeased Hitler?

World War I began after the assassination of Archduke Franz Ferdinand, heir to the Austro-Hungarian throne (an empire in central Europe). He was shot dead in his car (below) on June 28, 1914, in Sarajevo, now capital of Bosnia-Herzegovina. The gunman was Gavrilo Princip, a student who wanted the region to be free of Austro-Hungarian influence. Princip had blown an earlier chance to kill Ferdinand. But the Archduke's driver missed a turn and was backing up as Princip walked by. A month later, **Europe 216** was at war.

After **World War I 294** ended on November 11, 1918, the victors wanted to ensure that Germany would not fight any more wars. The Treaty of Versailles (1919) wrote the rules of the peace—Germany had to accept or be invaded by the victors (Britain, France, and the US, now known as the Allies). The Treaty prevented Germany from having an air force, submarines, or tanks and limited the size of its army. Germany lost its empire. Plus, the Germans had to pay compensation for the damage the war had caused and accept all responsibility for it.

In the late 1930s, Britain tried to appease Hitler's Germany. So, rather than challenge his plans, Britain gave Hitler more or less what he wanted. In March 1938, Germany created a union with Austria (the Anschluss) that had been forbidden by the Treaty of Versailles. The British didn't take any action. There was another crisis in September 1938, as Hitler demanded that parts of Czechoslovakia should be under German control. Again, Hitler got what he wanted. Many in Britain backed the policy because they thought it would prevent war. The policy of appeasement ended in March 1939 when Germany invaded the rest of Czechoslovakia (right).

For Germans, the terms of the Treaty seemed harsh and unfair. Nazi leader Adolf Hitler's promises to reverse the Treaty and make Germany strong again proved popular. If the Allies hadn't blamed Germany for the war and had made a fairer settlement, maybe there would have been less bitterness. It's possible that Hitler (right) might never have become German Chancellor in 1933, and another war could have been avoided.

The Austrians declared war on Serbia, who they blamed for the assassination. Russia backed Serbia and prepared for war with Austria-Hungary. Once that had happened, the other countries were drawn into war one by one. On one side, Russia, France, and Britain (the Entente). On the other, Austria-Hungary and Germany (the Central Powers). So, without the Archduke's missed turn, there wouldn't have been any assassination and no reason for war. But some other event might still have led to war anyway. It only took two countries to fall out for all the others to be dragged in.

WARS I AND II HAVE BEEN DIFFERENT?

IF...

...The Luftwaffe had won the Battle of Britain?

...Japan hadn't attacked Pearl Harbor?

Throughout the 1930s, Japan had been expanding its territory in Asia (including the invasion of China). This raised tensions with the US, which didn't like the growing power of Japan. The Japanese launched a surprise attack (below) against the US naval base at Pearl Harbor on December 7, 1941. It was a major success for the Japanese. The Americans were outraged and the nation declared <u>war 174</u>. Nazi Germany (which had made a deal with Japan) also declared war on the US.

The battle took place over the summer and fall of 1940. German forces had overrun Europe and only Britain, an island, remained to fight alone. The Germans had to destroy the Royal Air Force (RAF) to launch a successful invasion. At first, the Luftwaffe (German air force) targeted British airfields and aimed to destroy as many fighter planes as possible. Then, in September, Hitler ordered a switch to bombing British cities in retaliation for a British raid on Berlin. This gave the RAF breathing space to recover. The proposed invasion of Britain was canceled, but the bombing raids on its cities continued.

It is not certain that the German invasion would have succeeded even if the RAF had been destroyed. It was poorly planned and the troop and supply ships would have run into serious trouble with the Royal Navy. But if the Battle of Britain had been lost, Prime Minister Winston Churchill (below) might have had to resign. His successor might then have made peace with Hitler. The Germans could then have concentrated exclusively on fighting the Soviet Union.

Without Pearl Harbor, it is possible that the United States and Japan would still have gone to war. The US was demanding that the Japanese withdraw from China. The Americans had also put a block on Japan's <u>oil 070</u> supplies. Japan, expanding its influence in Asia, was bound to clash with the US. American public opinion might have been more divided on the issue, though. It would also have been more difficult for the US to support Britain and the Soviet Union in fighting the Nazis.

When Germany invaded Poland in September 1939, World War II began. Some think that if Britain had taken a harder line with Germany from the beginning then the war could have been avoided. But Britain's rearmament was far behind Germany's. Without the extra years to build up forces, it isn't certain Britain could have held out against <u>Germany 244</u>.

My family came to watch me. They're among more than three million fans from around the world who came to watch the Games live. Four billion people watched them on **TV 330**, too.

I'm one of 11,099 athletes at the Olympic Games in Athens, 2004—the largest ever, from a record-breaking 202 countries. We're carrying our national flags for the closing ceremony.

Tanzania

Venezuela

Togo

Djibouti

Thailand

Tonga

Turkmenistan

Turkey

I'm carrying the Turkish flag. We came 22nd at these Games, with gold medals in weightlifting, and silver medals in **boxing 052** and wrestling. We've never won a bid to host the Olympics.

Jamaica

Glowing with pride

Singing to the Greek music

Sweating in the 82 °F (28 °C) heat

We're all here thanks to Baron Pierre de Coubertin (1863-1937), a French nobleman. It was his idea to revive the Olympic Games. A sports lover, he boxed, rode horses, fenced, and rowed (you'd want him on your team).

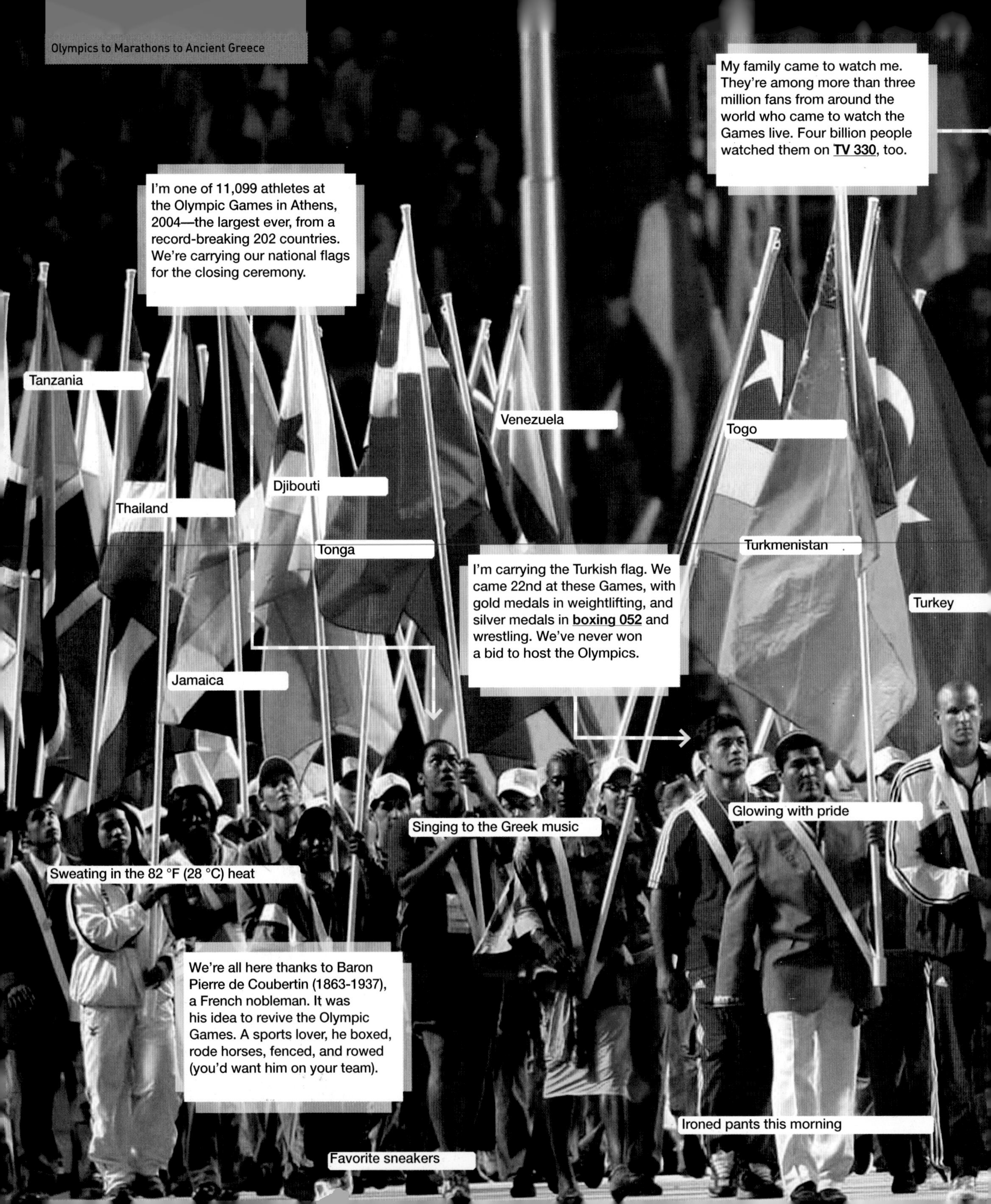

Ironed pants this morning

Favorite sneakers

I'm a Greek athlete. The Games originated in **ancient Greece 240** in 776 BC. The modern Games started again in Athens in 1896. They happen every four years and feature 28 sports.

Russia

Chile

Greece

Aruba

Algeria

Fiji

India

Aching hand

Sending a cell photo message

These feet have run 26 miles (42 km) today in a marathon. We've just come from the marathon medal ceremony. To train, male contenders run about 90 miles (145 km) per week.

Nasty blister

They can navigate

Birds don't have **maps 068**—so how does the Arctic tern (left), a type of seabird, make it from the Arctic to the Antarctic, on the opposite side of the globe, every year? Birds make such amazing journeys, called migration, by following coastlines, rivers, and mountain ranges, monitoring the Earth's magnetic field (with tiny grains of a mineral called magnetite in their heads) and observing the stars or using the **Sun 168** for guidance. Many birds migrate in flocks, a bit like an aerial bus party.

They're intelligent

Forget calling your friend a "bird brain"—unless you're being kind. Scientists claim some crows are supersmart and can even solve problems as fast as four-year-old children. Carrion crows (above) drop walnuts on roads and wait for **cars 113** to crack them open. The Clark's nutcracker, found in North America, has one of the best memories in the animal kingdom. During late August and early September it buries some 30,000 pine seeds over up to 8.5 square miles (22 km^2). During the next eight months it retrieves them, even those under snow.

GUESS WHAT? IT'S NOT A MAN'S WORLD. IT'S A BIRD'S WORLD!

What springs to mind when you say "bird"? Geeky bird watchers with binoculars? Bird droppings on cars (or your head)? Squawking swarms circling the playground, waiting to gobble up leftover snacks? Well—we don't give our feathered friends the respect they deserve. This army of winged wonders boasts an amazing range of skills and rules the world from above...

They're all around us

Can you remember the last time you went out and didn't see, or at least hear, a bird? There are a whopping 100 billion birds in the world and nearly 9,800 different species. They are EVERYWHERE. The only major threat to them is man. Due to the environmental damage people cause with their constant farming, forestry, building construction, and **pollution 070**, 10 percent of all bird species may disappear by the year 2100. But scientists believe that most birds will continue to adapt to these changing conditions—don't doubt it.

They can talk

Some (such as the parrot, left) probably hold more intelligent conversations than you hear on the playground. In the 1980s and 1990s an African grey parrot called Alex acquired a vocabulary of more than 100 words, under the guidance of US professor Irene Pepperberg. The bird could say the right words for colors, shapes, and 50 different objects. He even knew when to say "no" (unlike some of us) and phrases including "come here" and "calm down." In addition to talking to us, other birds have their own **languages 016** or song "dialects," which they pass down through generations—or just steal from each other. For example, when New Zealand saddlebacks want to infiltrate a new territory, a male bird will hang around and listen to the neighborhood lingo. As soon as a territory-owning male dies, they swoop in, talking fast to take over the area within 10 minutes. Smooth.

They can fly

This rather obvious ability is the main reason birds have been doing so well for so long. Their impressive party-trick (how cool would it be if we could "take off" in the playground?) means they travel faster and farther in the hunt for food than other animals. From a normal flying height of 500 feet (150 meters), species such as hawks pick out prey or threats with incredible vision. Even a duck (such as the gray teal, above) can reach speeds of 60 mph (100 km/h), while a peregrine falcon can stoop (dive) as fast as 200 mph (320 km/h).

They're superadaptable

Since they evolved from **dinosaurs 012** 150 million years ago, birds have had total command of the skies and more. Key to their survival is their ability to adapt. Penguins (such as the emperor penguin, left) for example, are better suited to the Antarctic cold than any other animal on Earth. Their short feathers trap air and warmth in a snug layer round the body. Desert gray gulls can survive the heat of South America's Atacama Desert, where the sun-blasted sand reaches temperatures of 122° F (50° C), despite having to fly elsewhere to find food.

HOW TO

CONFUSE AN ANGRY SEAGULL

Sometimes the scavengers aren't just after your ice cream. Seagulls will peck people's heads to protect their young. So, if you accidentally upset mama gull, put your sunglasses and your baseball cap on back-to-front. The crazy pecker will think you have two faces and won't know where to aim its beak (just don't blame us when the fashion police arrest you).

"THEY'RE COMING! THEY'RE COMING!"

In 1963, Alfred Hitchcock (1899-1980) adapted Daphne du Maurier's novel *The Birds* into a smash-hit horror film about birds mobbing people in a California coastal village. The fearsome flying creatures become so violent that people are forced to barricade themselves in their homes. Viewers everywhere were terrified since the film showed how defenseless we would be if our winged neighbors turned on us. An English director, Hitchcock made more than 50 feature films 034 during a career that spanned six decades. His other celebrated movies include *Psycho, Rear Window, Vertigo,* and *North by Northwest.* The so-called "master of suspense" continues to influence filmmakers today. Scary stuff.

DID JAMES WATT MAKE THE MOST EXCITING MACHINE EVER?

Your idea of an exciting machine may be the latest game console. But for life-changing inventions, it would be hard to beat the steam engine. Although Scotsman James Watt (1736–1819) didn't actually invent the steam engine, he did transform it from an inefficient machine to a device that helped launch the Industrial Revolution in Britain in the 1760s. This saw the introduction of complex machinery, factories, and new forms of transportation. In 1764, Watt was given an early steam engine to repair. Studying it, he realized that too much of the steam was heating the engine itself rather than powering other machines. He introduced a separate condenser to cool spent steam, so the engine retained heat. His improved model changed people's lives. Powering a **train 159**, it let people travel around quickly for the first time. Attached to factory machinery, it meant products were made faster—so there were more things to buy and sell, more jobs, and more money to be made. By 1850, the revolution was spreading to the rest of the world. Go for it!

THEN
18TH CENTURY

A 12-year-old girl working in an English factory would work bent over a textile machine from six in the morning to seven at night, with only a short break for some lunch.

NOW
21ST CENTURY

The same girl today spends six hours at **school 166**, does an hour's homework, and 10 minutes (maybe) of housework. When would you rather live?

MAKING AN INVENTION WORK FOR YOU

One machine on its own can't change the world—which is where 18th-century industrialist Richard Arkwright (top left) comes in. Arkwright took James Watt's invention and used it in his textile (or cloth) factories (left). This faster, stronger machine was capable of mass-producing textiles (so lots of the same thing was made quickly) and made him more money. Two-thirds of Arkwright's 1,900 workers were children. Some were as young as six (childrens' hands were more nimble than adults and they worked for little money). Arkwright was a very rich man when he died.

In the early 20th century, Henry Ford developed the first mass-produced **motorcar 070**, the Model T. By improving production methods, Ford (bottom left) reduced the time it took to make a Model T from 14 hours to one hour and 33 minutes. Each car was therefore cheaper to make, so Ford could undercut the price of other cars on the market. By 1927, Ford had sold more than 15 million Model T cars. He took something seemingly complicated and expensive and made it accessible to everyone. In the 1980s, **Bill Gates 058** did something similar in personal computing with his software.

TOP FIVE WAYS STEAM IS STILL GOOD FOR YOU

Steam might seem an outdated mode of power, but it still enhances the way we live today

- Gigantic steam turbines in power plants are the source of most of the world's electricity.

- From clothes to car engines, all kinds of everyday items can be cleaned with the help of some trusty steam.

- Steaming vegetables is an excellent way of cooking them, while retaining key **nutrients 176**.

- Inhaling steam can help clear your airways if you're feeling congested with a cold.

- Our coffees would be much less frothy (there would be no cappuccinos) if it weren't for a tasty dose of steam.

Where does God live?

Different religions have different ideas about where to find God, or gods (and what God means). They also have different ways to bring God alive for themselves...

Basilica of St Peter

Charity project

Western Wall

Menorah

Christianity

The **Basilica of St. Peter** in the Vatican (a city-state within Rome) is a vast Christian church. It is named after St. Peter, who was a follower or disciple of Jesus Christ. Christians believe Jesus was the son of God, who died to make up for all the wrong humans have committed. For Roman Catholic Christians, St. Peter was the founder of the Christian Church—all popes (the pope is the Roman Catholic leader) are considered his successors. However, there are more than two billion Christians in the world and many other different types of Christianity, too.

This **charity project** in India is supported by Caritas, a Christian charity organization. For many Christians, doing good works is an important part of their faith. When Christ was alive 2,000 years ago, he said that poor people were blessed and that his followers should serve them. Christians have also been inspired by a story Jesus told about a man (a Samaritan) who helped another man who was supposed to be his enemy. It meant that compassion and love is for everyone, no matter their beliefs or status. Christ often taught through parables (stories that have symbolic meanings), and many of them were about the importance of faith and love.

Judaism

The **Western Wall** in Jerusalem is the remains of a temple destroyed by the **Romans 286** in AD 70 and is considered the holiest place of the Jewish world. Judaism was one of the earliest monotheistic religions (meaning that there is one, all-powerful God to worship). The set of laws that tells Jews how to behave is called the Halakah. This describes what Jews can eat (kosher foods), who they can marry (other Jews), when not to work (Friday evenings and Saturday, the holy day), and how to treat God. Today, there are some 18 million Jews in the world.

The **menorah** is a seven- or nine-candle holder and one of the oldest symbols of the Jewish faith. The candles are lit from right to left during Hanukkah (or Chanukah), the eight-day Jewish Festival of Lights. The celebration takes place in November or December and commemorates the Jews' struggle for religious freedom. A menorah is found in every synagogue, the Jewish center for worship, education, and community. Synagogues are led by a religious leader called a rabbi.

Mosaic tiles

Mecca

River Ganges

Diyas

Islam

Mecca, in **Saudi Arabia 046**, is the spiritual home of Islam. One of the duties of being a Muslim is to make the hajj (religious journey) to Mecca at least once in a lifetime. Around three million people a year make the pilgrimage. While in Mecca, they visit the Kaaba, which is the most sacred building in Islam. Traditionally, they walk around the Kaaba seven times before throwing stones at three pillars that represent the devil. The other duties (known as the Five Pillars) for a Muslim are: praying five times a day, reciting the Islamic creed (acknowledging a belief in God), fasting during Ramadan (the ninth month in the Islamic calendar), and giving part of their earnings to the poor.

A mosque is where Muslims go to pray. But you will never find actual images or pictures of God (known as Allah to Muslims) there. To try to represent Allah visually would be to think you had special access to him and would be wrong. So mosques are often covered with quotations from The Koran, the holy book of Islam. **Mosaics** are used as decoration and to spell out the word "Allah" in Arabic.

Hinduism

Hindus consider the **Ganges River** sacred. It springs from the Himalaya **mountains 074** and flows for about 1,500 miles (2,400 km) across northeast India to the Bay of Bengal. Many Hindus believe the river itself is a goddess called Mother Ganga. Even though it is now very polluted, they come here to wash themselves in her holy water. Mother Ganga is one of many gods or goddesses that Hindus believe in. This belief in more than one God makes Hinduism different from most other modern religions. However, Hindus see all of these gods as aspects of one absolute, overall reality known as Brahman. Believers must follow a proper Hindu lifestyle in order to add up good karma (the sum of a person's actions)—the more they do so, the more they will receive goodness in return. Karma extends over many lives, as Hindus believe in reincarnation (where the spirit is reborn in a new body).

The **diyas** is an earthenware oil lamp traditionally placed in windows and doors during Diwali, the Hindu festival of lights (from late October to mid-November). It marks the Hindu new year, but also celebrates the victory of good over evil and hope for the future.

Bhodi tree

Mandala painting

A Langar

Golden Temple

Buddhism

Around 528 BC, a man sat under a **bhodi tree** in India and was "enlightened" (the tree is also known as the "tree of awakening"). He became known as the Buddha, and for those who follow his teachings—Buddhists— becoming enlightened is their goal. But what is enlightenment? It is an awakening, an awareness of the nature of the universe. Buddhism is different from other religions in that there is no God or gods who created the world. Instead, the emphasis is on personal spiritual development. This involves overcoming hatred and being released from desire.

Buddhists try to stop wanting things by doing something called meditating—this is achieved through chanting or concentrating on their breathing. They attempt to let their desires and thoughts fade away.

A **mandala** is a painting or diagram that represents the universe. They are used in meditation and were introduced by the Buddha as an aid to achieving enlightenment. There are different designs of mandalas—some of which can be made of sand—each teaching a different lesson. They may take many days to complete. However, once finished, they are destroyed. This is a reminder that in life nothing lasts **forever 249**.

Sikhism

The **Golden Temple** at Amristar, in the Punjab region of India, is the holiest of places for Sikhs. Completed in 1604, it is a gurdwara, a place of worship (though Sikhs can pray at any time and in any place). Gurdwaras don't have priests or religious pictures, as God has no physical form. Each one has a copy of the Adi Granth, the Sikh scriptures. The congregation sits on the floor, as everyone is equal before God. Sikhism originated in **India 142** in the 15th century and now has about 20 million followers. It was established by a guru (teacher or prophet) called Nanak. The guru introduced the wearing of

a turban as a sign of religious identity. He also suggested that Sikhs should wear the Five Ks: Kesh (hair that is not cut), Kangha (a wooden comb), Karra (a steel bracelet), Kirpan (a sword), and Kachera (cotton underwear).

A **Langar** is a free food kitchen attached to a gurdwara. Anyone can eat there without paying. Many Sikhs work in the kitchen, because by helping other people they also serve God. It is a part of the three duties of a Sikh: Nam Jaona (always keeping God in mind), Kirt Karna (living honestly), and Vand Chhakna (caring for others).

Remember learning to read?

"What is this?" said John.
"What is that?" said
Katie. Then the words
and pictures spoke.

"Look at me!" said
the spaceman.
"Look at me!" said
the doggy.

Why is the Mona Lisa beautiful?

BEAUTY
IS IN THE EYE OF THE BEHOLDER?

"Everything has its beauty, but not everyone sees it."
(Confucius)

"Beauty is only skin deep."
(Angelina Jolie)

"Beauty is power, a smile is its sword."
(Charles Reade)

"ANYONE WHO KEEPS THE ABILITY TO SEE BEAUTY NEVER GROWS OLD."
(Franz Kafka).

"BEAUTY IS NOT CAUSED. IT IS."
(Emily Dickinson)

"A thing of beauty is a joy forever."
(John Keats)

Don't know what the fuss is all about

It is called the most beautiful painting in the world. But the woman in the *Mona Lisa* looks nothing like the **supermodels 262** on magazine covers today. When Leonardo da Vinci painted her, during the **Italian Renaissance 148**, average-sized women (neither thin nor overweight) were considered the most attractive. This trend started with the ancient Greeks, who thought harmony and balance were essential in all areas of life, including the body. Later, in the 16th and early 17th centuries, rounded, voluptuous women were considered the most beautiful, as seen in paintings by Peter Paul Rubens, a famous Flemish artist. Today, average-sized or rounded women are generally considered average-

looking. Instead, it's often the slimmest people, with the most dangerously jutting cheekbones and tight, toned muscles, who are regarded as beautiful today.

But ideas of beauty don't only change if you're living in a different decade, they depend on where you live, too. In China, for example, having a fat belly symbolizes happiness, luck, and generosity. But in places like Europe it may suggest greed and laziness. Wabi-sabi, on the other hand, is the Japanese idea that beauty exists in imperfect, impermanent or incomplete things (so even your half-done homework can be beautiful!). One thing that almost never changes, however, is that the people who best fit their society's "beauty mold"

are the most desired and, often, the most successful.

The rise of the **mass media 330** during the 20th century has resulted in everyone's ideas of beauty becoming more and more similar. Now, people no longer just want to look like the prettiest person in their village or on their street. They want to look like the amazingly good-looking (and digitally enhanced) celebrities they see on TV, in magazines, and in the movies—even if they're from the other side of the world. Crazy, huh?

WHAT'S THE BIG DEAL ABOUT DA VINCI'S PAINTING?

The *Mona Lisa* is just a portrait of a woman making a funny face, isn't it? Yet few works are as famous. Its power may be due to **Leonardo da Vinci's 254** techniques. For example, if you look carefully, the corners of the mouth seem to move up and down. This may be because he painted the **smile 078** slightly blurry, so it seems clearest in your peripheral vision (when you look from the corner of your eye). But perhaps the big deal about the *Mona Lisa* is that it raises questions: its power and its beauty lie in its lasting mystery.

The things we do for beauty

+ LARGE EYES >
+ POINTY NOSE >
+ 70% WAIST >

= BEAUTIFUL

Get sliced up, reshaped, and sewn back together

In 2004, nearly 12 million people had cosmetic surgery in the US alone. Treatment can be dangerous, expensive, and gruesome. In a nose job, nasal bones are cut and can be deliberately broken. After-effects can include permanent scars and difficulty breathing. The "ideal" nose can cost upward of $4,000.

Inject poison into our foreheads

Botulinum toxin (Botox) is a poison created by bacteria in the soil. It is so toxic that 100 grams is enough to kill every human on earth. Injections of small doses have become popular as a way of softening facial lines. Botox works by paralyzing (freezing) muscles for months. Other wrinkle treatments are derived from cow collagen and even rooster combs (their fleshy crests).

Give up chocolate (or try to)

Diets to lose weight work when we take in less energy than we use. This energy comes from food. Eating less of fatty and sugary foods, such as chocolate, can help weight loss. Increased body image awareness and health concerns (an estimated billion people worldwide are obese) have made diets very popular in the past 20 years.

THE PSYCHOLOGY OF BEAUTY

Evolutionary scientists argue that physical beauty boils down to pure science. Healthy-looking men and women with symmetrical faces and strong bone structure are more attractive, regardless of their cultural heritage. **Evolution 206** suggests that attractive people are those that show signs that they will have strong children. Another evolutionary sign of a beautiful woman is a 70 percent waist-to-hip ratio (their waist is 70 percent of the size of their hips). This supposedly shows a woman's ability to have children. Child-like facial features (large eyes, round cheeks, and a small nose) also increase attractiveness. This might be because a younger person has more time to have children, and therefore is more likely to pass genes on to descendants. This all happens without you being aware—as though you have been programmed.

HOW TO

DRAW A FACE BEAUTIFULLY

It's much easier than drawing an ugly one. The secret is to make all the features completely symmetrical. So, after you have drawn a face shape, draw a line straight down the middle. Then, use these proportions to line everything up perfectly:

Eyes: halfway between the top of the head and the chin.
Bottom of the nose: exactly halfway between the eyes and the chin.
Mouth: halfway between the nose and the chin.
Top of the ears: line up with the center of the eyes.

Corners of the mouth: line up with the center of the eyes.
Bottom of the ears: line up with the bottom of the nose. Now you have your very own *Mona Lisa*—time to add a smile!

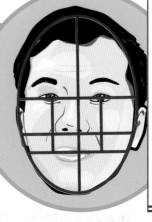

WHO WAS THAT LADY WITH THE MYSTERIOUS SMILE, ANYWAY?

Mona Lisa was probably a person called Lisa Gherardini. She was a young Italian woman, married to a wealthy Italian silk merchant and important government figure. But there are more doubtful theories as to her identity. She could be Isabella of Aragon, the Duchess of Milan. Or, she might just be Leonardo himself. If you take a self-portrait drawing of the artist, then merge it using a computer with an image of the *Mona Lisa*, the two faces line up perfectly. Wasn't he pretty?

How to make this outfit the height of fashion

Put it on the catwalk

Today, Paris is not the only fashion center with famous designers—New York, **London 159**, and Milan have all joined the gang. Twice a year, designers show their new fashion collections at special shows—there are the spring/summer shows and the fall/winter shows. These take place months before the actual season. For example, fall/winter collections are shown in spring. This allows time for the top stores (whose buyers sit in the front rows) to place their orders, and for the factories to stitch the items together. Journalists also attend the shows and write about them in magazines and **newspapers 330**. Then the readers know what will be in fashion.

Sell it through a chain

Most people buy clothes from chain stores. Sometimes, these look mysteriously like designer clothes. And sometimes they are—many top designers create affordable off-the-rack look at the catwalks, then quickly copy these clothes. However, regular stores also different in design, and probably not as good quality, but cheaper. It's a knock-on effect that's all part of the fashion world.

Make it by hand in Paris

Paris has been the fashion capital since the 19th century. While ordinary folks bought their clothes from neighborhood tailors, wealthy people got theirs made at fashionable ones. If these tailors were famous and lived in Paris, they became known internationally as "couturiers" (that's just French for "tailor"). All the other clothes-makers copied their designs. In the 1920s, an elegant French woman named Coco Chanel invented modern clothes for women—regular-looking (but very chic) skirts and pants. Today, you can still buy couture clothes made by hand in Paris, but it helps if you are a pop star, since they are very expensive.

Keep it retro

The true test of fashion is not how quickly it goes out of fashion or for how long it's in fashion, but how often it comes back into fashion. Styles from other decades get **recycled 310**. They are called "retro" looks because they are retrospective (they look to the past!). There's not much fashion that hasn't been seen before. Watch out! You could be dressing just like your mom and dad did when they were teenagers.

Get someone famous to wear it

Celebrities are a good source of publicity. Having **famous 218** people sitting in the front row of a fashion show helps boost "profile"—it gets written about in the press, and the star's glamour rubs off on the label. Also, if an actress wears a dress, say, to the Academy Awards, there will be lots of photographs of it in the magazines. It's free advertising for the designer (and a free frock for the actress).

Sew in a label

Fashion is all about labels. There are two types of label in a piece of clothing. One tells the brand label—the other—the brand label—it was has boring instructions about size and washing. The other—the brand label—it was who created it. If it is a top designer label, such as Prada or Ralph Lauren, it was probably expensive. This isn't because the clothes are hand-made (they are made in factories). People pay more to wear a designer name—it has value beyond the actual worth of the garment (you look cool, or at least rich, because you wear it).

Surf the trend

Fashionable clothes relate to current trends (what's hip and happening), which is why everyone seems to bring out the same style at the same time. It's not that designers are copying each other, but because they are influenced by similar things—the films, magazines, music, and whatever else is going on. It's called zeitgeist (which means "the spirit of the times" in German).

Ready to wear

Ready-to-wear was invented after **World War II 178** when fashion-followers in Europe and the US realized that it was silly to spend such a lot of cash on couture. Also, **teenagers 276** didn't want to dress like their parents and demanded their own styles. In the 1960s, Parisian designers like Yves Saint Laurent decided they would design stylish clothes and then get a factory to mass-produce them.

Usually, a famous fashion label also produces a range of perfume. Most people can't afford to buy designer labels (a designer handbag can cost as much as a small car), so they might buy the smelly stuff instead. They get the same designer label at a fraction of the price, and the designer makes hefty profits from it.

FASHION STINKS!

WHERE ARE ALL THE CATS?

In the US, the elevated, narrow stage the models walk up and down at shows is called a runway (the models walk in a straight line like an airplane preparing for takeoff). In the UK, it's a catwalk (it's so narrow that only a cat could walk it without taking a tumble), and in Australia it's a parade (models everywhere are trained to walk in a special way to show off the clothes).

TO PLAY:

Grab a counter, fetch a friend, and find some dice. Each player has his or her own country (make up a name for it, if you like). Take turns rolling the dice and move your counter. The first to establish a democracy wins.

Independent courts are a good thing for democracy. In the 2000 US Presidential election between George W. Bush (left) and Al Gore (right), the outcome was so close that it ended up with the Supreme Court (the highest court in the US). This decided that Bush had won.

CENSORSHIP

This is when the authorities force the media 330 only to report what they want them to. It means voters can't find out the truth and is bad for democracy.

MOVE 3 PLACES BACK

CONSTITUTIONAL EQUALITY

Everyone of adult age has the right to vote. No one can be excluded because of race, gender, or whether they have unfortunate hair.

MOVE 2 PLACES FORWARD

LET'S PLAY DEMOCRACY

A democracy is a political system, first thought up by the **ancient Greeks 240**. It is often described as government by the people: in a modern democracy, everyone can vote in elections, so everyone has an equal say.

REGULAR ELECTIONS

Rules are set up to make sure that there are limits on how long a government can govern before more elections are held. This helps prevent dictatorships, where the rulers can't be voted out.

MOVE 1 PLACE FORWARD

FREEDOM OF SPEECH

Your country passes laws so people can openly express their opinions. Everyone gets to make up their own mind about what they believe.

LEAP FORWARD ALONG THE BLUE LINE

START HERE

COUP D'ETAT

Disaster! The government has been overthrown by the army in a coup d'état (French for "a blow to the state"). No one gets to vote for anything—the military is in charge.

GO BACK TO THE START

In 1967, a group of army officers seized power in Greece through a coup d'état. Their leader, Georgios Papadopoulos, became prime minister. Democracy was finally restored in 1974.

RIGGED VOTING

The election has been set up to favor a particular political party. So it can't be a democracy.

GO BACK ALONG THE PINK LINE

THE ELECTION

Congratulations. Your country holds free and fair elections. A democratically chosen government takes power.

VOTING SYSTEM

The United Nations sends inspectors who confirm that your country's voting system is fair, and that people can cast their vote in private (known as a secret ballot).

MOVE 3 PLACES FORWARD

CORRUPTION

Uh-oh. The police, judges, and politicians take bribes and bend the rules to gain wealth and influence. This is bad for democracy, where everyone is supposed to obey the same laws.

MOVE 3 PLACES BACK

Until the early 20th century, women were not allowed to vote in **Britain 200**. Campaigners, known as suffragettes, struggled to win this right for women. In 1918, after years of sometimes violent struggle, British women over the age of 30 were finally given the right to vote. American suffragettes won their voting rights in 1920.

POLITICAL PARTIES

Competing political parties are set up. They publish manifestos. These set out their policies and goals— what they will do if elected into government. They are allowed to criticize each other.

MOVE 1 PLACE FORWARD

Is it raining?

Uh-oh, there must be clouds around. They form when water condenses (turns from a gas into drops of liquid). As the air cools, the condensed droplets increase in size until they are heavy enough to plop down as rain. **Gravity 024** then pulls the drops to the ground. Rain is one form of precipitation—others are snow, sleet, and hail. These occur when it's cold enough for the water droplets to freeze. Any region which receives very little precipitation is called a desert. The driest desert in the world is the Atacama, on the coast of Chile. On average, it only receives 0.004 inches (0.01 cm) of rain per year.

What is the weather doing right now?

Is it windy?

Wind is the air moving. It's caused by differences in air pressure. When air heats up, it rises. As it moves upward, the air underneath becomes thinner—this is low pressure. If the air nearby isn't heated as much, that air will be thicker (high pressure). The air is pushed from the high pressure zone into the low pressure area, creating a wind. The fastest winds are found in tornadoes (up to 300 mph or 480 km/h). The Asian Monsoon (from the **Arabic 046** word "mausin," meaning season) is not as strong as that, but affects a large area across southern Asia. It brings heavy rain in the summer months, but reverses direction in the winter and provokes a dry phase. The Doldrums, meanwhile, is an area at the equator known for its lack of wind—boats can be stuck there for days.

Weather forecasting

Scientists called meteorologists predict the weather by constantly measuring things like the wind, rain, clouds, and sunlight. Thousands of weather stations around the world, plus satellite and radar readings, record weather conditions. These measurements are crunched by superpowerful **computers 058** to produce a forecast—either for a few days or for months ahead (called a long-range forecast). Accurate prediction is tricky, because weather is so complex and interconnected (what happens in one part of the world affects the conditions somewhere else).

How weather affects us

What the weather is doing can change your state of mind. Heat waves can make people bad tempered and give them headaches. High temperatures also provoke the release of chemicals in the body that make it hard to concentrate (as you may have noticed during math class). On the other hand, sunlight can help raise spirits and boost energy.

Are there any clouds?

Clouds are made of millions of tiny water droplets (or ice crystals if they are very high up). Air always holds some water as vapor (gas)—so you can't see it. As it rises, it cools and water in the air condenses to form clouds. These are classified by type, such as "cumulus" (meaning they are piled up). If clouds are "cumulonimbus"—large and dense at high altitudes—you could have a thunderstorm on your hands. Lightning is a giant spark of **electricity 300**, caused by electrical discharges between clouds or between a cloud and the ground. Vibrations caused by the energy release are thunder (coming after the lightning because it travels at the speed of sound, which is much slower than the speed of light). If you count the seconds between lightning and thunder, you can tell how far away (or close!) a storm is—each second is equivalent to a distance of 1,000 ft (300 m).

Why the weather repeats itself

The seasons (spring, summer, fall, winter) are caused by differences in how the Sun heats the Earth during the year. The Earth is tilted on its axis. When the North Pole is pointing toward the Sun, the Northern Hemisphere receives more sunlight and the Southern Hemisphere less (making it summer in the north and winter in the south). Six months later, everything is reversed and the Notherners need their coats and bobble hats.

HOW TO

PREDICT THE WEATHER

Forecasting is a modern science. But for centuries, people relied on "weather lore," based on observations of the natural world. Many examples are simply **folk tales 014**, but some have a basis in science.

• "Clear Moon, frost soon": If there are no clouds, the Earth cools more rapidly and frost may form.

• "Closed pine cone, rain is on its way": It closes to protect the seeds in moist air.

• "Red sky at night, shepherds' delight. Red sky in the morning, shepherds take warning": The red sunset indicates good weather could be heading in from the west. A red sunrise warns that rain is on its way.

GOING, GOING, GONE?

Please help us find our **BEAUTIFUL CYCAD TREE!**

HAVE YOU SEEN OUR WELL-LOVED MARINE TURTLE?

HAVE YOU SEEN

THE GIANT PANDAS?

MISSING:
Gorilla

FOUND

NEW ZEALAND STORM PETREL

THE GIANT PANDAS?

LAST SEEN:
In southwest <u>China 118</u>. Now, there are only 1,600 left. Their survival is so threatened, they may become extinct (all die out for good).

REASONS FOR DISAPPEARANCE:
Large areas of natural forest where pandas live have been cleared for <u>**agriculture 086**</u>. Plus, some people hunt pandas to stuff and display them.

WILL RESPOND TO:
Offerings of bamboo. Pandas spend up to 14 hours a day eating the stuff, even though their ancestors could eat meat (they're veggies by choice).

CHANCES OF SURVIVAL:
Quite high. China is investing around $1 billion a year in their conservation, scientific assessments, and protecting forest reserves.

Gorilla

LAST SEEN:
The four subspecies of gorilla all live in Africa. They are some of the world's most endangered animals.

REASONS FOR DISAPPEARANCE:
Human threats, such as illegal hunting for food and body parts. Africa's growing human population is spreading into gorilla territory. The rain forests, the gorilla's habitat, are being chopped down. People also pass on diseases to gorillas. The apes have not developed the immunities (ability to fight illness) that humans have and perish once they become infected.

WILL RESPOND TO:
A cozy nest. Gorillas spend a lot of their time sleeping. They're placid vegetarians, unlike the scary creatures portrayed in <u>**films 034**</u>.

CHANCES OF SURVIVAL:
Shaky. Even if they are not being poached, they are often killed accidentally by traps set for other animals.

CYCAD TREE

LAST SEEN:
In Africa, Asia, and Central America. Now, 52 percent of cycad species (they look like palm trees, with a branchless trunk and a spiky crown of leaves) are threatened. They are the most endangered plant group known.

REASONS FOR DISAPPEARANCE:
Cycads live in endangered habitats such as tropical forests, and reproduce infrequently.

WILL RESPOND TO:
Beetles and small bees. Recent research has revealed that little <u>**insects 232**</u> carry cycad pollen between trees.

CHANCES OF SURVIVAL:
Medium. International law forbids some cycad seed trade. Steps have been made to protect their natural environments, and breeding programs set up at cycad nurseries. Genebanks have also been created to store genetic information, in case any species dies out.

MARINE TURTLE

LAST SEEN:
Swimming the seas or crawling onto tropical beaches around the world. Now, six out of the seven species are endangered.

REASONS FOR DISAPPEARANCE:
People have built over turtles' nesting beaches and destroyed coral reefs where they find food. Turtles are killed for their meat, shell, eggs, and calipee (their body fat—used in soup). They get tangled in fishing nets and litter, and run over by boats. New predators, such as dogs and racoons, raid their beaches. Could it be any worse for them?

WILL RESPOND TO:
Light. Under natural circumstances, the sea is the lightest place on the beach at night, as no vegetation shades it from moon or starlight. Newborn turtles head for light to reach water. However, building and road lights confuse them, and they often head inland.

CHANCES OF SURVIVAL:
Slim. 50,000 marine turtles are killed annually in southeast Asia and the South Pacific. They face so many threats, it will take huge conservation efforts to reverse their decline.

NEW ZEALAND STORM PETREL

LAST SEEN:
This sea bird hadn't been seen since 1850 and was presumed extinct. It was then spotted in January 2003. Had it come back from the dead?

REASONS FOR DISAPPEARANCE:
The petrel breeds on the Barrier Islands, off the coast of New Zealand, which used to have a large rat population. The rodents ate the birds' eggs and young. Now, the rats are in decline, so the petrels can reestablish themselves.

WILL RESPOND TO:
Mashed-up fish. This tempted one onto a fishing boat, where it was rediscovered.

WHERE HAVE THEY BEEN?
Good question. The species may have survived for 150 years on the predator-free Hauraki Islands nearby (now that's what you call an extended vacation).

THE 5 MOST DANGEROUS BITS OF LITTER

PLASTIC BAGS

If left floating in the ocean, sea turtles mistake them for their favorite food—jellyfish. They swallow the bag, then suffocate, choke, or starve.

SUPERMARKET CARTS

Believe it or not, farm animals and wildlife are often found stuck in them and badly injured. (That's before they've been packaged and put on supermarket shelves.)

SIX-PACK RINGS (PLASTIC THAT HOLDS CANS TOGETHER)

These cause around six million seabird deaths and more than 100,000 sea mammal deaths annually. The plastic takes 450 years to decompose.

POLYSTYRENE

Animals mistake the material (used for disposable cups or protective parts of boxes) for food. It clogs up their stomachs and poisons them. Polystyrene never fully decomposes.

DOG POOP

This is animal litter and it's dangerous to us humans. The toxocara canis roundworm is found in around 50 percent of dog droppings. It can cause a dangerous infection. Watch where you tread.

Quick goodbyes:
The big waves of extinction

IN THE HISTORY OF THE world, there have been five "extinction periods." These are times when high numbers of animals and plants have become extinct relatively quickly. They may have occurred due to climate change or natural disasters, such as tsunamis caused by a large asteroid or comet crashing into Earth. The "big five" occurred at the end of the Ordovician, Devonian, Permian, Triassic, and Cretaceous periods. The last wave happened 65 million years ago when the **dinosaurs 162** died out. Experts say we are now in the sixth extinction crisis. Species are currently dying out up to 1,000 times quicker than they would at a natural rate. Unlike other periods, this one is caused entirely by one species—humans. Gulp.

WHY BIODIVERSITY MATTERS

BIODIVERSITY describes the variety of all living things on Earth. Animals and plants are dependent upon one another in many different ways. For example, birds eat fruit grown on trees in rain forests. After digestion, they process it into poop, which they drop everywhere, including far-off parts of the forest. This helps distribute the trees' seeds widely. In biodiversity, if one species dies out, the habitat becomes unbalanced. So, if there were no birds, the trees could not spread as easily. Biodiversity is currently being disturbed in the North Sea, the natural habitat for plankton (tiny floating organisms). **Global warming 266** is heating up the ocean, forcing the plankton to move to colder waters farther north. In turn, this movement is drastically affecting all other sea life, including sea birds, as plankton forms the base of the whole ocean food chain.

COULD JURASSIC PARK HAPPEN?

IN THE 1993 HOLLYWOOD film, scientists re-create dinosaurs using a sample of **DNA 258** found in the blood of ancient mosquitos. The blood-sucking insects had bitten a dinosaur and then immediately become preserved in amber (fossilized tree resin or sap) for millions of years. But could this happen in real life? NO! Even if such a greedy mosquito were miraculously discovered, DNA would not remain intact for longer than 10,000 years. But if it did survive, creating a dinosaur would involve linking all the DNA bits together in the correct order—without knowing what that order was.

NUMBER OF SPECIES DISCOVERED EVERY YEAR
15,000

NUMBER OF SPECIES CURRENTLY THREATENED WITH EXTINCTION
15,000

Answers from page 079: B and C are faking their smiles.

United Kingdom

Population
**60.4 million—
going up**

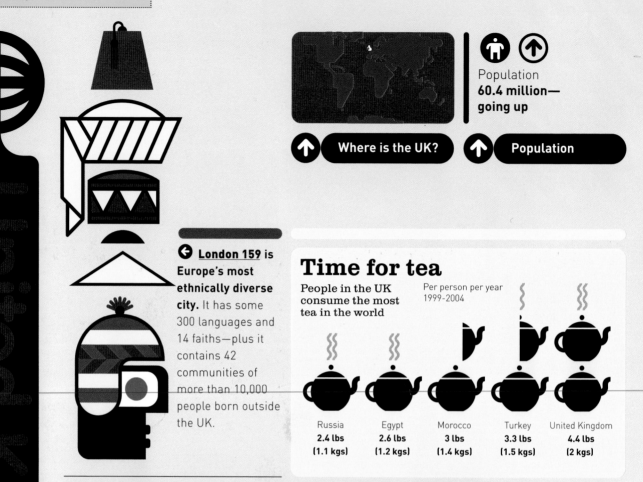

↑ **Where is the UK?**

↑ **Population**

← **London 159** is Europe's most **ethnically diverse city.** It has some 300 languages and 14 faiths—plus it contains 42 communities of more than 10,000 people born outside the UK.

Time for tea

People in the UK consume the most tea in the world

Per person per year 1999-2004

Russia	Egypt	Morocco	Turkey	United Kingdom
2.4 lbs (1.1 kgs)	**2.6 lbs (1.2 kgs)**	**3 lbs (1.4 kgs)**	**3.3 lbs (1.5 kgs)**	**4.4 lbs (2 kgs)**

Population density

England has the highest population density in the UK—and Scotland has the lowest

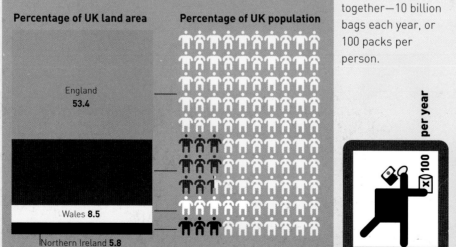

Percentage of UK land area

England
53.4

Wales **8.5**

Northern Ireland **5.8**

Percentage of UK population

❯ People in the UK eat more **potato chips 176** than the rest of Europe put together—10 billion bags each year, or 100 packs per person.

per year

x100

❯ The first English Duke was created in 1337. There are more than 3,000 people with **hereditary titles** (passed through generations), including the royal family.

France has about the same size population as the UK, but it is more than **twice the size**

UK + UK = France

↑ **Nation knowledge**

Soccer

The English Premiership is the richest football league in Europe with revenues of 2.5 billion dollars.

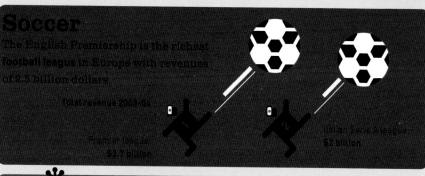

Total revenue 2003–04

Premier League **$3.7 billion**

Italian Serie A league **$2 billion**

Dialects

=

At least 34 different dialects (varieties of language used by people from particular areas) are spoken in the UK, including Cockney in London, Glamorganshire in west Wales, and Brummy in Birmingham. Cockney uses phrases that rhyme with words, instead of the words themselves (so, "frog and toad" means road). It was first spoken by thieves during the 1500s, as a secret code.

Tourist sights

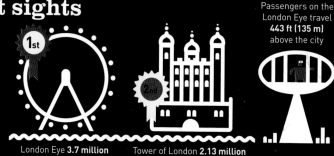

The London Eye is the most popular paid-for tourist attraction in the UK

Number of visitors in 2004

1st

2nd

Passengers on the London Eye travel **443 ft (135 m)** above the city

London Eye **3.7 million**

Tower of London **2.13 million**

Annual rainfall

Belfast	Glasgow	Manchester	Bergen
38½ in	**36½ in**	**34¼ in**	**81½ in**
(978) mm	(931) mm	(873) mm	(2,074) mm

↑ **Belfast is the wettest city in the UK,** followed by Glasgow and Manchester. But Belfast gets half the rain that hits Bergen in Norway—the wettest place in Europe.

↓ To gain a **taxi driver's license in central London,** drivers must have a **knowledge** of the 25,000 streets within a six mile (10 km) radius of Charing Cross train station. It takes two to four years to learn.

↓ **People in the UK buy more music than anyone else.** They spend $3.7 billion on recorded **music 305** every year.

TAXI

the ALIENS are Here!

WHERE? You probably haven't seen them as they are found in the depths of the seas and oceans. Less than 10 percent of this saltwater world has been explored—we know more about the geography of the **Moon 170**. The oceans are, on average, about 2.5 miles (4 km) deep. And they cover more than 70 percent of the world's surface (the Pacific alone is larger than the Earth's total land mass). Which means, there's a lot of room for weird and wonderful life forms.

MOST of our knowledge of ocean wildlife comes from what we eat—the **fish 208**, crab, lobster, and prawns that end up on our plates. But there are thought to be more than 30 million species living in the seas and oceans, most of these undiscovered. Many have peculiar lifestyles—and rather funny names.

TAKE the coffinfish: it dwells on the ocean floor and walks on small leglike fins. Or the Pacific spookfish that uses its long snout like a metal detector to scan for the electrical impulses of its prey on the sea floor. The anglerfish (below) has a "rod" that it can wiggle to lure prey nearby so it can gobble them up—whole. Life has seemingly spread everywhere in the ocean. In 1960, a submersible called the *Trieste* went to the deepest known point—the Mariana Trench, 36,089 ft (11,000 m) down—and saw fish.

THERE are creatures that make their own light chemically. This process is called bioluminescence (try saying that with a mouthful of mussels). It's rare among land animals (fireflies and some worms can do it), but popular in the ocean (check out the beaming deep sea squid, above). The black dragonfish uses the technique like a flashlight to find food. Other creatures use it for defense, such as the shrimp that vomits a glowing cloud to distract predators. Bioluminescent organs on the body can also make effective **camouflage 128**. Seawater scatters light, making the creature hard to see.

CHEMOSYNTHESIS (the process of creating energy from chemical reactions) is a whole other life system that has developed on the very bottom of the oceans. Tubeworms, fish, crabs, and some 300 other species have all adapted to life in darkness. Plants can't survive because they need sunlight to **photosynthesize 010**—and there's none at these depths. Instead, the deep sea life feeds on bacteria. Now, for the really crazy part… Hydrothermal vents are formed when the Earth's **tectonic plates 318** crack. This releases hot fluid. Also released are minerals (hydrogen sulfides) that feed the bacteria that feed the fish. This life system was only discovered in the last 30 years. Before, scientists had dismissed it as an impossibility.

SEA DEPTHS

ZONE:
Photic—sunlight can reach
DEPTH:
Upper 650 ft (200 m)
LIVES HERE:
Most marine life,
including nearly
all phytoplankton

ZONE:
Mesopelagic—
twilight zone
DEPTH:
650-3,300 ft
(200-1,000 m)
LIVES HERE:
Black dragonfish,
tubeworms

ZONE:
Bathypelagic—deep sea
DEPTH:
Below 3,300 ft (1,000 m)
LIVES HERE:
Pacific spookfish,
gulper eels

HOW HUMANS MAKE THE OCEAN WEIRDER (AND MORE DANGEROUS)

OVERFISHING

The oceans are being depleted because of man's appetite for seafood. Two-thirds of species in the north Atlantic are being overfished. Fish that used to be abundant, such as cod, have been fished almost to extinction in some places. Lobsters— which can live for 70 years and never stop growing—could once be found off New England weighing 20 lbs (9 kg). Now, the average weight is just over 2 lbs (1 kg), because they have no time to grow. One of the worst aspects of industrial fishing is the gigantic trawling nets that sweep up everything in their path. As much as a quarter of the fish caught in nets is unwanted. Nets also entangle larger creatures, such as **dolphins 130** and sharks, drowning them.

POLLUTION

For decades, the US, Russia, China, and European nations, among others, dumped canisters full of radioactive waste into the sea. It was a case of "out of sight, out of mind," as no one knows what effect any leaking canisters would have on the wildlife (Godzilla-style mutations are unlikely, though). Farm chemicals and toxic (poisonous) materials from factories end up in the ocean. This is not only bad news for the fish, but humans, too. Chemicals, such as lead, get into the **food chain 310** and contaminate the seafood people eat, causing health problems. Other major polluters are oil spills (around 250,000 sea birds were killed by the *Exxon Valdez* spill in Alaska in 1989), garbage dumping and gasoline from boat engines.

GLOBAL WARMING

Climate change (**global warming 266**) is also affecting the ocean. Warmer waters damage or kill algae (stuff like sea weed and kelp) that some fish feed on. There are then fewer algae-eating fish around, which means less food for those animals that would normally eat them. This has a knock-on effect up the food chain. Rising sea levels, caused by melting ice caps, may also affect the delicate balance of the ocean life.

CAREFUL WHERE YOU SWIM

BERMUDA TRIANGLE

This area of the Atlantic Ocean between Puerto Rico, Bermuda, and Florida has a reputation for supernatural disappearances. In 1945, a flight of US naval planes was lost, and many other planes and vessels have disappeared. However, the US Coast Guard says that there is no evidence to suggest strange goings-on.

MARY CELESTE

In 1872, a cargo ship, the *Mary Celeste*, left New York harbor and was later found adrift in the Atlantic Ocean. There was no one on board, and one lifeboat was missing. Everything else on the ship was untouched. Why she was abandoned is a mystery. The legend grew after Arthur Conan Doyle (creator of Sherlock Holmes) wrote about it.

Spot the (real) mermaid

Answer: No. 2, the manatee (because sailors used to mistake them for mermaids — maybe they all needed glasses).

HOW *SHIPPING* MADE NAGASAKI

Nagasaki is a port city on the southern tip of Japan. The first contact between Europeans and Japanese was in Nagasaki—when Portuguese ships landed in 1549. But foreign influences worried Japan's rulers and contact with foreigners was banned in 1637. The only exception was in Nagasaki. The city fully reopened to overseas trade in 1859 and rapidly became Japan's principal shipping port. By the 20th century, some seriously large ships were sailing out of Nagasaki. The

Musashi battleship, launched in 1940, was the largest and heaviest ever constructed. After World War II, Nagasaki began competing with cities around the world to build cargo ships. In the 1960s, __Japan 028__ and other countries including the US made vast ships, known as supertankers. Each was capable of transporting over 250,000 tons of oil. Today, tankers such as the *Tenryu*, built in Nagasaki in 1999 to carry 281,000 tons of oil, are the largest moving things ever built. Japanese shipbuilders are

now planning computer-guided supertankers that could cross the oceans with no need for a crew.

Luxury cruise ships also come supersized. In 2004, the *Diamond Princess* (left) was completed in Nagasaki. At 113,000 tons, it is one of the largest passenger ships in the world, with room for almost 4,000 passengers and crew.

BIG ISN'T ALWAYS SO BRIGHT

At every moment of every day, tankers are shipping oil around the globe. Slow-moving, but very big, they have to be sailed very carefully. In March 1989, a supertanker called the *Exxon Valdez* ran aground on the Alaskan coast. Its hull cracked and 35,000 tons of crude oil gushed out across an area of outstanding natural beauty. The bill for the cleanup operation was $3.6 billion. It wasn't the first such disaster, but it was the most expensive. Since then, all tankers have been built with double hulls to combat leaks.

THREE HEARTY PIRATES

GRACE O'MALLEY (c.1530-c.1603)
Grace was born into a wealthy Irish family, but engaged in piracy against English ships throughout her life. She was called the "Pirate Queen of Ireland."

BARTHOLOMEW ROBERTS (1682-1722)
Known as "Black Bart," Roberts was the most successful pirate in history, capturing 456 vessels. He was also one of the gentlest pirates in history—he hated cruelty, swearing, and drunkenness.

JOHN BOYSIE SINGH (1908-1957)
Born in Trinidad, Singh was a gangster and gambler before turning to piracy. From 1947 to 1956, he and his gang terrorized the waters between Trinidad and Venezuela. He was caught and hanged in 1957.

THE DAY THE BOMB DROPPED

During World War II, on August 6, 1945, the US dropped an __atomic bomb 060__ on Hiroshima, a seaport. Three days later, another was dropped on Nagasaki, because of its importance as a shipyard and naval base. The Nagasaki bomb, codenamed

Fat Man, destroyed a third of the city and killed 40,000 people. In the face of such devastation, Japan surrendered and the __war 174__ was soon over. Nagasaki was rebuilt, though some rubble remains as a memorial. The Hiroshima and Nagasaki bombs are the only nuclear attacks in world history to date.

THE PANAMA CANAL, OPENED IN 1914, CUTS THROUGH CENTRAL AMERICA, JOINING THE ATLANTIC AND PACIFIC OCEANS. SHIPS HAVE TO PAY A TOLL DEPENDING ON THEIR SIZE AND CARGO. THE SMALLEST TOLL EVER PAID WAS 36 CENTS, BY ATHLETE RICHARD HALLIBURTON, WHO SWAM THE CANAL IN 1928.

It is fast, immensely powerful — and lethal.
It is incredibly maneuverable, with awesome acceleration.
It has a precise and coordinated detection capability.
It has a deadly weapons system.
It is defensively camouflaged.
It is feared by its enemies.
It has been 5.5 million years in the making.

What is it?

EVOLUTION AT WORK: NATURAL SELECTION

Have you ever been told that you have your **father's** eyes or your grandma's smile? Well, it just might be true—**you are a descendant** of your parents and grandparents, and they have passed down some of their characteristics to you. Scientists have developed a theory that explains how every **species** alive today is a revised version of an earlier one. Go back far enough (seven million years) and you'll have the same ancestor that **apes** have (making chimps your cousins). Go back really far (three billion years) and your (extremely) distant ancestor is little more than a blob of bacteria (pretty easy to buy a birthday present for). This is what evolution is all about.

How we have evolved from simple structures such as bacteria into complex multicellular **organisms** is all about **natural selection**. It happens like this: in nature, not all plants and animals survive in their **ENVIRONMENT**. Some get eaten, die of disease, or starve. Those that adapt best to their environment (a furry coat in the winter, for instance, or good eyesight to spot dangers) have the best chance of living long enough to find a partner and mate. The **offspring** will then inherit the adaptations that helped their parents survive, making them more likely to survive themselves. With each new **generation**, the good adaptations become more common and the species gets better at coping with its environment.

Evolution also works by **mutation**—where the **genes 258** (the instructions carried in cells) of the offspring are different from the parents'. This difference may be **tiny**, but if it is enough to help the individual survive (and reproduce); the change can be passed on to future generations, too. By the way, the evolutionary process is still at work—in millions of years, very different creatures could be roaming the planet.

A.

Though it may sound like a fearsome man-made weapon, the answer is, in fact, a cheetah. Over millions of years, the cheetah has adapted to its habitat in Africa and Asia superbly well. It has developed a flexible spine, powerful heart, and thin body to make it the fastest of hunters. Keen eyes help it spot a meal, then strong jaws suffocate its prey. And its camouflaged, spotted coat allows it to arrive for dinner almost unannounced. The reason the cheetah is so good at what it does is that over the ages, cheetahs that didn't do as well at catching food were less likely to survive and, most importantly, to have offspring. This process, of evolution through natural selection, is the reason everything living is here today—including you.

EVOLUTIONARY TIMELINE

OR HOW LIFE GOT FROM A SIMPLE CELLULAR BLOB TO YOU

3.5 BILLION
First simple organisms—little more than basic cells—appear in early oceans

WHAT ARE THE INGREDIENTS FOR LIFE?

Scientists know which substances were around 3.5 billion years ago to create life—methane, water, ammonia, plus a dash of energy in the form of lightning. But experiments using these elements to create life from scratch have failed. Some scientists wonder if primitive life arrived on asteroids from space, while various **religions 185** offer other answers.

HOW MR. DARWIN CHANGED THE WORLD

CHARLES DARWIN (1809-1882) would probably have been an unknown minister instead of a world-famous naturalist if it hadn't been for his decision to take a voyage around the world in 1831. The man who made revolutionary ideas of evolution famous embarked on a ship called the *Beagle* and, though a poor sailor, spent the next five years at sea. He came back to Britain with crates of specimens from all kinds of exotic places, but didn't produce his theory of natural selection for nearly 30 years (it took a while to go through the specimens—and besides, he had 10 kids to bring up). *On the Origin of Species by Means of Natural Selection* caused a huge uproar when published in 1859, especially its suggestion that humans were related to apes. Ministers everywhere were very unhappy. Though the book was a sell-out, it wasn't until the mid-20th century that Darwin's ideas became widely accepted, when people understood more about how genes work.

MILITARY ARMS RACES

USSR vs. USA

For 50 years from 1949 both <u>superpowers 260</u> strove for global superiority in nuclear weapons (and both ended up with enough bombs to annihilate each other many times over).

BRITAIN vs. GERMANY

In the run-up to <u>World War I 178</u>, each country spent millions on having more of the biggest and best battleships than the other. Then they slaughtered each other by the millions in France and Belgium.

FRANCE vs. GERMANY

Also in the run-up to World War I, a contest was on for who could mobilize (be ready for war) the quickest. It was believed that Germany could be prepared in two days, while France could only manage it in three.

CASTLES vs. SIEGES

During the <u>Middle Ages 148</u>, castle designers and attackers attempted to outdo each other with superior defenses (stronger walls, hot oil to pour on soldiers) battling against extreme assault weapons (siege towers, battering rams, huge catapults). What fun.

THE BILLIONS-YEAR-OLD ARMS RACE

In a military arms race, two or more countries compete to gain an advantage by getting bigger or better weapons than the others. An evolutionary "arms race" is pretty similar—except that evolutionary time runs over thousands of years and it is the process of natural selection that improves the weapons. Cheetahs become better at catching gazelles because the ones that are faster, with better eyesight and sharper teeth are more likely to survive and breed. At the same time, gazelles get better at evading cheetahs because the ones that have coloring that blends into the grass, that move more quickly, or have sharper reactions also survive to **breed 106**. The cycle continues and the balance that is typical of arms races is maintained. The cheetah-gazelle arms race will continue for as long as both species survive.

FRANKENSTEIN'S MONSTER

IN THE 19TH CENTURY, PEOPLE THOUGHT LIFE COULD BE COOKED UP IN A LAB—ALTHOUGH IT WAS DANGEROUS TO TRY. MARY SHELLEY'S *FRANKENSTEIN* (1818) IS THE STORY OF A SCIENTIST (DR. FRANKENSTEIN) WHO MAKES A MURDEROUS CREATURE FROM DEAD BODY PARTS...

2.5 BILLION
Oxygen is now present in the atmosphere—setting the stage for new, more complicated life forms to evolve

ALL THIS TIME AND STILL NO FISH

1.5 BILLION
Small but complex cell organisms emerge,
able to reproduce sexually (two different
creatures mate to make some more)

YEARS AGO

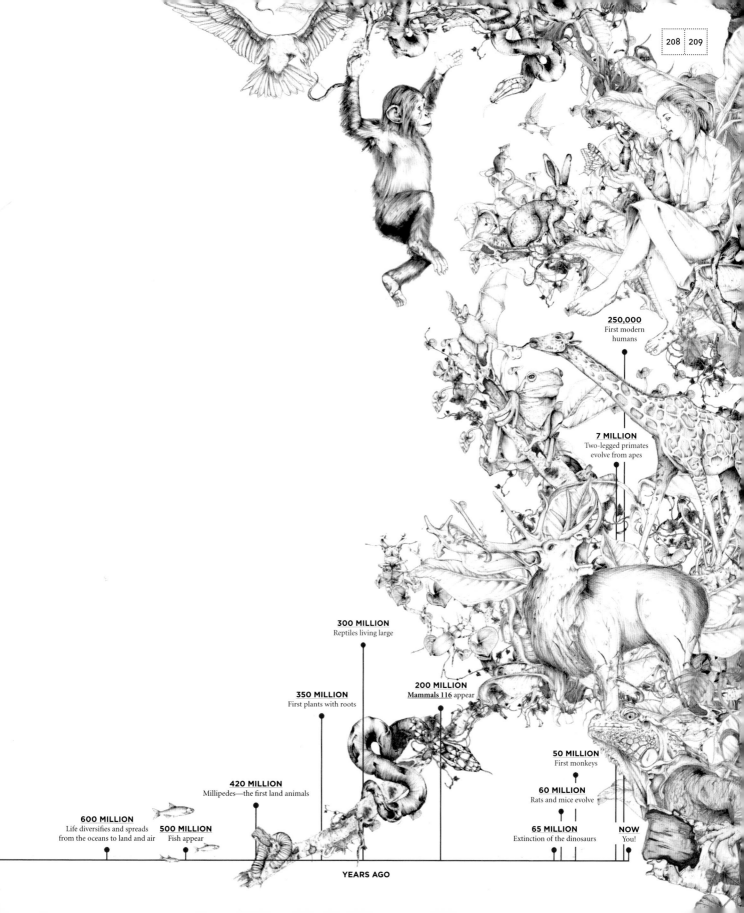

250,000
First modern humans

7 MILLION
Two-legged primates evolve from apes

300 MILLION
Reptiles living large

350 MILLION
First plants with roots

200 MILLION
Mammals 116 appear

50 MILLION
First monkeys

420 MILLION
Millipedes—the first land animals

60 MILLION
Rats and mice evolve

600 MILLION
Life diversifies and spreads from the oceans to land and air

500 MILLION
Fish appear

65 MILLION
Extinction of the dinosaurs

NOW
You!

YEARS AGO

HOW MUCH SLEEP DO WE NEED?

BABIES: AROUND 17 HOURS A DAY ● **OLDER CHILDREN:** NINE OR TEN HOURS A NIGHT ● **ADULTS:** SEVEN TO EIGHT HOURS A NIGHT ● **GIRAFFES:** TWO HOURS A DAY ● **BATS:** 20 HOURS A DAY

WHERE DID YOU GO LAST NIGHT?

Can you remember the amazing places you went to? When you dream, you can travel the world and move back and forth through time. And then you wake up and forget most of it

Sleep is a huge part of your life. If you live to the age of 75, you will have spent an incredible 25 years asleep (possibly more if you watch a lot of daytime TV). Scientists still don't know exactly why we sleep and why we dream, but they do know it's vital to our well-being—you can't live without it.

Stages of sleep

In adult humans there are two main types of sleep. Rapid Eye Movement (REM) sleep comes and goes through the night and makes up about a fifth of our sleep time. During REM sleep, our **brain 038** is very active, our **muscles 156** are very relaxed, and our closed eyes move quickly from side to side (hence the name). This is when we dream. The second type is non-REM sleep, which is when our brain is quiet, but we move around. During this time our body repairs itself after the wear and tear of the day. Each night we move between REM and non-REM sleep about five times. Dreams last for around 10 minutes early on, but get longer toward the morning (up to 45 minutes).

Why do we sleep?

No one knows for sure. It could be that sleep is a simple energy-saving device to help us use our bodies as efficiently as possible and recharge our batteries. It also seems that sleep is a time when our bodies do a lot of growing. But the better question may be, why are we awake so much? Like any animal, humans need to eat, drink, and reproduce. We need 14 or so hours a day for all of that. The rest of the time it makes more sense for the body to be using up precious energy to sleep.

Taking out the garbage

Sleep also seems to function in putting our brains in order. Dreams are a way for the brain to sort through all the information it has taken in and get rid of some of the stuff it doesn't need. Which is perhaps why our dreams are so forgettable (who wants to remember garbage?). Sleeping and dreaming also help us to improve our memories and to file information away more efficiently.

Working the nightshift

On the whole, human beings are awake during the day and asleep at night. This is because our bodies operate on 24-hour clock cycles called circadian rhythms. Some jobs require people to work at night (for instance, nurses and policemen), which disrupts these rhythms. This can result in tiredness and increased stress. Some animals love to work a permanent night shift. These nocturnal animals include mice, badgers, hedgehogs, and bats (who hang upside down when they go to sleep). It is thought these animals may have evolved to be awake at night so they can avoid other animals that would kill them in the day—or to catch other nocturnal animals for their own dinner.

WHAT HAPPENS IF WE DON'T SLEEP ENOUGH?

DAY 1

The longest time a human has been recorded as staying awake for is 18 days—and at the end of it the person was a total wreck (but after some catch-up sleep, was as good as new). Lack of sleep makes concentration difficult and affects how you look. The good news is that lost sleep is easily caught up: a 15-minute nap after lunch can work wonders. Next time you're caught dozing in class, try explaining that you're improving your health—zzzzzzzzzzzzzz...

DAY 18

BABY STEPS

Sleepwalking is a mild sleep disorder fairly common in children—around one in five goes for a wander in the night. While sleepwalking, someone gets out of bed and walks around. They are still asleep. Often, they won't communicate and may have a blank stare on their faces. They may even eat a snack (a cheese sandwich, perhaps) and go outside. Once awake, though, they probably won't remember what they've been doing.

In your dreams

Dreams usually involve images in a storylike sequence, though sensations and thoughts also play a part. They don't usually make complete sense and can be scary (then it becomes a nightmare). Cultures have long believed that dreams have special messages. Roman leaders paid a lot of attention to their dreams (they were supposedly a sign from the gods), while the Egyptians thought that the gods revealed themselves in dreams. **Sigmund Freud 239** believed that dreams required special attention since they were signs of frustrated desires (things we want but can't get). **Artists 322** and writers took up these ideas—in the 1920s, Surrealists began using dream "logic" as a means of artistic inspiration. Look at *The Persistence of Memory* by Salvador Dali (above)—it's sort of like being in a dream.

LIGHTING UP THE MODERN WORLD

Switching off the lights is the last thing you do at night—but who first turned them on? Thomas Edison (1847-1931) was a US scientist who in 1880 perfected the electric **light bulb 236**. He then developed the power system that brought **electricity 300** from the generating plant into homes. (The first commercial power plant opened in New York City in 1882.) Light bulbs did exist before 1880, but not very good ones. Edison's British rival Joseph Swan produced an effective bulb at about the same time as Edison did—so they went into business together.

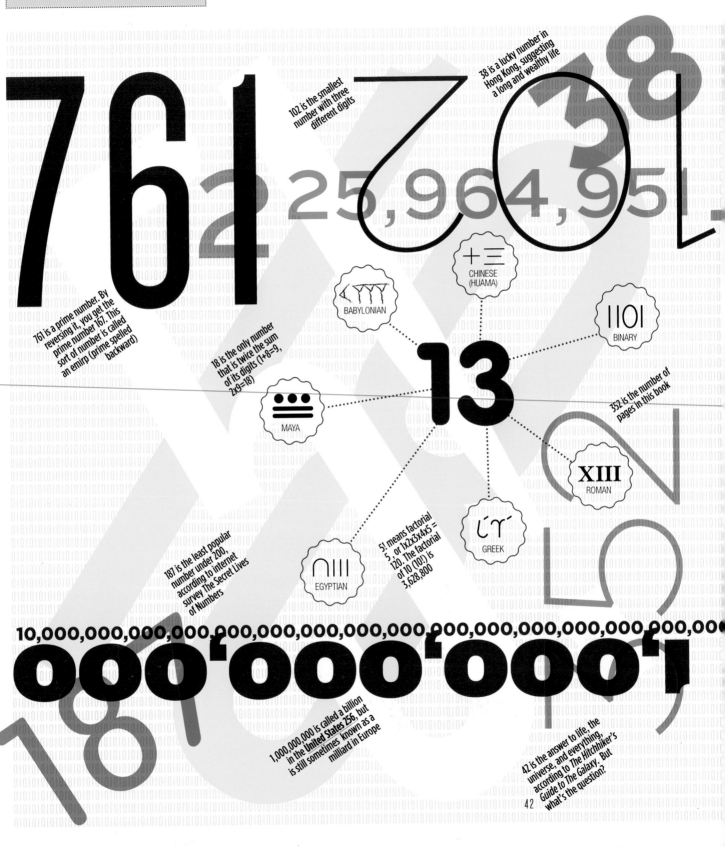

761

102 is the smallest number with three different digits

38 is a lucky number in Hong Kong, suggesting a long and wealthy life

25,964,951

761 is a prime number. By reversing it, you get the prime number 167. This sort of number is called an emirp (prime spelled backward)

18 is the only number that is twice the sum of its digits (1+8=9, 2×9=18)

13

CHINESE (HUAMA)

BABYLONIAN

1101 BINARY

352 is the number of pages in this book

MAYA

XIII ROMAN

187 is the least popular number under 200, according to Internet survey The Secret Lives of Numbers

5! means factorial 5, or 1×2×3×4×5 = 120. The factorial of 10 (10!) is 3,628,800

GREEK

EGYPTIAN

10,000,000,000,000,000,000,000,000,000,000,000,000,000,000,000,000,000,000,000,000

1,000,000,000

1,000,000,000 is called a billion in the **United States** 256, but is still sometimes known as a milliard in Europe

42 is the answer to life, the universe, and everything, according to *The Hitchhiker's Guide to The Galaxy*. But what's the question?

42

$2^{25,964,951}-1$ is the largest known prime number. To write it in full would take up this entire page

3.14159265358979323846264338327950288419716939937510582097494459230781648

π (pronounced "pi") allows you to calculate the circumference of a circle (the length of its boundary) when you only know the diameter (the width of the circle). It begins 3.14, but continues on and on...

2 is the only even prime—a number that is divisible only by itself or one

1,148 is the possible number of ways to fold a strip of 9 stamps

168 is the number of hours in a week (there are never enough)

2,434 is the number of legal king moves in chess

5,050 is the value of the first 100 numbers added together

10,000,000,000,000,000,000,000,000,000,000,0 00,000,000,000,000,000,000,000,000,000,000, 000,000,000,000,000,000,000,000,000,000,000,0 00,000,000,000,000,000,000,000,000 is known as a googol. Mathematicians use the abbreviation 10^{100} instead

0,000,000,000,000,000,000,000,000,000,000,000,000.000,000,000,000,000

292 is the number of ways to make change for a US dollar using pennies, nickels, dimes, quarters, and 50 cent pieces

32 is the average number of **teeth 078** in an adult's mouth

120 is sometimes called a great hundred, from the ancient German

YOUR NEXT COLD IS ONLY A SNEEZE AWAY

THERE'S A CERTAIN GROUP, which you may have come across, that leads a jet-set lifestyle. Its members travel all over the world and seem to have access to everyone—including the rich and famous. They might sound like a glamorous crowd, but the truth is the members of this particular group are a nasty bunch, and they travel not to vacation or to party, but to infect people. These are viruses, and viruses cause all kinds of illnesses, including the common cold, chicken pox, and measles...

WHAT IS IT? A virus is a piece of __DNA 258__ (or its chemical cousin, RNA), which is the same stuff that makes up your genes (the instructions for making and maintaining your body). Viruses are tiny (about one millionth of an inch long, or 2.5 millionth of a centimeter)—so small that 50,000 rhinoviruses (the stuff that cause colds) could fit along one millimeter (0.039 inches). Think about that the next time you sneeze without covering your mouth.

WHAT DOES IT WANT WITH YOU?
A virus cannot reproduce on its own—it needs the cells in a host body to do that. To begin with, it has to find a way in. Viruses enter human bodies through our noses, mouths, or breaks in the skin. Most viruses (including the common cold) are transferred from one human to another through mucus (the sticky stuff that comes out of your nose when you blow it). Wart and planter's wart viruses can be caught by touching something that an infected person has touched (ick). Some viruses can be transferred through close physical contact, like touching and kissing (double ick).

INVADING YOUR BODY Once it has found its way into you, the virus finds a host cell in which it can make more viruses. It has its own genetic instructions for reproducing, but unlike human cells, viruses do not contain enzymes (needed for important chemical reactions). So, the virus brazenly uses the enzymes in your cells instead (it's kind of like breaking into a sock factory and using the equipment and materials there to make gloves). The new viruses exit the host cell (which it has killed—but don't worry, you have plenty more), and look for other cells to take over. Then the process repeats itself and your cold gets worse.

HOW YOU FIGHT BACK Your body isn't doing nothing while all this is going on. The intruder (the virus) is detected and your __immune system 084__ is put on full alert. It can quickly deploy an army of white blood cells (which are licensed to kill) to attack the virus. It also has the ability to raise the body temperature, causing a fever. This may make you uncomfortable, but it does the virus no good at all—it slows down the rate of viral reproduction until the virus is unable to operate any more (kind of like turning the heat up on the bad guys).

HOW YOUR COMPUTER GETS A COLD (OF SORTS)

Computer viruses act in a similar manner to biological ones. They spread from computer to computer 044 using email systems. Once in a machine, they make copies and may send themselves to everyone in the address book. Some computer viruses are harmless pranks, but others cause damage by erasing data and changing programs. There may be 50,000 viruses in existence, with as many as 10 a day released into cyberspace.

Flu virus

SYMPTOMS: Stuffy nose, body aches, cough. Like a cold, but worse.
SPREAD: Like a cold, through coughing and sneezing.
DEADLINESS: In the US, 36,000 people die each year from the flu.

THE TOP 5
most common excuses for avoiding school

1. I've got a stomach ache
2. Honest, I've got a really bad stomach ache
3. I've got an earache
4. I was contacted by an alien last night, and I have to help him phone home
5. My stomach ache is worse today

PANDEMICS: (REALLY) BIG KILLERS

A pandemic is when an outbreak of disease spreads over a vast region, infecting a large section of the population

BLACK DEATH

Not all fast-spreading diseases are viruses. The Black Death is the name given to a disease called the bubonic plague that was rampant during the mid-14th century. Caused by a bacterium (tiny organism), it was most likely spread by fleas carried by rats. In **Europe 216**, one-third of the population died from the disease, and its killing spree did not end until the 1600s.

FLU

The flu can be (very) deadly. A Spanish Flu virus outbreak between 1918 and 1919 killed up to 50 million people worldwide. Scientists now believe it may have been a lethal form of bird flu, and are worried that something like it could cause a new pandemic today.

HIV

HIV (Human Immunodeficiency Virus) is a particularly nasty virus because it targets and attacks the body's defense mechanism. HIV may be spread through unprotected sex with an infected person or contact with their blood. HIV causes AIDS (Acquired Immune Deficiency Syndrome), a condition where the immune system is attacked until it is destroyed. Without any defense, the patient could die from an infection (even a common cold) that the immune system would normally easily deal with. There are more than 40 million people worldwide infected with HIV.

HOW TO AVOID SPREADING A VIRUS

COVER your mouth or nose when you sneeze or cough.
MAKE sure you wash your hands regularly—especially after going to the bathroom, preparing food, shaking hands with someone, or touching a surface that lots of other people have touched.

AVOID contact with other people's body fluids (nice).
LOOK after your general health—it will help to keep your immune system in top condition.
FAILING THAT, wear a snorkel and mask at all times.

Red ribbons are worn as a sign of support for those who have HIV

Who was he? A German monk and professor of theology (religion).
What did he do for Europe? He reinterpreted the Bible, boldly challenging the Catholic Church. Luther's beliefs came to be known as Protestantism. Some countries, such as England and Holland, broke away from the Catholic Church and became Protestant. The split in Christianity led to the Wars of Religion (1562-1598) in France and affected European politics for centuries.
He said: "The fewer the words, the better the prayer."
Did you know? Apparently, Luther decided to be a monk after he was almost struck by a bolt of lightning.

Martin Luther (1483-1546)

Who was he? Also called King Charles the Great, he is often regarded as the founder of France and Germany.
What did he do for Europe? He united large parts of western Europe. His kingdom stretched from northern Spain to Italy to Germany—bigger than anything in the west since the Roman Empire. Charlemagne converted his peoples to **Christianity 185** and encouraged education and learning.
He said: "To have another language is to possess a second soul."
Did you know? Some genealogists (people who study **family trees 010**) believe that the majority of people in western Europe are descended from Charlemagne.

Charlemagne (c.742-814)

Who was he? Gaius Julius Caesar was a Roman politician and military leader. He established himself as dictator of the Roman Republic.
What did he do for Europe? He conquered many countries, including Gaul (modern France) and Spain, bringing many European peoples under a single rule for the first time. The **Romans 286** introduced a common system of laws —elements of which are still in place today. The Roman language, Latin, became the basis of the western European languages.
He said: "I came, I saw, I conquered" ("Veni, vidi, vici").
Did you know? The month of July is named after Julius Caesar. Before Caesar, it was called Quintilis (not quite as catchy).

Julius Caesar (c.100 BC-44 BC)

EUROPE IS ALL ABOUT PEOPLE

★ ★ ★ ★ ★ ★ ★

Europe is a continent, but it is also an idea. It's an idea shaped by individuals and based on a common history that has grown over thousands of years—right up to today's European Union

Who were they? A hugely successful Swedish band.
What did they do for Europe? They won the Eurovision Song Contest in 1974 with the song "Waterloo," which brought them huge international fame. The Eurovision Contest was an event devised by a Frenchman called Marcel Baison to help draw the cultures of Europe back together after **World War II 294**.
They said: "ABBA will never reform!" (And they didn't.)
Did you know? At one point, they were Sweden's biggest export—even bigger than car maker Volvo.

ABBA (1972-1983)

Catherine the Great
(1729-1796)

Who was she? Catherine the second, Empress of **Russia 328**.
What did she do for Europe? She modernized Russian society, bringing it closer to the rest of Europe. Her interest in culture helped set the scene for later Russian writers such as **Leo Tolstoy 114**. It is partly through her efforts that Russia can be considered a part of Europe.
She said: "I praise loudly. I blame softly."
Did you know? Catherine probably ordered her own husband's death.

Johann Wolfgang von Goethe
(1749-1832)

Who was he? A German thinker and politician.
What did he do for Europe? Goethe's scientific and philosophical writings had a major impact on European thinking, influencing the likes of naturalist **Charles Darwin 206** and philosopher **Friedrich Nietzsche 042**. His literary work inspired other writers and musicians, including **Beethoven 022**.
He said: "Divide and rule, a sound motto—unite and lead, a better one."
Did you know? Goethe discovered the intermaxillary bone in the jaw, which was important for proving the similarity between man and animals.

Napoleon (1769-1821)

Who was he? Emperor of France.
What did he do for Europe? After Napoleon became ruler of France in 1799, he started conquering large parts of Europe. A hugely successful general, he eventually overstretched his armies and fought his last battle in 1815 at Waterloo. However, he had set up a modern administrative and legal system (including decimal weights and measurements) that remained important in many countries.
He said: "'Impossible' is not in the French language."
Did you know? In his lifetime, he wrote some 33,000 letters.

Karl Marx (1818-1883)

Who was he? A German philosopher and radical writer.
What did he do for Europe? He believed that **capitalism 050** benefitted only a few wealthy people. He thought there should be a revolution that would do away with inequalities, and property would be shared. Known as communism, this was hugely influential on political thought, and the 1917 Russian **revolution 138**.
He said: "From each according to his ability, to each according to his need."
Did you know? Marx is buried in Highgate Cemetery in London, England.

Winston Churchill (1874-1965)

Who was he? British prime minister during World War II.
What did he do for Europe? By helping to win the war against Nazi Germany, Churchill preserved the culture and freedom of Europe. After the war, he supported the development of the European Common Market, an economic agreement between the governments of Europe. This eventually became the modern European Union, which in 2005 consisted of 25 countries.
He said: "We must build a kind of United States of Europe."
Did you know? He won the Nobel Prize for Literature in 1953 for his historical writings.

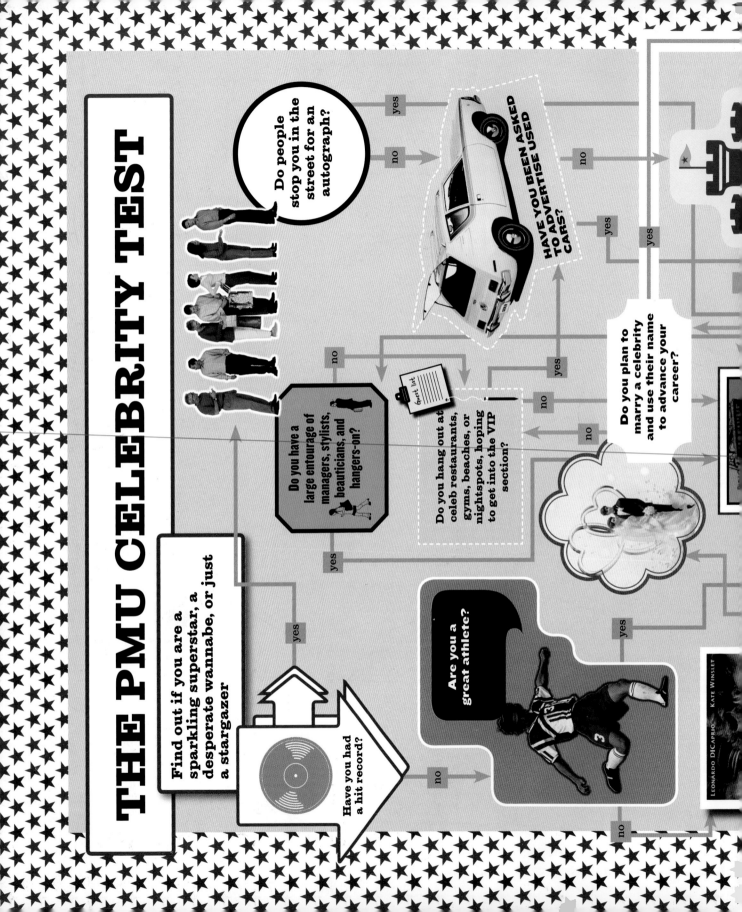

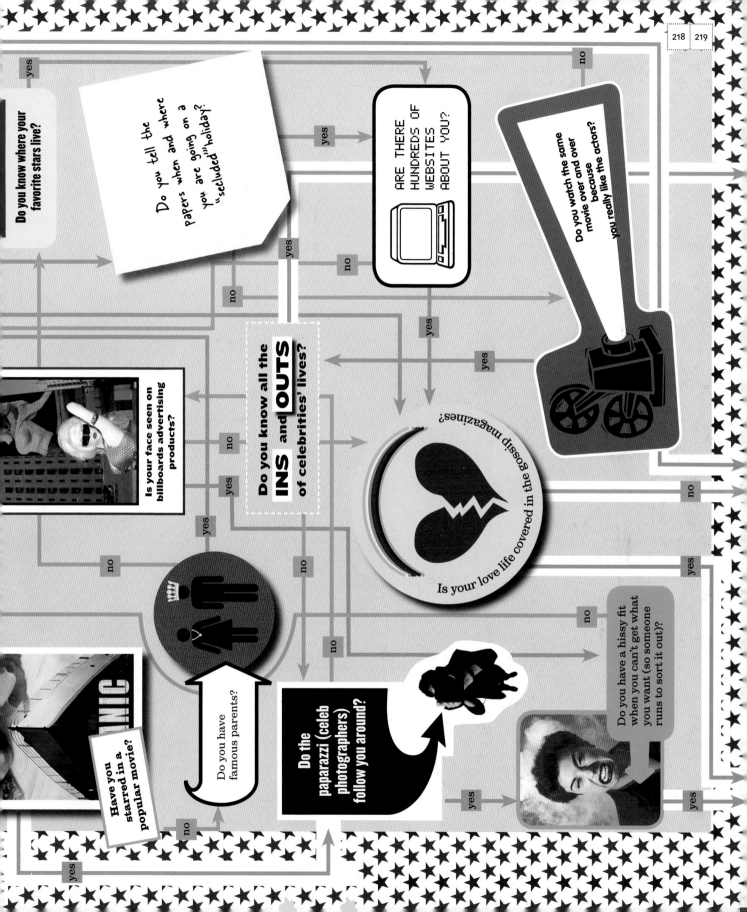

STARGAZER

No celebrity, but what a fan. You know everything there is to know about your favorite celebs, and follow the twists and turns of their complicated lives. But remember not to take this too far by following them around, as that is called stalking and could get you in a lot of trouble. Some fans take things to extremes, like Mark Chapman, who shot and killed John Lennon (one of **The Beatles 305**) in 1980 because he resented the man he had once admired. He also wanted to be famous—and achieved it, through murder. Not recommended!

WANNABE

Keep trying. You're on the way to fame (possibly), but you have to keep working the angles, hustling for attention. Don't be put off because you aren't stopped in the street, people can't quite remember your name or aren't sure what you have done. Don't forget, you can be famous for just being famous—you don't actually have to achieve anything or have talent. Just try to be seen in the right places with the right people and accept every offer to appear on every reality show or in any magazine. All publicity is good publicity!

CELEBRITY

Oooh, get you. Your natural home is on a red carpet smiling for cameras. But you *hate* that you can't step out the front door in sweat pants to go to the stores without the paparazzi (those pesky celeb photographers) taking a picture. You're pampered, looked after, and expect everything to be done right this minute. But in the pages of the magazines you're thoughtful, considerate, and always such a nice person. You don't like all the fuss, but you know you wouldn't be anything without the mass **media 330** (the magazines and TV shows, etc.).

Mental MEMORABILIA

The cult of celebrity can do funny things to people. Ordinary folks have paid a fortune for objects just because they were once owned, touched, or within a 100-mile radius of their favorite idol

What?
The guitar played by rock star Jimi Hendrix at Woodstock, a famous 1960s music festival.

Going, going, gone, for:
$368,000
Rockin' the bank balance.

What?
The bat used by Babe Ruth, the famous 1920s baseball player, to hit the first home run at the New York Yankees' new stadium.

Going, going, gone, for:
$1.26 million
Way out of the ball park.

I AM YOUR FATHER

What?
Darth Vader's helmet from Star Wars.

Going, going, gone, for:
$5,500
What a bargain—and so useful for keeping your head warm in winter.

What?
John Lennon's piano (decorated with his cigarette burns).

Going, going, gone, for:
$2,700,000
English pop star George Michael splashed the cash— proving that you can be both a celebrity and a crazy fan.

Victoria

Napoleon

Tom

Will

David

Madonna

Julius

DEAD FAMOUS

Sometimes celebrities only hit the big time after they're dead—perhaps because they kept their talents hidden (or maybe it was just bad timing)

John Kennedy Toole
(1937–1969)

The American writer was so depressed by failing to get his novel, *A Confederacy of Dunces*, published that he committed suicide. His mother didn't give up, and 12 years later the book won the prestigious Pulitzer Prize.

Emily Dickinson
(1830–1886)

Unpublished, reclusive, and almost unknown during her lifetime, she is now seen as one of the greatest American poets of the 19th century.

Vincent van Gogh
(1853–1890)

The Dutch painter had little success while alive, but later became recognized as one of Europe's greatest **artists 322**. He's also famous for slicing off part of his ear (people told him it was silly – but he just wouldn't hear of it). Unfortunately, he committed suicide at the age of 37.

WHY ARE WE ALL SO *OBSESSED* WITH CELEBRITY CULTURE THESE DAYS?

Cultural expert Dr. Jo Littler shares her ideas with PMU

Celebrities are not just *anybody*. So a society with celebrities in it is an unequal society: not everyone is worth the same as everybody else.

TYPES of celebrity have existed for a long time. Think of the **face 110** of an emperor on a Roman coin—that was his way of getting famous and of showing he was the boss. But celebrity has not always been the same. Before the 17th and 18th centuries, it was mainly the ruler (the emperor, the king, or queen) and religious figures who were famous. The rise of **capitalism 050** and the expansion of the middle classes changed all that. Busy, self-made men and women gained fame through the expanding media. Since then, more people have become celebrities—and more people have become aware of not being them.

TODAY, there is a greater emphasis on how "anyone" can be a celebrity. Media coverage of celebrity has mushroomed with the advent of new technology. And because all of us are interested in how we compare to other people, celebrity has tremendous power. We can relate to celebrities in a number of ways: for example, by offering glimpses of what we would like to be, or for living a life we might want.

CELEBRITY, in all its various forms, shows how it's increasingly possible for us to live very differently from our parents. But its very existence continues to show up divisions of wealth and status.

HOW TO PERFECT YOUR CELEBRITY SIGNATURE

FIRST, DECIDE THE SIGNATURE YOU WANT: BIG OR SMALL, FULL NAME OR JUST INITIALS? THEN, PRACTICE, PRACTICE, PRACTICE—UNTIL IT'S TOTALLY ILLEGIBLE. IT MUST LOOK LIKE YOU SIGN AUTOGRAPHS ALL DAY LONG.

1.

Your Name

2.

perfect!

PRIME TIME ENTERTAINMENT
1601
3,000 people pack out The Globe in London, England

During the Elizabethan era (1558-1603), talented playwrights were ten a penny. The most famous of them all was William Shakespeare. He wrote many of the period's blockbusters, including *Macbeth*, *A Midsummer Night's Dream,* and *Hamlet*. All writers were inspired by medieval stories to create new tales. History plays were common. Comedies, such as Ben Jonson's *The Alchemist*, were well-liked too. But tragedies (plays with sad endings) were the most popular, for example, Shakespeare's *Othello* or *Doctor Faustus* by Christopher Marlowe.

'We're the wealthiest here. I'm a doctor. Behind me are nobles who own large estates. Queen Elizabeth I loves plays—though she's never been here. She granted the aristocracy rights to maintain acting groups.'

"That Shakespeare, he's the poster-boy of Elizabethan theater and English literature. A tradesman's son, he was a London playwright by 1592. I predict he'll be famous for centuries."

"I'm a Puritan, a type of very strict **Christian 185**. I believe that lots of fun things, such as games and dancing, are immoral and evil. As for theaters, those young boys dressing up as women are disgraceful. I'm going to do my best to get this place shut down—you mark my words."

"I agree! Did you know he writes 14-line poems, called sonnets, as well as plays? I hear he's written nearly 150. Some are addressed to a young man, others to a mysterious 'dark lady'—but no one knows who they're really for. I like to imagine it's me as Shakespeare's awfully good-looking!"

"Watch out for those playwrights. Christopher Marlowe was killed in a tavern brawl. Shakespeare has associates in the London underworld and earns extra income with questionable money-lending. And that Ben Jonson killed an actor in a duel."

"I admit it. I ate the last bag of hazelnuts."

"O villain, villain, smiling, damned villain!" (*Hamlet*)

BEAR BAITING
Near the Globe, the popular Elizabethan blood sport of bear baiting took place in a "bear garden." Bears were tied to posts and dogs set on them. Spectators gambled on the outcome. Nasty.

VERY PUBLIC TOILETS
People had to pee outside. The streets must have looked like a yellow river. Nice.

BOX OFFICE
Money for performances was collected in boxes, which were put in a room backstage—that's where the name "box office" comes from.

SHOWTIME
The Globe was built in 1599 by brothers Richard and Cuthbert Burbage. The first play staged may well have been Shakespeare's *Julius Caesar*. It is thought a **flag 228** advertised each performance. Black meant tragedy, red meant comedy.

"To be, or not to be... me, William Shakespeare. Bet you never knew I was an actor, too!"

"I'm a 13-year-old boy playing a woman. I live with the family of one of the older actors and get voice training from the theater company. I also have an excellent memory and have been acting for three years already."

TIRING HOUSE
So called because it was where the actors changed their attire (not because it wore them out).

"I'm trying to remember my lines. Our costumes are really elaborate to make up for the lack of scenery. It's also something to look at for the people who don't understand everything that's going on..."

"Look at that gold medallion—must be super expensive!"

YARD
People standing in front of the stage were the poorest people present. They were known as groundlings.

"Goodnight, goodnight! Parting is such sweet sorrow." (*Romeo and Juliet*)

"All that glistens is not gold." (*The Merchant of Venice*)

"Okay, bye. (I didn't think the date had gone that well...)."

Q: Who is the modern Shakespeare?

A: It's Shakespeare himself, believe it or not. His plays and writings continue to be regarded as the best in English literature—or even the world. His plots have been used as the basis for **films 034** in nearly every genre, from cartoons to romantic comedies.

TRY BEING A BOY FOR A DAY

Try being a boy for a day. You have a fight with your mom. When things get heated, lose it and snap at her—or just storm off to your pal's house for a few hours. When she tries to talk things out, don't listen.

Boys' and girls' hormonal levels are different (hormones are chemical messengers that instruct the body to perform certain actions). Boys have less of the estrogen hormone than girls. When **girls 080** are under stress, estrogen prolongs the production of a chemical called oxytoxin, which has a calming effect. But male hormones appear to reduce oxytoxin's effect. So, although it seems male and female teenagers can be equally defiant (be honest!), the sexes tend to react differently to tension. Some research has shown girls adopt a "tend and befriend" approach, such as talking things through with family. Boys are more likely to have a "fight or flight" reaction—starting a conflict or wanting time alone. This hormonal difference probably evolved from **prehistoric 234** times, when calmer females were likely to be better carers. But in hunting situations, it was more effective for males to fight or flee. Today, the male reaction means they are more prone to certain stress-related diseases than females. Chill out, guys!

If you forget some fact during a conversation, wing it. Once you've mastered the art of appearing to know what you're talking about, you'll even start believing yourself!

Everything we say, whether male or female, is said in a certain tone of voice, at a certain speed, with a certain choice of words, and at a certain volume. This creates our individual speaking pattern, called our linguistic style. But there are real contrasts in the way boys and girls speak. Differences between the sexes are attributed to nature (we're born like it) or nurture (what we learn growing up). Or maybe it's a little of both. On the side of nurture is Deborah Tannen, a Canadian expert in linguistics (the study of language). According to Tannen, girls learn to downplay knowledge to avoid appearing boastful, while boys use words that "big up" their abilities and intelligence. So, a boy and girl may say exactly the same thing, but the boy will be more believable, since he will say it with more assurance. Tannen believes that this is not a built-in difference. Rather, it's a pattern of behavior gradually learned from the people around us.

You get hit on the nose by a ball. It really, really hurts, but whatever you do, don't cry. If you possibly can, laugh it off. (Even if your nose is broken and gushing with blood, and you think you're about to pass out.)

Until recently, it was believed that boys act differently from girls when they get hit in the face purely because they are taught by people around them to hide any sign of weakness. However, this doesn't explain the fact that male and female babies respond to **pain 084** differently just six hours after birth (come on, we don't learn that fast). In 2005, British academics discovered that girls feel pain in more bodily areas and more often during their lives than boys—explaining why boys always seem tougher (except when they stay in bed for a week with "man flu," i.e., a common cold). Other experts say boys and girls process pain differently in the brain. And they predict that different painkillers will soon be created for each sex. Up until the 1990s, females were often excluded from drug studies since scientists believed males and females were biologically identical (their bodies were the same) except for their reproductive organs. They've since discovered that many diseases affect the sexes differently. For example, the buildup to a heart attack causes chest pain in males, but only vague, flulike symptoms in females. Now, a gender-based medicine movement is in full swing.

Pick your most boyish interest. It may be sports, computer games, or music. Bone up—which are the best players/games/bands around at the moment?

Play a contact sport. Hustle, get in your opponent's face. Get hostile. Don't be afraid!

Make some medals to reward yourself for your greatest accomplishments. Don't worry about appearing big-headed: the more impressive the achievement and medal, the better.

Practice your throwing— until you can throw a really long way. Impressive, no?

Why do boys and girls usually have such different interests? Famous psychologist **Sigmund Freud 239** believed boys' and girls' contrasting interests are set from birth. He said, "Anatomy is destiny," meaning girls' and boys' different bodies are better at different things. For example, some research has suggested that boys use more of the part of the brain (the right side) that controls spatial awareness. This could be one of the reasons they are often more interested in **sports 052**— they may be better at judging distances and figuring out team tactics. Sheri Berenbaum, an American psychology professor, has completed research that also appears to support Freud's point. She studied girls born with higher levels of a male sex hormone called androgen, and found they showed more interest in sports and less in "typical" girl pastimes, such as dolls. So, the more male hormones you have, the more likely you are to have "boyish" interests. However, all these natural differences start out very small and subtle—and then society magnifies them. So, a boy may start off only intrigued by soccer, but with encouragement from his friends and family, he will become obsessed with the game (and even learn the off-side rule).

Boys are more aggressive than girls. This isn't the case with every boy, but statistics show it is the case with the majority. In the United States, for example, more than 82 percent of violent offenders are male. **Evolutionary 206** biologists (people who study how humans have changed) say this is because aggression is an essential part of human development: when resources are low, males fight for supplies for their family's survival. Boys' and girls' aggression rates are also linked to their different hormones. One type of hormone found in both boys and girls is called testosterone. But boys produce substantially more of it per day than girls. Testosterone plays a large part in **puberty 274** development, but it can also be linked to aggression. For example, body builders who abuse drugs called steroids (that increase testosterone levels to promote muscle growth) can become very hostile. But scientists are wary of solely blaming (poor, old) testosterone, as a hormone alone cannot "activate" a behavior.

Individual achievement, for most boys, equals success. Boys usually find it easier to communicate such success proudly to others, whereas girls often believe that if they brag, they won't be liked. Again, the reason for this is a combination of biological and social reasons. Boys tend to value solo achievement more than they value what people may think about them, because society teaches them that to succeed in this way is masculine. Girls are often taught that forming healthy relationships with others will make them better females. However, these contrasting definitions of success may also be partly explained by other reasons. Unlike boys, girls are born physically equipped to raise children. Some research has suggested that, on average, they have a larger deep-limbic brain system than boys, which may increase their ability to bond with others. By just one day old, girls look longer at faces, while boys look longer at inanimate (lifeless) objects, such as mobiles over their cribs (probably trying to figure out a better way of making them). Even girls' more acute sense of smell may be linked to their mothering role—it may have developed so they could recognize their offspring. But who cares about all that when you're the best and there's bragging to be done?

Dr. Janet Hyde, an American psychologist, completed radical research about gender differences (the different ways boys and girls behave) in 2005. After studying the psychology of boys and girls for over 20 years, she discovered that the two sexes are alike in almost every way. There are only a few differences between them, such as the fact that boys throw farther and are more physically **aggressive 154**. So, according to Hyde, all those other distinctions, such as the idea that girls are more emotional, or that boys are better at reading maps, are actually myths. They only become true because society encourages them to be true (she's definitely on the side of nurture, not nature). Hyde even states that it is very harmful to stereotype boys and girls in ways that have so often been done in the past. So, girls grab your toolkits and boys lace up your ballet shoes: it's time to bust down those old gender constraints and be as "boyish" or "girly" as you like...

ARE YOU A BOY? TURN TO PAGE 80

The Universal Declaration of Human Rights was adopted by the United Nations in 1948. A little like a guarantee for living, it sets out your freedoms and rights as a human being

L I

Articles 1-5

All human beings are born free and equal, and have the same **rights** whatever their race, sex, religion, or beliefs. Everyone is entitled to life, liberty, and security. No one shall be held in slavery, or **tortured.**

Articles 6-12

Everyone is entitled to equal protection from the **law.** No one may be arrested without just cause, and everyone is entitled to a free, fair, and independent trial. Everyone must be presumed innocent until proven guilty.

Articles 13-17

Everyone has the right to a nationality, and no one may be deprived of their nationality or denied the right to change it. Anyone may leave any country and may seek asylum (refuge) abroad. They may hold **property** and may not be deprived of it.

LAW
In 1215, a group of barons forced King John of England to sign a document called the Magna Carta. This meant that no man was above the law—not even the king. The document has influenced modern law, including the Universal Declaration of Human Rights. In 1948, Eleanor Roosevelt (wife of US President Franklin D. Roosevelt), who helped to write the Declaration, called it "a Magna Carta for all mankind."

RIGHTS
In the past, people have been singled out because of their skin color or beliefs. In the 1960s, in the southern states of the US, black people had to use separate schools, restaurants, and buses. Martin Luther King, a Baptist minister, led a protest known as the civil rights movement. He helped secure equal rights for the black population in 1964. In 1968, he was murdered.

TORTURE
Torture was routinely used in **Europe 216** during medieval times as a punishment or to extract confessions. (A particular favorite was the rack: the body was stretched until the joints dislocated. Ouch.) Today, states don't admit to torturing people, but human-rights charity Amnesty International believes that torture is still used in over 130 countries.

Martin Luther King

PROPERTY
What's yours is yours—but it hasn't always been like that. From the 16th century, European settlers seized land in North America from the **Native Americans 096**. Thousands were relocated in the west, but the settlers took these lands too. Eventually, the Native Americans were confined to reservations. This was a very clear violation of their Human Rights.

Native American camp in 1890

"GET UP, STAND UP"

The famous hit reggae song "Get Up, Stand Up," released in 1973 by Bob Marley (1945–1981), encouraged followers of the Rastafarian religion to defend their rights and faith. Reggae is a style of pop music from Jamaica that Marley helped make world famous.

F E

A USER'S WARRANTY

Articles 18-21
Everyone may hold whatever religious or political belief they choose, and discuss ideas and spread them to others freely. They may form associations (groups) and hold peaceful assemblies. Everyone has the right to take part in the government of their country. The authority of the **government** *will be based upon the will of the people, expressed in regular, free elections.*

GOVERNMENT
This is all about <u>democracy 194</u>—or as US President <u>Abraham Lincoln 093</u> put it, "Government of the people, by the people, for the people." The concept of democracy originated in ancient Athens, but didn't really make it big until the 20th century. Of the 192 countries in the world today, 120 are democracies.

Education (a good thing)

Articles 22-27
Everyone is guaranteed the right to work for equal pay, to leisure time, to an adequate standard of living, to an **education***, and to take part in the cultural life of their community.*

EDUCATION
Despite what you may think, going to school is important. Since the <u>Enlightenment 150</u>, education for all has come to be seen as essential to a nation's prosperity. But there are still more than 770 million adults worldwide who can't read or write, two-thirds of them are women. Imagine how much more difficult life would be if you couldn't read (you wouldn't be learning about this for a start).

Free speech

Articles 28-30
These rights imply a **duty** *to one's community. These rights may not be used contrary to the purposes of the United Nations, and nothing in this document may be interpreted as allowing the removal of any of the rights it* **guarantees***.*

DUTY
You may have rights, but with them come responsibilities (a bit like being allowed out to meet friends, but agreeing to look after your little brother when you get back). In this way, everyone has a part to play in protecting democracy and respecting other people's rights.

GUARANTEES
Rights can be a bit tricky if taken to extremes. For example, the right to free speech often comes into conflict with other rights. If someone wants to say how much they hate certain types of people, this may provoke racial hatred. So, all rights have to be balanced. Sure, you have the right to set up your own <u>weblog 064</u>. But posting extracts from your friend's diary would violate her right to privacy (no matter how juicy they are).

TALKING LOUD

Flags are more than just colorful pieces of cloth for waving at the Olympics. The shapes, colors, and designs are often chosen to communicate a message or idea—they are a way of speaking to us. Flags can be traced back to the ancient Egyptians, who carried poles with carvings of symbols attached to the top (the flapping fabric came later). In the Middle Ages, soldiers carried flags so they could tell who was on their side

R

U

O

K

Before radio, people on ships used to wave flags to other vessels to spell out messages, using a system called semaphore

THE FLAG THAT CAN'T STAY STILL

The Red Cross is a worldwide organization that looks after the victims of war. It was formed by a Swiss man named Henry Durant in the 1860s and named after its flag: a red cross on a white background. This is the opposite of the Swiss flag (a white cross on a red background).

The flag symbolizes the cross on which Jesus was crucified. This is fine for Christian countries, but there are plenty of people who follow other religions. So a new flag was created for **Islamic 186** countries. This flag has a red crescent (a symbol of Islam) instead of a cross.

But, of course, there are other religions, too. So, in 2005 a third option —the red crystal—was adopted as a symbol that doesn't carry an extra religious message.

HOW TO MAKE YOUR OWN FLAG

Most flags are designed from similar elements. You can make your own in just a few simple steps:

1. Choose a basic shape

2. Add a second shape (optional)

Or invent one

3. Color the sections

4. Add a design (optional)

A soccer linesman's flag signals

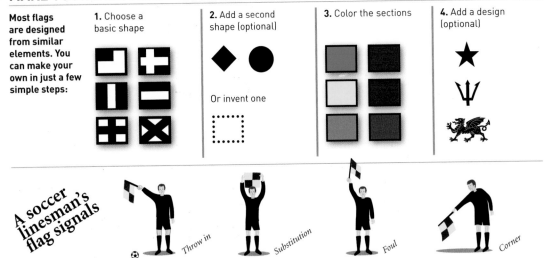

Throw in   *Substitution*   *Foul*   *Corner*

South Korea

Soviet Union

Pirate

Spain

Israel

Power, authority, and belief— all on a flag

Take a look at South Korea's flag. The circle in the middle (called the yin-yang) and the black lines around it (part of what's called the **I-Ching 255**) relate to ideas from ancient Chinese philosophy about the harmony, balance, and peace of the world. The **color 128** white is also a traditional symbol of peace. The flag is designed to make a statement of South Korea's peaceful beliefs.

As a communist country, the Soviet Union believed that power should belong to the workers rather than to business, or royalty. This is reflected in the flag. Its red color signified the blood of the working people who were seen as the most important part of society. The hammer stood for industrial workers, and the sickle (a blade for cutting crops) represented agricultural workers. The yellow star referred to the five fingers of the worker's hand, and also the five inhabited continents of the world (which perhaps shows how the communists thought their beliefs would spread).

The color black in flags is often used to signal mourning or death. Think of the famous pirate flag called the Jolly Roger (a white skull and crossbones on black). There were variations on this design—a skull and two swords, or just an arm holding a sword—but almost all incorporated black. **Pirates 204** would sail up close to a ship they were planning to attack, then fly their Jolly Roger. The flag was intended to scare victims witless so they would surrender and hand over the booty. If not, the pirates would fly a red flag, signaling that they were ready to fight (and had finished feeding their parrots). Bummer.

The coat of arms on the Spanish flag is a symbol of the monarchy (king and queen)—it is a way of expressing tradition and unity. Similarly, the blue Star of David on Israel's flag is a symbol of the Jewish religion which unites the country.

graffiti

Sometimes people want to express a message that others will see, but they don't have an outlet, such as a flagpole or the **media 330**, so they end up writing on walls. This is known as graffiti (from "graphein," the Greek word for writing), and it's been around since the **ancient Egyptians 100** (they used to scrawl on tomb walls). Graffiti can be a way for people who feel ignored to make political expressions. During the 1970s, street gangs in New York wrote a "tag" (or nickname) on walls to state their presence. Using spray paint, they were soon decorating subway trains in elaborate murals. Writing on property is illegal (it's vandalism), but there were genuine artistic talents, such as Jean-Michel Basquiat, whose work ended up in art galleries. Love it or hate it, graffiti is here to stay.

WHEN CAN YOU EAT A FLAG?

The next time you eat a pizza, remember that you are eating a flag (not literally—you'd choke on the pole). The Italian flag is green, white, and red, so in 1889, a baker called Raffaele Esposito used the colors to cook up a meal for King Umberto and Queen Margherita, who were visiting his town. He chose basil (green), mozzarella (white), and tomato (red). He put them together on a piece of bread and invented the Margherita pizza (but remember, waving it around will make a mess).

Apologies for all the "ologies"

Vexillology is the study of flags. It's just one of the many weird and wonderful studies with their own "-ology." Buzzing, stings, and honey—these are all part of apiology, the study of bees. Professional clock-watchers are experts in horology, the study of time. Ever wanted to send a secret message? If you knew cryptology, then you'd be able to create secret codes. Some people even study baths and how they help us relax. This is called balneology.

Population
**45 million—
falling**

In South Africa, more people are sick with **HIV/AIDS 214** than anywhere else in the world. In 2003, **5.3 million** South Africans had the virus.

10

South Africa is the **10th** largest wine producer in the world

↑ **Nation knowledge**

Top gold producer
Percentage of the world's gold

1. South Africa	14%	
2. US	11%	
3. Australia	10%	

South Africa is also the world's fourth largest producer of diamonds. The world's biggest producers of diamonds by value are:

Botswana **$2.57 bn**

Russia **$1.8 bn**

Canada **$1.67 bn**

South Africa **$1.2 bn**

Angola **$0.8 bn**

↓ South Africa is poor at sharing its wealth. In 2000, the **poorest** 20 percent had just 3.5 percent of the income. The **richest** 20 percent had a 37 percent share of the income.

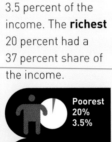

Poorest 20% 3.5%

Richest 20% 37%

→ There are more **cell phones 144** in South Africa than in any other country in Africa—more than **one-third of the population** has a cell phone. Egypt, in second place, has half the number of cells—despite having 30 million more people.

All talk...

English is the most commonly spoken language in South African public life. But it only ranks joint fifth as a first tongue for the people who live there.

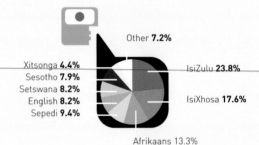

Other **7.2%**

Xitsonga **4.4%**
Sesotho **7.9%**
Setswana **8.2%**
English **8.2%**
Sepedi **9.4%**

IsiZulu **23.8%**

IsiXhosa **17.6%**

Afrikaans **13.3%**

Hello

Save the rhino

South Africans are committed to preserving their country's wildlife. In 1895, there were just 20 white rhinos left in the world. Now, there are 10,400, mostly in South Africa, thanks to conservation efforts.

Record-breaking land mammals live there...

Largest
African Elephant

Smallest
A tiny shrew

Tallest
Giraffe

Fastest
Cheetah

Plus 900 bird species, 6,000 different spiders, and 23,200 different plants

Where is South Africa?

➜ South Africa has the third highest **literacy** rate in Africa: more than **85 percent** of the population over the age of 15 can read and write.

African Literacy		
1	Seychelles	91.9
2	Zimbabwe	90.7
3	South Africa	86.4
4	Equatorial Guinea	85.7
5	Mauritius	85.6

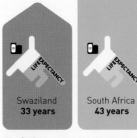

Swaziland **33 years** · South Africa **43 years** · Andorra **83 years**

Life expectancy

South Africa has one of the **lowest life expectancies** in the world. The average person born in 2005 will only live to be 43.

The Truth and Reconciliation Commission

was created to investigate crimes committed during South Africa's apartheid era (March 1, 1960 to May 10, 1994, the day of President **Nelson Mandela's 242** inauguration). It was part of the country's peaceful change from minority to majority rule (now everyone could vote, rather than just a relatively small, white population).

8000

125

21,000

Petitions for amnesty (people would confess to crimes in return for exemption from punishment) **received by the Commission**

People granted amnesty

Victim testimonies heard between 1996 and 1998

There is more grassland than anything else

South Africa is a grassy place: 55 percent of the country is **covered in savannah** (grassland), with shrubs and small **trees 010**.

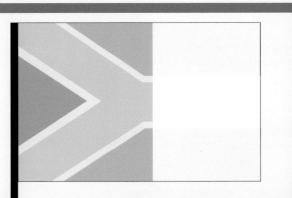

South Africa...

Growing up would mean some dramatic changes. Being a **teenager 274** is nothing compared to the metamorphosis (total form change) experienced by a monarch butterfly (left), cave moth (below left), or luna moth (third right). They emerge as caterpillars (top of the page), then grow to full caterpillar size, before turning into a pupa. Generally after a few days, the pupa splits and a butterfly or moth emerges.

You could be a wingless flea (left) and jump vast distances. Fleas power-jump from one warm-blooded animal—a **cat 101**, say—to another in search of a blood meal. Energy for jumping is stored in a flea's back legs which enable the 0.08-in (2-mm) long flea to make a 12-in (30-cm) leap. That's equivalent to you vaulting a 60-story building.

IF YOU WERE AN INSECT...

You might be amazingly strong like a worker ant. Worker ants put the average bodybuilder to shame. They can use their jaws to lift and carry food (leaves, seeds, other animals) up to seven times their own weight. They can even drag food 25 times their weight. That's like you pulling a hippopotamus along with your **teeth 078**!

You would have a hard shell (or exoskeleton) covering your body. Every insect has this. It helps protect them from enemies. However, exoskeletons don't stretch. So, like other insects, shield bugs (below) have to shed their old exoskeleton before their bodies can grow. They then generate a replacement shell.

You could glow in the dark. Fireflies (left)—from the beetle family, the largest insect group with more than 350,000 species—use a chemical reaction in their abdomens to produce light flashes. It's a kind of a come on. At night, males send out flashes, then wingless females (glow-worms) respond with their own flashes. The male swoops down to find his mate. Some females sneakily flash to lure males of other species—then eat them.

You could fly. Dragonflies (above left) are among the best fliers in the world. Like many insects, they have two pairs of wings rather than one set. The front and hind wings beat alternately (other insects with four wings beat them all together), giving incredible flight control. In pursuit of prey, such as mosquitoes (second left), dragonflies engage in aerial maneuvers that would make human fighter pilots green with envy.

Spiders say: eight legs rule

Having eight legs means arachnids (they get annoyed if you call them insects) can move, at high speed, not only forward and backward, but sideways, too. Plus, they can multitask. While the back two pairs of legs are holding on to the web and drawing out silk from the spinnerets, the front legs are wrapping prey in silk, ready to eat later.

You might, like an earwig, have three pairs of legs attached to the thorax—that's the middle of the three body sections that all insects have (the head's in front and the abdomen's behind). This arrangement allows the earwig (below) to scuttle along at high speed. Plus, you would smell, feel, and taste through that pair of antennae sticking out of your head.

You and your 80,000 sisters would share one mother, like a worker honeybee (above). (And if you think that's a large family—an estimated 30 million insect species exist altogether, living in every type of habitat aside from the sea.) As a honeybee, it would be your job to look after your mom, the queen, nuture her eggs, and go out looking for nectar and pollen. After a short, hard life of six weeks, you'd die from exhaustion. Oh dear.

You could have an amazing disguise to hide from enemies. Many insects do this, adopting the guise of sticks (stick insect, above), leaves (leaf insect, right), flowers (orchid mantis, left), or bark (bark bug, second left). The caterpillar of the viceroy butterfly even looks like a bird dropping. Eeew!

You could see the world through compound eyes. Each eye of the housefly (below) is made up of hundreds or thousands of light-detecting units. Each unit contributes a "spot" of light, so the housefly "sees" a dotted image of the outside world (a bit like the pixels of a **TV screen 128**). A fly's eyes (and brain) are very good at registering movement, which is why the annoying little critters are so difficult to swat.

Nanotechnology

The smallest insects are tiny—only visible with a microscope. But imagine even tinier things, the size of **atoms 060**. This is the nanoworld, where things are measured in nanometers (billionths of a meter). Scientists developing nanotechnology hope to make things, such as powerful computer chips, out of atoms. It may even become possible to construct microscopic robots (nanobots) to be injected into a person's body to fight disease.

How would a prehistoric man cope in New York City today?

He'd wonder where everyone had come from

For much of human history, the world was sparsely populated. It is thought that 100,000 years ago there were as few as 10,000 human adults in the population. Early humans survived in groups of 10-20 related individuals, living a nomadic (traveling) life. There are probably more people in this picture than they would have met in a lifetime. It was only during the agricultural era, when people settled and grew crops, that the global population really increased. It is estimated that during this time (2,000 to 10,000 years ago), the population grew from six million people (less than the population of modern **London 159**), to 250 million. That's peanuts, though, compared to the six billion-plus people in the world today.

If he were lost, he'd have trouble asking for directions

Crucial in the development of humans has been language ability. Around a million years ago, our distant relatives would have had basic **language 054** skills, though these would have been limited to grunts (similar to some teenage talk, then). The fossil record shows that 150,000 years ago, our ancestors were physically capable of making the kind of fast and flexible speech you are used to. The brain was large enough (pictured, a cast of an adult's skull). The mouth and throat had also made the necessary adaptations for complex speech.

Sophisticated language has given humans a huge advantage in the world. It means that the past and future can be talked about and plans made. It also allows information to be shared and passed on, even through generations.

Humans can learn from being told, and not just by experience and watching (the way chimpanzees, for example, learn).

WHICH AGE IS IT?

Prehistoric refers to the time before recorded history, when things weren't written down (writing dates from around 3300 BC). The Roman poet Lucretius labeled these periods (in order) Stone Age, Bronze Age, and Iron Age, according to the technology. Stone tools date back 2.5 million years. Hard metals, such as bronze, were first produced in **Sumer 086** in the fourth millennium BC. They were used to make weapons and ornaments (like this bronze statue). And iron was being worked by 2500 BC in what is now Turkey.

He would expect to hunt for his food—not go to McDonald's

Prehistoric man foraged (found **plants 018**, nuts and the like) or hunted for his supper. Tools helped him do this. More than two million years ago, a distant member of the human family, *Homo habilis* (meaning "handy man"), was using tools. Some animals use tools (chimpanzees utilize sticks to get at termites and eat them). But *habilis 278* had foresight and planning and was able to craft sharp stone flakes with precision. These weren't used to slay animals, but to butcher already dead ones. Neanderthal man (a relation of humans, extinct by around 25,000 years ago) also used tools, but these were more sophisticated. They included axes and spear points (pictured) used for hunting.

Our species, *Homo sapiens*, created stone devices and introduced antler and bone into toolkits (useful for making more elaborate clothing). Crucially, we properly tamed fire. It had been used for cooking, perhaps for a million years or so, but *sapiens* also used it to aid hunting. So-called "fire stick farming" may have been used 45,000 years ago. Bright *sapiens* knew that if he burned brushland in regular cycles, new plants would grow. This attracted animals that could then be hunted.

He'd wonder why there were giant pictures hanging in the sky

Obviously, our prehistoric man wouldn't know anything about modern **advertising 312** billboards. But he would have known something about **art 322**, a key indicator of creative minds at work. Around 40,000 years ago, there is the earliest evidence of human art in southwestern Europe. Some 10,000 years later, cave paintings had become elaborate with processions of animals and mysterious shapes—as seen at Lascaux in France (pictured).

What they mean and why they were painted is unknown. They may have had something to do with religious or magical practice—they may be attempts to influence the behavior of animals they hunted. Whatever the purpose, the art died out 9,000 years ago, as mysteriously as it had begun. It would be another 6,000 years before the world saw great art again.

He wouldn't be here— he'd be in Africa

Archeologists can't be sure when modern humans, known as *Homo sapiens* (pictured), first evolved. (The **fossil 162** record is patchy at best, and archeologists are fond of arguing about dates.) One hotly debated theory is that humans appeared abruptly in Africa some 120,000-250,000 years ago. They then spread across the rest of the world—there is evidence that they were in Europe 40,000 years ago and had reached Siberia (the top right of Russia) 25,000 years back. From there they crossed into the Americas. They must have used boats to reach Australia (possibly as far back as 60,000 years ago). Born ramblers.

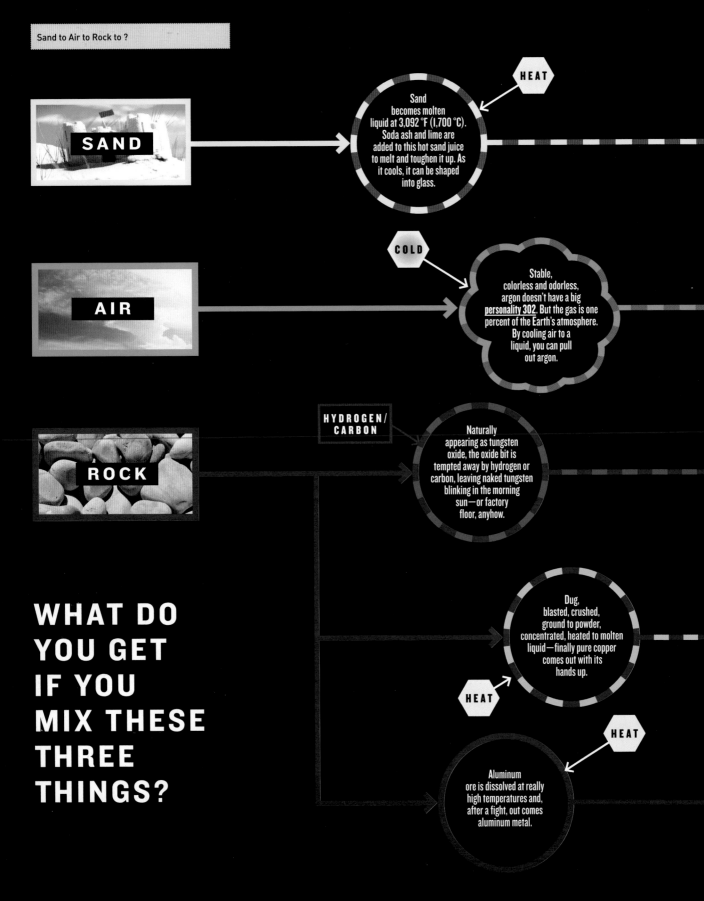

SAND

AIR

ROCK

HEAT

Sand becomes molten liquid at 3,092 °F (1,700 °C). Soda ash and lime are added to this hot sand juice to melt and toughen it up. As it cools, it can be shaped into glass.

COLD

Stable, colorless and odorless, argon doesn't have a big **personality 302**. But the gas is one percent of the Earth's atmosphere. By cooling air to a liquid, you can pull out argon.

HYDROGEN/ CARBON

Naturally appearing as tungsten oxide, the oxide bit is tempted away by hydrogen or carbon, leaving naked tungsten blinking in the morning sun—or factory floor, anyhow.

Dug, blasted, crushed, ground to powder, concentrated, heated to molten liquid—finally pure copper comes out with its hands up.

HEAT

HEAT

Aluminum ore is dissolved at really high temperatures and, after a fight, out comes aluminum metal.

WHAT DO YOU GET IF YOU MIX THESE THREE THINGS?

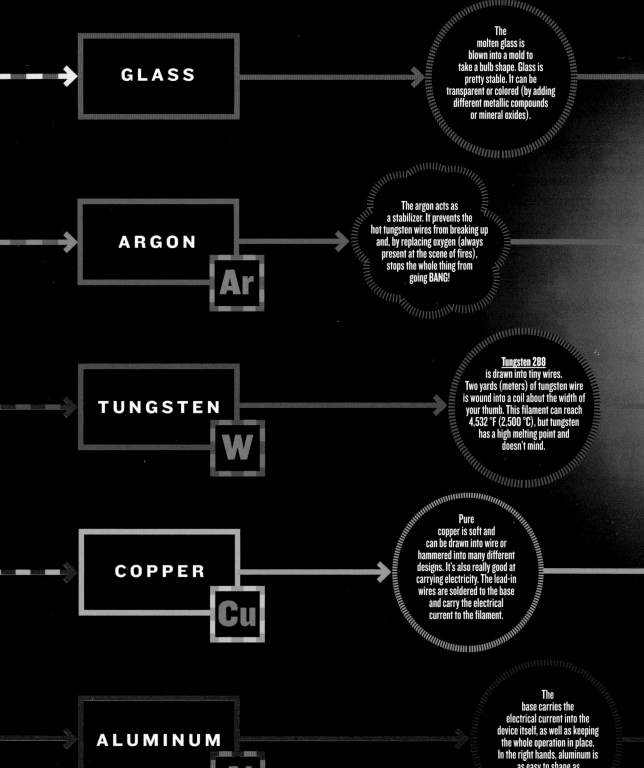

GLASS

The molten glass is blown into a mold to take a bulb shape. Glass is pretty stable. It can be transparent or colored (by adding different metallic compounds or mineral oxides).

ARGON **Ar**

The argon acts as a stabilizer. It prevents the hot tungsten wires from breaking up and, by replacing oxygen (always present at the scene of fires), stops the whole thing from going BANG!

TUNGSTEN **W**

Tungsten 288 is drawn into tiny wires. Two yards (meters) of tungsten wire is wound into a coil about the width of your thumb. This filament can reach 4,532 °F (2,500 °C), but tungsten has a high melting point and doesn't mind.

COPPER **Cu**

Pure copper is soft and can be drawn into wire or hammered into many different designs. It's also really good at carrying electricity. The lead-in wires are soldered to the base and carry the electrical current to the filament.

ALUMINUM **Al**

The base carries the electrical current into the device itself, as well as keeping the whole operation in place. In the right hands, aluminum is as easy to shape as modeling clay.

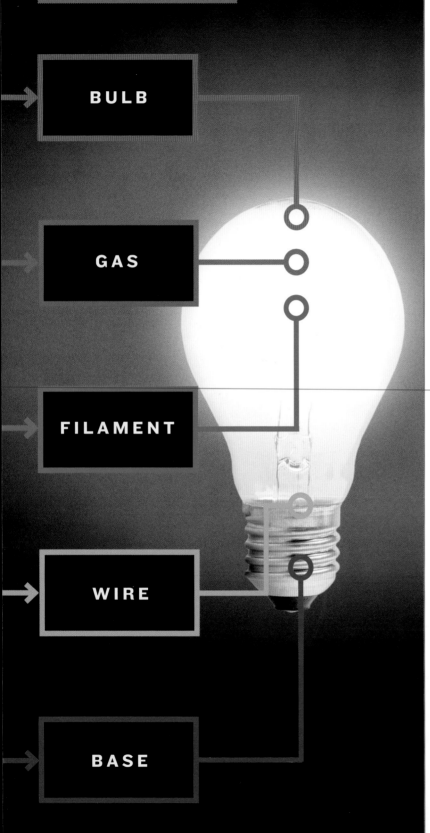

BULB

GAS

FILAMENT

WIRE

BASE

What are you thinking?

Your body language can give some pretty obvious clues to what you're thinking. Open palms mean you're interested in what's going on. But standing with your arms and legs crossed means you probably want to be left alone. And if you're lying, chances are you won't look people in the eye, you'll wave your hands around too much, sweat, and even bite your fingernails.

Facial expressions tell a lot about what we're thinking—often without us knowing it. Scientist Paul Ekman discovered that humans use about 3,000 different facial expressions to show their feelings. Many are the same all around the world, such as <u>**smiling 078**</u> and wrinkling our noses to show disgust.

Your voice also gives you away. Through tiny changes in tone, it reveals details such as your emotional state or how you feel about the person you're talking to. If your voice rises at the end of a sentence, you might be insecure about what you're saying (or Australian).

And your inner state of mind is also revealed by your outward appearance. Hiding behind your bangs tells other people

that you're insecure. If you wear flattering clothes, you're proud of your body. The way you look reveals things about your tastes (for instance, what music you like) and attitude (are you outgoing or shy?).

Where's my cake?

HOW TO
TELL WHEN SOMEONE (REALLY) LIKES YOU

Reading body language is not exactly a science. But by keeping a close eye on the person you're talking to, you can figure out whether or not they find you completely repellent. Look out for these signs to tell if they've got the hots for you! Only, don't jump to conclusions. One of these points on their own doesn't mean anything. You need to collect the set to score a definite crush...

1. They watch your mouth and look intensely from eye to eye.

WAS FREUD A BIT BONKERS?

I'm a little insecure

I'm not going to lie to you

I like you

Don't embarrass me

I need to go to the

Sigmund Freud (1856-1939), an Austrian doctor, had some pretty crazy ideas. After all, he made his patients lie on his couch and talk about their problems. He thought nearly everything they said was really about sex. He invented the Oedipus complex, where boys want to kill their fathers and marry their mothers. And he was partial to the **drug 280** cocaine. Surely all that makes him a little nuts?

Actually, no. Freud laid the foundations for modern psychiatry (the study and treatment of mental illness). He believed that the unconscious (the part of the mind you are unaware of) has a lot to do with your behavior. That's why he got his patients to talk so much—to uncover their hidden fears and desires (this was called pyschoanalysis). He believed that the mind was split into three parts. The id is the instinctive "me, me, me" part. The superego is the sensible part that makes you follow rules. And the ego is the conscious self stuck in-between.

Freud's theories dominated psychology (the study of the mind) until the 1960s. But modern psychiatrists are critical—Freud's method wasn't very scientific and not everything is to do with sex. No single school rules the psychology roost today. Instead, there are varied approaches to treating patients. Cognitive therapy tackles how the brain deals with information. Social psychology looks at the effects of society on the individual. Evolutionary psychology focuses on how **evolution 206** has shaped the mind. They all use different methods in their treatments. But the couch is still popular.

The dark side of obedience

In the 1960s, psychologist Stanley Milgram set up an **experiment 326** to find out what ordinary people were prepared to do when asked by someone in authority. In the test, the 'subject' was asked to give painful electric shocks to another participant (who was actually an actor, and not being hurt at all). Milgram found that nearly two-thirds of people were willing to inflict what they thought was considerable pain on someone else just because the scientist in charge told them to. The study showed how easily normal people can cause suffering when they blindly obey authority (but don't bother trying this line with a policeman).

Madmen who made the world

Because you don't always have to think straight...

Nebuchadnezzar II (died: 562 BC) Ruler of Babylon. In later life, he imagined he was a goat and ate grass (saying "baaaah" was probably easier than saying his name).

+++++++++++++++++++

Peter the Great (1672-1725) Czar of Russia. Peter was over 6 ft 9 in (two meters) tall and liked hanging out with dwarves and people with funny faces. When he was 52, he filled his house with fireworks, set fire to it, and marched around beating a drum.

* * * * * * * * * * * * * * * * * *

George III (1738-1820) King of England. He was put in a straitjacket to control his ravings. Modern studies suggest he was afflicted with porphyria, a maddening disease possibly set off by arsenic. (No wonder he lost Britain's American **colonies 096**.)

2. The pupils in their eyes swell and they blink more often.

3. When they first see you, their eyebrows rise and fall (be alert—it only lasts one fifth of a second).

4. They point their body in your direction.

5. If they mimic you (you sip your juice, they sip theirs)—you might just have scored!

THE ALPHABET TO ODYSSEUS OF WHAT THE ANCIENT GREEKS DID FOR US

THE ANCIENT GREEKS WERE A SMART BUNCH. FROM THE FIRST OLYMPICS IN 776 BC TO WHEN THE ROMANS TOOK OVER IN 146 BC, THEY OPERATED A SMART, MODERN CIVILIZATION THAT STILL INFLUENCES THE WORLD TODAY. RESPECT IS DUE

CHEWING GUM

The ancient Greeks chewed mastiche, a resin from the bark of the small, mastic tree ("mastic" is another word for chew). They liked it because it kept their breath smelling sweet. Whether or not chewed lumps of gum got stuck to the ancients' sandals is, sadly, lost to history.

COMPUTER

Obviously, the ancient Greeks didn't have laptops. But they did create a complex system of gears and dials to calculate the motions of the Sun, Moon, and planets. A 2,000-year-old device was found in the Mediterranean Sea in 1900 and has been called the world's oldest computer.

FIRE EXTINGUISHER

Ctesibius (285-222 BC), a clever engineer, created an early fire extinguisher using a force pump. This worked by compressing water in a cyclinder, then using a piston to shoot it out. Take that!

FLAME-THROWER

Fire has always been used as a weapon. By the time of the ancient Greeks, people were shooting fiery arrows every time a war broke out. The Greek flame-thrower dates to 424 BC. It was a hollow wooden tube that held a cauldron of burning sulfur, charcoal, and pitch at one end. It only had a range of 16 ft (5 m), but it could sure mess up an enemy **ship 273**.

ALPHABET

Around 1500 BC, the Phoenicians (later the Greeks' neighbors) created an alphabet with no vowels (a-e-i-o-u), like txt tlk. In the eighth century BC, the Greeks adapted this to include vowels. With 22 letters, it laid the foundation for today's alphabet. Alpha and beta, the first two letters, created the word "alphabet".

CRANES

Archeologists suspect that cranes were used to build in ancient Greece: simply because some of the stuff they had to move was so incredibly heavy. What we're certain about is that the crane was used in Greek theater, to make actors fly around like the **gods 185**.

DEMOCRACY

Cleisthenes, a Greek statesman, introduced demokratia ("people power") to Athens in about 510 BC. **Democracy 194** today refers to a political system where the government is selected by vote. In ancient Greece, 5,000 free men (women, slaves, foreigners, and children were excluded) held regular meetings to discuss how things should be run.

ASPIRIN

Hippocrates, a physician known as the "father of medicine," used a powder from the willow tree to relieve **pain 084**. After a small gap of some 2,200 years, the ingredient was named salicin. A German scientist then used it to create aspirin.

THEATER

The first actor recorded in history, Thespis, lived 2,500 years ago. Ancient Greeks adored stories and poems, and speakers like Thespis would read these to audiences. Then one day, Thespis shocked his audience by leaping onto a cart and "acting" the story. **Actors 222** today are sometimes called thespians.

LIGHTHOUSE

The lighthouse of the city of Alexandria was one of the **Seven Wonders 308** of the ancient world. Credited to the astronomer Ptolemy, it was built around 300 BC. Apparently, the light at the top (mirrors reflecting fire or sunlight) could be seen up to 300 miles (483 km) away.

PHILOSOPHY

The founder of modern **philosophy 042** was called Socrates (469 BC-399 BC). He believed that the more you knew, the better person you were. But angry Greeks disagreed with his ideas and he was forced to drink a lethal poison. Plato, his pupil, later invented universities and homework (the fool!).

VENDING MACHINE

Heron (10 BC-70 AD), an inventor, created a slot machine that is the basis for modern vending machines. Just like today, you inserted a coin. The weight of this lifted a lever, which opened a valve and shot out some water. (Luckily, the snacks have developed since.)

ODYSSEUS

Odysseus was one of the original Greek heroes. The concept and the word "hero" derives from Greek myths (stories). Heroes were dead characters who could still influence the living—a kind of bridge between gods and man. Odysseus won the battle of Troy in Homer's epic poem *The Odyssey* by hiding Greek troops in a large wooden horse (who would ever guess?).

OLYMPICS

The first **Olympic games 180** took place nearly 3,000 years ago. Back then, Greece was divided into many city-states (called polis). Each one wanted to show that it was the best, so they sent athletes to Olympia (a sacred site for worshipping top god Zeus) to compete. Running, boxing, and wrestling were all performed at these early games.

GUESS WHAT? THE GREEKS CALLED THEMSELVES HELLENES. "GREEK" WAS A NAME GIVEN TO THEM LATER BY THE ROMANS

SHOWER

The first image of showers with plumbed-in water can be found on an ancient Greek vase from the fourth century. It shows four **athletes 052** bathing under water sprays. Other than the showerheads, which had images of boars and lions, the showers look just like the ones that you should use more often.

LEVER

A lever may not sound impressive. But third-century BC mathematician Archimedes made everyone realise how important it is. The device paved the way for modern necessities. Scissors, pliers and (essential) hair straighteners would be useless without it.

WAS NELSON MANDELA A TERRORIST?

A terrorist is someone who uses violence, or the threat of violence, to intimidate or terrorize governments or societies to achieve a political goal. Nelson Mandela is a famous South African politician who fought to abolish the racist laws of his country. As part of this struggle, he used violence to get the government to change its policies. So, does that mean he was a terrorist?

Terrorism—today

In the Middle East, the Palestinians and Israelis disagree about the borders of their countries. Some Palestinian groups, such as Hamas, make terrorist attacks on Israel. These include using suicide bombers against civilians. They claim to be fighting a war of liberation against Israeli oppression, using **asymmetrical warfare 294**.

ETA is the name of an organization founded in 1959 that believes a part of Spain (and France), called the Basque Country, should be a separate nation. ETA has organized attacks all over Spain. Its bombs have often killed innocent people.

Al-Qaeda (meaning "the base") is an international terrorist group with radical Islamic goals, including the establishment of a new Caliphate. Al-Qaeda has admitted responsibility for the attacks on the US on September 11, 2001 (known as 9/11), when thousands of innocent people died. Al-Qaeda has been connected to bomb attacks in many other countries, including the UK, **Spain 164**, Saudi Arabia, and Kenya.

WHO ARE YOU CALLING A "TERRORIST"?

There are other figures who, like Mandela, have been described as terrorists but have became politicians.

Menachem Begin

In the 1940s, Menachem Begin wanted Jews to have their own state and became involved in armed rebellion against British rule in Palestine. On his orders, the King David hotel in Jerusalem (where the British had a head-quarters) was bombed, killing 91 people. In 1948, Israel was created, with Begin becoming Prime Minister in 1977.

From 1948 to 1992, **South Africa 230** lived under a regime called apartheid (from the Dutch word meaning "separateness"). Under this system, white people had more **rights 226** than the indigenous black Africans and other nonwhites. For example, nonwhites were not allowed to enter cities without carrying a special book, like a passport, which contained information on them. Nonwhites were not allowed in the same hospitals and schools as whites. Nonwhites were not even allowed to travel on the same buses as whites. The country was as good as color-coded, with the whites having the best of everything.

As a young man, Nelson Mandela decided these laws were wrong. He joined a political party

called the African National Congress (ANC) and helped organize protests against racism. The protests were peaceful, but the white government would not tolerate them. In 1960, there was a huge protest by Africans in a black town called Sharpeville. The police opened fire, killing and injuring hundreds of protesters. In response, hundreds of Africans rioted in anger. But instead of listening, the white government decided to make political parties like the ANC illegal.

This meant that no protests of any kind were permitted. Mandela decided that the only way now to protest was through violent acts. He created a new group called "Umkhonto we Sizwe", which means "Spear of the Nation" (known as MK

for short). Its goal was to attack the symbols of apartheid, such as military and industrial sites. Mandela was captured and imprisoned in 1962. The South African government called him a terrorist.

MK did not set out to kill innocent people. But incidents such as the 1983 bomb blast in Pretoria that killed 17 were bound to hurt bystanders. By the 1980s, the ANC itself was described as a terrorist organization by the UK and the US governments. (Mandela, in prison at the time, still supported the armed struggle.)

While in prison, Mandela was a symbol of resistance against white oppression. He refused to be intimidated by his jailers or to make a deal to secure his release. Only free men can negotiate, he

famously said. He became a focus for antiapartheid campaigners around the world. **Pop 305** bands wrote hit songs about him. Likewise, MK described its members as "freedom fighters," not terrorists. They argued that the end (abolition of apartheid) justified the means (armed struggle).

In 1990, after much international pressure (and 28 years in prison), Mandela was set free. He negotiated with the South African President to bring an end to apartheid. In 1993, he received the Nobel Peace Prize. And 1994 saw the first multiracial elections in the country. Mandela was elected president. He is now considered a global statesman for peace, not a terrorist.

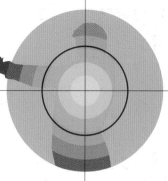

THE FIRST ASSASSINS?

The Assassins (or Hashshashin to give them their Arabic name) were a secretive Islamic sect specializing in political killings. Thought to be active from the 8th to the 14th century, they were feared throughout the Middle East. They were very skilled killers, often targeting their victims in public.

2004
635 DEATHS FROM TERRORISM WORLDWIDE
275,000 DEATHS FROM INDIAN OCEAN TSUNAMI

TERRORISM—THEN
THE WORD "TERRORISM" COMES FROM THE FRENCH WORD "TERRORISME," WHICH WAS FIRST USED IN THE 1790s. THEN, IT REFERRED TO THE VIOLENT METHODS USED BY THE GOVERNMENT AGAINST ITS OPPONENTS (THE REVERSE OF WHAT IT IS NOW).

Martin McGuinness

From the 1970s to the 1990s, the Irish Republican Army (IRA) was involved in a violent struggle against British rule in Northern Ireland. Martin McGuinness was a senior IRA member (arrested in 1973 for carrying explosives) who later became involved in the peace process. He was appointed Minister of Education for Northern Ireland in 1999.

Yasser Arafat

Yasser Arafat led the Palestine Liberation Organization (PLO) from 1969 until his death in 2004. Land had been taken from **Palestinians 046** when the state of Israel was created. The PLO used hijackings (as above, in 1970) and assassinations to further its cause. In the 1990s, Arafat negotiated a peace deal with Israel that won him the Nobel Peace Prize in 1994.

⊥ Germany is the wealthiest country in Europe. The top five richest countries in Europe by **gross domestic product** (amount of goods and services produced) are:

1. Germany: $2.365 trillion
2. UK: $1.782 trillion
3. France: $1.737 trillion
4. Italy: $1.609 trillion
5. Russia: $1.408 trillion

⊥ The Germans invented the highway, or autobahn.

The first **autobahn** opened between Cologne and Bonn in 1932. The autobahn system today stretches 6,800 miles (11,000 km). On many German highways, there is no speed limit.

Meet the neighbors

Germany is at the heart of Europe. In addition to having a coastline to the north, it shares a border with nine countries.

Denmark 42 miles (68 km)

Netherlands 359 miles (577 km)

Poland 283 miles (456 km)

Germany

Belgium 104 miles (167 km)

Czech Republic 401 miles (646 km)

Slovakia

Luxembourg 86 miles (138 km)

Austria 487 miles (784 km)

France 280 miles (451 km)

Hungary

Switzerland 208 miles (334 km)

Keep it green

Germany is a green place. Nearly a third of the country is covered with <u>trees 010</u>.

Farm land 54.1% **Forest 29.4%** **Towns and cities 11.8%**

Other 4.7%

Each household creates 1,279 lbs (580 kg) of trash per year. But Germans are committed to <u>recycling 310</u>, too.

Waste recycling

1990 less than 15%

2003 58%

Germany...

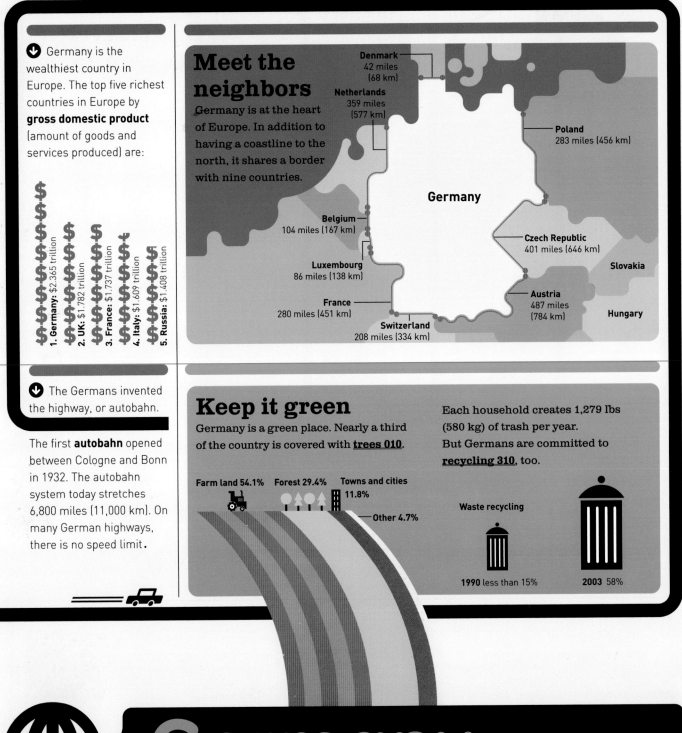

Most popular sports

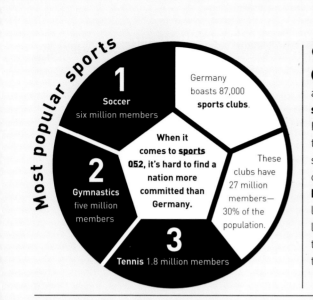

1 Soccer six million members

2 Gymnastics five million members

3 Tennis 1.8 million members

Germany boasts 87,000 **sports clubs**.

When it comes to **sports** 052, it's hard to find a nation more committed than Germany.

These clubs have 27 million members—30% of the population.

→ Brothers Adolf (known as Adi) and Rudolph Dassler started making **sports shoes** in their hometown of Herzogenaurauch, near Nuremberg, in the 1920s. But they fell out and in 1948 set up separate companies. Adi's was called **Adidas**, while Rudolph named his **Puma**. Adidas registered its three stripes logo in 1949. Puma trademarked its leaping cat in 1968. Both are still based in the town, and both are among the world's top five sporting goods companies.

Exports and imports

Germany exports more than any other country in the world. Top **exports** in 2004 (million euros):

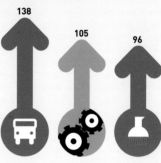

138 Motor vehicles, trailers and semitrailers

105 Machinery and equipment

96 Chemicals and chemical products

Germany is the world's second biggest importer (after the US). Top **imports** in 2004 (million euros):

66 Chemicals and chemical products

62 Motor vehicles, trailers and semitrailers

41 Machinery and equipment

Food and drink

Germany is famous for its beer. The country exports 12.9 percent of the beer it produces each year— that's 2,899,130 pints (1,371,800 liters).

The Germans like their meat—and they're pretty keen on potatoes, too. They eat 2.8 billion lbs (1.27 bn kg) of **meat** and sausages per year.

Mr. (or Mrs.) Average German consumes each year...

245 pints (115.8 liters) of beer

134 lbs (61 kg) of meat and sausages

84 lbs (38 kg) of potatoes

74 lbs (34 kg) of ready-made potatoes (chips, fries, mashed, etc)

↓ Where is Germany?

↓ Nation knowledge

 Population **82 million— holding steady**

 Only 15 percent of Germans were **under 15 years** of age in 2005.

 In 2005, there were nearly as many **old ladies** as children.

 By 2050, every third person will be over **60 years old**.

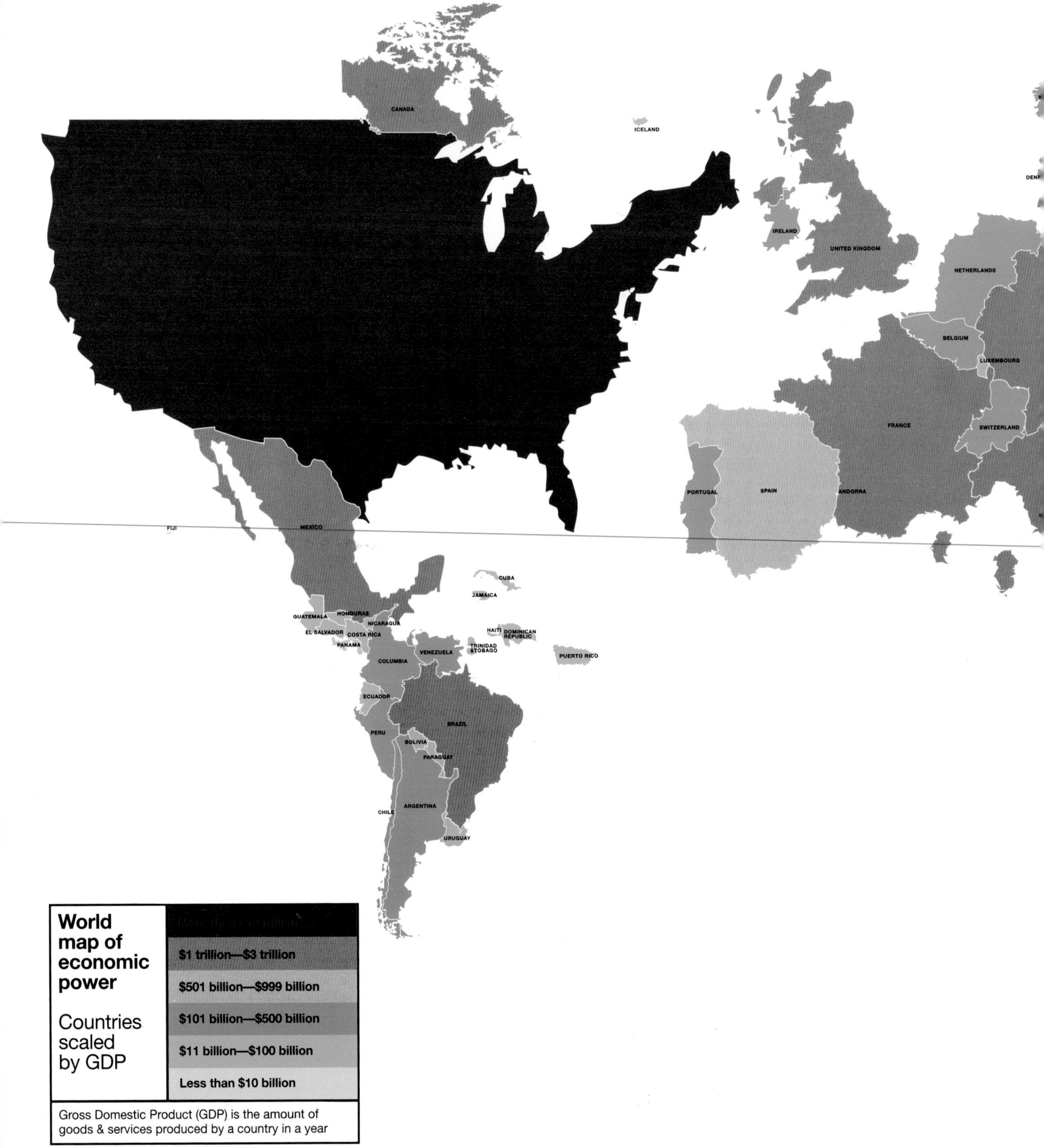

CANADA

ICELAND

DEN

IRELAND

UNITED KINGDOM

NETHERLANDS

BELGIUM

LUXEMBOURG

FRANCE

SWITZERLAND

PORTUGAL

SPAIN

ANDORRA

FIJI

MEXICO

CUBA

JAMAICA

GUATEMALA

HONDURAS

NICARAGUA

HAITI

DOMINICAN
REPUBLIC

EL SALVADOR

COSTA RICA

PANAMA

TRINIDAD
&TOBAGO

PUERTO RICO

COLUMBIA

VENEZUELA

ECUADOR

BRAZIL

PERU

BOLIVIA

PARAGUAY

CHILE

ARGENTINA

URUGUAY

World map of economic power	
	More than $3 trillion
Countries scaled by GDP	$1 trillion—$3 trillion
	$501 billion—$999 billion
	$101 billion—$500 billion
	$11 billion—$100 billion
	Less than $10 billion

Gross Domestic Product (GDP) is the amount of
goods & services produced by a country in a year

"The countries of the developing world will be the economic superpowers of the 21st century"
Discuss

WAR: WHAT IS IT GOOD FOR?

WAR IS BAD, BUT IT DOES PRODUCE ONE GOOD THING: TECHNOLOGICAL INNOVATION

RADAR TO MICROWAVE OVEN

The microwave was invented in 1947 after a scientist realized that the chocolate bar in his pocket melted when he went near a military radar. The first "Radarange," as it was then called, was so big and expensive that it was only used in restaurants. Not until the 1970s did microwaves as we know them today became common in household kitchens.

V2 ROCKET TO MAN ON THE MOON

In the 1940s, the Germans were at the forefront of rocket technology. Their V2 missile was launched against **Allied 294** cities, including Paris and London, in 1944. At the close of the war, the US grabbed as many V2 parts and scientists as it could get hold of, including the leader of the rocket program Wernher von Braun. He became head of the US's space rocket program that put a man on the **Moon 048** in 1969.

MINUTEMAN BALLISTIC MISSILE TO GAMEBOY

Silicon chips were developed for the US Air Force in the 1960s to improve the guidance computers on their nuclear missiles. The "chips" soon found their way into the consumer market, and are now in everything from watches to iPods to Gameboys.

ARMY RATIONS TO A CAN OF BAKED BEANS

During the French Revolutionary Wars, **Napoleon's 022** troops needed food rations that wouldn't rot. In 1809, sweet-maker François Appert figured out how to preserve food inside vacuum-sealed glass jars. A pleased Napoleon awarded him 12,000 francs. In Britain, Peter Durand developed Appert's ideas to store food in tin canisters. The idea traveled to the USA and, in 1895, preserved foods entrepreneur Henry Heinz put baked beans and tomato sauce into a can. Yum!

B-2 BOMBER TO CAR NAVIGATION

The Global Positioning System (GPS) uses a minimum of 14 satellites in orbit around the Earth to figure out precisely where you are. It was developed in the 1970s and 1980s to guide weapons such as the B-2 bomber and cruise missiles. Today, anyone can use the system, from pilots to lost drivers.

LAND MINES TO NOTHING GOOD

Land mines just blow people up. They are so nasty that 122 governments signed a treaty in 1997 to try to ban them—because they end up killing and maiming innocent civilians long after any conflict has ended. What a waste.

ARPANET TO ONLINE SHOPPING

In 1968, the US military experimented with a computer network linking together a small number of universities. More computers joined the network, but by 1979 there were only 110 hosts (connected computers). It only really took off with the home computing revolution, becoming what is now known as the **internet 330**. Today, there are in excess of 350 million hosts.

AIRPHIBIAN: Fed up with being stuck at airports with no way of getting into town, American inventor Robert Fulton Jr. created an **airplane 304** in 1945 that could convert into an car. Although over 6,000 prototypes were made, the weight of the parts meant the idea failed to take off. Literally.

CEMENT FURNITURE: Even the best get it wrong sometimes. Thomas Alva Edison, inventor of the **light bulb 211**, the phonograph (the earliest method of sound recording) and the motion picture camera, fell down when he tried to introduce cabinets and pianos made from concrete. Nice try, but the concrete furniture was far too heavy to move and was darned expensive, too. The concept went down like a concrete balloon.

EUREK-EH?

SOME INVENTIONS DON'T QUITE WORK OUT

JUMPING SHOES: To try to get kids to run and jump more, American couple George and May Southgate invented jumping shoes in 1922. You placed the shoes over your regular ones and held them in place with a buckle. Rather like grasshoppers, they had six strong and springy legs (only these were made of steel) to help the wearer jump farther. But then they realized that kids couldn't actually walk in them. Minor detail...

CHICKEN GLASSES: The UK patent office has previously recorded such successful patents (inventors' ideas) as the flush toilet and aspirin. But it has also registered many that never quite made it. Among more amusing failures are spectacles for chickens (to stop them from pecking each other's eyes out, obviously), two-person gloves (so couples can hold hands in cold weather) and coffins equipped with alarms (for people accidentally buried alive—whoops).

WHAT TIME IS IT?

(turn the page)

It may be 9 a.m. in Boston, 8:30 p.m. in Kabul, and midnight in Beijing. The world is split into 24 time zones. These mean the Sun is always directly overhead at 12 noon—wherever you are

When did time begin?

It depends which calendar you ask. The various ones in use today haven't existed since the dawn of time (whenever that was...). People invented and began using them at different points in history, and each backdated to when time "officially" began. For example, people in the <u>US 256</u> and Europe mostly use the Gregorian calendar, a Christian calendar decreed and named after Pope Gregory XIII on February 24, 1582. According to this, the "initial epoch" was when Christ was born, AD 1 (or "Anno Domini," which means "in the year of the Lord" in <u>Latin 054</u>). Years that passed before Christ's birth are counted backward from AD and marked BC (Before Christ). The Chinese calendar has a different idea. It counts years in cycles, with no particular cycle specified as the initial one. And according to the Hebrew calendar, the initial epoch was AM 1 ("Anno Mundi," Latin for "in the year of the world"). If we translate this into the Gregorian calendar, Hebrew time began in 3761 BC.

Why does time fly only when you're having fun, then go really slowly when you're doing homework?

Distinct from clocks, time zones, and official measurements, everybody has their own "personal" sense of time. This goes more quickly when we're completely absorbed in an activity (reading a great book, trying our best in an exam) and more slowly when we're wishing an activity was over (homework, a boring bus trip). Try to record your personal time today. Do some activities—some fun, some dull. Decide how long they took in "personal time," then look at a clock or watch to find out how long they took in actual time. You'll find the two differ quite a bit. This explains why a world in which everyone ran around without an agreed official time would be utter chaos. For a start, no one would arrive at <u>school 166</u> at the same time (if their "personal clocks" said they had to go at all).

Have we always used clocks to tell the time?

<u>Ancient Egyptians 100</u> first used a water clock. It measured time by letting water flow out of a container through a tiny hole. Since the rate of flow was difficult to control, water clocks were never very accurate—although they are still used in parts of northern Africa. The hourglass was first used during the 14th century to measure time at sea. Fine sand flows from one glass bulb into another through a narrow tube. The problem with the hourglass, of course, is that it can measure only one given time. Ancient Egyptians (clearly very busy people) also invented the sundial. This measures time by the position of the sun as it casts a shadow on a flat surface marked with hours of the day. As the sun's position changes, so does the time indicated by the shadow. The good old clock, however, is our most reliable timekeeper. Sunlight isn't necessary, and it is now a lot more accurate then when 13th-century Italian monks created the first clocks to measure intervals between prayers.

What does time look like?

Superclever philosophers have been battling this one out for years. **Isaac Newton 024** believed that time and space form a container for events, kind of like a bucket. No, really: he argued that this container is as real as the objects it contains. But other smarties figure that time doesn't look like anything at all. It is an abstract framework we use to help keep events in order. And, therefore, it doesn't flow, it can't contain anything and time travel is impossible. To further stir up the brain-busting debate, some suggest time is circular and that we have an infinite past and infinite future. (Contrary to rumors, time looks nothing like a sheep playing poker in a leotard.)

Spacetime— is that what aliens use to measure time in outer space?

No. It actually refers to the extremely important discovery made by **Albert Einstein 132** in 1915 that time and space are relative. Eh? Let's use an example to explain. You're standing still on a hill and see two firecrackers explode in the sky at the exact same time. Your friend Suzy, however, is running down the hill at half the speed of light to buy popcorn (faster than is humanly possible—she's very hungry) and sees one firecracker exploding before another. Einstein's theory means you're both correct: for you, the firecrackers did explode at precisely the same time, while for Suzy the explosions actually did occur seconds apart. Time and space are "different" for you and Suzy because you are moving at different speeds. That's why we say they are "relative": one affects the other. If Suzy had been running even more quickly (unlikely, considering how much popcorn she eats), she would have seen an even bigger gap between the explosions. Time and space, therefore, shouldn't always be treated as distinct things, but should be linked together. Rather imaginatively, Einstein named this partnership "spacetime."

Why do people in the States say "time is money"?

Benjamin Franklin, one of the leaders of the **Revolutionary War 138**, first said those words to a young tradesman in 1748, and they've been in use ever since. The richest nation on the planet, the US has always had a strong work ethic. The concept of the "self-made man or woman" is central to the national identity. This is the idea that the more time you spend working, the more successful you shall be (of course, if the boss at your Saturday job mumbles the phrase, it's because you shouldn't be texting your friends). People in places like Kenya, for example, have different perceptions about time and the best way to spend it. Kenyans contentedly chat with friends for hours, enjoying and savoring time spent building and maintaining relationships without anxiety about meeting this deadline or that one. **French 290** people traditionally spend a lot of time dining every day. A sociable mealtime with family and friends is an important daily activity that mustn't be cut short. The contrasting ways in which cultures spend time tells us lots about the way we live.

Have we always used seconds, minutes, and hours?

No—not the same kind of seconds, minutes, and hours, anyway. Ancient Romans and Greeks measured their hours according to sunlight. One hour was one twelfth of the time between sunrise and sunset. However, this meant the length of the hours would change when they had more sunlight in summer and less in winter—so they had to adjust their clocks constantly. These days, the second is the unit of time that dictates all the rest. It is our standard unit of time. This is set according to more advanced means than sun or sand—it's set according to 200 **atomic 060** clocks in 50 different laboratories around the world. Between them, they ensure our measurement of every second is absolutely accurate—so that every minute is just right. And so is every hour, day, week, month, year, decade, century (you get the idea...).

What time is it now?

While you've been blowing your mind with time knowledge, the sneaky thing's just continued passing by. Time waits for no encyclopedia reader, buddy.

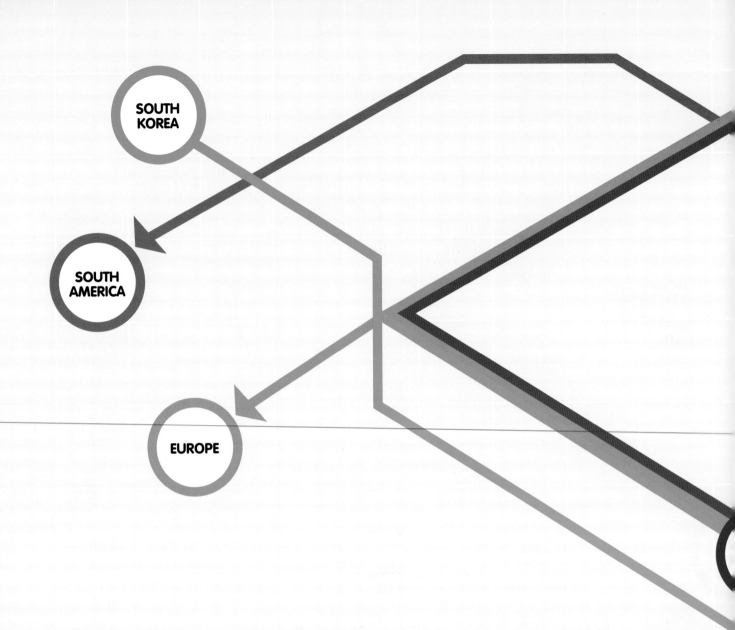

Imagine how far this book has traveled

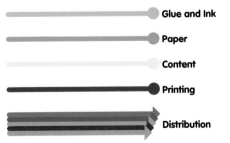

● Glue and Ink
● Paper
● Content
● Printing
➤ Distribution

SOUTH KOREA

SOUTH AMERICA

EUROPE

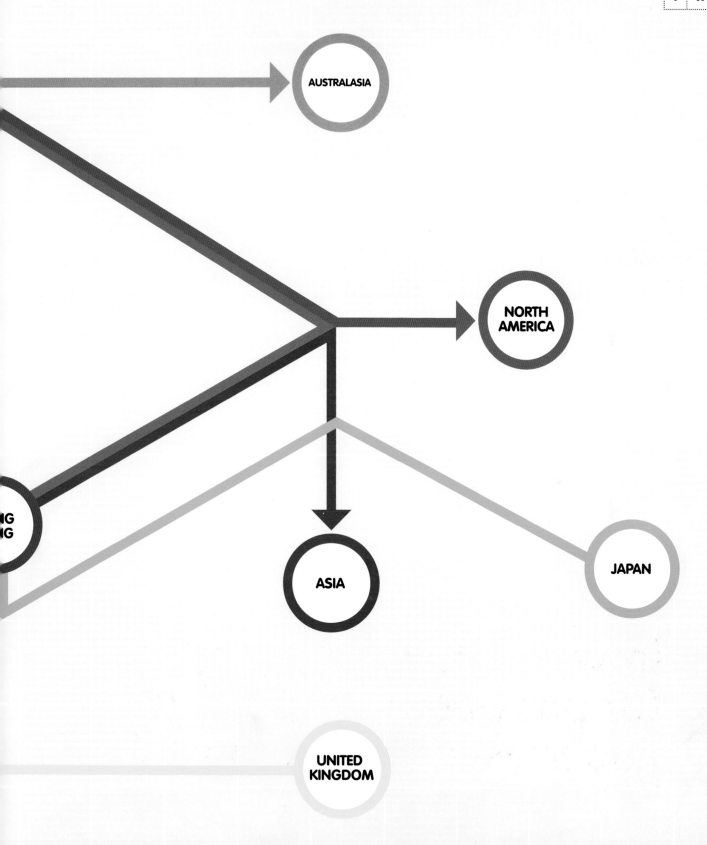

ROBOT

Leonardo created the earliest known design for a humanoid mechanical robot. It's not known how far he got with his ideas, but the mechanical man was designed to move its jaw and head, sit up, and wave its arms. This was 200 years before the first mechanical robots were built. And it was in 1948 that the first electronic robot was made.

SUBMARINE

Over 100 years before the first working submarine was tested in London's Thames River, Leonardo had the idea on his drawing board. It was big enough for one person and had a conning tower (the piece that sticks up) like modern subs.

HOW **LEONARDO DA VINCI** MADE THE FUTURE

Most people have one job. Leonardo da Vinci (1452-1519) had at least eight. He was a painter, sculptor, architect, musician, engineer, anatomist, mathematician, and inventor. He lived in an era known as the **Renaissance 148**.

When he wasn't painting the *Mona Lisa* **190**, Leonardo was designing bridges or dissecting human bodies. Since Leonardo's time, people who have many different skills are often referred to as "Renaissance men."

Some of the things Leonardo described were so ahead of their time that they weren't built until 400 years later. He never published his notebooks and they remained obscure until the late 19th century. So nobody could try out his ideas.

HELICOPTER

Leonardo was fascinated with flying machines. In 1483 he came up with a design for the first helicopter. At the time, there wasn't the technology to make a working model. It wasn't until the 1940s that helicopters became practical.

PARACHUTE

Probably never tested as a full-scale model, Leonardo's parachute was made of linen cloth tucked over a **pyramid 314** of wooden poles. There was no harness—so if you let go you'd be in trouble. But the design has been shown to work.

TANK

Leonardo's "covered chariot" was designed to smash through enemy ranks. Reinforced with metal plates, it was powered by men cranking handles. Troops were supposed to fire weapons from the upper turret. The first tank was used by Britain in **World War I 294** in 1916.

VEGGIE DA VINCI

For part of his life, Leonardo da Vinci was a vegetarian. People who didn't eat meat were pretty unusual in Europe at the time. But vegetarianism has been a feature of **Hindu 186** and Buddhist societies for thousands of years. Lucky animals.

* FAMOUS FICTIONAL FUTURES *

FILMS

THE MATRIX

Humans are an energy source for the machines that really run the world. A group of rebels fights the system, mostly wearing sunglasses and black coats.

RELEASED 1999

2001: A SPACE ODYSSEY

Director Stanley Kubrick's epic story about the fate of mankind. It used groundbreaking special effects, which would become ever more important for big budget science fiction films.

RELEASED 1968

METROPOLIS

A silent movie directed by Fritz Lang about a **dystopian 104** future. It is set in a city where the "planners," who run the place, live in luxurious skyscrapers, while the workers are kept below ground.

RELEASED 1927

BOOKS

THE TIME MACHINE (1895)

A time traveler goes far into the future to discover a peaceful planet, in H. G. Wells' popular novel. But, beneath the surface, something sinister lurks. Ooooh.

BRAVE NEW WORLD (1932)

Aldous Huxley's future has a world where poverty and war no longer exist, but neither do things like art, philosophy, family, or religion.

NEUROMANCER (1984)

Written by William Gibson, this sci-fi novel depicts a future filled with hackers, intelligent computers, and virtual reality. Sound familiar?

PREDICTING THE FUTURE IS A DIFFICULT BUSINESS

HIT!

Math genius Charles Babbage came up with the idea of the **computer** in 1837. His version was steam-powered and called the Analytical Engine.

...Science fiction writer Arthur C. Clarke came up with the idea of **satellites** that could be used to send telecommunications around the globe in 1945—20 years before the first one was launched.

...The **fax machine** was invented in 1842—seven years before the telephone. A Scottish physicist and clockmaker, Alexander Bain, devised a system using swinging pendulums scanning lines of metallic type.

MISS!

Flying cars were meant to solve the problems of traffic jams. The first one was designed in 1917, but none have been hits.

...During the 1960s **underwater living** was considered the solution to overpopulation. French undersea explorer Jacques Cousteau even built an underwater station for "aquanauts."

...Futurologists predicted that by 2000 **robots and computers** would be doing most of the work, giving humans almost unlimited leisure time. Still waiting...

MAYBE!

Another Arthur C. Clarke idea was the **space elevator** to take men and materials into space, instead of using rockets. No one expects to see one until at least 2018.

...**Nanotechnology**, the building of materials and machines at the microscopic scale, was first outlined by physicist Richard Feynman in 1959. It would allow for computers the size of atoms.

...**Space vacations** were predicted a long time before the first tourist went into space in 2001. More regular trips to the edge of space are planned to start in 2008—but they will be expensive.

NOSTRADAMUS, a Frenchman who lived nearly 500 years ago, is the best-known prophesier of the future. His book of four-line poems is said to predict everything from the **French Revolution 138** to Adolf Hitler to the **9/11 attacks 242**. Critics point out that his meanings are very ambiguous and are made to apply to an event after it has happened.

THE SCIENCE OF THE HEAVENS

Leonardo da Vinci wasn't the only scientist making exciting discoveries during the Renaissance (though he may have been the hardest working—he left behind 13,000 pages of notes). Nicolaus Copernicus (1473-1543, above) overturned ideas that the Earth was at the center of the universe. His "heliocentric" theory put the Sun at the center of the **solar system 168**. Later, Johannes Kepler (1571-1630) figured out the laws of planetary motion, and provided evidence for Copernicus's theory.

FORETELLING THE FUTURE

TAROT

A pack of cards with symbolic characters. Users divine (predict) the future by interpreting the arrangements of the cards.

ASTROLOGY

The layout of the heavens when you are born is supposed to affect your personality and destiny. Astrologers draw up horoscope charts to make predictions.

I CHING

An ancient Chinese text (also called *The Book of Changes*) that can be used for the purposes of divination.

Wish you hadn't said that?

"Maybe only five computers."
Thomas Watson, chairman of IBM, forecasting the world market for computers, 1943

"The Americans have need of the telephone, but we do not. We have plenty of messenger boys."
Sir William Preece, chief engineer at the British Post Office, 1878

"Who the hell wants to hear actors talk?"
Harry Warner, head of Warner Brothers, on the new technology of talking movies, 1927

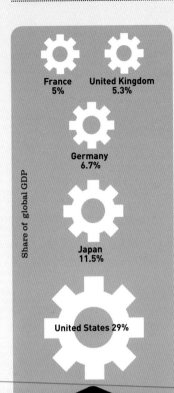

France 5%

United Kingdom 5.3%

Germany 6.7%

Japan 11.5%

United States 29%

Share of global GDP

Economy

The US has the world's biggest economy

The US has **1,740** separate TV channels

About **80%** of middle and high school students take part in organized activities after school and on weekends—most have something scheduled nearly every day.

⬆ **Nation knowledge . . .**

◯➔ **89 percent of people in the US have shopped online.** Online shopping is growing fast. In 2005, Americans spent 30 percent more online during the Thanksgiving and Christmas holiday periods than in 2004.

A small, well-off 18% of online shoppers account for 46% of online spending

Online shopping The last three
items shoppers are most likely to have bought are:

Books **28%**

Clothing/accessories/shoes **25%**

Videos/DVDs/games **22%**

"Cyber Monday" is one of the US's biggest online shopping days of the year. Many sites offer special deals in time for Christmas. On Cyber Monday, November 28, 2005, peak online traffic reached more than 1.8 million visitors per minute.

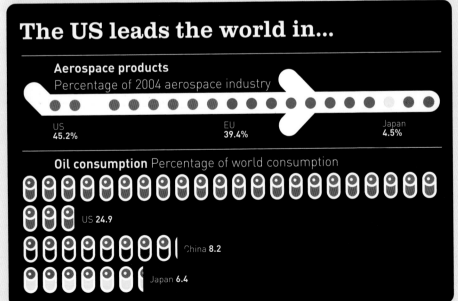

The US leads the world in...

Aerospace products
Percentage of 2004 aerospace industry

| US 45.2% | EU 39.4% | Japan 4.5% |

Oil consumption Percentage of world consumption

US **24.9**

China **8.2**

Japan **6.4**

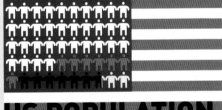

US POPULATION IN 2003

◯ **197.3 m** were non-Latino white
◯ **39.9 m** were Latino
● **38.7 m** were African American
◯ **13.5 m** were Asian

In 2000, 47 million people (**18 percent of the population**) spoke a <u>**language 016**</u> other than English at home.

HOLLYW★O♥OD

Population
295.7 million—going up

38.8 million people in the US watched the 2006 Oscars. The 1998 awards scored most viewers, 55.2 million in the year *Titanic* won 11 awards.

↑ **Nation knowledge**

↑ **Where is the USA?**

Eating and exercise

30 percent of US adults aged 20 and older—over 60 million people—are **obese**.

Among US children and **teens 276** aged 6 to 19 years, 16 percent (over 9 million young people) are considered **overweight**.

74 percent of 15-year-old US boys and 54 percent of 15-year-old US girls exercise twice a week or more.

The US was ranked first at the 2004 Summer Olympics in Athens, Greece. Its team won 103 medals in total, including 35 gold medals.

❯ **76.5 percent** of all Americans own a **car**, more than any other country in the world. **Traffic congestion** adds 30 minutes to the average American's drive to work each day—that's nearly **5 days a year**.

US
76.5%

Luxembourg
68.6%

Malaysia
64.1%

Australia
61.9%

Defense spending

In 2004, the US alone accounted for 47 percent of the world's total defense spending

Yellowstone National Park, located in the states of Wyoming, Montana, and Idaho, was the first national park in the world. Of the park's 3,400 square miles, 99 percent remains undeveloped

↑ **US gospel music sales** have increased more than **80 percent** between 1995 and 2004, from $381 million to over $700 million. In 2004, gospel sales were higher than **jazz** and **classical** combined.

1951 2005

↑ From 1951 to 2005, the US received 56 percent of **Nobel Prizes** awarded in Medicine, Physics, and Chemistry.

Say hello to yourself

How does your body know how to grow? How does it know where to put your arms and legs? Why do you have brown hair and your sister blonde? The answer is deoxyribonucleic acid—or, to give it a name most people can pronounce, DNA. These three letters describe a string of chemical units that act as a recipe for making a person. It is very tiny but very, very long—if you unraveled all the DNA in your body, the thin thread would stretch to the **Moon 170** and back many times. DNA is wound into a double helix shape (like a twisted ladder). It contains four different types of chemicals units (known as bases). These are connected like rungs on a ladder—and it is their precise arrangement that dictates things such as your height and eye color

Double helix

The structure of DNA (the double helix shape) was discovered in 1953 by British scientist Francis Crick and American James Watson, working together at Cambridge University in England. They won the Nobel Prize for their work in 1962.

Base pairs

The "rungs" of the DNA ladder are formed from four different bases. These can combine in two ways only: guanine goes with cytosine, while thymine is matched with adenine. The Human Genome Project (1990-2003) identified the sequence of the three billion base pairs that make up human DNA, as well as the makeup of the genes. In other words, what makes a human being.

Genes

A gene is a section of DNA containing information that may control a specific characteristic, such as your eye color. Each gene may have just a thousand base pairs or several hundred thousand. Each of us has about 35,000 genes—99.9 percent of which are the same as anyone else's. The 0.1 percent difference is enough to make you **unique 302**. As bossy as it is, DNA is only an instruction—it falls to something called RNA (ribonucleic acid) to actually make things happen.

This translates DNA's coded information so the body's biological machinery can produce proteins. Proteins are complex substances found in all living things (humans have 200,000 different proteins). The proteins do the hard work of getting toenails to grow and red blood cells produced—everything, in fact, to keep you alive.

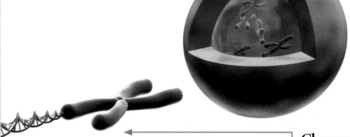

Chromosomes

Lengths of DNA are packed tightly into chromosomes. Humans have 23 pairs of chromosomes (that's 46 in total). Each pair is made up of one chromosome from your mom and one from your dad, which is why you can end up looking a bit like both of them. Which bits of your parents' chromosomes you end up with is completely random, so every child inherits a different set. If your parents hadn't **bonded 106** exactly when they did, you wouldn't be "you"—there would be a different set of chromosomes making up a different person (don't think about that for too long).

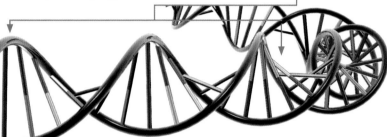

Cells

There are 23 pairs of chromosomes stored in the nucleus of just about every cell in your body. It is estimated there are some 10,000 trillion cells in each person, and most contain the full set of genetic instructions needed to make you "you." But cells don't use all of this information, they just use what they need to get their jobs done—such as growing skin or making sure your ears have enough wax in them. Genes can be switched on or off like a light, and different cells will have different genes turned on according to what they do. Not that you have to tell cells what to do—they do it all automatically (you'd never get anything done if you had to order your cells around all day). When a cell reproduces (they actually split to form two cells), all the genetic information is recorded again, much in the same way a computer stores digital data to a disk. Occasionally—perhaps one time in a million—one of the bases will end up in the wrong place. That may not be a big deal—it just gets lost in among all the other bases. But, sometimes, this may result in a slight change to the body. It is this small tendency to error that allows for **evolutionary 206** development (mistakes aren't always a bad thing).

A superpower is an extremely powerful nation with the ability to influence events on a global scale. A superhero is a man or a woman possessed with special powers such as the ability to fly, or phenomenal strength, which he or she will generally use to fight crime or rescue people in danger. But if one were to take on the other in a fight, who would win?

THE UNITED STATES OF AMERICA *Vs.* SUPERMAN

Tricky bout, this one. Since World War I, the US has been quick to act as a force for international order, but Superman is *the* cleancut superhero. As an immigrant (from the dying planet Krypton) come to enrich his adopted nation, he actually embodies the American Dream (poor boy makes good).

The **US 256** emerged as a superpower in 1945 and set about creating a massive consumer economy (with plenty of shopping malls) and a large military. Its ideological archenemy was the communist Soviet Union and, during the period known as the **Cold War 294**, both nations built up massive nuclear arsenals. But it was the US that ultimately emerged as the most powerful country in the world.

It now spends more on its military than the next 12 most powerful countries combined. While the Man of Steel may be faster than a speeding bullet and stronger than a train, he couldn't compete with the resources of America— and would be too busy looking for a phonebooth to notice the stealth bombers overhead.

Winner: THE UNITED STATES OF AMERICA

SUPERPOWER ACTION FIGURE COLLECTION

PRIME EAGLE™

BATTERIES NOT INCLUDED

FEATURES LAUNCHING MISSILE!

MILITARY MIGHT

$ MASSIVE CONSUMER ECONOMY

MOST POWERFUL COUNTRY IN THE WORLD

US

Made in USA

DAD, WILL YOU BUY ME A SUPERPOWER?

RED BEAR™

BATTERIES NOT INCLUDED

FEATURES
RETRACTABLE CLAWS!

STRONG LEADER INCLUDED

BIG NUCLEAR ARSENAL

LOADS AND LOADS OF TANKS

USSR

Made in USSR

USSR
Vs. THE INCREDIBLE HULK

This is a contest of brute strength. In the green corner, a large monster in ripped pants—The Incredible Hulk. In the red corner, the mighty Soviet Union (USSR). Born in 1922, the USSR wasn't a superpower until after **World War II 178** when dictator Joseph Stalin (1879-1953) led it into a period of huge industrial-military growth (lots of tanks and coal, not much in the stores).

The Hulk isn't anything unless he's angry—he's just mild-mannered scientist Dr. Bruce Banner. Stalin was also someone you wouldn't want to make angry. Stalin was a communist, which was meant to be all about sharing property and wealth and social justice. But he spent much of the 1930s imprisoning and executing anyone considered an "enemy" of the people. Millions died, from intellectuals to peasants. After Stalin's death, things picked up a bit (and there was more in the stores) but the USSR collapsed in 1991, unable to compete economically with the US.

The USSR's only chance against The Hulk is not to make him angry, but that's unlikely. The Hulk's skin protects him from all modern artillery, so nukes are useless. The Hulk could pick up the USSR and hurl it into **space 102**—end of contest.

Winner: THE INCREDIBLE HULK

BRITISH EMPIRE
Vs. THE FANTASTIC FOUR

A fight determined by brawn and brews. The British Empire reached its peak in the early 20th century—it was the largest ever, covering 14 million square miles (36 million square km). It emerged during the mid-19th century when it was reaping the benefits of the **Industrial Revolution 184** and its navy dominated the seas.

Though some countries such as India were ruled directly during this period, Britain would also control some territories (such as China) without formal rule (setting up their own government).

The Fantastic Four got their special powers after passing through a radiation storm. They may look as though they could give the Empire the runaround, but the Brits have a few tricks up their sleeve. Mr. Fantastic could never stretch from Canada to **India 142** to Australia like the British did. And The Invisible Girl couldn't hide from 500 million subjects. Plus, between the four of them, they wouldn't really know how to make a decent cup of tea.

Winner: BRITISH EMPIRE

MORE
SUPER THINGS
OVER THE PAGE

LION MIGHTY™

BATTERIES NOT INCLUDED

FEATURES
LAUNCHING BOWLER HAT!

INDUSTRIALLY ADVANCED

LITTLE COUNTRY BIG BITE

STIFF UPPER LIP INCLUDED

Made in UK

MORE SUPER THINGS

SUPERNOVAS

A supernova is an exploding star that can shine like a billion suns for a few weeks. This happens when a big star dies and its core implodes (bursts inward). Or when a white dwarf (a burned-out star) in a double-star system (two stars connected by **gravity 024**) becomes unstable and explodes. There goes the neighborhood.

SUPERMARKETS

Supermarkets have been around since the 1920s, supplying people with food, beverages, and household goods. Before then, sales clerks measured out goods and served customers. Supermarkets are self-service and make it hard for small shops to survive, but are great if you want 47 kinds of chips in one place.

SUPERPOWER
ACTION FIGURE COLLECTION

BATTERIES NOT INCLUDED

MIGHTY KHAN™

FEATURES
BIONIC ARM!

AWESOME HORSE-MANSHIP

TOTALLY RUTHLESS

FANTASTIC MILITARY STRATEGY

Made in Mongolia

THE MONGOL EMPIRE *Vs.* SPIDERMAN

A tough contest for the kid Peter Parker, who got his powers after being bitten by a mutant spider. He can walk on walls, fling webs, and is blessed with the strength of a spider. This may not sound very impressive, but spiders can hang upside down carrying 170 times their own body weight. But he is up against the power of the Mongols, who controlled an empire from China to Europe containing 100 million people.

In 1206, Genghis Khan (c.1162-1227) united the nomadic tribes of what is now northwestern **China 118** and started expanding territory. His hordes were seemingly unstoppable and ruthless (defenders had the choice of surrendering or

dying: this policy saw the population of China fall by half during 50 years of Mongol rule). Still, they developed trade routes and an extensive postal system and, due to his strict governance, the empire had very low crime rates.

Spiderman's motivation doesn't come from a desire to conquer regions, but from the murder of his Uncle Ben. Despite his powers, it has to be said that Spiderman is too much of a nice guy to

beat up Genghis or match the military might and discipline of the Mongol armies, which were huge.

Winner: THE MONGOLS

ROME
Vs.
THE X-MEN

Long-awaited epic battle that sees the great Mediterranean power—with conquests from Britain to Egypt—take on the mutants. **Rome 286** dominated Europe from the second century BC (when rival Carthage was beaten) to AD 476, which marked the end of the Western Roman Empire. In that time the Romans built (really straight) roads all over Europe, had **trade 324** links as far as India and China, and introduced methods of architecture, law, and government that are still used today.

Unfortunately, many of Rome's emperors had personality problems. Caligula (AD 37–41) was so insane that he ordered his army to cancel an invasion of Britain and collect seashells instead. And Nero (AD 54–68) was so nasty he had his own mother executed.

Storm, one of the mutant X-Men, can control the weather and could command winds to scatter the well-trained Roman legions. Wolverine, who has accelerated healing powers, could survive the poisonings that Roman leaders were so fond of. And brainy Professor X would be more than a match for Roman generals. In fact, the emperors were such a treacherous bunch, they would be too busy stabbing each other in the back to deal with the X-Men.

Winner:
THE X-MEN

SUPERPOWER
ACTION FIGURE COLLECTION

BATTERIES NOT INCLUDED

WOLFIUS™

FEATURES
BITING METAL TEETH!

HIGHLY TRAINED LEGIONS

INCLUDES WORKING CIVILIZATION

BONUS UNSTABLE EMPERORS

Made in Rome

SUPERSTRUCTURES

A superstructure is the part of a building above the foundation or base (it is also the part of a ship above the main deck). Houses made of brick or wood have walls strong enough to hold up the floor, ceiling, and roof. Taller buildings, like **skyscrapers 314**, need a frame—all the weight is transferred down columns to the building's base. The walls hang from the frame.

SUPERSONIC

Anything traveling faster than the speed of sound (about 700 mph or 1,100 km/h) is called supersonic. The British came up with the blueprint for the first supersonic plane, but the US built it in 1947. Many modern fighter aircraft, much loved by superpowers, are supersonic. The last supersonic passenger aircraft, the Concorde, made its final flight in 2003.

SUPERMODELS

Glamorous and beautiful, supermodels are the elite **fashion 192** models who appear on glossy magazine covers. They first appeared in the 1980s. The original five supermodels were Cindy Crawford, Naomi Campbell, Christy Turlington, Linda Evangelista, and Claudia Schiffer. Like **movie stars 036**, supermodels score by projecting an attitude the camera just loves.

A (VERY) LONG STORY

The Great Wall isn't the only thing that made Ancient and Imperial China great...

1. THE GREAT WALL
Forget those photographs of a large stone wall snaking dramatically along a Chinese hill top. The original Great Wall was actually built of local materials, usually beaten dirt reinforced with brushwood and covered with pine or oak boards. More than 300,000 soldiers under the command of the first emperor, Qin Shihuangdi, built the first wall around 214 BC to keep out unruly foreigners from the north. It wasn't until the 1400s that the Ming emperor ordered the wall to be rebuilt and strengthened in stone.

2. THE TERRA-COTTA ARMY
Although he only ruled China for 11 years, the first emperor, Qin Shihuangdi, was determined to go out in style. When he died in 210 BC, he was buried—at Lintong in Shaanxi province—in a tomb guarded by 7,000 warriors made of terra-cotta (baked clay). Each warrior's hair and face was individually modeled on real soldiers. Apparently, the more lifelike the soldiers were, the more effective they would be in guarding the emperor in the afterlife.

3. CHANG'AN
In the seventh century AD, Chang'an (modern-day Xi'an) was the capital of China and had a population of more than a million people, making it the largest city in the world. Surrounded by a 22-mile (37-km) wall, Chang'an was laid out on a grid plan, much like a modern city in the US. It was divided into 108 wards, or districts, each one surrounded by its own wall. There were further subdivisions, making it reasonably easy to find out where someone lived—and for the government to monitor their movements.

GUESS WHAT?

HENRY PU YI, THE LAST EMPEROR OF CHINA, GAVE UP HIS THRONE IN 1912 WHEN HE WAS ONLY SIX. HE WAS A GARDENER IN BEIJING WHEN HE DIED IN 1967

4. BEIJING
The Chinese emperor was known as the "son of heaven," as he took his authority from the Chinese supreme god Tian, or heaven. His palace was in the Forbidden City in Beijing, capital from 1279 to the present day. His throne sat on a square platform representing Earth 170. Above, a round ceiling represented heaven. Between the two sat the emperor, linking his human subjects to heaven and Earth.

5. MANCHURIA
Given their all-around skill and inventiveness, you would have thought the Chinese could have ruled themselves. But China's emperors have often been foreigners. The Yuan or Mongol 262 dynasty of emperors (ruled 1279–1368) came from Mongolia, in the north, while the final Qing or Manchu dynasty (1644–1912) came from Manchuria. At one point, the Chinese were so spoiled for choice they had a "Five Dynasties and Ten Kingdoms" period (907–960)—which got very confusing for everyone.

6. THE GRAND CANAL
Look closely at a map of China and you soon realize that all the rivers 140 flow roughly from west to east. This made carrying goods north and south very difficult. The Sui dynasty Emperor Yangdi (ruled 604–17) solved this problem by getting thousands of forced laborers to dig a canal from Yangzhou, via the Sui capital of Luoyang, up to what is now Beijing in the north. This made it easier to transport grain and troops to the north.

7. THE SILK ROAD

Well, it wasn't actually made of silk, nor was it really a road (more a collection of routes). But, from about 100 BC until sea routes replaced it in the 1400s, the Silk Road was one of the most important trade routes in the world. It stretched 4,350 miles (7,000 km) from Loyang, west through central Asia and Persia to the Mediterranean Sea, and then, finally, by boat to **Rome 320**. Chinese merchants traded expensive silks, porcelain, tea and salt, in exchange for gold.

8. QUFU

In 551 BC—when China was a series of small, warring kingdoms, rather than a unified empire—this unremarkable place in Shandong province was the birthplace of Kong Qiu. Also known by his westernized name, Confucius, he was a teacher and **philosopher 042** who believed in kindness, respect, and the family. It is thanks to his teachings that the Chinese still see themselves as one great family, including the living, the dead, and the unborn.

9. MACAO

MacWhat, you may well say. Well, a little bit of history is what. In 1999, its Portuguese owners gave Macao—two islands and a peninsula situated on the opposite side of the Xi (Pearl River) estuary from Hong Kong—back to China. And so ended 442 years of Portuguese rule over Macao, and the end of European **colonial 096** rule in Asia. Macao was the last European colony on the continent.

OH NO, YOU CAN'T!

It is commonly believed that you can see the Great Wall of China from space. Well, you can't (unless you've got space-based radar or a very, very high-powered telescope). The wall is the longest man-made structure on Earth, at more than 2,500 miles (4,000 km). But at 20 ft (6 m) across, it is no wider than an average street, and you can't see your road from space.

Man-made objects you CAN see from the **International Space Station 102**, with the naked eye:

* Major cities standing out from the surrounding countryside

* Trails from airplane jet engines and, sometimes, sunlight glinting off the planes themselves

* Man-made satellites orbiting the Earth

* The effects of human **environmental damage 266**, such as deforestation

Humans are already using **half** of the planet's **fresh water**. By 2025, this could be more than 70 percent.

As many as **88 million people** could have their homes **flooded** during the 2080s.

World energy **consumption** could **increase** by more than **50 percent** by 2025.

Up to a third of all **animal and plant species** (about a million species) could be made **extinct** because of **climate** change by 2050.

The ice cap on **Mount Kilimanjaro 074** could be completely **gone** by 2025. More than 80 percent of the ice field has disappeared since the mountain was first mapped in 1912.

WHAT MIGHT HAPPEN NEXT?

The temperature on planet Earth is climbing. If it continues to rise, these predictions could become reality...

The **last remaining rain forests** could be completely **chopped** down in the next 40 years.

By 2020, greenhouse gas **emissions** (such as carbon dioxide and methane) could **rise by 50 percent**.

By 2030, the number of **cars 113** in the world could **double**.

GUESS WHAT?

THE AVERAGE AMERICAN SENT 44,000 LBS (20,000 KGS) OF CARBON DIOXIDE INTO THE ATMOSPHERE IN 2002, FIVE TIMES AS MUCH AS THE AVERAGE MEXICAN

TEMPERATURE TIME BOMB

↓

What happens as the planet gets warmer?

1 °F / **+0.6 °C**	2 °F / **+1 °C**	3 °F / **+1.5 °C**	4 °F / **+2 °C**
Current level of global temperature increase since 1860 (the year it was first recorded)	Oceans and Arctic ecosystems are damaged (**birds 182** and fish die out as their food becomes scarce)	**Greenland ice sheet begins to melt**	Sea level rise forces millions to leave the coasts. Arctic ecosystems collapse and the walrus and polar bear are made extinct

The recipe for global warming

1 Burn coal and oil at a vigorous rate. These quickly emit a blanket of gases (carbon dioxide, methane, etc.) that sticks in the Earth's atmosphere. Less of the Sun's heat is able to escape, so temperatures rise rapidly.

The Earth is naturally heated by the "greenhouse effect": some of the Sun's warming rays are trapped in the atmosphere, while others bounce back into space. The increased presence of carbon dioxide, methane, and other gases in the atmosphere stops these rays from leaving Earth. This causes global warming.

2 Make matters worse by removing a small section of the Earth's solar shield—the ozone layer—at the North and South poles. Mourn the loss of animal life in these areas.

The ozone layer, high up in the atmosphere, protects us from harmful ultraviolet (UV) radiation. Increased levels of UV in Antarctica have already upset the food chain there, devastating the penguin population. UV also causes skin cancer in humans and animals, and can damage crops and plants, too.

3 Stand far back and wait for increased <u>hurricanes 136</u>, tropical storms, droughts, floods, and rising sea levels to hit the planet.

As the globe warms up, huge Antartic ice sheets will melt, causing sea levels to rise up to 20 in (50 cm) by the end of the century. Combined with thermal expansion of seawater (when a hotter global temperature increases <u>sea 202</u> levels), this would cause floods in low-lying cities, including London and New York. Natural disasters, such as hurricanes, thrive on higher temperatures, and deserts could spread and become even hotter.

Ingredients for a healthy planet

•
Replace the light bulbs in your home with long-lasting, low-energy ones.

••
Take out your bike and bike helmet and use them to get to stores and school. Walk instead of taking the car. When the distance is too long, take the bus or a train.

•••
Prepare your <u>recycling 310</u> bins and dispose of your wastepaper, cardboard, glass, and metal accordingly. For best results, do this at <u>school 166</u> as well as at home.

••••
Plant trees.

•••••
Campaign for wind farms, solar power plants, and hydroelectric power. Persuade your parents to switch to renewable energy.

••••••
Switch off the TV and computer when you're not using them. No, really.

•••••••
Chill out and let the planet cool.

4-6 °F /**+2-3 °C**	6 °F /**+3 °C**	8-10 °F/ **+4-5 °C**
The Amazon rain forest is wiped out, along with other forest and grassland ecosystems	Millions at risk from flooding and other natural disasters. Diseases such as **malaria 280** spread like the plague	**Permanent extreme weather (cyclones, blizzards, etc.) affects harvests in some areas. Millions starve**

HOW A PIG INVENTED A TEMPERATURE SCALE

German physicist Daniel Fahrenheit developed the Fahrenheit scale for measuring temperature in 1724, a few years after inventing the mercury thermometer. To set the scale, he decided the average human body temperature was 100 °F (it's actually more like 98.6 °F). Rumor has it he took a pig's temperature instead, thinking it would be the same as a man's.

WAS WILLIAM WILBERFORCE A FAILURE?

William Wilberforce (1759-1833) was an English political activist who never gave up. His ambition was to ban slavery (when one person is owned by another). At the time he was born, British ships carried black slaves from Africa to the West Indies, where they were sold to work on plantation farms. The British economy depended on the system. Wilberforce spent his career campaigning to destroy it. Inspired by his Christian faith, he believed every man and woman was extremely precious. In 1780, he was elected to the English parliament. From 1788, he made proposals to ban slavery every year. For the next 18 years, every one was rejected. Wilberforce suffered death threats, the decline of his physical health, and a nervous breakdown. In 1807, his dream was finally realized when parliament abolished the British slave trade. However, slaves already living in the British Empire 260 remained captive. Wilberforce kept on fighting as a member of the Anti-Slavery Society. One month after his death in 1833, the society's efforts were rewarded in the Abolition of Slavery Act. This freed all slaves in British territory. Today, slavery is against the law in almost every country. However, in 2006, it was estimated that millions of illegal slaves still existed around the world.

The descendants of slaves should be able to claim compensation (payment for damages) from governments. **DISCUSS**

THE STORY OF THE BLUES

When 19th-century American slaves suffered the "blue devils," or low spirits, they turned to music.

Their blend of praise songs, shouts, and chants became known as "the blues." After the slaves were freed, a blues movement developed in the northern city of Chicago. The style influenced most American and European music, from jazz, rock'n'roll 152, and country, to pop and modern classical.

SLAVERY TODAY

Even now, slavery in one form or another continues illegally in almost every country in the world. At least 20 million people, mainly in south Asia, are enslaved in bonded labor—they are forced to work long hours in awful conditions to repay a "loan." However, they may never repay it, and the loan gets passed down through generations. Meanwhile, human trafficking (when people are sold for work) is one of the fastest growing crimes across the world. Around 800,000 people, mainly women and children, are trafficked each year between countries. Thousands also work in factories, known as sweatshops, under conditions comparable to slavery. These are found everywhere from the US to China. Workers (often children) make products, such as clothes and electronics, in dangerous conditions for minimal pay. The goods are then sold for huge profits 050.

HARRIET JACOBS: ONE BRAVE LADY

Harriet Jacobs (1813-1897) was born into slavery, as her parents were slaves in North Carolina. At 13 years old, she was sold to Dr. James Norcom, who mistreated her and, later, her two children. In 1835, she escaped and, after help from a neighbor, spent several years hiding in an attic not even 9.8 feet (three metres) long at her grandmother's house. In 1842, she sailed to Philadelphia where slavery had been abolished. There she wrote a book, under the name Linda Brent, entitled *Incidents in the Life of a Slave Girl*. When printed in newspapers, her story shocked readers. In 1861, the book was published, nine years after the fictional *Uncle Tom's Cabin* first told its own slavery story. Such books helped shape US public opinion against slavery.

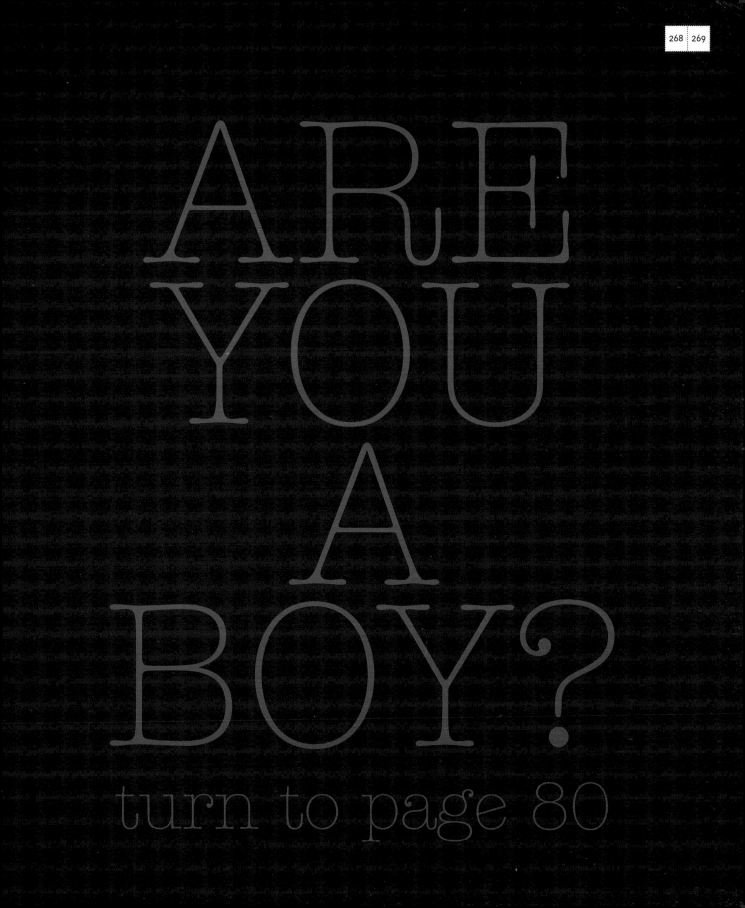

ARE YOU A BOY?

turn to page 80

The (brief) history of medicine in six chapters

1. TREPANNING—KIEV, UKRAINE, 7000 BC

The earliest known surgery is called trepanning: a hole is made in the skull, leaving the tissue around the brain intact.

Prehistoric surgeons used sharpened rocks 318, shells, and flints on their patients. They were probably attempting to release "evil spirits" to treat disease.

Skulls have been found that suggest patients survived—and came back for more. These days, trepanning is used to relieve pressure on the brain caused by leaking blood.

2. STITCHES—EGYPT, 2000 BC

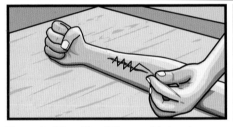

The ancient Egyptians 100 were able to suture (stitch up) wounds with a needle and thread.

After stitching, raw meat was applied to the wound, followed by a dressing of herbs, honey, and bread. Tasty.

The wound healed up—raw meat prevented bleeding and honey stimulated white blood cells (the body's defenses). Moldy bread might have contained penicillin 280 that deterred infection.

3. LEECHES—LONDON, ENGLAND, 1833

For hundreds of years, it was believed (wrongly) that too much blood was what made a person sick. So, doctors used to put bloodsucking worms called leeches on patients' skin to get blood out.

Bloodletting peaked in 1833, when London hospitals were getting through seven million leeches a year. They were thought to cure everything—headaches, obesity, hemorrhoids, eye disorders, even mental illness 239.

Better understanding of anatomy put an end to bloodletting and, by the 1960s, the practice had generally died out. But leeches are still sometimes used today to control blood flow during plastic surgery.

4. PAIN RELIEF—GEORGIA, 1842

"Ether frolics" were parties where guests would take the drug ether for fun. Surgeon Crawford Long went and noticed that when people hurt themselves, they didn't feel pain.

Long realized that ether could be used to dull the pain of surgery. In 1842, he removed a tumor from a patient's neck after knocking him out with an ether-soaked towel.

Long continued to use ether to remove other tumors, to amputate toes and fingers, and to relieve the pain of childbirth 158. Today, special doctors called anesthesiologists are in charge of putting patients to sleep during surgery.

5. NURSES—SCUTARI, TURKEY, 1854

In 1854, British nurse Florence Nightingale visited her country's military hospitals in Turkey. Conditions were disgusting: more soldiers were dying of disease than from injuries. Patients were not cleaned and everything was dirty.

Nightingale and her staff started cleaning the hospital and reforming medical care. As a result, fewer soldiers died 108. Nightingale established rules that gave nurses responsibility for a healthy environment and diet.

Nightingale became known as the "lady with the lamp" because she would care for her patients day and night 056. Thanks to her efforts, nurses became the backbone of medical treatment—as you'll see in any modern hospital today.

6. HEART SURGERY—CAPE TOWN, SOUTH AFRICA, 1967

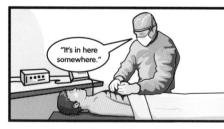  

Surgeon Christiaan Barnard transplanted the heart of a car accident victim into a 59-year-old man in December 1967—the first ever open-heart transplant.

Sadly, the patient died 18 days later from pneumonia. The drugs used to prevent his body from rejecting the new heart also stopped his body from fighting off other illness.

In 1974, safer drugs were developed to encourage a body to accept a transplanted organ. Today, open-heart transplants are a routine medical practice. Doctors can also transplant kidneys 134, lungs, bone marrow, and the liver.

WHO ON EARTH WAS CHRISTOPHER COLUMBUS?

WE CORNERED HIS GHOST TO FIND OUT

Americas

Who are you?

I'm an explorer and trader born in the 1400s. I'm famous for bravely crossing the Atlantic Ocean and reaching what is now known as the Americas, on October 12, 1492.

Were you really the first person to find the Americas, or did someone else get there first?

As cool as it was a few centuries back when everyone thought I was the first, some **Vikings 064** beat me to it. Those sneaky horn-heads came over from Greenland in the 11th century to set up a short-lived colony. The experts also believe that a small community of people arrived from Asia 20,000 years ago. They would have walked the 994 mi (1,600 km) across the former Bering land bridge that connected present-day Alaska with Siberia (how exhausting!). The Native American population then grew from this small group of hikers. But Europe didn't have a clue America existed until I went there and shouted home about it. I introduced the Old World (mainly Europe) to the New, and the word spread via the **printing press 292**.

Where were you from?

Okay... it could have been Genoa, a city in northern Italy. Everyone believed this for years. Then rumors started flying that I was from the Aragonese Empire (an ancient Spanish regime), Galicia (a community in the northwest of Spain), or Portugal. But wherever I was born, I landed on American soil flying the flag of Castile, a kingdom in **Spain 164**.

Why did you sail west around the world when everyone else was going east?

The eastern route had become so common —every sailor and his dog was taking it. Sure, people thought I had cabin fever when I suggested going in the opposite direction. Not because they believed the world was flat (they didn't)—no, they thought the long journey would kill us. But I was sure the western route could be easier and quicker. To tell you the truth, I misread my maps and thought the world was smaller than it actually is. It didn't help that the map itself was wrong. Stupid thing was 13 centuries old! Still, without my poor map reading, I may never have thought the route was possible—and would never have reached America.

So how did you get there?

We took three ships: *Santa Maria*, *La Niña*, and *La Pinta*. King Ferdinand of Aragon and Queen Isabella of Castile paid the bills. My crew got so homesick and frightened that they threatened to hurl me overboard and sail back to Spain. But we got there in five weeks, and didn't run out of food or get marooned. Which was nice.

Some say you were a hero. Others think you were a villain. Which is true?

I'll let you decide on that one. In the US, they celebrate Columbus Day—it's a national holiday. Loads of Americans, especially those of Mediterranean descent (like me), think I'm a heroic symbol of the American "can-do" attitude. But others see me as an evil rogue who treated Native Americans badly and who kicked off the Atlantic **slave trade 268**. I am so disliked in Venezuela that they renamed Columbus Day "The Day of Indigenous Resistance" in honor of the nation's native groups. But these opinions are more to do with today's politics than how things were in my lifetime. Honest.

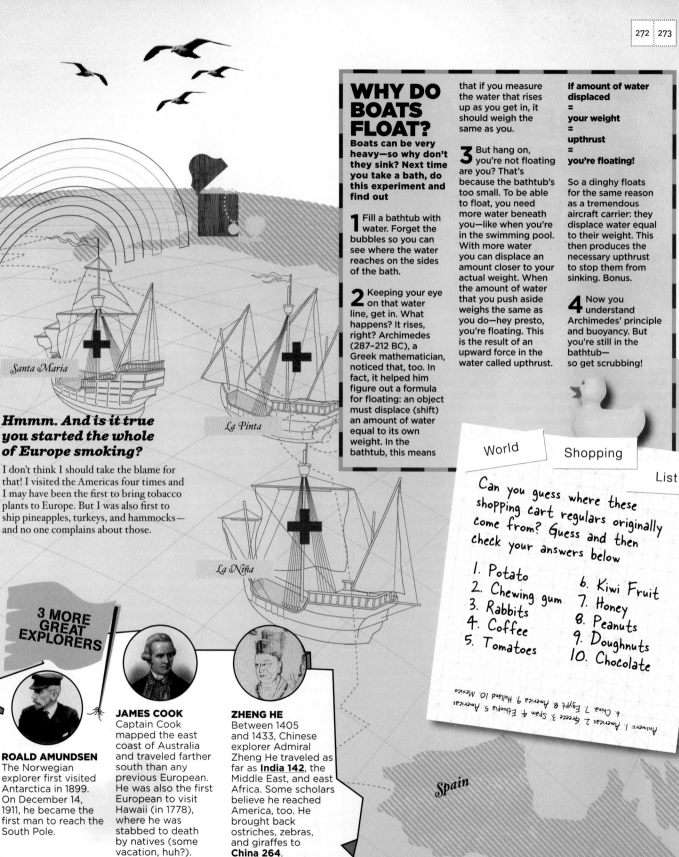

Santa Maria

La Pinta

La Niña

Hmmm. And is it true you started the whole of Europe smoking?

I don't think I should take the blame for that! I visited the Americas four times and I may have been the first to bring tobacco plants to Europe. But I was also first to ship pineapples, turkeys, and hammocks—and no one complains about those.

3 MORE GREAT EXPLORERS

ROALD AMUNDSEN
The Norwegian explorer first visited Antarctica in 1899. On December 14, 1911, he became the first man to reach the South Pole.

JAMES COOK
Captain Cook mapped the east coast of Australia and traveled farther south than any previous European. He was also the first European to visit Hawaii (in 1778), where he was stabbed to death by natives (some vacation, huh?).

ZHENG HE
Between 1405 and 1433, Chinese explorer Admiral Zheng He traveled as far as **India 142**, the Middle East, and east Africa. Some scholars believe he reached America, too. He brought back ostriches, zebras, and giraffes to **China 264**.

WHY DO BOATS FLOAT?

Boats can be very heavy—so why don't they sink? Next time you take a bath, do this experiment and find out

1 Fill a bathtub with water. Forget the bubbles so you can see where the water reaches on the sides of the bath.

2 Keeping your eye on that water line, get in. What happens? It rises, right? Archimedes (287–212 BC), a Greek mathematician, noticed that, too. In fact, it helped him figure out a formula for floating: an object must displace (shift) an amount of water equal to its own weight. In the bathtub, this means that if you measure the water that rises up as you get in, it should weigh the same as you.

3 But hang on, you're not floating are you? That's because the bathtub's too small. To be able to float, you need more water beneath you—like when you're in the swimming pool. With more water you can displace an amount closer to your actual weight. When the amount of water that you push aside weighs the same as you do—hey presto, you're floating. This is the result of an upward force in the water called upthrust.

**If amount of water displaced
=
your weight
=
upthrust
=
you're floating!**

So a dinghy floats for the same reason as a tremendous aircraft carrier: they displace water equal to their weight. This then produces the necessary upthrust to stop them from sinking. Bonus.

4 Now you understand Archimedes' principle and buoyancy. But you're still in the bathtub—so get scrubbing!

World Shopping List

Can you guess where these shopping cart regulars originally come from? Guess and then check your answers below

1. Potato
2. Chewing gum
3. Rabbits
4. Coffee
5. Tomatoes
6. Kiwi Fruit
7. Honey
8. Peanuts
9. Doughnuts
10. Chocolate

Answers: 1. Americas 2. Greece 3. Spain 4. Ethiopia 5. Americas 6. China 7. Egypt 8. America 9. Holland 10. Mexico

Spain

BEING A TEENAGER IS AWESOME!
(BUT IT STINKS TOO)

STARE AT THE CENTER OF THE ILLUSTRATION. SLOWLY BRING THE PAGE TOWARD YOUR FACE. WATCH THE LOVE-STRUCK TEENS KISS!

MATTHEW, 16, WRITES… It really is very confusing. You get to do all this new stuff like sleeping late and hanging out all day with your friends. But a lot of the time you don't notice how good life is. Friends that you make in your teens can last forever—it's not much fun hanging out by yourself, is it? You'll start to appreciate your friends more (and probably Britney Spears/this week's pin-up as well). You can hang out all day, listen to music or whatever, and never get bored. That's a pretty big achievement for a teenager! Pretty much every teen loves music in some shape or form, whether it's hip-hop, rock, dance ,or whatever. And most teens like it loud: contrary to adult beliefs, music sounds way better turned up, anyway. Parents may tell you to turn the music down, but in fairness they are just trying to protect your ears. Believe it or not, your parents were teenagers once upon a time (they've just forgotten). Personal hygiene is important to teenagers. Not quite as important as sleeping, but still important. Sadly, this requires certain sacrifices—such as showering and using deodorant. Which brings us to laziness. Parents call you lazy. But they only see you chilling at home. At school, you spend all day learning about stuff, hurting your brain. Parents also hate PlayStation and TV 014, but playing PlayStation improves hand-eye coordination (foolproof excuse). Anyway, there will be lots of changes, but just live with them. Everyone has to go through them. Oh, and don't forget to wear your clothes as crumpled as you want.

JAMES DEAN… I KNOW THE NAME. WHO IS HE?

All teenagers idolized him. Adolescents everywhere related to the way he stood up to the authorities and struggled to gain recognition in the world—just like them. An actor from Indiana, he starred in three 1950s films, including *Rebel Without a Cause* (1950), about a boy who braved the bullies. At 24, Dean died in a <u>car 113</u> accident. His favorite jeans-&-T-shirt outfit is still popular with teens today.

WHICH CAME FIRST: LEGS OR JEANS?

Now we all wear jeans—but there was life before blue denim. In 1873, Levi Strauss, a merchant from Bavaria, Germany, and tailor Jacob Davis were granted a patent for their blue jeans with reinforcing rivets. Mine workers in California loved them immediately. By the 1930s, American actors wore them, so movie-goers did too. Movie stars James Dean and Marlon Brando made them so hip in the 1940s that schools and movie theaters banned them. Since the 1960s, they've become everyday wear everywhere.

WHAT WE LIKE
First crushes
SATURDAY JOBS (FIRST PAY CHECK)
Sleeping until noon
FORMING OUR OWN BANDS
Wearing a different trend every week
TEXTING 144 FRIENDS WHEN THEY'RE
SITTING NEXT TO US
A different pop star every month
GOSSIPING ABOUT HOOKING UP
Dyeing our hair

TEEN–O–METER

Parents and their stupid rules
TEACHERS
Eye contact with adults
BEING TREATED LIKE A KID
Speaking in complete sentences
BEING SPOTTED OUT WITH
GRANDAD BY CLASSMATES
Concentrating on anything for more than
half an hour (unless it's TV or PlayStation)
BLANK SPACES ON BEDROOM WALLS

WHAT WE DON'T

EMBARRASSMENT®
Please read carefully before flushing

AGE
13 to 19-year-olds.
DOSAGE
Several times daily—increase dose if you have a crush on someone.

DEFINITION
Uncomfortable mental and physical state.
SYMPTOMS
Blushing, sweating, fast pulse, pumping adrenalin, stammering, nausea, light-headedness, desire to flee (and, sometimes, hide).
CAUSES
If you're a teenager, it feels like the whole world is out to make you look ridiculous. Embarrassment hits when you feel ashamed of something you've done or said (like calling your teacher "mommy"), or if you see something that makes you feel awkward (your parents dancing).
REMEDY
Grow up. Literally. People feel less embarrassed as they get older, and gain more self-confidence. But even adults still squirm and blush in some situations (like when your dad forgets to zip up his pants after going to the bathroom).

WHEN YOUR GREAT-GRANDPARENTS WERE ADOLESCENTS...

...they dressed and acted like mini-adults. Many were sent to fight in wars, while others had to work as apprentices or junior clerks—sometimes at just 14 years old. Whatever they were doing, they had to grow up and act like adults as fast as possible. Only in the 1950s did youths in the US and Europe get to spend more time with their friends—plus they had extra cash in their pockets (provided by a booming economy).

They spent this on records, movies, and clothes. New music called **rock'n'roll 305** encouraged teens to rebel, dress differently, and fight for their beliefs—or just fight a lot. At around the same time, adolescence was extended in **Japan 028**. Until the beginning of the 20th century, Japanese children were considered grown-ups as early as 12. But in 1948 a national "coming of age" day was introduced, making people legal adults at 20. A new subculture had been born across the world—and it was called "teenager."

For the answers to your most perturbing pubescent problems...

"Why is it SO embarrassing being a teenager?"

ASK PICK ME UP!

"I have so many zits on my face, back, and chest that small children mistake me for a human connect-the-dots game. I've stopped eating junk **food 176**, but the zits haven't cleared up. I feel like a freak. Please help!"
BLOTCHED AND BLEMISHED, AGE 16

PMU: *You'll only look like a freak if a kid manages to draw all over you. Many, many people get zits (even during adulthood) and people notice them a lot less than you think. Zits occur when sebaceous glands (cells in the skin that produce oils) become blocked with dead skin cells and bacteria. Your face, back, and chest have lots of these glands. That's why they're the places with most zits. Poor diet is not the only cause of bad **skin 134**, but eating healthily can help. Hormones and stress are major reasons, explaining why teenagers suffer so much. Follow a strict cleansing routine and, if that fails, see a doctor.*

"Arggh! I've got hair on my genitals and under my arms! And I smell funny! What's going on?"
W. BEEST, AGE 13

PMU: *You're becoming a wolf. No, seriously, the new, thicker hair is perfectly natural. It protects certain areas of the body, regulates temperature, and catches natural, attractive odors called pheromones. Of course, with your overactive teenage chemicals and hormones, unless you wash regularly these scents smell about as attractive as a pair of old sneakers after soccer practice. So, please, don't dodge the soap!*

"Everywhere I go, someone is waiting to humiliate me. At school, it's my teacher, asking me difficult questions in front of the class. At home, my little sister shows my old **dinosaur 012** pajamas to my friends whenever they come around. And last week, my dad got mad at me in front of everyone, because I wasn't waiting outside at exactly midnight when he came to pick me from a house party! Now everyone calls me Cinderella!"
CONSTANTLY CRINGING, AGE 15

PMU: *I know a great store for glass slippers, if you're interested (they only sell one-of-a-kinds!). Jokes aside, all teenagers feel awkward. An army of chemicals called hormones is partying in your bloodstream, transforming you from child to adult. These extra hormones completely upset your emotions and sense of perspective. You're a blank canvas grasping to find an identity. How other people perceive you becomes far too important—you think they can tell you who you are. The key to surviving all this is to hang in there. As you grow older, you'll become proud of your quirks and stop caring what other people think so much. Once you're grown-up, you can drive yourself home from parties at sunrise, if you want.*

Teenagers have higher levels of a hormone called melatonin in the mornings than young children and adults, which makes it harder for them to wake up

Eighty-five percent of 16 year olds in the UK would choose professional qualifications over being a **celebrity 218**

Eighty percent of Canadian teens play computer games for an average of five hours per week

Twenty-one percent of Belgian teenagers are woken up between one and three times a month by their cell phones. Eleven percent are woken once a week, and three percent every night

In Osaka, Japan's biggest entertainment center after Tokyo, unaccompanied youths under 16 are banned from establishments with a karaoke machine after 7 p.m.

In **Brazil 072**, teenagers go to school for only four hours a day.

One percent of Chinese teens are willing to let parents make decisions for them. Seventy-four percent believe they should lead an independent life

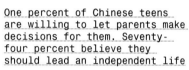

The average US teenager spends just over 10 hours a week with friends outside school—and just under eight hours messaging or talking on their cell phones to them

Seventy-three percent of girls in Bangladesh are married by the age of 15

odd

Spot

the

1. QUAGGA
2. PROTHALYCINUS
3. DAWN MONKEY
4. CAROLINA
   PARAKEET
5. NESODON
6. DINORNIS

one

out

14.
15.
16.
17.
18.
19.
20.
21.
22.
23.
24.
25.
26.
27.

7. CAVE BEAR	10. MASTODONSAURUS	14. SIVATHERIUM	18. UINTATHERIUM	22. SPECTACLED	25. OKAPI
8. EOHIPPUS	11. INDRICOTHERIUM	15. HOMO HABILIS	19. AUROCHS	CORMORANT	26. ARSINOITHERIUM
9. NEANDERTHAL	12. SYNDYOCERAS	16. MEGALOCEROS	20. GLYPTODON	23. DIRE WOLF	27. LYSTROSAURUS
MAN	13. WOOLY MAMMOTH	17. HENKELOTHERIUM	21. TASMANIAN WOLF	24. DODO	

What's all the fuss about drugs?

WHAT IS A DRUG?

A drug is a chemical or substance that affects your body in certain ways. Medicinal drugs are used to prevent and treat disease. Recreational drugs—some legal such as alcohol, some illegal such as marijuana—change the way you feel and can be highly addictive.

MEDICINAL

NATURAL BEGINNINGS

While many drugs are synthetic (man-made), some come from natural sources. Taxol, for example, is a **plant 018** chemical used to treat tumors. A hormone used by women going through menopause (the end of a woman's fertile years) derives from pregnant horses' urine. Tasty. Such drugs have helped develop biopharming: when crops or livestock are grown to make use of their medicinal parts.

RECENT ADVANCES

These days we also suffer recently recognized illnesses such as **HIV 214** (only discovered in 1983) and depression. Different drugs are required—and scientists are hot on the case. HIV-associated deaths in the US fell from 50,877 in 1995 to 15,798 in 2004 after the introduction of new treatments. Scientists predict that by 2050 the number of cancer sufferers will have halved through the use of preventive drugs.

BATTLING BACTERIA

In 1928, medicine took a huge leap forward. Alexander Fleming (1881-1955), a Scottish scientist, discovered penicillin. This is a type of antibiotic—a drug capable of killing or stopping the growth of bacteria (the tiny microorganisms that cause many diseases). Antibiotics have proved effective against fatal diseases such as cholera and the plague.

WAR ON DISEASE

Some diseases aren't easily scared off. Malaria, spread by mosquitoes, was eliminated from the developed world in the 1950s. But it still exists in Africa and Asia, claiming two million lives a year. The trouble is, the parasite that causes malaria (living in its human or mosquito host) has become resistant to drugs used to kill it.

GUESS WHAT?

TO RELIEVE HEADACHES, ANCIENT EGYPTIANS CHEWED BARK CONTAINING THE ACID USED IN MODERN ASPIRIN

ALCOHOL

The first drug in recorded history is alcohol. **Ancient Egyptians 100** drank beer more than 5,000 years ago. Today, alcohol is found in a huge variety of drinks. Some people can become addicted to alcohol, causing great disruption in their lives. Long-term excessive consumption also causes liver damage and other health problems.

SO HERE'S THE FUSS

Some people take drugs when they're not ill, for the effects they have on the body and mind. This is known as recreational drug use. Many recreational drugs are very addictive. Although legal, the nicotine in cigarettes and the alcohol in drinks such as beer and wine can cause serious harm to our health. Illegal drugs, such as marijuana (the most widely abused illegal drug in the world), cocaine, and heroin, can cause psychological as well as physical harm.

CAFFEINE

This chemical is found in coffee, tea, chocolate, and soft drinks, and is the world's most widely available drug. Around 80 percent of people in the **US 256** consume caffeine on a regular basis. One of its main effects is releasing adrenalin in the body, encouraging alertness. But it can also prevent sleep, cause irritability, and become addictive.

RECREATIONAL

LEGAL OR ILLEGAL?

Some recreational drugs were once sold for medicinal use—hard drugs like heroin and cocaine were sold as medicines in Europe during the 19th and early 20th centuries. Around the same time, marijuana (from the cannabis plant) was easy to buy at drugstores in the US. From the 1920s, most of the western world began banning recreational drugs.

NICOTINE

A cigarette habit is hard to kick because the active drug in tobacco is nicotine, which is highly addictive. Smoking tobacco affects the brain, making people feel stimulated yet relaxed. But it's unhealthy, as it can cause cancers and heart disease. Worldwide tobacco-related deaths are predicted to rise from four million per year in 2005 to 10 million per year by the 2030s.

ALMOST AS ADDICTIVE

Estimates suggest that over six percent of the 189 million internet users in the US are addicted to the web. Their dependency can be almost as harmful as drug addiction. In the UK, 26 percent of cell phone users are classified as "cyborgs," or people who can't imagine life without a mobile. In Australia, around 20 percent of regular exercisers are addicted to exercise, either psychologically or physically (there is such a thing as being too buff, then).

THE WHEEL

may seem an obvious invention, but it doesn't exist anywhere in nature. And the great **Inca, Aztec, and Mayan civilizations 298** only used wheels for children's toys. Humans first started using the wheel in earnest in Asia, probably around 6,000 years ago (no one's absolutely certain). Ancient civilizations were doing well when it came to beekeeping and cave painting, but they wanted to make better pots. The first wheel was a flat disk on which potters spun their clay. But there was still a problem when it came to moving stuff around. So someone came up with the idea of using rollers—probably **tree 010** trunks—that were placed under a heavy object to make it trundle along. And then someone else (perhaps the other guy's brother, who knows?) figured out that they didn't need the whole roller. What they needed was two rolling parts on each side and a bar to join them together. The bar became an axle, the rolling parts the wheels, and this *Flintstones*-ish creation is basically the same as what we use today on cars and **bikes 088**. The next step was to adapt it for horses. So around 2000 BC, the citizens of Mesopotamia (in today's Middle East) invented the two-wheeled chariot and the four-wheeled cart. And soon people were zipping around all over the place, carrying supplies and dropping in on relatives unannounced. Spoked wheels, like the ones on your bike, quickly followed—Egyptians used them on their chariots. And this was still the most common wheel right up until the automobile pushed horses off the road in the early 20th century. Meanwhile, the wheel has had a second life as an instrument of technology. Behind almost every man-made thing that moves, even in the smallest way, there's a wheel. Take a look and see...

FAN The mechanical, rotating fan emerged during the **Industrial Revolution 184**. Its blades spin on an axle

PAINT ROLLER Invented by Norman Breakey, a Canadian, in 1940. It comprises a broad wheel, an axle, and a handle

PLANE Wheels are needed for takeoff and landing, plus navigation (the gyroscope), and propulsion (the engine)

CLOCK The little cogs that power the mechanical **clock 249** are all just little wheels

MOVIE PROJECTOR The machine that beams the movie onto the movie screen is a maze of spinning wheels

THE DARTBOARD It may be round and flat but it doesn't use an axle, so it's no wheel

TANK "Caterpillar" track was invented in the early 20th century. Wheels turn the track but don't touch the ground

BENCH PRESS Dumbbells aren't wheels, dumbo. But some benches use pulleys and they do use wheels

THE MAGLEV TRAIN uses magnets to hover off the track, so no wheels (at least none that roll)

HOW TO

DO A PERFECT WHEELIE

1. Make sure you're nowhere near a road or cars. Strap on your safety gear. Set the seat low and select a medium gear. Here we go!

2. Put your weight over the handlebars. Set your pedals at 11 o' clock. Push down on the pedal and at the same time pull up on the handlebars.

3. Lean back. Straighten your arms, sit on the seat, and continue pedaling. Feel ready for a unicycle?

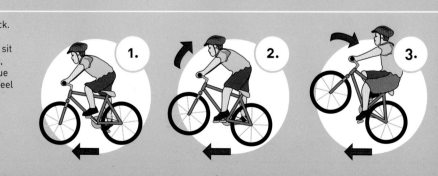

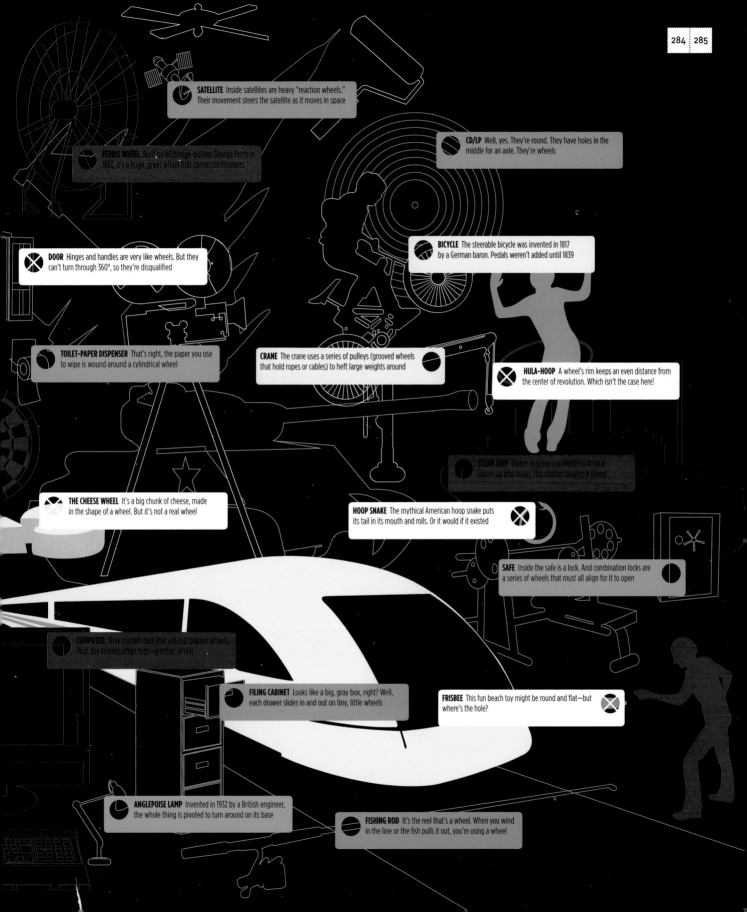

SATELLITE Inside satellites are heavy "reaction wheels." Their movement steers the satellite as it moves in space

CD/LP Well, yes. They're round. They have holes in the middle for an axle. They're wheels

FERRIS WHEEL Built by US bridge-builder George Ferris in 1893, it's a huge, great wheel that carries thrillseekers

DOOR Hinges and handles are very like wheels. But they can't turn through 360°, so they're disqualified

BICYCLE The steerable bicycle was invented in 1817 by a German baron. Pedals weren't added until 1839

TOILET-PAPER DISPENSER That's right, the paper you use to wipe is wound around a cylindrical wheel

CRANE The crane uses a series of pulleys (grooved wheels that hold ropes or cables) to heft large weights around

HULA-HOOP A wheel's rim keeps an even distance from the center of revolution. Which isn't the case here!

STEAM SHIP Steam engines use steam to drive a piston up and down. This motion powers a wheel

THE CHEESE WHEEL It's a big chunk of cheese, made in the shape of a wheel. But it's not a real wheel

HOOP SNAKE The mythical American hoop snake puts its tail in its mouth and rolls. Or it would if it existed

SAFE Inside the safe is a lock. And combination locks are a series of wheels that must all align for it to open

COMPUTER They contain fans that are just bladed wheels. Plus, the screens often turn—another wheel

FILING CABINET Looks like a big, gray box, right? Well, each drawer slides in and out on tiny, little wheels

FRISBEE This fun beach toy might be round and flat—but where's the hole?

ANGLEPOISE LAMP Invented in 1932 by a British engineer, the whole thing is pivoted to turn around on its base

FISHING ROD It's the reel that's a wheel. When you wind in the line or the fish pulls it out, you're using a wheel

Q: Why is the Roman Empire like McDonald's?

A: Both are (or were) set on world domination (of a sort)

ROMAN EMPIRE

COMPARATIVE CVs

CV stands for curriculum vitae—Latin for "course of one's life." Academics use it to sum up their skills and experience for employers.

OCCUPATION
Empire.

BORN
According to legend, the city of Rome was founded in 753 BC near the Tiber River in Italy, by Romulus and Remus (sons of **Mars 172**, the Roman god of war).

EARLY LIFE
Got rid of its tyrant kings to became a republic in 510 BC. For the next 250 years, the Romans battled their way (slowly, bloodily) across Italy. On the way, they trampled rival civilizations, including the Etruscans and the Samnites, and even some stray **Greeks 240**.

CAREER
After trashing the rival city of Carthage (in north Africa) in 146 BC, the Romans took control of the Mediterranean and branched out across **Europe 216**. Rome became the Roman Empire in 27 BC.

EXTENT OF WORLD DOMINATION
Most of Europe (as far as Germany and Scotland to the north), the top part of Africa and the Middle East (aside from the parts owned by the **Persians 120**).

QUALIFICATIONS
Vast army, straight roads (so the army did not waste time walking around bends), skill at winning battles.

STAFF
As many as 645,000 troops under Emperor Diocletian (reigned AD 284–305). Large numbers of administrators, such as tax collectors.

REVENUE
No figures available, but it would have taken an awful lot of denarii (Roman money) to run the Empire.

SLOGANS
SPQR, which stood for "Senatus Populusque Romanus" (the senate and the people of Rome). This was used on coins and army standards. The senate was the main law-making body of the Roman Republic.

World peace

The Roman Empire itself was mostly peaceful, so the period of its power was known as the Pax Romana—the "Roman peace." McDonald's has the "Golden Arches Theory of Conflict Prevention," invented by US journalist Thomas Friedman. He observed that no two countries with a McDonald's have ever gone to war with each other. NATO countries did bomb Serbia in 1999. But then NATO is an organization, not a country, so it has no McDonald's of its own.

HOW TO

RUN A FRANCHISED EMPIRE

A franchise (from the French word for freedom) is when a company allows another firm to produce and sell its products. Seventy percent of McDonald's restaurants are franchised. The Romans, too, got locals to be governors, administrators, and soldiers, making it simpler to run its own Empire.

1. Build identical-looking roads and install decent plumbing. Make Latin an international language.

2. Divide empire up into manageable chunks (provinces) and let the locals govern themselves (under Roman law). Even let one of the locals become emperor for a time, like "Philip the Arab" (ruled AD 244–249).

3. Take a leaf out of McDonald's book: adapt to local markets. In **Muslim 186** countries, for example, McDonald's doesn't serve bacon for breakfast, because Muslims don't eat pork. So, when running a large empire, do things differently in different places.

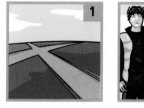

McDONALD'S

OCCUPATION
Fast-food company.

BORN
May 15, 1940, San Bernardino, California. In the first restaurant opened by brothers Richard and Maurice McDonald, a hamburger cost 15 cents.

EARLY LIFE
Serving hamburgers and barbecued food.

CAREER
1948
Introduced "Speedee Service System," a fast-food assembly line for making hamburgers.

1955
Chief executive officer Ray Kroc opened the first franchised restaurant, in Des Plaines, Illinois. First day's takings were $366.12.

1967
First restaurant outside the US opened in Canada.

1968
First Big Mac sold.

1971
First Asian McDonald's opened in Tokyo, **Japan 028**, followed by the first European McDonald's in the Netherlands.

EXTENT OF WORLD DOMINATION
By 2005, McDonald's was operating in 119 countries, serving 48 million customers each day through more than 30,000 restaurants.

QUALIFICATIONS
Big Mac, Chicken McNuggets, Drive-thru.

STAFF
1.5 million.

REVENUE
$20.5 billion (2005).

SLOGANS
"I'm loving it,"
"Mac your day."

THE ROMAN ARMY

The Roman army consisted of soldiers from all over the Empire (they were each expected to serve for at least 25 years). The main part of the army was made up of infantry. A section of 80 infantry was called a century and had a centurion in charge. A legion was made up of 59 centuries (plus support staff such as messengers and cooks). The army had around 30 legions in total.

LITHIUM: A crystal, called lithium niobate, is used to produce electronic filters in TVs and **cell phones 144** (who ever said crystals were only good for sparkling?).

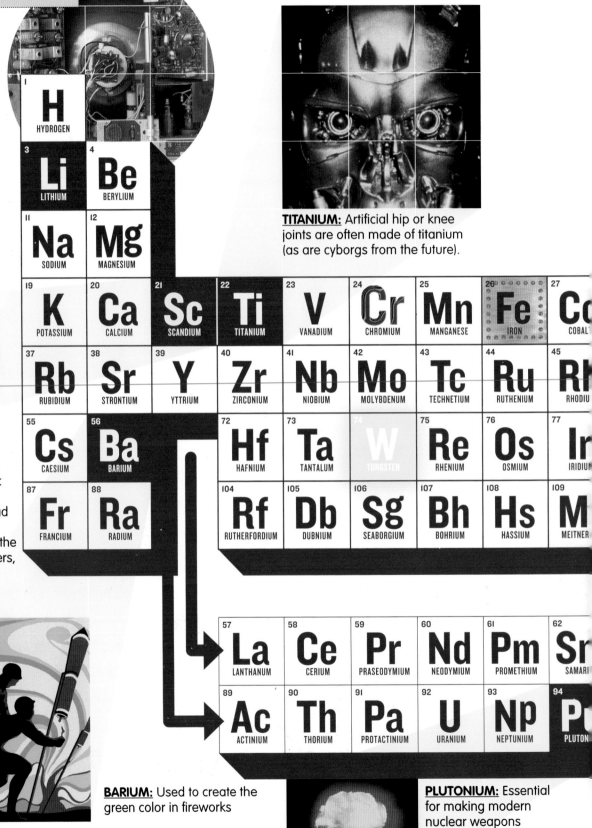

TITANIUM: Artificial hip or knee joints are often made of titanium (as are cyborgs from the future).

SCANDIUM:
Russian chemist Dmitri Mendeleev first presented his periodic table in 1869. Only about 60 elements had been discovered, but Mendeleev predicted the properties of four others, including Scandium.

BARIUM: Used to create the green color in fireworks

PLUTONIUM: Essential for making modern nuclear weapons

GOLD: If all the world's gold were squished together, it would form a cube just 65 ft (20 m) on each side. That's a very small cube in a very big world. No wonder it's so expensive.

PHOSPHORUS: Provides the spark in matches

ZINC: Used in batteries

MERCURY: Used in thermometers

| 2 **He** HELIUM |

| 5 **B** BORON | 6 **C** CARBON | 7 **N** NITROGEN | 8 **O** OXYGEN | 9 **F** FLUORINE | 10 **Ne** NEON |

| 13 **Al** ALUMINIUM | 14 **Si** SILICON | 15 **P** PHOSPHORUS | 16 **S** SULPHUR | 17 **Cl** CHLORINE | 18 **Ar** ARGON |

Ni NICKEL | 29 **Cu** COPPER | 31 **Ga** GALLIUM | 32 **Ge** GERMANIUM | 33 **As** ARSENIC | 34 **Se** SELENIUM | 35 **Br** BROMINE | 36 **Kr** KRYPTON |

Pd PALLADIUM | 47 **Ag** SILVER | 48 **Cd** CADMIUM | 49 **In** INDIUM | 50 **Sn** TIN | **Sb** ANTIMONY | 52 **Te** TELLURIUM | 53 **I** IODINE | 54 **Xe** XENON |

Pt PLATINUM | 79 **Au** GOLD | 80 **Hg** MERCURY | 81 **Tl** THALLIUM | 82 **Pb** LEAD | 83 **Bi** BISMUTH | 84 **Po** POLONIUM | 85 **At** ASTATINE | 86 **Rn** RADON |

Uun UNNILIUM | 111 **Uuu** UNUNUMIUM | 112 **UuB** UNUNBIUM |

Everything in the world is on these pages

The periodic table is a list of elements (substances that can't be broken down into anything simpler), including those artificially created by scientists. Each element is arranged by atomic number (how many <u>protons 060</u> it has) and is shown with its symbol (e.g., H for hydrogen)

Eu EUROPIUM | 64 **Gd** GADOLINIUM | 65 **Tb** TERBIUM | 66 **Dy** DYSPROSIUM | 67 **Ho** HOLMIUM | 68 **Er** ERBIUM | 69 **Tm** THULIUM | 70 **Yt** YTTERBIUM | 71 **Lu** LUTETIUM |

Am AMERICIUM | 96 **Cm** CURIUM | 97 **Bk** BERKELIUM | 98 **Cf** CALIFORNIUM | 99 **Es** EINSTEINIUM | **Fm** FERMIUM | 101 **Md** MENDELEVIUM | 102 **No** NOBELIUM | 103 **Lr** LAWRENCIUM |

EINSTEINIUM: Named after the great Albert

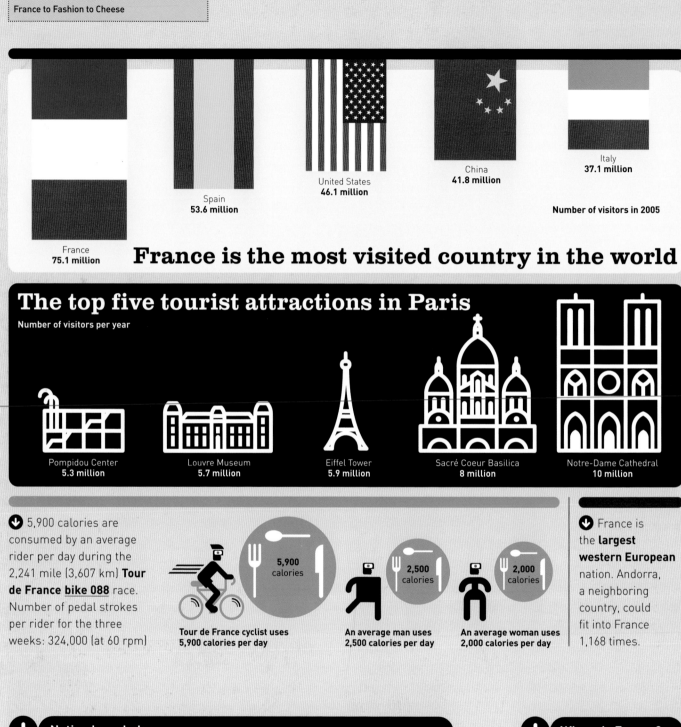

Spain
53.6 million

United States
46.1 million

China
41.8 million

Italy
37.1 million

Number of visitors in 2005

France
75.1 million

France is the most visited country in the world

The top five tourist attractions in Paris

Number of visitors per year

Pompidou Center
5.3 million

Louvre Museum
5.7 million

Eiffel Tower
5.9 million

Sacré Coeur Basilica
8 million

Notre-Dame Cathedral
10 million

⬇ 5,900 calories are consumed by an average rider per day during the 2,241 mile (3,607 km) **Tour de France bike 088** race. Number of pedal strokes per rider for the three weeks: 324,000 (at 60 rpm)

5,900 calories

Tour de France cyclist uses 5,900 calories per day

2,500 calories

An average man uses 2,500 calories per day

2,000 calories

An average woman uses 2,000 calories per day

⬇ France is the **largest western European** nation. Andorra, a neighboring country, could fit into France 1,168 times.

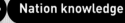

⬇ Nation knowledge

Population **60.7 million**—predicted to soar to **75 million** by 2050, making it the **largest population in the European Union**

Birth rates are steady, but the number of **deaths** is in decline

Life expectancy is strongly increasing: men = 76.7 years women = 83.8 years

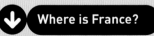

⬇ Where is France?

➡️ The **Train à Grande Vitesse** (TGV—High speed **train 159**) was introduced in 1981. Three major routes run from Paris: north to Lille-Calais, southwest to Nantes and Bordeaux, and southeast to Lyon and Marseille.

In 2001, TGV Réseau set the train speed endurance record: 663 m (1,067 km) at 190 mph (306 km/h)

In 1990, the TGV reached its fastest ever speed: 320 mph (515 km/h)

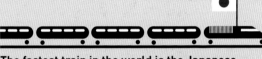

The fastest train in the world is the Japanese Maglev, which reached 361 mph (581 km/h) in 2003

⬇️ France is the second-largest **agriculture exporter** in the world, after the US. It is Europe's leading producer and exporter of farm products. 54 percent of France is used for agriculture.

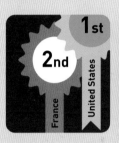

1st United States

2nd France

⬇️ France ranks fifth among the world's top 70 car producers, making more than 3,600,000 vehicles every year.

3,600,000 per year

⬇️ Over 2,000 **fashion 192** journalists flock to Paris every year to catch its **two fashion weeks:** one showcasing the spring/summer collections in October, and the other the fall/winter collections in February or March.

Wine and cheese party

France is the world's biggest exporter of cheese. The French also consume the most cheese, munching 54 lbs (24.5 kg) per person per year. Most is eaten as a separate dish between the main meal and dessert.

The French love wine—on average, a French person drinks 99 pints (47 liters) per year, just behind the Italians, who drink 113 pints (54 liters). In 2004 they produced a wine surplus (more than they could drink or sell) of over 12.7 billion pints (6 bn liters).

How the French eat cheese

80% — for cheese course

20% for cooking

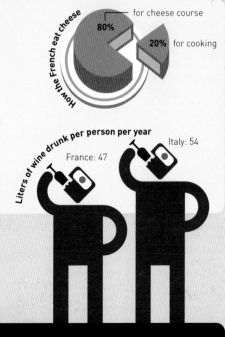

Liters of wine drunk per person per year

France: 47   Italy: 54

France...

FROM PAMPHLETEERS TO BLOGGERS

Pamphlets—printed works under 100 pages in length and usually unbound—were the forerunners of today's online blogs. They became popular when Gutenberg's invention of movable type provided a cheap and easy way to publish opinions. They could be printed and circulated much more quickly than books. Thomas Paine (1737–1809), an Englishman living in the US, is famous for his political pamphlets. He was a radical who opposed the British monarchy and believed **colonies 096** should be independent. His writings were influential on the **Revolutionary War 138** (he's also famous for bringing the first tea bags to the US). Today, you're more likely to find a blogger than a pamphleteer. Weblogs are internet sites that have opinions, articles, diaries—anything, in fact, that a blogger writes. And they are considered democratic because anyone can do one: nothing has to be printed or distributed, and millions around the world can read your blog—if anyone thinks it's interesting enough.

DON'T BELIEVE EVERYTHING YOU READ

PRINTING WAS first invented by the Romans over 2,000 years ago. A senator named Printius Copyius made a basic printing press to produce some leaflets that advertised the sale of his house. It didn't really catch on, though—it was easier to dictate to a scribe.

It's thought that an Irish monk, Casey O'Manure, came across Copyius's manuscripts in the 10th century and built a printing press himself. But he destroyed it when he realized that it would ruin his job as a page illustrator for gold-leaf Bibles.

It wasn't until the 16th century that printing finally took off as an easy way to print crossword puzzles, which were then all the rage. However, the evidence is that this whole story is a a tall tale—just one big pack of **lies 110**. Remember, you can't always believe everything you read.

There's one other false fact on these pages. Do you know what it is? (Answer at the bottom of the page.)

PROPAGANDA

Propaganda is information used by governments and political groups to influence how people think:

EMOTION USED MORE THAN LOGIC TO GET IDEAS ACROSS!

OFTEN OVEREXAGGERATED OR UNTRUTHFUL!

BIASED TOWARD A GROUP OR IDEA!

PROPAGANDA is often used during war as a way of boosting morale or messing with the enemy's head. Planes can drop leaflets on enemy troops to undermine their reasons for fighting. Propaganda also helps "dehumanize" the enemy, so people hate them. During **World War I 178**, stories were spread about German troops killing babies in Belgium. The stories weren't true, but they helped convince many Americans to join the war.

THE HISTORY OF PRINTING (HONEST)

READ ALL ABOUT IT... TRUE TALES FROM THE WORLD OF PRINTING FROM EARLIEST BEGINNINGS TO THE BOOK THAT'S IN YOUR HANDS

THE CHINESE invented printing in the sixth century BC and their first books date back to the ninth century AD. But the printing press, the machine to do the job, wasn't created until the mid-1400s. This was refined by a German goldsmith called Johannes Gutenberg (1398-1468). His method was known as movable type and involved reusable letters that could be arranged into whatever word combinations were required. In 1455, he printed copies of the Bible (the "Gutenberg Bible"), which sold for 300 florins each (at least five years' allowance). By the end of the 15th century, the printing press had spread across Europe, and by 1539 it had reached as far as Mexico City.

GUTENBERG'S printing method really did change the world. It has been called the most important invention of the millennium. Before Gutenberg, books were very expensive and copied out by hand, often with elaborate illustrations and adornments, such as gold leaf. It fell to the church—monks, mainly—to do the laborious work of copying, so books tended to be religious.

MOVABLE TYPE changed all that. During the 16th century, religious reformer **Martin Luther 216** reached a large audience throughout Germany with his printed pamphlets. His translation of the Bible helped standardize German. Before this, most Bibles had been written in **Latin 054**. And so, national languages took on more importance.

PRINTING HELPED to create a community of scientists who swapped information about their latest discoveries. It also meant that anyone who could read had access to all types of knowledge. With books, people could learn alone—just like you can with this one.

The Daily Truth

NEWS
WITH YOUR CORNFLAKES

The newspaper in its modern form has its origins in Germany in the early 17th century. (The first handwritten newspaper dates back to AD 713, when *Mixed News* was published in **China 264**.) But newspapers really took off at the end of the 19th century in Europe and the US. Printing methods were more efficient, and more people than ever could read because of improved education. A morning paper gave people something to do when eating breakfast. Today, there are thousands of titles worldwide, although reading news on the internet is becoming popular. Journalists

"PICTURES FAKED AND DISHONEST STORIES"

write for newspapers and are expected to tell the truth and not make things up. But newspapers can often be biased because they may be owned by the government or a proprietor who has strong political opinions, or who simply wants sensational stories to sell the paper. US media mogul William Randolph Hearst was one such owner, who had **pictures 076** faked and printed dishonest stories in his *New York Morning Journal* in the late 1890s.

🔥 BOOK BURNING

Knowledge is power. For that reason, books can be considered dangerous. The ideas contained in their pages might inspire a revolution or bad behavior. As a result, books are sometimes burned in dramatic acts of censorship. The Nazis burned thousands of books that they didn't like, including works by such famous authors as Thomas Mann and H. G. Wells. More recently, books, including J. K. Rowling's *Harry Potter* series, were burned by some Christian church groups in the US, who believed the stories promoted witchcraft.

And it's not always books that face the flames. In 1948, children, overseen by priests, burned comics in New York state. **Beatles 305** records were thrown onto fires in the 1960s, after singer John Lennon described his band as more popular than **Jesus 185**. In Ray Bradbury's futuristic novel *Fahrenheit 451*, all books are burned to prevent the population from learning new ideas. Beware.

ADVERTISING techniques are often similar to those of propaganda. **Adverts 312** rely heavily on repetition, slogans, and emotional appeal. sell products used to

THE GOEBBELS TECHNIQUE
Dr. Joseph Goebbels (1897-1945) was propaganda minister for the Nazi party in Germany during World War II. He stirred up hatred against Nazi enemies, such as Jews and communists. His technique was to repeat a lie so often that people would believe it was the truth.

WARS AREN'T WHAT THEY USED TO BE

WHY DEMOCRACIES DON'T GO TO WAR

As a rule, <u>democratic 194</u> countries don't go to war with each other. Though historians like to find exceptions (technically, Finland was at war with Britain in 1941, for example), democracies are usually eager to promote peaceful relations that encourage trade. Membership of international organizations, such as the United Nations, also helps.

WAR	WHEN IT HAPPENED	MAIN PLAYERS	WHERE THE ACTION WAS	FAVORED WEAPONS
ONE HUNDRED YEARS' WAR	1337-1453	ENGLAND vs. FRANCE: fighting over who should rule France	FRANCE	Long-sword, longbow and, later, firearms, cannon, and, supposedly, the two-fingered salute (the French cut the bow-fingers off captured archers. English bowmen would wave their intact fingers to say, "I still have mine.").
FRENCH REVOLUTIONARY WARS	1792-1815	FRANCE vs. EUROPEAN MONARCHIES: the French wanted to be rid of royalty in Europe and run the place themselves	Across EUROPE, from Spain to Russia	Deadly effective artillery (cannon) and firearms (muskets), plus lance, sword, and aerial balloon for checking out the troops.
WORLD WAR I	1914-1918	CENTRAL POWERS (Germany, Austro-Hungary) vs. ENTENTE (UK, France, Russia, plus US after 1917): clash of the world powers	EUROPE (mostly Belgium, France, and Russia), but also Turkey, Palestine, Africa	Machine gun, artillery, rifle, poison gas, and planes made of wood and pieces of fabric. Mass production of very efficient weapons meant there were plenty to go around.
WORLD WAR II	1939-1945	AXIS (Germany, Italy, Japan) vs. ALLIES (UK, Russia, plus US after 1941): a.k.a., everyone versus fascism	A real WORLDWIDE war: Europe, North Atlantic, Middle East, Far East	Tank, bomber, and fighter aircraft, artillery, machine gun, rifle, grenade, radar (an instrument for detecting aircraft and ships), aircraft carrier, <u>atomic bomb 204</u>.
COLD WAR	1945-1989	EASTERN BLOC (Soviet Union and Eastern Europe) vs. NATO (US and Western Europe): a.k.a., communism versus <u>capitalism 050</u>	The WHOLE WORLD was threatened	In theory, enough nuclear weapons to destroy the world. In practice, a lot of talk but not much action. Phew!
VIETNAM WAR	1964-1975	US & SOUTH VIETNAM vs. NORTH VIETNAM & VIET CONG REBELS: the US fights communism	VIETNAM (and occasionally Cambodia and other parts of southeast Asia)	Helicopter, AK-47 assault rifle, land mine, booby trap, napalm (nasty liquid explosive), B-52 bomber.

"All men should be expected to fight for their country" Discuss.

BEST TACTICS	WHAT'S SO DIFFERENT?	WHAT ABOUT ORDINARY FOLKS?	THE RESULT	WARFARE RATING
Initially, the English ruled the battlefield with their longbows (at Crécy in 1346, the outnumbered English cut down the French with their arrows). Later, the rise of cannon and handguns put the French back in contention.	It marked the end of the Age of Chivalry (when there were strict rules about fighting) and the decline of the noble warrior class. For the first time since the fall of Rome 262, there were standing (permanent) armies in Europe.	With farms laid to waste and famine across much of France, it wasn't a great time to be a peasant. (Then again, it never is.)	The English lost and future kings remained French. Well, up until the Revolution in 1789. (That caused a lot more trouble—see below.)	BRUTAL AND IN-YOUR-FACE
Large, defensive fortresses became pointless as armies swamped an area and lived off the land. Cavalry (forces on horses) was now less important than massed infantry (soldiers on foot) supported by mobile artillery.	Armies were much bigger than before. In 1794, France had more than one million soldiers. Before this, an army of 100,000 would have been huge. Early industrialization 184 meant there was a musket for every man.	Revolutionary zeal and conscription (forced recruitment) in France meant normal citizens became soldiers—it was the duty of all men to fight for their nation.	France lost and got its king back (for a while, anyway). The rest of Europe kept its monarchies. But the larger scale of war meant casualties aplenty: four million were killed.	A RIGHT ROYAL DISASTER
Defenders with machine guns and artillery could cut down thousands of men in just minutes 250. Attacking enemy trenches (going "over the top") was often suicidal. Tanks were first used in 1916 but kept breaking down.	Soldiers lived in trenches (miserable, wet, lots of rats). The battles were huge and more about destroying men and equipment than gaining ground. It became a war of attrition (about which side could keep going the longest).	Some aerial bombardment of cities, causing fear rather than great damage. Because so many soldiers were being killed, conscription was widely used across Europe.	Germany and its buddies lost, but the seeds were sown for a sequel (see below). Some 8.5 million soldiers were killed, with as many as six million civilian casualties.	GREAT BIG WAR
The German Blitzkrieg ("lightning war") was initially successful—they used tanks and dive bombers to smash through enemy lines. Radio brought instant communication between troops and command, speeding everything up.	At the start of the war in 1939, the Poles still used cavalry. By the end, the atomic bomb had been dropped. While plenty was new—air power was crucial and tanks dominated the battles—soldiers still had to do the fighting. Some things don't change.	Both sides used bombers to carry the war beyond the frontlines—entire cities were destroyed. Nazi policies targeted any civilians they didn't like, and the Soviet population was caught up in much of the brutal fighting in the Soviet Union 329.	After six years, 50 million people were dead (including six million Jews who were murdered by the Nazis in the Holocaust). Fascism was finished but the Cold War was starting up (see below).	AS BLOODY AS IT GETS
A standoff. Both sides had nuclear weapons and these acted as a deterrent to either side starting a war. This doctrine was suitably known as MAD (Mutually Assured Destruction).	The superpowers 260 did have "proxy" wars. They would intervene and support countries in local conflicts rather than fight each other directly. This happened in Vietnam (see below) and also Afghanistan in the 1980s.	In the event of a "hot war" and nuclear conflict, cities would have been the main targets. Everyone knew whole countries could be destroyed with millions killed in a matter of hours.	In 1989, communism began to collapse, bringing the Cold War to an end. Democracy, capitalism, and the US were left to dominate international politics.	HERE'S A WAR THAT NEVER WARMED UP
The US wanted to stop South Vietnam from becoming communist. The Viet Cong used guerilla warfare (ambushes, booby traps, surprise attacks) because they couldn't have beaten the world's mightiest army in a straight fight.	The Americans were frustrated by an enemy that didn't necessarily wear uniforms or line up in neat rows to fight. So-called asymmetrical warfare has since been used in Afghanistan (against bigger USSR) and Iraq (against much stronger US).	The distinction between combatant and civilian was further blurred. Rebels and peasants looked the same to US forces—even when they could find them in the dense jungle. Villages were cleared and bombed, the peasants bearing the brunt of it, yet again.	The US lost this conflict and Vietnam became communist. Two million Vietnamese and 58,000 US soldiers had been killed.	RUMBLE IN THE JUNGLE

www.imagineawor

dwithoutpaper.com

AND THEY DIDN'T EVEN INVENT THE WHEEL...

Central and South America were home to peoples who were skilled engineers, architects, and inventors. They developed advanced societies, at times more sophisticated than anything in Europe 216. But they didn't always get it right...

MISSES

HITS

INVENTING NOTHING

The Maya were great astronomers. They made careful observations to measure the phases of the Moon, the timing of eclipses, and the movements of several of the planets. The mathematics involved required them to invent the number zero—as early as the seventh century AD. Not bad, considering they did this nearly 1,000 years before Europeans caught on to how useful nothing could be when doing addition.

POWERFUL PYRAMIDS

The Egyptians built **pyramids 314** in which to bury their pharaohs (kings). Three thousand years later, peoples of Central and South America built vast pyramids on which to worship their gods and kill their enemies (the Aztecs may have sacrificed anything between 20,000 and 80,000 captured enemies when they dedicated a new temple in their capital, Tenochtitlán, in 1487). Some Mayan pyramids were 230 ft (70 m) high.

A LOST CITY

The Incas were stunning stonemasons, building towns and fortresses out of stone so carefully cut and placed that they could survive for centuries. One such site was Machu Picchu, a religious center so high up and remote in the Peruvian Andes that when the Spaniards conquered the Inca Empire in the 1530s, they didn't find it. An American archeologist, Hiram Bingham, spotted it from the air in 1911, and it soon became a popular **tourist 122** site, attracting 500,000 visitors a year by the late 1990s. Fearful of the damage that mass tourism was doing to the area, the Peruvian government restricted numbers on the Inca trail leading to the site to only 500 a day.

LOTS OF STRING

The Incas built an empire that stretched the length of South America, built a road system as good as many today, and constructed some fabulous cities. But they didn't have the ingenuity to devise a simple writing system. They were quite content to use string, knotted and tied, to create a method of recorded statistics for everything from the annual harvest to the size of the population. This was kind of clever, but still a "miss."

MISSING WHEELS

The Maya and other people of the region, just like all kids today, liked to play with toys. They made little figures of animals and put them on miniature **wheels 282** so they could pull them around. But then they had a mental block and did nothing else with those wheels, like making them bigger and sticking them under a cart or wagon.

THE SPANISH

Unfortunately, the Aztecs and Incas were no match for the Spanish. They arrived in Mexico in 1519 armed with guns and carrying deadly diseases. The natives were quickly overcome. The Aztecs made things worse by mistaking the Spanish conquistador (conqueror) Hernán Cortés for their chief god, Quetzalcoatl, and worshipping him. The Incas also fared badly against the Spanish adventurers who arrived in South America in the 1530s. They were recovering from a major civil war and didn't notice at first what the Spanish were up to. Plus, most of the Incas' neighbors were happy to form an alliance with the Spanish—they didn't want to be used as sacrificial victims in the Incas' temples any more. And every Inca decision had to be made by the the emperor. So, once conquistador Francisco Pizarro captured him in 1532, no decision to **fight 154** could be made. Oops.

5 **TOLTECS**

NO.	PLACE	DATE (APPROX.)	REASONS TO KNOW ABOUT THEM
1	Gulf coast of Mexico	1200–200 BC	The Olmecs carved huge stone heads
2	Oaxaca Valley southern Mexico	400 BC–AD 950	The Zapotecs devised a calendar and were the first people in the Americas to write, using hieroglyphs or pictures
3	Valley of Mexico	200 BC–AD 700	Teotihuacan was a vast capital city—one of the largest in the world, with as many as 200,000 inhabitants
4	Yucatan Peninsula	AD 300–1400	The Maya developed complex writing skills, built temple pyramids, and were skilled astronomers
5	Valley of Mexico	AD 900–1200	Great architects—the Toltecs' capital, Tula, had ceremonial temples and flat-topped pyramids

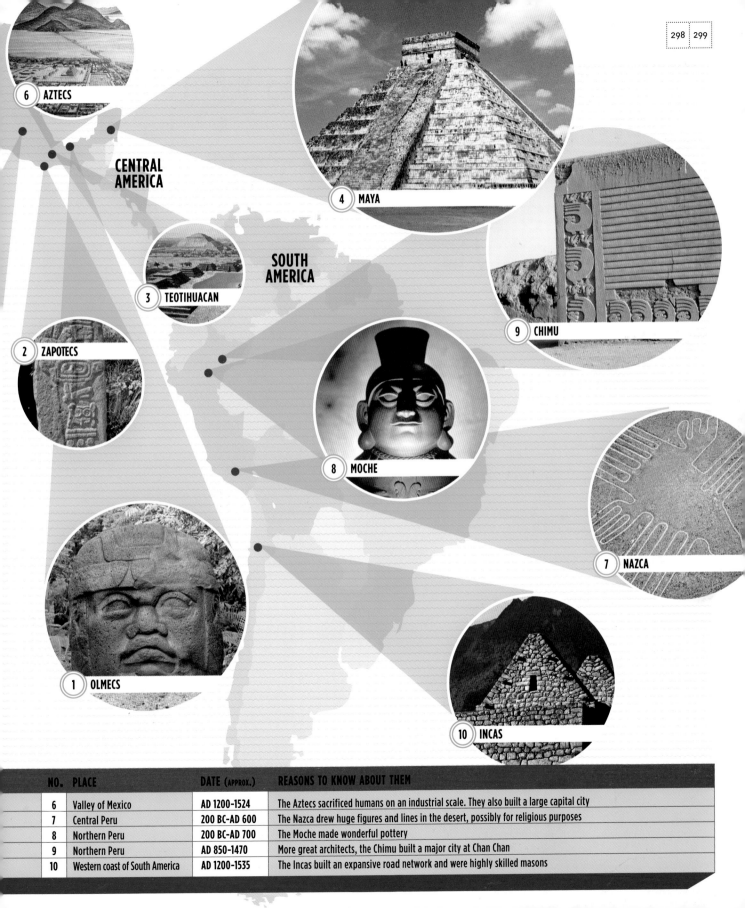

6 AZTECS

CENTRAL AMERICA

4 MAYA

3 TEOTIHUACAN

SOUTH AMERICA

9 CHIMU

2 ZAPOTECS

8 MOCHE

7 NAZCA

1 OLMECS

10 INCAS

NO.	PLACE	DATE (approx.)	REASONS TO KNOW ABOUT THEM
6	Valley of Mexico	AD 1200-1524	The Aztecs sacrificed humans on an industrial scale. They also built a large capital city
7	Central Peru	200 BC-AD 600	The Nazca drew huge figures and lines in the desert, possibly for religious purposes
8	Northern Peru	200 BC-AD 700	The Moche made wonderful pottery
9	Northern Peru	AD 850-1470	More great architects, the Chimu built a major city at Chan Chan
10	Western coast of South America	AD 1200-1535	The Incas built an expansive road network and were highly skilled masons

HOW ELECTRICITY AND MAGNETISM CAN SAVE YOUR LIFE

COPPER WIRE

ELECTRON

ELECTRON FLOW

INSULATION

What are magnets?

Magnets attract certain materials—not because they are particularly charming, but because they create a force called a magnetic field. This is invisible, though you can see the field's trace if you sprinkle iron filings on paper around a bar magnet. The lines loop from one end of the magnet to the other. These ends are known as poles (north and south)—this is where the magnetic field is strongest. Opposite poles (north-south) attract each other, but matching poles (such as north-north) repel.

As with electricity, electrons play a big part in creating magnetism. All electrons create tiny magnetic fields. In most materials, the electrons are facing in different directions and the fields cancel each other out—no big deal.

A magnet, though, has electrons that are a bit different. They face in the same direction, creating regions of magnetism called domains (remember, these are really, really tiny). These domains themselves face in the same direction, combining to create a strong magnetic field. A magnetic material, such as iron, will have domains facing in different directions (fig 1), unless a magnet is brought close so that they all line up (fig 2).

The **Earth 170** itself acts like a giant magnet with its two poles. It creates a magnetic field that is crucial in protecting us from harmful rays from the Sun.

An electromagnet, as used in an MRI scanner, is made of wire coiled round an iron core. When an electric current flows through the wire, a magnetic field is created.

Electricity at work

Electric currents are created by the movement of tiny particles called electrons. Usually these are firmly in orbit around the center (or the nucleus) of **atoms 060**. But in certain materials, called conductors, electrons are loosely held to their atoms (this occurs in most metals, for example).

An energy source, such as a battery or generator, causes electrons to leave their atoms. An electron jumps into the neighboring atom, causing that electron to become detached and move off, to jump into the next atom. In this way, a chain reaction is set up (similar to falling dominoes) that creates an electrical current. This all pretty much happens at the speed of light, so when you switch on the TV, electricity powers it up in an instant. Copper is often used in electrical wiring because it makes an excellent conductor; the electrons move through it easily (pictured above).

In nonconducting materials, or insulators, the electrons are held firm to their atoms—they aren't going anywhere. Things such as plastic and wood block electrical currents. Most cables have an insulating layer covering the electrical wire to prevent hair-raising electrocutions.

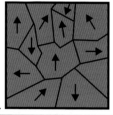

1.

2.

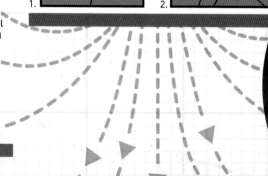

The incredible MRI machine

The image of the man (right) looks as if his body has been sliced from head to toe. It is made by a Magnetic Resonance Imaging (MRI) machine (far right). Invented in 1971, this uses electricity and magnetism to allow doctors to "see" inside a patient's body without operating. It is especially useful for looking at soft tissue, such as the **spinal cord 044** and the brain, where it can be used to detect tumors. MRIs can also create moving images—useful for checking whether the heart is working properly.

A typical scanner consists of a tunnel, into which the patient is moved by a motorized bed (cool!). Concealed in the tunnel walls are powerful electromagnets, producing a magnetic field around the patient. This makes the trillions of hydrogen atoms in the body line up to face in the same direction (imagine soldiers on parade). Then, a burst of radio waves (directed at the body area to be scanned) causes the hydrogen atoms to spin. After their brief workout, the atoms line up again, facing the magnet. The clever bit is that, as they do this, they give off small radio signals. The scanner then processes these signals into images, like the one you see here. Pretty neat, huh?

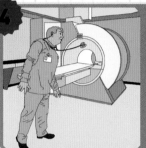

Leave big metal objects such as chairs, oxygen cylinders, industrial floor polishers, metal ladders, and forklift trucks (oh yes) outside the MRI room—or they will get pulled inside the scanner.

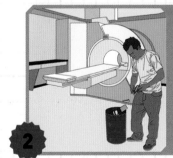

Don't carry small metallic objects such as scissors, stethoscopes, keys, pens, or clipboards. These will be pulled out of hands or pockets and fly toward the opening of the MRI scanner.

Don't go armed. In the US, in 1999, a police officer lost his revolver when it was ripped from his holster, hit the scanner and fired a shot into the wall.

Credit cards and bank cards are best left at home. The magnetic field will erase the coding on the cards, rendering them useless.

PREDATORY SHARKS

At close range, a shark uses special electrosensors to pinpoint a prey's position. The prey's **muscles 156** create weak electrical currents. These are picked up by tiny, jelly-filled pores in the shark's snout. Getting close, the hungry shark follows the electrical trail and slices into its victim with razor-sharp teeth. Yikes!

ANIMAL MAGNETISM

NAVIGATING BIRDS

How do Arctic terns make their annual 25,000-mile (40,000-km) migration from Arctic to Antarctic and back without getting lost? How does a homing pigeon return to its owner? It seems that these and other **birds 182** navigate by detecting the Earth's own magnetic field—the invisible lines of force between the north and south poles.

DON'T EVEN GO THERE

There are five good reasons to remember that the powerful magnets on **MRI machines 316** are always switched on. And all of the following have happened to poor fools who forgot that. For real...

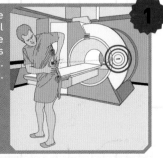

Stay away if you have embedded shrapnel or maybe bullets. The machine's magnets will yank them out. Which will hurt. A lot.

NO

Language Parents always complain that young people "speak their own language." But what would it be like if the words you write or speak couldn't be understood by anyone else? It would hardly be a language at all. Languages are systems of words shared by two or more people to convey needs, ideas, and feelings. If you've ever been on vacation somewhere where you can't speak the language, you'll know how difficult it is to communicate. Even a secret code needs one other person who can decode it again. For 1,500 years nobody could understand the markings on the Rosetta Stone, an Egyptian artifact from 196 BC (now in the British Museum in London, England). No one knew the language. But then, in the 19th century, a French professor studied the stone and figured out what the hieroglyphic symbols meant (it wasn't "mind your own business"). Unless you want to spend the rest of your life talking to yourself (tempting at times), don't make up a language unique to you.

YES

Your biometrics The modern world can sometimes feel like a **science fiction movie 057**. Technology can now recognize your fingerprints, voice, iris (the colored ring of the eye), the way you type on a computer, and even how fast you're reading this book (okay, the last one is made up). This is called biometric testing. In the future, your iris print may be contained in a computer chip on your passport as a form of identification. Although the pattern of your iris is unique to you, however, there is always the possibility that it could be faked (with a contact lens, perhaps). If someone wanted to steal your identity (perhaps to get hold of all your millions!), they could try to forge your biometric details and pretend to be you. You are biometrically unique, but future technologies might be able to copy that uniqueness.

YES

Dreaming That's right—the dream you had where your feet turned into bananas and you kept slipping is pretty unique (and seriously weird). Dreams are often thought of as mixed-up versions of events and feelings we experience when we're awake. No two people have exactly the same waking experiences, so your **dreams 210** will never be the same as anyone else's. Though some dream events may be common (showing up at school naked except for your shoes, for example), no one can dream your dreams for you. Everybody deals with experiences in their own way, according to their memories and personality. Which is why other peoples' dreams always sound so crazy.

ARE YOU UNIQUE?

Ever wondered if there is another you in the world? Someone who looks, acts, and talks the same? Stealing all your best lines?

YES

DNA differences You have 10 trillion cells in your body. Can you imagine the chaos that would occur if they didn't know what they were supposed to do? **DNA 258** tells your cells exactly that. DNA is a ladderlike molecule that stores information on how you will grow and how to maintain your body. It decides many aspects of you, like hair color and height, and affects things like whether you are good at math or not ('It's not my fault, sir... It's my DNA!'). Every time your body makes a new cell, this genetic information is passed on. But although the DNA in each of your cells is the same, nobody else's DNA will be quite the same as yours (unless you have an identical twin). This means that using someone's DNA is a great way to identify people (and even solve murders). It is also a good way of finding out if you are related to someone, since relatives share certain DNA patterns. You contain DNA from both your parents, so it is related to theirs, but still unique.

NO

Social position How would you feel if you were told that everything you like is directly related to what your parents' jobs are, or even which street you live on? You may feel as if you decide which clothes, **music 022**, and food you like, but some sociologists (people who study how society works) believe those tastes are all affected by your social position. This is known as "class." It is also related to things like your family's level of education. For example, if your parents have lots of books in their house, it follows that you will grow to understand, and even like (come on, admit it), some of those books. Your family's wealth is also important— richer families will tend to have more luxuries (such as expensive cars or food), and there will be more money for children to have private tutoring, take trips, or learn musical instruments. Sure, there are ways of bucking these patterns, and no one has to be stuck in the same social class forever. But the fact remains that most people choose things they like from what is familiar and affordable to them.

NO

Falling in love When two people fall in love, they often feel as if they invented the emotion. Each experience of love feels utterly unique and personal. But we can also think of romance as being very unoriginal. Try and think of romantic movies depicting a couple falling in love: they run through fall leaves hand in hand and watch the **sunset 327**. It's all filmed through a misty camera lens, and they spend a lot of time staring meaningfully into each other's eyes (feeling queasy yet?). Even in real life, there are certain patterns of behavior that everyone experiences. When you see someone you've got a crush on, your heart might beat faster, you may sweat more, and you might even go weak at the knees. These are physiological (body) reactions that many of us share. And if you ever get to the kissing part, it will (hopefully) be pleasant, but it is hardly a unique experience. People have been locking lips for centuries. Indeed, many human emotions and behaviors (not just love) are universal.

NO

Branding you People like to be different. Just look around the next time you go to school. Whether you have to wear a uniform or not, people always find ways of trying to look unique—by wearing the latest sneakers, carrying a trendy bag, or wearing fancy jewelry. People want to stand out from the crowd (especially if the crowd is wearing a particularly unflattering school uniform—just who invented them?). But are these **fashionable 192** people really being more individual? Take a look at what they use to set themselves apart. Often, it is an item sporting a brand name or logo such as Nike, Levi, or Chanel. Brands carry messages, whether obvious marketing messages from their advertisements or home-grown messages that people make between themselves (as to what is and what is not "cool"). Just when people think they are expressing their individuality, they might only be following a different crowd. If millions of people buy Nike sneakers, how can wearing them make you unique?

YES

Where you live Lots of zoos are home to African elephants. In many ways, these elephants are the same as the thousands of wild ones roaming national parks in Africa. But, of course, captive elephants are not really the same. Wild elephants are nomadic—they are free to wander. Elephants in zoos live in a small compound and are given food every day. Free elephants would find the existence of a captive elephant very confusing, and zoo elephants wouldn't know how to survive in the wild. We humans also adapt to and are shaped by our environment. This doesn't just mean the **birds 182**, animals, and trees around us, but also the kind of buildings we live in, the people we meet and the type of school we go to. If you could live two lives—one, say, growing up in the countryside, and the other in a city—your environment would influence your clothes, the way you speak, your interests, your knowledge, your health, and your friends. You might not even recognize yourself!

NO

DNA similarities Well, your DNA is unique to you, but it is also on average 99.9 percent the same as anyone else's—it's only that 0.1 percent that makes you "you." So, when it comes down to it, people are a whole lot alike. Humans are also remarkably similar to other species. For example, mice and humans each have about 30,000 genes (a gene is a section of DNA), yet only one percent of those are unique to either organism. However, humans and mice don't use all the genes in their DNA—humans, for example, have genes for a tail, but it isn't activated, so you don't actually grow one. Too bad!

YES

Your memories The way you remember things is not quite the same as anyone else. This is because you see and remember events from a viewpoint particular to you. You can share memories with your friends and family, but when they talk about your seventh birthday party, they are thinking about it from a different point of view. They might remember the way you cried when you didn't get that Barbie doll or Lego set you wanted, while you might remember the joke candles on the birthday cake that wouldn't blow out (still infuriating!). Of course, even your own unique memory can let you down or change over **time 249**. Memories can decay or be influenced by other people's suggestions, but the whole range of your memories still remains only yours.

Unique Facts

Some people, animals, or places have unique features that make them one of a kind

Archeologists have tasted the honey found in the tombs of Egyptian pharaohs, leading some to think it is the only food that never goes bad.

The only continent with no snakes or other **reptiles 146** is Antarctica. Ophidiophobes (people who are afraid of snakes) take note.

The only country where cows have rights like people do is India (Hindus consider the cow a sacred animal). So, watch out how you milk them—they might sue you.

The hyoid bone in the throat is the only floating bone in the body—the only bone not joined to another. It is held in place by three sets of muscles.

Bats are the only **mammals 116** that can flap their wings and fly (rather than lazily glide), while giraffes are the only animals born with their horns.

HOW *PLANES* HELPED PUT CHICAGO ON THE MAP

The city of Chicago is not only famous for its skyscrapers, blues music, and gangsters—it's also known for its aviation. In the 1920s, Chicago's central location proved ideal for moving mail around the US. Car magnate <u>Henry Ford 184</u> and plane-manufacturing firm Boeing were among the companies contracted to fly mail in and out of the city. In 1932, a century after the city was founded, Chicago's Midway Airport was the world's busiest airport. Plane technology advanced: biplanes, with two parallel wings, were replaced by monoplanes, and by the 1950s, propellers were out and jet technology was in. Jet engines, known as gas turbines, burn gases that blast backward to thrust the plane into the sky. This greatly improved the speed and range of aircraft. The Boeing 707, which first flew in 1954, became the icon of the age. It could fly 141 passengers over a distance of 4,000 miles (6,400 km). Modern airliners, such as the Boeing 777 (left), are designed on computers and contain some three million parts.

After World War II, Chicago built a new airport, named O'Hare. It soon overtook Midway as the busiest airport in the world. These days, more than 70 million people each year <u>travel 122</u> through O'Hare. In 2001, Boeing made Chicago the site of its world headquarters. The company's newest plane, the 787 Dreamliner, is due to fly in 2008. Designed for fuel efficiency, it will carry up to 290 people 10,000 miles (16,300 km). Care for a trip?

A CURE FOR AIRSICKNESS

Ellen Church (above) was a registered nurse who took flying lessons and wanted to be a pilot. Instead, in 1930, she became the first flight attendant, flying with US airline Boeing Air Transport (now United Airlines) on its earliest passenger routes. Other nurses were also hired as flight attendants—a comfort to passengers in an era when flying still seemed dangerous. They dispensed earplugs, <u>chewing gum 240</u>, and smelling salts. Hot meals were introduced in 1936 and the first male flight attendants were hired in 1950. But it wasn't until the mid-1960s that stewardesses were allowed to marry!

LOOK! UP IN THE SKY...

US space agency NASA is developing a "highway of the sky" that will use small aircraft as a flying taxi service. Planes with just four passenger seats will avoid overcrowded airports and use small landing fields. Meanwhile, superfast planes (such as NASA's X-43 prototype, above) that reach the edge of space could reduce the seven-hour flight from London to New York to a mere half-hour.

DID FLYING START WITH BIRDWATCHING?

Humans have long had a fascination with joining the birds in the sky. Over 500 years ago, <u>Leonardo da Vinci 254</u> sketched a machine with flapping wings, dubbed an ornithopter. Powered flight didn't come until 1903, when American bicycle mechanics Orville and Wilbur Wright (below), an airplane made of wood and cloth. With Orville at the controls, it flew 120 ft (37 m) across sand dunes in North Carolina. This was the world's first sustained, powered flight, lasting 12 seconds.

IF AIR TRAVEL WERE 99.99 PERCENT SAFE THERE WOULD BE THREE FATAL AIR CRASHES EVERY DAY OF THE YEAR. IN FACT, AIR TRAVEL IS 99.9999996 PER CENT SAFE. MORE AMERICANS DIE BY FALLING FROM LADDERS EACH YEAR THAN BY FLYING ON COMMERCIAL AIRLINES.

BEATLES
FOR
SALE

★HOW THE BEATLES
PATENTED POP

(Because they were the first group to do all
the things pop groups do. Don't believe us?
Turn the page...)

George

Paul

Ringo

John

THE MANAGER

Behind every famous pop star is a manager. They handle the (boring) business side of things, dealing with record companies and making sure the band gets all its hard-earned pennies. They can be ruthless, too. Brian Epstein, The Beatles' manager, got rid of original drummer Pete Best because he didn't like his haircut (among other things).

THE SONGWRITING PARTNERSHIP

Before The Beatles, pop stars usually performed songs written by other people. Even big names such as Elvis Presley and Frank Sinatra did not write their own material (the cheats). John Lennon and Paul McCartney changed all that. Between them, they wrote most of The Beatles' songs.

It makes financial sense for performers to write their own songs—they receive a royalty (or fee) every time the song is played on the radio, or used in a film or **advertisement 312**. They also get paid every time someone else performs a version of the song. The Beatles' song "Yesterday," written by McCartney, is the most recorded pop song in history, as well as the most played on radio.

Brian Epstein

Pete Best

(Didn't make the cut)

Frank Sinatra

The Beatles are the biggest pop group in history. From Liverpool in the north of England, John Lennon, Paul McCartney, George Harrison, and Ringo Starr were only together from 1962 to 1970, but their sales have exceeded a billion records—more than any other artist. The Beatles didn't just sell a bunch of records, though, they also changed the world. They started off as a boy band in matching suits, and ended up as icons for a new way of life.

BEATLEMANIA (OR, MENTAL FANS AND FAINTING GIRLS)

At first, none of the big record companies wanted to sign The Beatles. Finally, the group signed to EMI in 1962—and became a sensation. The Fab Four (as they were known) conquered Britain, and were an instant hit in the US. Their singles dominated the top five places in the singles chart. Their fans screamed so loud at their concerts that nobody could hear the music. Other bands wanted to sound like them—and look like them (some still do).

Sometimes, pop music can define a moment. In the 1960s, American singer Bob Dylan made "protest music" popular. The Motown record label, with artists such as Stevie Wonder and The Supremes, defined soul music. In the 1970s, Ozzy Osbourne's band Black Sabbath played so loud, they invented heavy metal.

Bob Dylan

Bill Haley

EARLY DAYS

The Beatles played rock'n'roll. This type of music was popular with **teenagers 274** in the 1960s. Rock'n'roll groups such as Bill Haley & The Comets used electric guitars, a fast drum beat, and a singer to create songs about girls and cars (mostly). The style was influenced by an earlier form of black American music called the **blues 268**.

The Supremes

Ozzy

(Likes it very loud)

Grandmaster Flash (& The Furious Five)

Sitar

★ TRYING EVERYTHING NEW
The Beatles performed their last-ever concert in 1966, at Candlestick Park in San Francisco. But they kept making more adventurous records. Indian instruments such as sitars (a stringed instrument) and tablas (a type of drum) joined the electric guitars. Tapes played backward introduced freaky new sounds.

In the early 1970s, German band Kraftwerk was one of the first bands to make songs by only using electronic instruments (some of which they made themselves). Sampling developed in the 1980s, meaning sections of music or sounds from one record could be played in another. It's been used in dance music ever since. It is now possible to make music on a computer without touching an actual instrument. But then you'd never get to play a sitar (shame).

★ IT'S MORE THAN JUST POP MUSIC
In July 1966, John Lennon said that The Beatles were "more popular than Jesus." He was trying to get across the idea that when a pop group gets really big, they become almost like a religion. But the remark upset many Christians.

By the late-1960s, The Beatles had their own company, Apple, which produced books, clothes, and films, as well as records. They were seen as leaders of an alternative youth culture, known as the counterculture, that didn't like authority and wanted to do things differently from the **older generation 108** (some things never change).

There have been other countercultures. In the mid-1970s, punk rejected the music of the time. Bands such as the Sex Pistols played angry, noisy music, expressing the frustrations that young people felt about the world. In the early 1980s, rap music did a similar thing. It originated in New York, where a person with a microphone would rhyme over records at parties. The likes of Grandmaster Flash and Run DMC made new music and defined a new attitude (check out the outfits, above!).

★ THE SPLIT
Musical differences or personal disagreements can ruin any band. When The Beatles split up in 1970, they were arguing about **money 058** (among other things) and who controlled the business.

One of the longest surviving rock groups is The Rolling Stones. The core members of the band have been together since the early 1960s, because they still enjoy touring together (and have become filthy rich doing it). The Irish band U2 has had the same members since they started in 1976, probably because they agreed always to share their money equally. (Or maybe they don't have many other friends.)

Bono of U2

★ POP MUSIC AS AN ART
By the mid-1960s, The Beatles were making records, such as *Revolver* (1966) and *Sergeant Pepper's Lonely Hearts Club Band* (1967), that could be called works of **art 322**. They challenged the notion that classical music is superior to pop, by showing that pop could be thoughtful and beautiful. Bands including The Beach Boys, Pink Floyd, Radiohead, and REM have all made albums that are complex and artsy. Today, downloads are shaking up music all over again. In 2005, 26.4 million tracks were (legally) downloaded in the UK, for example—a 355 percent increase on 2004's total. Since people are less likely to listen to albums from start to finish, acts are having to find fresh ways to make exciting music. (Some are even trying to write better songs!)

Run DMC

Brian Wilson

REM

Rolling Stones

SEVEN **COLOR** SHADES
AND THE **FEELINGS** THEY REFLECT
(BY DR. MAXO LUSCHER, COLOR PSYCHOLOGIST)

1 Orange-red: excited, independent
2 Bright yellow: optimistic, creative
3 Green-blue: persistent, assertive
4 Dark blue: calm, sensitive
5 Violet: mystical, intuitive
6 Brown: uncomfortable, aimless
7 Black: rebellious, strong

A LIST OF PHOBIAS

ABLUTOPHOBIA
FEAR OF WASHING OR BATHING
BIBLIOPHOBIA
FEAR OF BOOKS
BAROPHOBIA
FEAR OF GRAVITY 024
CHOROPHOBIA
FEAR OF DANCING
DROMOPHOBIA
FEAR OF CROSSING THE STREET
GENIOPHOBIA
FEAR OF CHINS
PAPYROPHOBIA
FEAR OF PAPER
PTERONOPHOBIA
FEAR OF BEING TICKLED BY FEATHERS
THAASOPHOBIA
FEAR OF SITTING
ZOOPHOBIA
FEAR OF ANIMALS

TYPES OF LIST

ALPHABETICAL
arranged in the order of the alphabet

ASCENDING VALUE
from the least to the most valuable

RELEVANCE
starting with the most closely connected item

CATEGORICAL
divided into separate groups

CHRONOLOGICAL
arranged in date order

HIERARCHICAL
ranked according to importance

NUMERICAL
listed by number 212

UNORDERED
arranged any old way

OLYMPIC VENUES

1948 – LONDON, UK
1952 – HELSINKI, FINLAND
1956 – MELBOURNE, AUSTRALIA
1960 – ROME, ITALY
1964 – TOKYO, JAPAN
1968 – MEXICO CITY, MEXICO
1972 – MUNICH, GERMANY
1976 – MONTREAL, CANADA
1980 – MOSCOW, USSR
1984 – LOS ANGELES, CA
1988 – SEOUL, SOUTH KOREA
1992 – BARCELONA, SPAIN
1996 – ATLANTA, GA
2000 – SYDNEY, AUSTRALIA
2004 – ATHENS, GREECE
2008 – BEIJING, CHINA
2012 – LONDON, UK

LIFETIME ACTIVITIES: 24 YEARS SLEEPING **9** YEARS AT LEISURE **9** YEARS AT SCHOOL **6** YEARS EATING **5** YEARS DREAMING **4** YEARS LOOKING FOR MISPLACED OBJECTS **3** YEARS SICK **2** YEARS ON THE PHONE **2** WEEKS WAITING FOR THE TRAFFIC LIGHTS TO CHANGE

VENUES AND RUNNING ORDER OF THE LIVE 8 CONCERTS, SATURDAY JULY 2, 2005:
Hyde Park (London) PALAIS DE VERSAILLES (PARIS) *Siegessäule (Berlin)* CIRCUS MAXIMUS (ROME) *Museum of Art (Philadelphia)* PARK PLACE (ONTARIO) *Makuhari Messe (Tokyo)* MARY FITZGERALD SQUARE (JOHANNESBURG) *Red Square (Moscow)*

KINGS AND QUEENS OF
DENMARK
AND WHEN THEY REIGNED

Frederik IV	1699-1730
Christian VI	1730-1746
Frederik V	1746-1766
Christian VII	1766-1808
Frederik VI	1808-1839
Christian VIII	1839-1848
Frederik VII	1848-1863
Christian IX	1863-1906
Frederik VIII	1906-1912
Christian X	1912-1947
Frederik IX	1947-1972
Margrethe II	1972-present

3 CUPS FLOUR
2 CUPS SUGAR
6 TABLESPOONS COCOA
2 TEASPOONS BAKING SODA
INGREDIENTS FOR A CHOCOLATE CAKE
1 TEASPOON SALT
3/4 CUP VEGETABLE OIL
2 TABLESPOONS VINEGAR
2 TEASPOONS VANILLA
2 CUPS COLD WATER

FIVE PLACES THAT HAVE MORE SHEEP THAN PEOPLE

	HUMANS	SHEEP
AUSTRALIA	19 MILLION	99 MILLION
NEW ZEALAND	4 MILLION	39 MILLION
MONGOLIA	3 MILLION	12 MILLION
FAEROE ISLANDS	46,000	68,000
MONTSERRAT	4,000	5,000

WISH LIST OF A 13-YEAR-OLD GIRL

1. TEENY, TINY MP3 PLAYER
2. SKATEBOARD
3. MY BROTHER TO BE SENT TO PRISON FOREVER
4. KICKBOXING LESSONS
5. NEW JEANS
6. EYESHADOW KIT
7. BIRTHDAY CAKE

WHEN FOODS WERE INVENTED

POPCORN	3000 BC
CROISSANTS	AD 1683
POTATO CHIPS	1853
CHEWING GUM	1875
COCA-COLA	1885
CORNFLAKES	1894
CHOP SUEY	1896
HAMBURGER	1902
ICE CREAM CONE	1904

A LIST OF THESE LISTS

1 A LIST OF THESE LISTS
2 SEVEN COLOR SHADES AND THE FEELINGS THEY REFLECT
3 WISH LIST OF A 13-YEAR-OLD GIRL
4 INGREDIENTS FOR A CHOCOLATE CAKE
5 WHEN FOODS 176 WERE INVENTED
6 TYPES OF LIST
7 THE SEVEN WONDERS OF THE ANCIENT WORLD
8 OLYMPIC VENUES
9 FIVE PLACES THAT HAVE MORE SHEEP THAN PEOPLE
10 PHOBIAS
11 LIFETIME ACTIVITIES
12 KINGS AND QUEENS OF DENMARK AND WHEN THEY REIGNED
13 TIPS ON HOW TO WRITE A TO-DO LIST YOU MIGHT ACTUALLY DO
14 VENUES AND RUNNING ORDER OF THE LIVE 8 CONCERTS

THE SEVEN WONDERS OF THE ANCIENT WORLD

1 THE GREAT PYRAMID OF GIZA 314 • 2 THE HANGING GARDENS OF BABYLON • 3 THE STATUE OF ZEUS AT OLYMPIA • 4 THE TEMPLE OF ARTEMIS AT EPHESUS • 5 THE MAUSOLEUM AT HALICARNASSUS • 6 THE COLOSSUS OF RHODES • 7 THE LIGHTHOUSE OF ALEXANDRIA

Tips on how to write a TO-DO LIST you might actually DO!

1 - Separate what you have to do into types of task—errand, project, gift-buying, etc.

2 - Prioritize by urgency—do you need to buy the gift first or finish your homework?

3 - Break down the tasks into manageable chunks—for example, first brainstorm gift ideas, then hit the mall, then gift-wrap it.

4 - Reorder the list as tasks get done and different things become important.

5 - Keep it somewhere you will look at it regularly.

6 - Check off each job as you go—and enjoy the satisfaction it gives you.

WHAT GOES AROUND COMES AROUND

1 [illegible] produces about 2,200 lb (one metric ton) of garbage. [illegible] Why not set off a chain of events that might mean your can of cola ends up as a [illegible] lemonade in its next life?

2 Put your soda can, and the rest of your recycling, out to be collected. Some houses have special bins or boxes for recycling garbage. There are also designated sites where it can be left. The aluminum can is the most recycled drink container on the planet—over 50 percent are recycled. In 2005, this amounted to 54 billion cans. Every week, the average family in a developed country gets through four glass bottles or jars, 13 cans, three plastic bottles, and 11lbs (5kg) of paper—most of which can be recycled. Recycling just one can saves enough energy to run a television for three hours. Aluminum cans are 100 percent recyclable, so they can be recycled indefinitely.

3 Your soda can, and all the other garbage to be recycled, is collected and taken to a recycling center. The different objects are separated, and anything that shouldn't be there is taken out (so please don't try to recycle your siblings, no matter how annoying they are). Your can of soda is put with all the other aluminum cans and sent to a reprocessor.

4 At the reprocessor, [illegible]

5 [illegible]

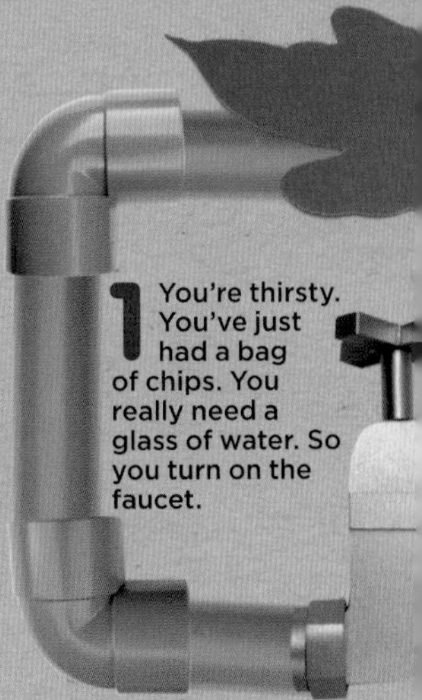

1 You're thirsty. You've just had a bag of chips. You really need a glass of water. So you turn on the faucet.

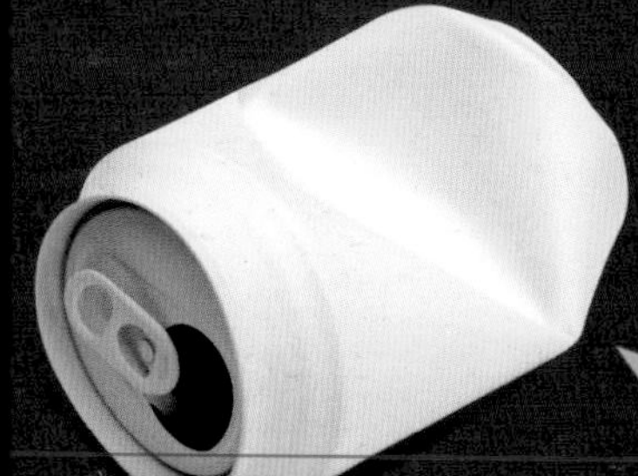

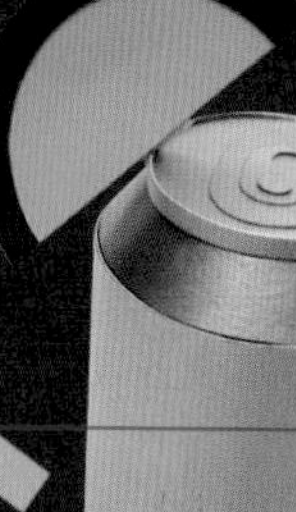

2 You're not thirsty any more, but now you really, really need to pee and have to run to the bathroom. So, you pee, flush it, and wash your hands (of course). Your job in the water cycle is complete.

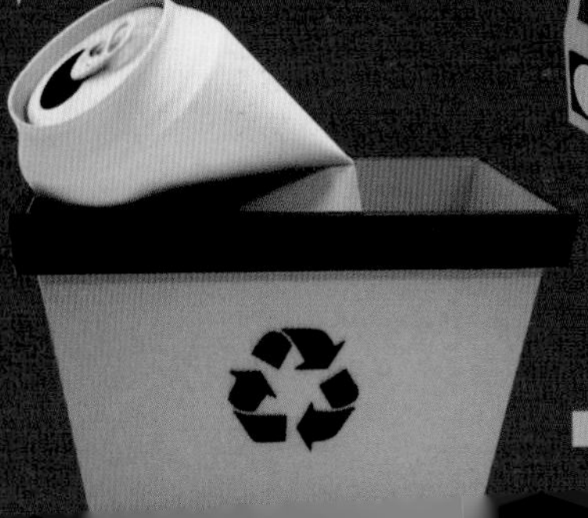

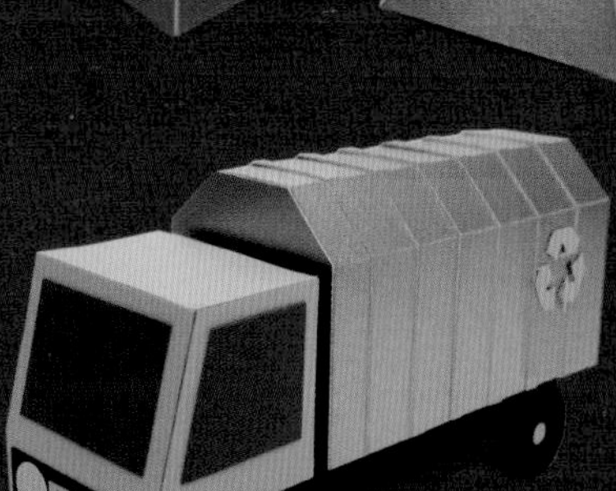

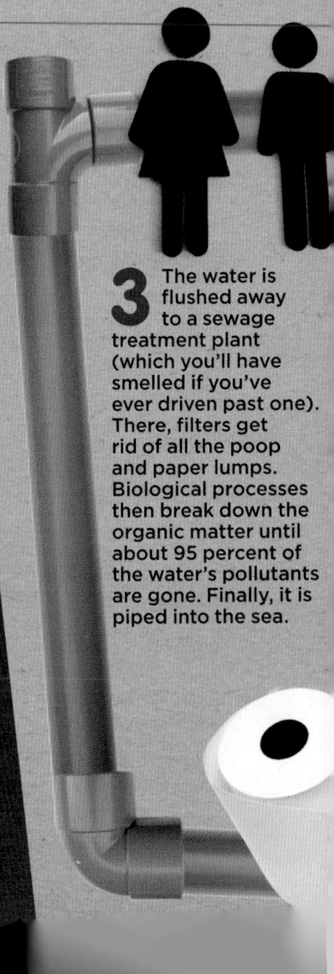

3 The water is flushed away to a sewage treatment plant (which you'll have smelled if you've ever driven past one). There, filters get rid of all the poop and paper lumps. Biological processes then break down the organic matter until about 95 percent of the water's pollutants are gone. Finally, it is piped into the sea.

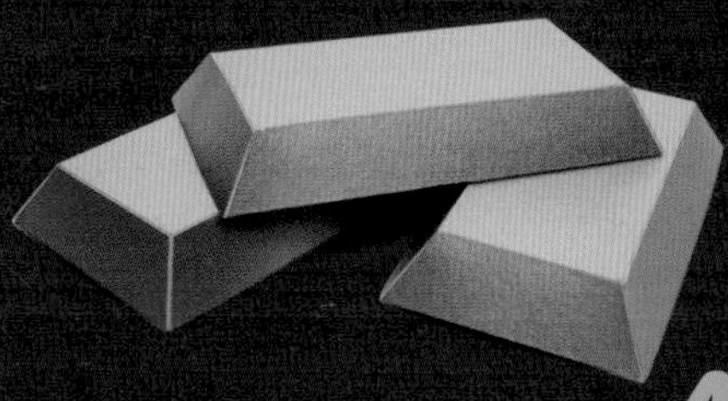

Water Cycles

7 The lake and **river 140** water is taken to a treatment plant and cleaned by running it through screens to get rid of debris like sticks and leaves. Then it is processed to remove algae (tiny plants), poisons, and to kill bacteria. These treatments are repeated. And, as a finishing step, a small amount of chlorine is often added. Finally, the water is clean enough to be stored in reservoirs or piped into homes and businesses. So, you're feeling a bit thirsty again. Turn on the faucet and, hey presto, you're glugging down somebody else's old (but clean) pee.

6 As these clouds rise, they get cooler, so they can't hold the water vapor any more. The vapor comes down as rain, hail, fog, or snow—depending on how warm it is. When it has fallen, the water runs down and across the Earth. Some of it goes into the soil, some into **rocks 318** and a lot runs into lakes and rivers.

5 Warm air then pushes this evaporated water up and turns it into **clouds 196** (which are not so much fluffy and floaty as wet and misty).

4 Heat from the Sun, evaporates the seawater (that is, it turns the water into a vapor).

Food Cycles

4 The **snake 146** is feeling very pleased with himself. So much so that he doesn't see the owl (a tertiary consumer) swooping down. Within seconds, he is history. But very tasty.

3 A secondary consumer (something a bit bigger, in this case a snake) spies the insect. He slithers across and swallows the animal before it sees him (proving there's a real gap in the market for animal eye tests).

5 The owl is very old. Sadly, the excitement of eating the snake kills her. She falls onto the ground, where she lies until bacteria and fungi decompose her body and it becomes part of the soil. The mineral nutrients that were once part of her body are transferred to the soil, creating fertile conditions for **plants 018**. So, there's this little green plant...

1 A little green plant is in a field, soaking up the energy in the sunshine. Using a process called **photosynthesis 010**, it collects this energy and uses it to grow.

2 A tiny animal (the primary consumer) eats the plant. Animals and fungi are consumers, and so are most bacteria. Instead of getting energy from the sunlight, they get it from other living things, or from their dead remains.

People in the US 256 see so many adverts each day that it's difficult to keep count. Estimates range from 245 to a total bombardment of 3,000 adverts per day. In 2005, the nation spent over $160 billion on advertising.

MAD
LO

Advertising is a method of promoting products or services so people buy them. Many ads detail the legal terms and conditions of the sale in very small print. These terms might reveal a deal is not as good as it seems. It is often made tiny so buyers don't bother reading it closely.

Many much-loved characters have been created by ads, such as the Michelin Man (born 1898) and Coca-Cola's 1931 Father Christmas, who popularized the red suit.

MICHELIN

Since 1995, internet advertising has exploded—almost literally. Pop-ups, banners, buttons—they're all over computer screens. Unrequested emails promoting goods aren't normal ads—they're spam. Though often annoying, spam is a cheap and easy way to target millions of people.

Advertising dates back to at least 3000 BC and the ancient Babylonians. Archeologists have found signs created by tradesmen, such as shoemakers and scribes, to promote their wares.

Most adverts are created by advertising agencies. They may employ marketing specialists, designers, writers (known as copywriters), economists, psychologists, researchers, analysts, product testers, and mathematicians (and probably a tea 200 maker, as well).

Hold on! Ads appear in many forms of media 330, including print, radio, and television. They're smuggled into movies too, when companies pay to have actors drink a particular brand or wear a certain label (known as product placement).

TV ads are the most dramatic, effective and expensive form of advertising. In the US, each 30-second ad shown in the annual Superbowl commercial break during the costs at least $2 million to air.

Attention! Perhaps the most popular TV ad of all time was created by Coca-Cola in 1971. It showed 500 young people in traditional dress from different nations, singing "I'd Like to Buy the World a Coke". Rewritten as a pop single, it became a hit around the world and the sheet music still sells today.

Generally, advertising is paid for, as opposed to publicity (for example, being mentioned in a newspaper article), which is usually free. It should also be distinguished from propaganda 292, public relations (about generating goodwill to a cause, product or person) and seasonal gift giving.

ANCIENT EGYPTIANS SAY:
SIZE MATTERS

The Great Pyramid of Giza (above, second from right), which was built by the Egyptians around 2560 BC, remained the tallest building in the world until the 19th century. It is 479 feet (146 m) high, and 20,000 workers probably took around 20 years to build it. All this effort was for one thing—to house the body of the pharaoh (or king) Khufu when he died.

Ancient Egyptians 100 expected to travel to the afterlife after dying. It was essential, though, that the physical body continued to exist for when they got there. Pharoahs had the privilege of getting their own tombs built. Pyramid construction dates back to around 2630 BC, with the earliest known example at Saqqara. Why they used the pyramid shape is uncertain—it may represent the rays of the Sun or symbolize a ramp to the sky.

Khufu began planning his pyramid as soon as he became pharoah. The location, on the west bank of the Nile River, was chosen because it was where the Sun "died" each night. It was built of granite and originally covered in brilliant white limestone, which was trimmed, giving a smooth appearance. It is estimated that more than two million individual blocks were used. These were cut from nearby quarries, hauled to the site, and put in place—all without the use of **cranes 240** or even basic rope pulleys. Ramps were probably used to raise the blocks, which were then levered into position. But despite the technological limitations, the pyramid is perfectly proportioned. Two other large pyramids were built at Giza before the Egyptians settled on smaller, but elaborately decorated tombs.

GOING UP

Unlike pyramids, skyscrapers don't need a large base to stay up. The floors and walls are supported by a steel skeleton instead. The first skyscraper, designed by William Le Baron Jenney, went up in Chicago, in 1885. Demand for office space near the city center drove a skyscraper boom. In 1920s New York, two buildings were in contention to be the world's tallest. At 40 Wall Street, the architect added two extra floors when he found out the projected height of the rival building. But this construction, the 77-floor Chrysler Building, had a surprise in store—hidden inside was a 125 ft (38.1 m) spire. This was hoisted on top one afternoon in November 1929—and the Chrysler became the tallest building on Earth (though some people say spires shouldn't count). By 1931, though, the nearby Empire State Building had stolen the honor.

CHRYSLER BUILDING

WHY BUILD BIG?

Throughout history, powerful people and groups have used big buildings to show off and to impress. Only 200 years ago, the biggest buildings were cathedrals and royal palaces. Today, they belong to banks or large corporations. Building upward is also useful in cities where space is tight—Hong Kong has many skyscrapers because it is an island with limited building space. The current tallest building in the world is Taipei 101, a finance building in Taipei, Taiwan: 1,667 ft (508 m) from bottom to top. But other, taller things are being planned all the time

THE PYRAMIDS' FAMOUS FANS

ALEXANDER THE GREAT
THE FAMOUS CONQUEROR PAID A VISIT IN THE FOURTH CENTURY BC. HE SUPPOSEDLY SPENT TIME IN KING KHUFU'S BURIAL CHAMBER.

MARC ANTONY
IF HE HADN'T FALLEN IN LOVE WITH THE EGYPTIAN **QUEEN CLEOPATRA 030**, ROMAN GENERAL MARC ANTONY MIGHT HAVE BEEN EMPEROR OF **ROME 262**. ON A TRIP TO EGYPT, HE SPENT A WEEKEND CLIMBING THE PYRAMIDS.

NAPOLEON BONAPARTE
INVADED EGYPT IN THE LATE 18TH CENTURY. SPENT THE NIGHT IN A PYRAMID. APPARENTLY, IT SCARED HIM WITLESS.

ISAAC NEWTON
THE GREAT SCIENTIST OF THE 1600s NEEDED TO KNOW THE DIAMETER OF THE EARTH TO FIGURE OUT HIS LAWS OF **GRAVITY 024**. HE DECIDED THAT THE PYRAMIDS COULD PROVIDE HIM WITH THIS INFORMATION DUE TO THEIR CLEVER CONSTRUCTION. HE WAS WRONG.

UNITED STATES OF ANCIENT EGYPT?
An unfinished pyramid features on the back of all US one-dollar bills. This comes from the Great Seal of the United States—an emblem of the nation completed in 1782. The pyramid symbolizes "strength and durability." It is unfinished to signify that the US will always "grow, improve, and build."

Meet the new boss

UNUSUAL ETYMOLOGIES

WORDS HAVE HISTORIES, AND ETYMOLOGY IS THE STUDY OF THE ORIGINS OF WORDS, SOME OF WHICH ARE RATHER STRANGE...

PYRAMID
The ancient Egyptian term for pyramid was "mer." The English word "pyramid" comes from the Greek, probably derived from "pyramis," a wheaten cake that resembled the shape of a pyramid.

HOT DOG
The hot is obvious, but why dog? Well... dog was a slang word for sausage because, back in the 1800s, dogmeat was sometimes used to make the sausage. Poor Fido.

After invading Britain in 1066, the Normans (from northern France) wowed the native Anglo-Saxons with their magnificent architecture. The locals had nothing to compare with the enormous cathedrals the conquerors built (such as the one in Durham, left). Thick walls were made even stronger with buttresses—supporting ribs that run up the outside walls. Creepy stone heads, called gargoyles, grinned or scowled from on high. The huge buildings could be seen for miles. They might have been built for the glory of God, but it was a good way to show the locals who was boss now.

HOW THEY MEASURE UP: BIG BUILDINGS IN MINIATURE

01. Taipei 101, Taipei, Taiwan, 2004, 1,667 ft (508 m)
02. Petronas Towers, Kuala Lumpur, Malaysia, 1998, 1,483 ft (452 m)
03. Sears Tower, Chicago (IL), United States, 1974, 1,450 ft (442 m)
04. Jin Mao Building, Shanghai, China, 1998, 1,381 ft (421 m)
05. CITIC Plaza, Guangzhou, China, 1997, 1,283 ft (391 m)
06. Shun Hing Square, Shenzhen, China, 1996, 1,260 ft (384 m)
07. Empire State Building, New York (NY), United States, 1931, 1,250 ft (381 m)
08. Central Plaza, Hong Kong, China, 1992, 1,227 ft (374 m)
09. Bank of China Tower, Hong Kong, China, 1989, 1,207 ft (368 m)
10. Emirates Office Tower, Dubai, United Arab Emirates, 1999, 1,165 ft (355 m)
11. The Center, Hong Kong, China, 1998, 1,135 ft (346 m)
12. John Hancock Center, Chicago (IL), United States, 1967, 1,129 ft (344 m)
13. Chrysler Building, New York (NY), United States, 1930, 1,047 ft (319 m)
14. Bank of America Plaza, Atlanta (GA), United States, 1993, 1,024 ft (312 m)
15. AT&T Corporate Center, Chicago (IL), United States, 1989, 1,007 ft (307 m)
16. Eiffel Tower, Paris, France, 1889, 984 ft (300 m)
17. Washington Monument, United States, 1884, 554 ft (169 m)
18. Cologne Cathedral, Germany, 1248–1880, 515 ft (157 m)
19. Cathédrale Notre Dame, Rouen, France, 1202–1876, 495 ft (151 m)
20. Great Pyramid of Giza, Egypt, c. 2560 BC, 479 ft (146 m)

WHERE ARE ALL THE CAMELS?
These days, camels are often used for transportation or to carry gear in the desert. But they weren't introduced into Egypt until the Persians 120 took over around 525 BC. The ancient Egyptians would have employed donkeys instead.

Sony releases its Betamovie camcorder. It's the first video camera for home-users. Kids everywhere say: "Don't! It's embarrassing."

1983

1965

The Moog synthesizer is invented by Robert Moog. It rhymes with "vogue," so forget the cow impressions.

1972

The first liquid crystal display (LCD) digital watch is produced by the Hamilton watch company. Called the Pulsar, its name is chosen to reflect the new "space age" in watches. (First step: digital watches. Next step: vacations on **Mars 172**.)

1979

Sony invents a portable audio cassette player with earphones: the Walkman. People can keep their passion for cheesy ballads private.

1958

The hula hoop is popularized by US company Wham-O (probably named after the sound of the hoop as it falls to the floor, yet again).

THIS IS THE MODERN WORLD
EVERYTHING YOU SEE HERE DIDN'T EXIST
LESS THAN A LIFETIME AGO

1957

The first AA-size alkaline batteries are produced. They are used to power radios.

H. Edward Roberts creates the first personal computer (PC), the Altair 8800—a kit of parts to be assembled by "enthusiasts." Geeks, is more like it.

1975

2006

The Airbus A380, a huge double-decker jumbo jet, is introduced. Planned to be a third bigger than the existing Boeing 747 jumbo jet, the upper decks offer bars (some with pianos) and lounges.

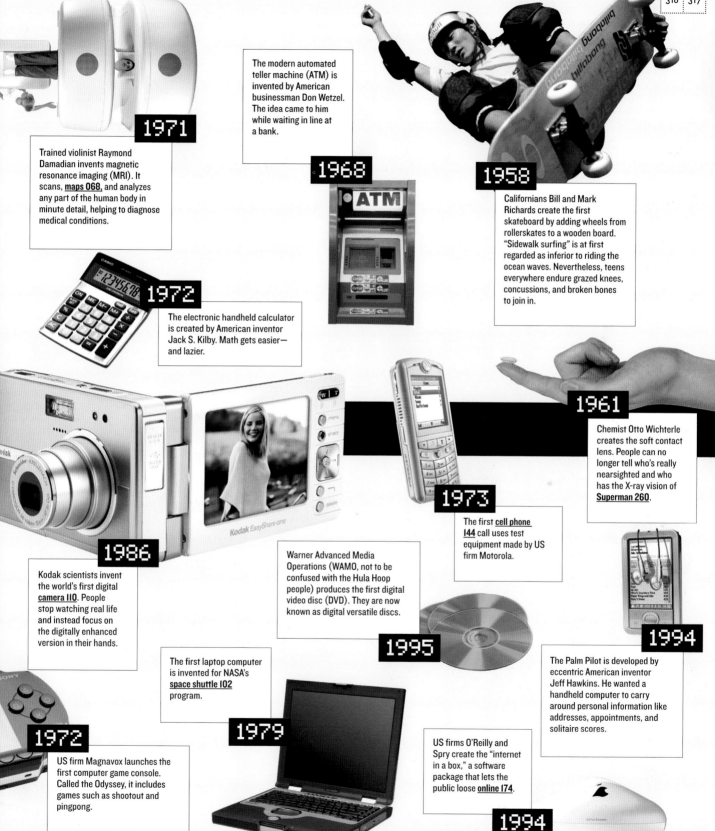

1971

Trained violinist Raymond Damadian invents magnetic resonance imaging (MRI). It scans, **maps 068,** and analyzes any part of the human body in minute detail, helping to diagnose medical conditions.

The modern automated teller machine (ATM) is invented by American businessman Don Wetzel. The idea came to him while waiting in line at a bank.

1968

1958

Californians Bill and Mark Richards create the first skateboard by adding wheels from rollerskates to a wooden board. "Sidewalk surfing" is at first regarded as inferior to riding the ocean waves. Nevertheless, teens everywhere endure grazed knees, concussions, and broken bones to join in.

1972

The electronic handheld calculator is created by American inventor Jack S. Kilby. Math gets easier— and lazier.

1961

Chemist Otto Wichterle creates the soft contact lens. People can no longer tell who's really nearsighted and who has the X-ray vision of **Superman 260**.

1973

The first **cell phone 144** call uses test equipment made by US firm Motorola.

1986

Kodak scientists invent the world's first digital **camera 110**. People stop watching real life and instead focus on the digitally enhanced version in their hands.

Warner Advanced Media Operations (WAMO, not to be confused with the Hula Hoop people) produces the first digital video disc (DVD). They are now known as digital versatile discs.

1995

1994

The Palm Pilot is developed by eccentric American inventor Jeff Hawkins. He wanted a handheld computer to carry around personal information like addresses, appointments, and solitaire scores.

The first laptop computer is invented for NASA's **space shuttle 102** program.

1979

1972

US firm Magnavox launches the first computer game console. Called the Odyssey, it includes games such as shootout and pingpong.

US firms O'Reilly and Spry create the "internet in a box," a software package that lets the public loose **online 174**.

1994

WHAT MAKES ICELAND THE WORLD'S FASTEST GROWING COUNTRY?

EURASIAN PLATE

NORTH AMERICAN PLATE

Hot springs and geysers are spectacular signs of lots going on below the surface

Fifteen interlocking tectonic plates shape the surface of the world

Iceland is growing in size by about an inch (a few centimeters) every year. The Earth's crust—the ground beneath your feet as well as the oceans—sits on 15 **TECTONIC PLATES**. These are solid layers of rock, about 60 miles (100 km) thick, which fit together like giant jigsaw pieces. They are constantly on the move. Iceland straddles two of these plates. The North American Plate pulls west and the Eurasian Plate pulls east (above)—and Iceland slowly grows.

All the Earth's plates (some of which are larger than continents) are moving in relation to each other and interact in different ways when they meet:

TRANSFORM BOUNDARY—this is when two plates grind past each other. Tension can build up and releases suddenly and violently, causing an __earthquake 136__. The San Andreas Fault running through California is an active transforming boundary.

CONVERGENT BOUNDARY—This occurs where two plates slide toward each other. Usually, one plate moves under the other, forming an oceanic trench. But sometimes, the two collide and compress, buckling the Earth's surface. This is how __mountains 074__ are formed over the course of millions of years.

DIVERGENT BOUNDARY—in this case two plates pull apart, which is what is happening in Iceland. It's the reason why the country is home to volcanoes, hot springs, and geysers (where boiling water spurts out of the ground like a fountain). The gap created by the plates is filled with hot liquid rock, called magma, which is pushed upward from deep in the Earth. Magma actually made a new island, Surtsey, off the coast of Iceland in 1963.

These processes mean the world is slowly changing shape. You know how the west coast of Africa looks like it would fit with the east coast of South America? Well, they used to be joined together. In fact, 250 million years ago, the world was just one continuous land mass, called Pangaea, surrounded by water. But, as the tectonic plates did their sliding and grinding, the seven continents we know today were formed: Europe, Asia, Africa, North America, South America, Australia, and Antarctica. Perhaps one day Iceland could end up as big as the largest continent, Asia—in the very distant future, that is.

ROCK HARD FACTS

Geologists (rock scientists) divide rocks into three types. Igneous rocks, such as granite (below), have solidified from hot molten rock. Sedimentary rocks, including sandstone and limestone (top), are made of small fragments of other rocks. These are squeezed together very slowly (in geology, most things happen very slowly), forming layer upon layer of rock. They're often formed under seas and oceans. But with heat and pressure (and plenty of <u>time 249</u>), limestone can be transformed into marble (above). This is an example of the third type: metamorphic rock, when the mineral content of a rock changes. Geologists can learn a lot about the structure, composition and history of our planet by studying rocks.

Why are there five rings on the Olympic symbol?

After all, each ring represents a continent, so there should be seven in total. Well, Antarctica doesn't compete (no one really lives there—penguins aren't allowed to enter the swimming competition). And the Americas are sometimes considered to be a single continent—so that makes five.

WHAT ARE YOU STANDING ON?

If there were a road, you could drive to the center of the Earth in about three days. It would be a pretty interesting journey, too…

Lithosphere
The name comes from the Greek *lithos*, meaning stone. The lithosphere includes the crust (the Earth's rocky skin) and upper mantle. It is made up of the tectonic plates.

Lower mantle
Made of different rocky materials. Unlike the cooler upper mantle, the lower part is hot because heat rises from the outer core. It is this heat that moves the tectonic plates.

Outer core
Nothing much here but hot, liquid iron. It's thought the movement of the liquid acts like an electrical motor to create the Earth's <u>magnetic 300</u> field.

Inner core
The pressures at this depth turn the liquid metal (nickel and iron) into solids. It's estimated to be hotter than the surface of the <u>Sun 168</u>: 13,000 °F (7,200 °C).

25 miles (40 km) — 0 Surface
450 miles (700 km)
1,800 miles (2,900 km)
3,200 miles (5,200 km)
3,960 miles (6,370 km)

GUESS WHAT?
THE ONLY NATIVE MAMMAL IN ICELAND IS THE ARCTIC FOX. ALL THE OTHERS WERE IMPORTED

WHOSE LAND IS IT ANYWAY? ☞ **ICELAND:** *named Ísland by Norwegian explorers, meaning "land of ice"* ☞ **ENGLAND:** *"the land of the Angles"—the Angles were the dominant tribe in the fifth century* ☞ **DEUTSCHLAND:** *from the old German word "diutise," meaning "the people"* ☞ **ARGENTINA:** *in Latin, argentum means silver. Argentina means "land of silver"*

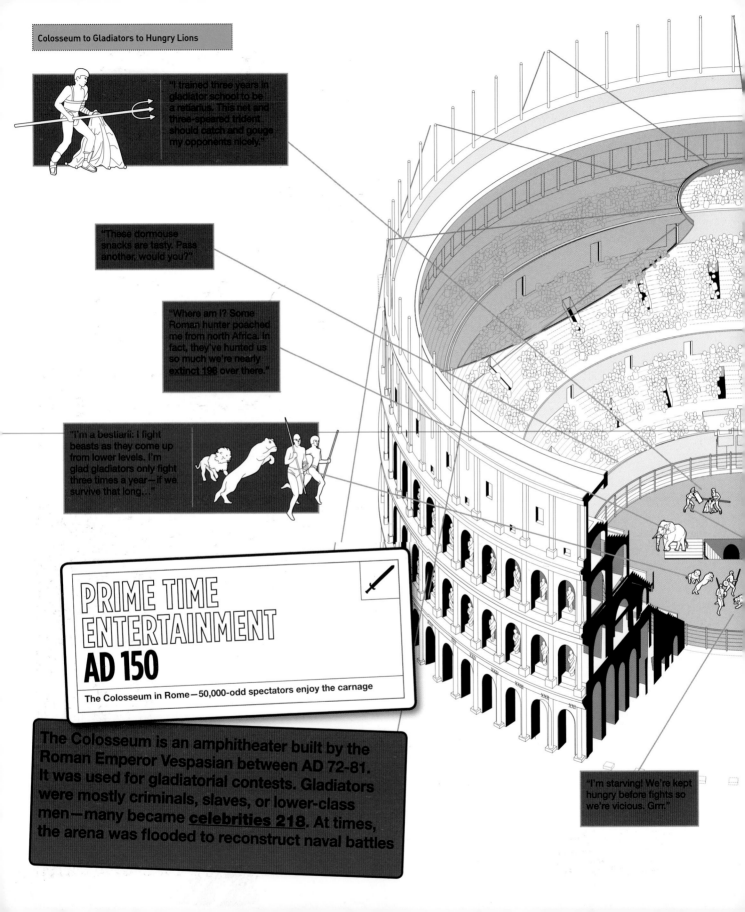

Colosseum to Gladiators to Hungry Lions

"I trained three years in gladiator school to be a retiarius. This net and three-speared trident should catch and gouge my opponents nicely."

"These dormouse snacks are tasty. Pass another, would you?"

"Where am I? Some Roman hunter poached me from north Africa. In fact, they've hunted us so much we're nearly extinct 196 over there."

"I'm a bestiarii: I fight beasts as they come up from lower levels. I'm glad gladiators only fight three times a year—if we survive that long…"

PRIME TIME ENTERTAINMENT
AD 150

The Colosseum in Rome—50,000-odd spectators enjoy the carnage

The Colosseum is an amphitheater built by the Roman Emperor Vespasian between AD 72–81. It was used for gladiatorial contests. Gladiators were mostly criminals, slaves, or lower-class men—many became celebrities 218. At times, the arena was flooded to reconstruct naval battles

"I'm starving! We're kept hungry before fights so we're vicious. Grrr."

"Watch the sandy floor soak up that panther's blood. I heard 5,000 animals were killed within the Colosseum's first 100 days."

"I wish contests took place daily, not just on spectacle days. Still, that's about 150 times a year..."

"My male students will learn lots about courage and strength here. Young boys watch all the killing and savagery like everyone else."

"We may not be aristocrats, but at least we get marble seats. There are archers over there, ready in case any animals get out of hand. Phew!"

"My private emperor's box is so comfortable. I avoid the riff-raff when I come in, too, with my four private entrances. Put more lions in the ring—spice it up!"

"I'm a Christian. The Romans 286 don't like us much, so I'm being mauled by small beasts to make sure I have a slow—owww!—death.'

"My fish-shaped helmet shows I'm a myrmillo. I volunteered to be a gladiator because I wanted to be famous. I'm going to win back my freedom and become a true legend."

"I've got my pottery shard ticket here somewhere..."

BUT IS IT ART?

Art isn't what it used to be—literally. What is called art has changed a lot over the centuries. Which things in this gallery are art?

ENTRANCE

1. Anonymous, Vase, 440-430 BC; ceramic

For the **ancient Greeks 240**, making or painting a vase wasn't art in a sense that we would understand today. In those days, art was the term used for all types of practical activities. According to Greek philosopher Aristotle, learning and mastering the rules of a particular trade were the important things. Painters, sculptors, and even shoemakers were judged on their skill, not their brilliant ideas. Poets and musicians were top dogs when it came to creativity. They weren't dependent on rigid rules, but inspired by the gods (supposedly).

ART FACTOR: only as artistic as a good shoe

2. Anonymous, Illuminated manuscript, 13th century

In Europe, books were made by monks before the innovations in **printing 292** in the 15th century. Whether religious works, psalms, philosophical texts, the monks carefully copied the words down and drew complex illustrations, often using gold leaf. But, despite their abilities, they were considered artisans (skilled workers)—not artists. Similarly, painters and sculptors were mostly anonymous, so it's not possible to tell who made what. They belonged to artisan guilds (like a youth club, but not as much fun). Painters were lumped in with doctors because they shared the same patron saint (St. Luke).

*ART FACTOR: as much artistic status as an **advertisement 312***

3. Michelangelo, Sistine Chapel ceiling, 1508-12; paint on plaster

The Sistine Chapel is a church in the Vatican (where the Pope lives in Rome). Michelangelo was asked by Pope Julius II to paint the ceiling—some task, considering it's 60 ft (18 m) up. By this time (the early 16th century), painters and sculptors were beginning to be more respected. The **Renaissance 148** had revived classical ideas of art, in particular **Plato's 042** belief that poets were divinely inspired. Such inspiration came from God (the Christian one, that is), and painters now basked in his glow, too. Michelangelo was described by his colleagues as "divine," and artists could now be considered "creators." It is also at this time that the idea of the "artistic genius" emerged—a person who was gifted but also eccentric.

ART FACTOR: a whizz-kid with a paint brush and scaffolding

4. Edouard Manet, *Le Déjeuner sur l'herbe* (Luncheon on the Grass), 1863; oil on canvas

When you think about the kinds of paintings that you see in museums—old-fashioned people in funny clothes—this is probably what you imagine. But when Manet first exhibited *Le Déjeuner sur l'herbe*, people were outraged and shocked, and many didn't consider it real art at all. For a start, they didn't approve of the subject matter—a naked woman lounging with two dressed men was considered indecent. Plus, Manet had adapted the composition (or arrangement) from an older painting, but used a new technique to paint it (which was considered a bit too bold). The people in the picture seem very flat, as though they are in a photograph, and it appears unfinished. Manet's interest in color and light, rather than making the people appear realistic, is a feature of "modernism." He is often considered the first modernist painter. And though he didn't set out to be controversial, he became a hero to those who wanted a new type of art.

ART FACTOR: art, but not as they knew it

5. Marcel Duchamp, *Fountain*, 1917; porcelain urinal

A men's urinal is obviously not art. It belongs in a public restroom. But in 1917 a French artist called Marcel Duchamp exhibited a piece called *Fountain*. It was a porcelain urinal that he had signed with a fake name. This blew the toilet lid off the idea that art was about portraying beauty. With many artists seeking a complete break with the past, art was being used to ridicule society's customs and beliefs. Duchamp also drew a moustache on a reproduction of the **Mona Lisa 190** and exhibited that. Thanks to Duchamp, anything could be art if the artist said it was. This attitude was to be hugely influential on 20th-century art.

ART FACTOR: it depends if an artist has got his hands on it

6. Andy Warhol, *Black Bean* (from Soup Can series), 1968; screenprint on paper

Hang on, this is a print of a soup can. It's not even a painting—it's created using a stencil and inks. How is that art (unless you really, really love soup)? Since Duchamp, what was considered art had become much broader, and artists could paint anything they wanted. Warhol was famous for being a Pop artist. As the name suggests, Pop Art was concerned with popular culture (music, fame, **fashion 192**, comics, shopping). In the 1950s and 1960s, Pop artists drew, painted, or photographed everyday things that people recognized. Warhol said he could find beauty everywhere, even in something dull like a soup can. He also produced his own wallpaper (including some brightly colored cow designs). This was now considered art and was even exhibited in a gallery.

ART FACTOR: hey, what isn't art?

7. Banksy, *Balloon Debate*, 2005; stencil on concrete wall

If art is anything and everything, then why should art even be in a gallery? After the 1960s, artists such as Richard Long and Christo made artworks that were simply too big or couldn't be shown in galleries. Banksy is a UK **graffiti artist 229** who is renowned for producing stenciled works on buildings, walls, and anywhere else he likes. He often uses a familiar image and changes part of it—to make you laugh but also to make you look again at what you are seeing. He has placed his own work in famous museums around the world (when no one was looking), in order to make you think about why any of the paintings on the wall are there. Banksy's real identity is not known—he claims to be uninterested in fame, and not even an artist at all.

ART FACTOR: art when no one quite knows what art is any more

Globalization, broadly speaking, refers to increased trade between companies around the world—in ideas, people, and goods. I run a multinational corporation—a large company that operates in many countries at once (**McDonald's 286**, Adidas, and Vodaphone are examples of multinationals).

We make laptops. We have factories in Ireland, China, and Malaysia. Our computers are designed in the US, at our HQ in Texas. Customers order them on the internet or over the phone (because they may not own a computer yet!).

A hundred years ago, I would have been charged special taxes to sell goods to other countries (import and export duties). The relaxation of these laws—plus cheaper transportation and more efficient communication between countries—has been a big factor in allowing international companies to work with each other. All these things together are what make my business possible.

I do my grocery shopping online, which means I don't have to travel to the store. But look at my kitchen table and you'll see more evidence of globalization: bananas from Costa Rica, beef from South America, and coffee from Jamaica.

In the past, the only goods that were available cheaply were those grown or produced nearby. But, as some trade restrictions (government laws and taxes) have been relaxed, it's become easier for **farmers 086** in other countries to compete with local farmers to sell their goods to my supermarket.

There's lots of debate about whether this is good or bad. On the plus side, it allows producers in poor countries to sell their goods overseas, and you get to buy more exotic things. On the downside, transporting goods around the world creates environmental pollution, and local farmers may be driven out of business by increased competition. It's an example of **capitalism 050**, but on a global scale.

WHAT ON EARTH DOES GLOBALIZATION MEAN?

Okay, so globalization affects trade, but you can also see it working when you get home from school and stick on the **TV 330**. Here in the Philippines, the most popular soap opera is *Alicia*, a Mexican program dubbed into Filipino.

Our broadcasters import all kinds of shows from around the world, and it's normal to see other cultures on TV. But 50 years ago, very few people ever got the chance to see what life was like in other countries, unless they were lucky enough to travel.

Satellite TV, which beams foreign channels to my set, allows me to find out more about foreign ideas. My family can watch news shows from Qatar or Chinese cooking shows—even British reality TV (if my mom lets me watch it!). This breaking down of cultural barriers between nations is yet another side to globalization.

I own a company that manufactures and sells sportswear. The clothing industry is among the most globalized of all—about 30 million people are making clothes and textiles worldwide.

I design my line at home in Scotland, but I have it made in China because the labor and factory costs are cheaper. We then fly the clothes to Europe, where they are shipped to stores ready to be sold to customers.

To make and deliver one T-shirt, we employ people in six countries, including all the suppliers and the companies we use for marketing and **advertising 312**. It may sound surprising, but using skills and resources from around the world is the most efficient way to create my clothing line.

I work in a call center in Bangalore, India, handling calls for a British insurance company. When people in Britain phone up with questions about their insurance policy, it comes through to me in India.

Thousands of companies, mainly in Britain and the US, employ call centers in India because the cost of labor is so much cheaper here. Contracting jobs to workers in other countries is known as "outsourcing," and has become possible because of sophisticated **communication links 144** around the globe. International calls have become much cheaper and computer networks easily connect my office in India to the UK head office.

Employing labor where it is cheapest and linking it to customers with information technology (stuff like computers) is another aspect of globalization.

WHAT WAS THE BATTLE OF SEATTLE?

The World Trade Organization (WTO) is a body that decides the rules for world trade. At its meeting in Seattle in December 1999, protestors turned up to demonstrate against the impact of globalization. They wanted fair trade for poorer countries and a better deal for the environment. Most of the protests were peaceful, but some became violent. Riot police clashed with thousands of demonstrators (all captured by TV cameras, of course) and 600 people were arrested. The "Battle of Seattle" put the issue of globalization on the front pages around the world.

WHEN IS A FACT A SCIENTIFIC FACT?

There's one, big simple concept in science. If you have an idea, you have to show that it works in the real world—whether that involves mixing chemicals in a test tube, smashing atoms in **accelerators 061,** or analyzing the wobble of a distant star with a radio telescope.

Science (from the Latin *scientia,* meaning knowledge) is all about coming up with a theory—or hypothesis, as it's known—that predicts how the world works. Hypotheses are tested by experiment, which work on the same basis as the ones you do in school. A procedure is carried out and the results observed. If facts are found that do not fit the hypothesis, you need to change the hypothesis.

Another hallmark of a scientific fact is consilience, which is when knowledge spans different fields of study. For example, **Charles Darwin's 206** theories about evolution mesh with our understanding of how eye color is passed down generations and how such traits are encoded in genes. This ties in with ideas of how differences between people are down to chemical "spelling mistakes" in their DNA.

Scientists don't always get it right. They make mistakes and sometimes even commit fraud (by falsifying results, for example). That is why facts and ideas must be repeatable, testable, and confirmable.

ONE VERY BIG EXPERIMENT

Scheduled for launch in 2016, LISA will be the largest scientific instrument ever constructed, consisting of three spacecraft positioned in a triangle formation, each separated by three million miles (five million km). Its task will be to detect elusive gravitational waves sent out by violent cosmic events, which were predicted by **Albert Einstein 132** in his Theory of General Relativity (published 100 years before, in 1916). To detect a gravitational wave, the incredible distance between the spacecraft must be measured by laser beams to an accuracy of 10 picometers —about one millionth of the diameter of a human hair.

SOME VERY CRAZY EXPERIMENTS

The best of these are celebrated each year by the Ig Nobel Prizes, awarded in Harvard University. Recent winners included experiments on exploding pants, the brain of a locust watching highlights from the film *Star Wars,* and the peculiar odors produced by 131 different species of frogs when feeling stressed. Who said science wasn't fun?

BIG FACTS FROM LITTLE ONES

In the third century BC, in Alexandria, Egypt, a librarian called Eratosthenes sized up the entire **Earth 170**—literally. He was able to calculate the planet's circumference (the distance around it) with a few assumptions and simple measurements. He knew that objects in the town of Syene (now Aswan) didn't cast a shadow at noon because the Sun was directly overhead. In Alexandria, he found the angle of sunlight at noon to be 7°. Because a circle has 360° in it, 7° is the same as ¹/₅₁ of a circle. This also meant that the distance between Syene and Alexandria was ¹/₅₁ of the circumference of the Earth. It was then a matter of multiplying this distance by 51 to estimate the circumference of the Earth. Eratosthenes was accurate to within a few hundred miles (or kilometers).

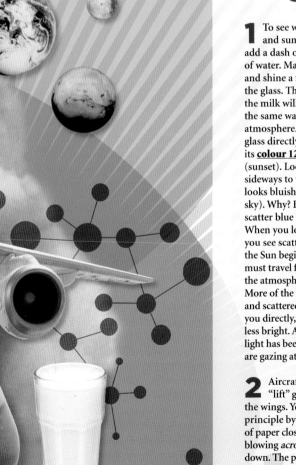

Try these experiments

1 To see why the sky is blue and sunsets are orange, add a dash of milk to a glass of water. Make the room dark and shine a flashlight through the glass. The particles in the milk will scatter light in the same way as those in the atmosphere. Gaze through the glass directly into the beam and its **colour 128** is yellow-orange (sunset). Look into the glass sideways to the beam and it looks bluish-white (daytime sky). Why? Because particles scatter blue light more than red. When you look up in the sky, you see scattered blue light. As the Sun begins to set, the light must travel farther through the atmosphere to reach you. More of the light is reflected and scattered. As less reaches you directly, the sun appears less bright. And most of the blue light has been scattered—so you are gazing at a reddish glow.

2 Aircraft fly because of the "lift" generated around the wings. You can test the principle by holding a piece of paper close to your lips, and blowing *across* it as it hangs down. The paper should defy gravity and rise—just as 18th-century Swiss mathematician Daniel Bernoulli said it would. Bernoulli's Principle states that a gas or liquid decreases in pressure the faster it flows. In theory, the **air pressure 196** below the paper is higher (because it's not moving), so it pushes the paper up.

3 With a couple of simple ingredients, you can have fun thinking you've undermined a theory of the great scientist **Sir Isaac Newton 024**. He came up with a theory about liquids that have a viscosity (thickness or resistance to pouring) that does not change with motion. These are called Newtonian fluids. But if you put cornstarch and water together you get something peculiar. It becomes stiffer and more crumbly the more you stir it. It feels like a solid. But once you stop stirring, it turns runny, almost like a liquid. This is a non-Newtonian fluid. You've beaten a great scientific mind... kind of.

Population 143.5 million—going down

In 2005, a third more people died than were born

61 **Life expectancy** for a person born in Russia in 2005 was **61 years for men** and **74 years for women** **74**

In Russia interesting facts

More than **80 per cent** of Russians belong to the **Russian Orthodox Church**. It is different to **western Christian churches:**
• Christmas Day falls on January 7
• Followers fast for more than half the year (179 days in total in 2006)
• They give up foods such as meat, dairy, wine, and cooking oil

Rags to riches in Russia...

Russia has more **billionaires** than any country except the US and **Germany 244**. They're also not short of millionaires.

20% of Russians live in Poverty

3 **Russians are billionaires**

88,000 **Russians are millionaires**

Most of the country's wealth is in the hands of businessmen, known as **oligarchs.** They made fortunes by taking over state-owned industries, such as oil and media in the early 1990s

Russia has 90,000 official architectural landmarks, with some dating back to the tenth century. They include the Winter Palace and Hermitage museum in St Petersburg and the Kremlin fortress and Red Square in Moscow. Even Moscow's metro stations contain intricate artwork and regal columns.

The Russian language uses the **Cyrillic alphabet**. Named after the Greek missionary Saint Cyril, it has 33 letters and is based on the Greek alphabet.

АБС

Russia's energy

Pipelines carry gas from Russia through eastern Europe and reach as far west as Italy and Germany

Oil pipelines 46,938 miles
75,539 km

Gas pipelines 93,210 miles
150,007 km

30% of world gas reserves in 2003

6% of world oil reserves in 2003

Russia...

↑ **Where is Russia?**

①1 ②2 ③3 ④4 ⑤5 ⑥6 ⑦7 ⑧8 ⑨9 ⑩10 ⑪11

↑ **Russia spans 11 time zones**—more than any other country in the world. When it's 7 p.m. in Kaliningrad, Russia's most westerly city, it's 8 p.m. in Moscow, 11 p.m. in Omsk, 2 a.m. (the next day) in Tiksi and 5a.m. in Pevek on the Arctic Ocean.

Russia is the coldest country in the world

The average annual temperature is **22 °F (-5.5 °C)**

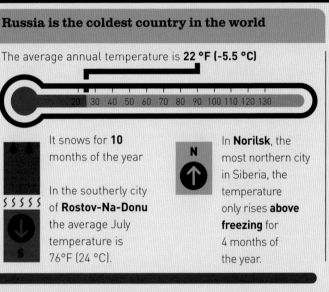

It snows for **10** months of the year

In the southerly city of **Rostov-Na-Donu** the average July temperature is 76°F (24 °C).

In **Norilsk**, the most northern city in Siberia, the temperature only rises **above freezing** for 4 months of the year.

→ Russia was the heart of the **Soviet Union**, a communist superstate created in 1922. It collapsed in 1991, and countries including **Lithuania, Georgia, Ukraine, and Azerbaijan** became independent. In 70 years, the USSR had six leaders. The dictator **Joseph Stalin 260**

ruled the longest: 29 years, from 1924 to 1953.

Russia is the largest country in the world.
Its total area is 6,595,600 sq miles (17,075,200 sq km), twice the sizeof the next largest country, Canada

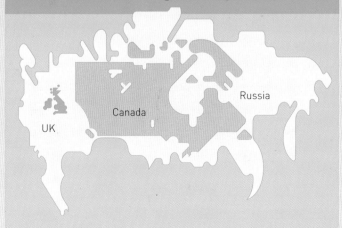

UK

Canada

Russia

The three most popular Russian dishes...

- pelmeni: ground meat wrapped in thin dough, like ravioli
- peroshki: small meat pies
- blini: small, thin pancakes

WITHIN...

IT'S NOT AN EVENT WITHOUT THE MEDIA

JOURNALISTS

The word "media" refers to mass forms of communication. Waving at your friend doesn't count (because only your friend sees it), but a news program does, because it is seen by millions. So how do different forms of media work? Live 8 was a huge global event. On July 2, 2005, there were concerts in 10 cities around the world as part of a global campaign to help the world's poor. Around 85 percent of the planet's population was able to tune in to the event through one of the many types of media there to cover it...

At the Live 8 concert in Johannesburg, South Africa, **Nelson Mandela 242** comes on stage. A boy in the crowd uses his cell phone to video Mandela's speech. He sends it to a friend as a video message. The message is received by a girl in Munich, Germany. She posts the footage on her **blog 064**. Within minutes, she has replies from thousands of miles or kilometers away. Digital video is composed of electronic data, so it can be transfered from phone to computer to the internet. Information can be shared almost instantly and the distinctions between types of media become blurred (blogs mix TV, newspaper, and online diary).

FANS

CAMERAS

BLOG

MOBILE INTERNET

Another fan accesses the internet via her phone, to check the coverage of the concert she is at. The TV cameras have picked out a girl in the crowd watching the concert on her cell phone—she realizes she is watching herself watching herself. Now that's weird.

LIVE RADIO BROADCAST

In the days before people had TV sets, radio was the best way to receive up-to-date news and listen to events (such as concerts) as they were happening. These days, radio programs still have huge audiences. Some 2,000 radio networks around the world covered Live 8. Radio programs continue to thrive partly because they allow people to do other things (driving, cleaning, breakdancing) while they're listening. But because there are no images the presenter has to describe clearly what is going on. Today, internet radio breaks down the national boundaries of radio—listeners can "tune in" to stations around the world.

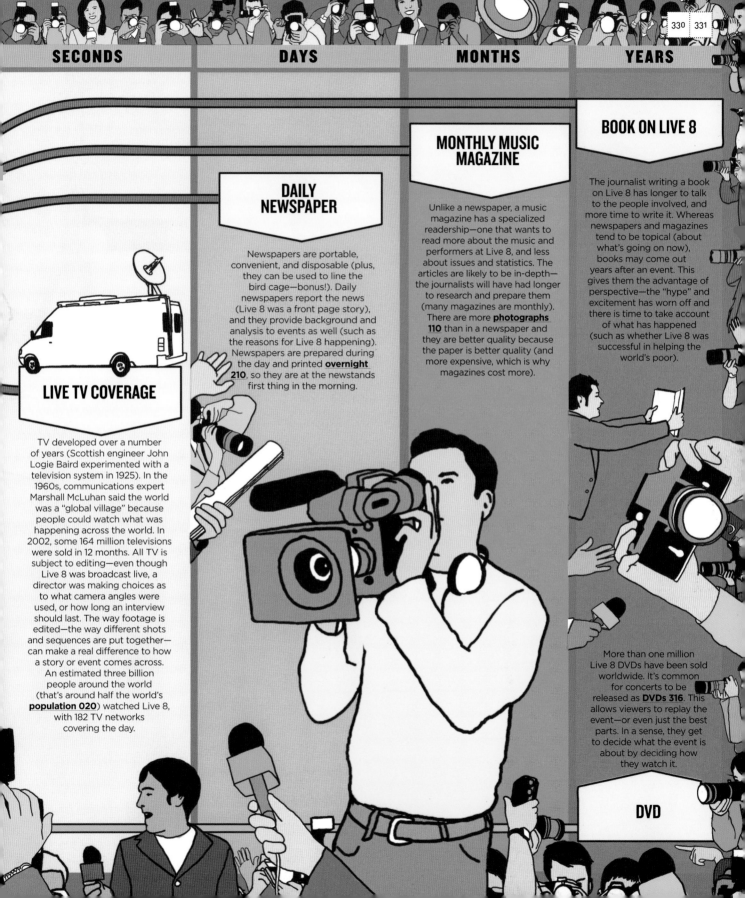

SECONDS

DAYS

MONTHS

YEARS

BOOK ON LIVE 8

The journalist writing a book on Live 8 has longer to talk to the people involved, and more time to write it. Whereas newspapers and magazines tend to be topical (about what's going on now), books may come out years after an event. This gives them the advantage of perspective—the "hype" and excitement has worn off and there is time to take account of what has happened (such as whether Live 8 was successful in helping the world's poor).

MONTHLY MUSIC MAGAZINE

Unlike a newspaper, a music magazine has a specialized readership—one that wants to read more about the music and performers at Live 8, and less about issues and statistics. The articles are likely to be in-depth—the journalists will have had longer to research and prepare them (many magazines are monthly). There are more **photographs 110** than in a newspaper and they are better quality because the paper is better quality (and more expensive, which is why magazines cost more).

DAILY NEWSPAPER

Newspapers are portable, convenient, and disposable (plus, they can be used to line the bird cage—bonus!). Daily newspapers report the news (Live 8 was a front page story), and they provide background and analysis to events as well (such as the reasons for Live 8 happening). Newspapers are prepared during the day and printed **overnight 210**, so they are at the newsstands first thing in the morning.

LIVE TV COVERAGE

TV developed over a number of years (Scottish engineer John Logie Baird experimented with a television system in 1925). In the 1960s, communications expert Marshall McLuhan said the world was a "global village" because people could watch what was happening across the world. In 2002, some 164 million televisions were sold in 12 months. All TV is subject to editing—even though Live 8 was broadcast live, a director was making choices as to what camera angles were used, or how long an interview should last. The way footage is edited—the way different shots and sequences are put together—can make a real difference to how a story or event comes across. An estimated three billion people around the world (that's around half the world's **population 020**) watched Live 8, with 182 TV networks covering the day.

More than one million Live 8 DVDs have been sold worldwide. It's common for concerts to be released as **DVDs 316**. This allows viewers to replay the event—or even just the best parts. In a sense, they get to decide what the event is about by deciding how they watch it.

DVD

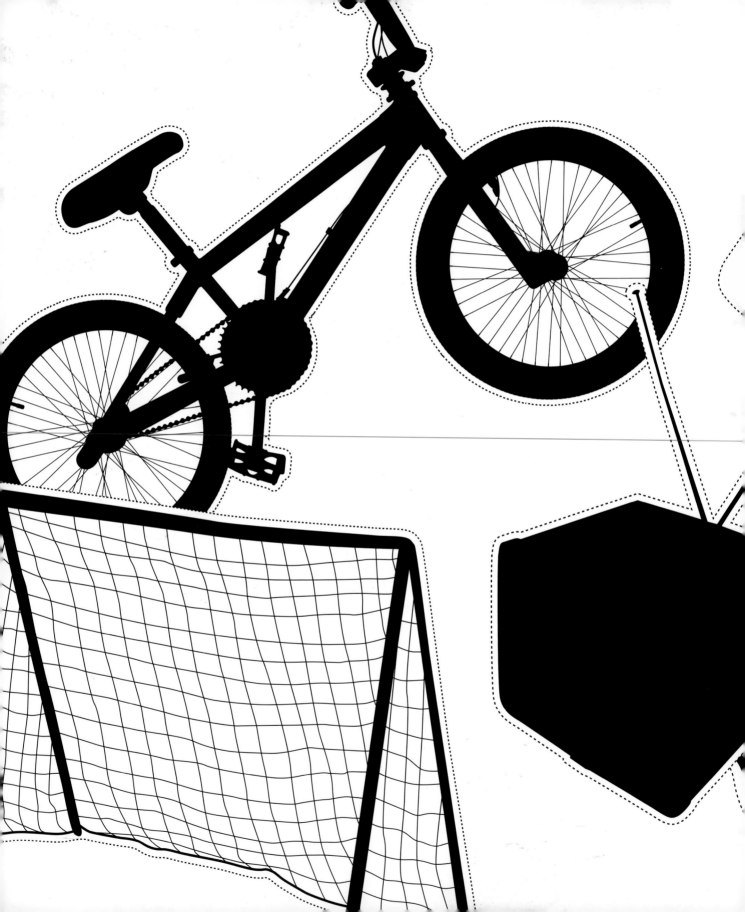

REMEMBER DECIDING TO PICK UP THIS BOOK?

Index

Note:
Bold type idicates the
main entry for that subject

J

K

L

M

N

O

oceans 199, **202–203**
Odysseus 241
oil
　consumption 256
　pollution 135, 203,
　204, 267
　production 46, 119, 328
okapi 278, 279
Olmecs 298, 299
"-ologies" 229
Olympics 52, 53, 74,
　180–181, 257, 308, 319
　Ancient Greece 52, 144,
　172, **241**
O'Malley, Grace 204
ontology 43
opposites 98–99
orchestras 40–41
Otto, Nicklaus 70, 71
outsourcing 325
owls 135
oxygen 10, 11, 134, 135,
　207, 289
ozone layer 267

P

paganism 11
pain **84**, 158, 224, 239
pain relief 109, 240, 271
Paine, Thomas 292
Palestine **47**, 242, 243
pamphlets 292, 293
Panama Canal 204
pandas 198
pandemics 215
Panjabi 54
Pankhurst, Emmeline 93
Papadopoulos, Georgios 195
Papua New Guinea 96
parables 185
parachutes 254
parasites 84
Paris 28, 192, 290, 315
Parks, Rosa 31
parrots 183
particles 60–61
Pasteur, Louis 108
Pavlova cake 87
Pearl Harbor 179
pee **134**, 135, 222, 280
Pelé **53**, 72
pencils 71, 83
penguins 183
penicillin 280
perfume 193
periodic table 60, **288–289**
Persepolis 121
Persians 39, 101, **120–121**,
　131, 315
Peter the Great 239
Petrarch (Francesco
　Petrarca) 149
pets 29, **130–131**
phalanx 65
pharaohs 100, 101, 314
pheromones 275
philanthropists 58
philosopher's stone 25
philosophy **42–43**, 45, 137,
　148, 151, 241, 265
phobias 303, 308
phosphorus 289
photography 76–77,
　110–112, 317
photosynthesis 10
pi 213
Picasso, Pablo 79
pigeons 144

Pioneer spacecraft 102
pirates **204**, 229
plague 130, 177, **215**, 280
planets 145, 151, **169–173**
plankton 199
plants 10, **18–19**, 83, 87, 198,
　199, 209, 311
Plato **42**, 241, 323
platypus 116
plots 14
Pluto 173
plutonium 288
Poland 29, 179, 295
politics 150, 177, 195, 292
pollution 70, 103, 122, 135,
　203, 204, 324
polygraph machines 100–101
polystyrene 199
Pompeii 136–137
Pony Express 144
poop 134, **135**, 154, 176, 199,
　310
Pop Art 307, 323
pop music 113, 152–153, 227,
　305–307, 308
popcorn 35, 309
popes 185
population **20–21**, 234
　Asia 29, 119, 142–143, 328
　Brazil 72, 73
　Europe 165, 200, 201,
　245, 290
　South Africa 230
　United States 256, 257
portraits 79, 110–111, 112, 190
Portugal 139, 164, 265
Portuguese 54
positrons 60
postal service 144, 304
potato chips 177, 200, 309
potatoes 177, 245
poverty 72, 143, 230, 328
pregnancy 158
prehistoric man 71, **234–235**
Premchand, Munshi 115
prime numbers 212, 213
Princip, Gavrilo 178
printing 62–63, 92, 150,
　292–293
profit 51
propaganda 120–121, **292**,
　293

property 226
proteins 70, 177, **259**
Protestantism 216
protons 60
Proxima Centauri 56, 57
psychiatry 239
psychoanalysis **42**, 239
psychology 45, 80, 128, **239**
puberty 158, 275
Puma 245
Punch and Judy 157
punk 22, **307**
puppets 157
Puritans 222
pyramids 45, 100, 298,
　314, 315

S

T

X

Y

Z

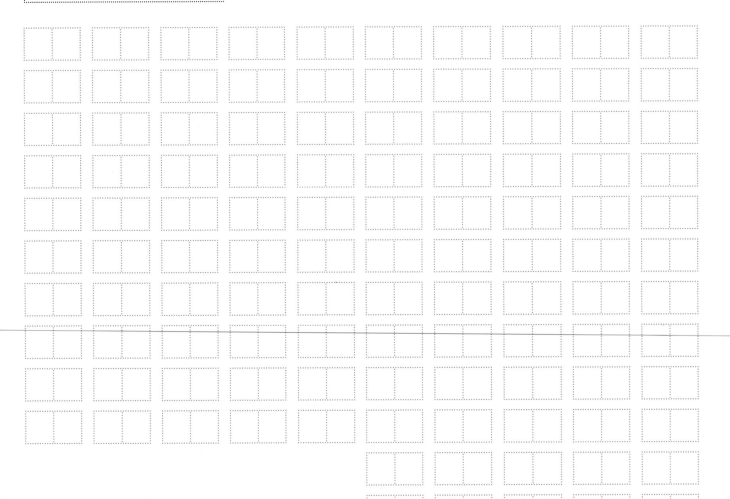

Credits

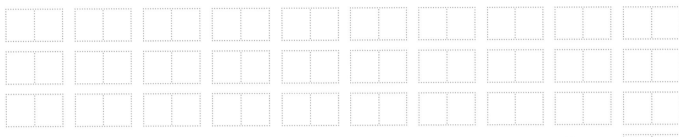

The publisher would like to thank the following for their kind permission to reproduce their photographs:

(Key: a-above; b-below/bottom; c-center; f-far; l-left; r-right; t-top)

The Advertising Archives: 105tc, 207br, 307bc, 307ca; Apple Corps Ltd. 306tc, 307c; **akg-images:** 65tc, 100cr, 101t, 101tl, 148br, 149b, 150bl, 150tl, 151bl, 151crb, 151tl, 217cl, 255c; British Library 273cb, 322tr; Peter Connolly 65cr; Eric Lessing 322bl; **Alamy Images:** 51tr, 101cr, 140tl; Alaska Stock LLC 87bl; Bill Bachmann 86bc; George Band 75cl; Wally Bauman 254crb; blickwinkel 267ca; Leland Bobbe 80tc, 81cr; Mark Boulton 267bc; Rahael Bowes 324-325c; Penny Boyd 131c; Brandon Cole Marine Photography 203bc; Paul Broadbent 147br; Buzz Pictures 80tl; Rosemary Calvert 155bl; Nick Cobbing 325b; Alan Copson 187fcl; Dattatreya 190; David Noton Photography 56-57c; Dynamic Graphics Group 29tl, 229; Andy Eaves 236tl; Elmtree Images 184bl (mill); Christer Engstrom 84; EuroStyle Graphics 113tr; f1 online 130b; Terry Fincher 194bl; Foodfolio 140t; Eddie Gerald 289tc; Jim Gipe 86br; Dennis Hallina 251t; David Hansford 249tl; Andrew

Harrington 206; Dallas and John Heaton 132tr (balloon); Andrew Holt 249bl; D. Hurst 187cl; Iconsight 105cr; ImageState 225tr; Imagestate 57cl; Jeff Greenberg 267tr; Andre Jenny 287crb; Vehbi Koca 186cla; Kos Picture Source 199ca; Katja Kreder 148-149c; Leslie Garland Picture Library 103c, 315b; Richard Levine 287bl; Yadid Levy 187fcr; Photofusion Picture Library 224bc; Joe Malone 88tr; Mary Evans Picture Library 221crb, 221tc, 273clb; Kirsty McLaren 227bc; Kader Meguedad 130c; Bernd Mellmann 318cr; David Moore 227br; Jeff Morgan 97bl (add on); Motoring Picture Library 225tc; Z. Okolicsanyi 254clb; On Request Images 140br; Troy and Mary Parlee 251bl; Paul Thompson Images 140cr; Phototake Inc. 267tl; Picture Partners 224c, 225bc; Popperfoto 112tl, 113cl, 132tl (Einstein), 178b, 178cl, 179b, 179l, 289b; Pictorial Press 326br; Profimedia.CZ s.r.o. 326bl; Den Reader 83fcl; Mervyn Rees 319c; Robert Harding Picture Library Ltd. 81bc, 186fcl; Ray Roberts 159tl; Royal Geographical Society 207tl; Steve Skjold 224-225b; Frantisek Staud 81tr; Steve Bloom Images 186cra; Stockfolio 195clb; Swerve 224tl; Peter Titmuss 249cr; Transtock Inc 304tl; Visual & Written SL 300-301cb; Visual Arts Library

286l; David Wall 267br; Rob Walls 204tl; Chris Warren 249br; James D. Watt 83cr; Maximilian Weinzierl 249tr; Janine Wiedel 83cl; Rob Wilkinson 251br; A. T. Willett 267bl; David Young-Wolff 225c; **Ariana Anast:** 276c, 277cla, 277tl; Ariana Anast 276cl; **Andrew N. Gagg's Photoflora:** 83ca; **Courtesy of Apple Computer, Inc.:** 317br; **The Art Archive:** 79crb, 211b, 287cr; Archaeological Museum Spina Ferrara 322tl; Dagli Orti 119br, 119cl, 120tl; Musée d'Orsay 322-323; Nasjonal Galleriet Oslo 91, 92; **Axiom:** Jenny Acheson 276br; Pierre Alozie 277c; Paul Quayle 277b; **Bridgeman Art Library:** 79br, 322cl; Bibliothèque Nationale, Paris 65fcr; Private Collection 273fclb; Galleria degli Uffizi, Florence 216tr; Germanisches Nationalmuseum, Nuremberg 216cra; Hermitage, St. Petersburg 217cla; Mauritshuis, The Hague 112bl; Metropolitan Museum of Art, New York 272tl; Musée de Torun/ Giraudon 255cr; Royal Castle, Warsaw 217tl; Southampton City Art Gallery 221tr; Wilberforce House 268c; **Buzz Pictures:** Neale Haynes 317tr; **CAFOD:** Catholic Relief Services 185cl; **Camera Press:** Keystone 195c; **Casio UK Ltd:** 316ftl, 317cla; **CERN:** 59bl; **Christie's Images Ltd.:** 220cr, 307cra; **Compaq**

Computer Corp.: 317bc; **Construction Photography. com:** 141cb, 141r; **Corbis:** 87cb, 136, 137br, 137tr, 155cr, 198ca, 216cr, 236l, 327cr; Alinari Archives 254tl; Paul Almasy 141cr; Archivo Iconografico S.A 45cl, 22tr; Brooklyn Museum of Art 286clb; Yann Arthus-Bertrand 299crb; Tony Aruzza 140-141r; Austrian Archives 286cra; Dave Bartruff 47cl, 187cr; Sophie Bassouls 44cr (Murdoch); Nathan Benn 299cb; Bettmann 39tc, 52, 53cr, 76-77, 84tl, 93bl, 93cra, 103br, 132bc, 132cla, 132tl, 132tr (classroom), 203br, 204cr, 217clb, 226bc, 226br, 235clb, 243crb, 304cl; Geneviève Chauvel 243br; Condé Nast Archive 192cl, 192cr, 192tl; Pablo Corral Vega 299br; Creasource 154-155c; Jim Cummins 141br; Gianni Dagli Orti 86bl; Deborah Betz Collection 132tr (Einstein); Henry Diltz 19cr; Najiah Feanny 287bc; Robert Fiocca 141ca; John Gilmoure 194cra; Louise Gouliamaki 229tr; George Hall 254bc, 254cra; Angelo Hornak 299cla; Hulton Archive 93tl, 275tl; Hulton-Deutsch Collection 44cr (Bronson); Wolfgang Kaehler 318c; Jonathan Kirn 141b; Danny Lehman 299bl; Charles & Josette Lenars 299cr, 299l, 299tl; Joe McDonald 327cra; Wally McNamee 44cr (Reagan); Gideon Mendel 242cla; David

Illustrator Credits

René Alejandro: 64
Henrick Andersson: 15
Izabella Bielawska:
    80-81, 224-225
Mr Bingo: 144-145
Nishant Choksi: 8-9
Austin Cowdall/New Studio:
    68-69, 166-167
Eboy: 94-95
Josefine Engstrom: 278-279
Grundy Northedge:
    28-29, 72-73, 118-119,
    142-143, 164-165, 200-201,
    230-231, 244-245,
    256-257, 290-291, 328-329
Ben Hasler/NB Illustration:
    88, 113, 159, 204, 301, 304
Roger Harris/NB Illustration:
    12-13
Graham Harvey: 168-173,
    258-259
Adam Hayes: 23, 42-43
Ciaran Hughes: 320-321
Rian Hughes: 50-51, 260-263
Ron Jonzo: 48-49, 109
Sam Louis Kerr: 226-227,
    240-241, 286-287
Yuko Kondo: 26-27
Jessica Langdon: 108, 191,
    228
Chris Leigh: 270-271 and
    'How to' boxes on 22, 75,
    85, 112, 117, 145, 183, 215,
    284, 238
Morgan Lloyd: 182-183
Chrissie Macdonald: 310-311
Al Murphy/Pocko: 114-115
Neil Murren: 208-209
Motomichi Nakamura/Pocko:
    157
Marcus Oakley: 10
Alison Puyaoan: 192-193
Andrew Rae: 25
Mikko Rantanen/Pocko:
    210-211
Paul Rigby: 66-67

Larry Ruppert: 188-189
Marco Schaaf/NB Illustration:
    34-35
Serge Seidlitz: 152-153
Andy Smith: 239
Stephen Sweet: 44, 70-71
Tado: 128-129
James Taylor/Debut Art:
    330-331
Matt Taylor: 274
Nik Taylor: 14
Elliot Thoburn: 138-139, 206
Mark Verhaagen: 86-87
Patrick Walker/Dust: 272-273
Graham White/
    NB Illustration: 222-223
Andrew Wightman: 264-265
Spencer Wilson: 44, 60
Steven Wilson: 282-285
Paul Wootton: 30-31, 156-158

Proofreading: Sandra
Ferguson and Terry Moore

Americanization:
Margaret Parrish